What they're saying about Jack Dunn and "From the Third Base Coach's Box":

"An outstanding book from an outstanding coach. Use it as the Gospel."

Harvey Koepf
Former Major League Scout

"The foundation of my baseball instruction was developed playing high school and Legion ball for Coach Jack Dunn. I have used his philosophies and drills at every level of professional baseball over my 34 years of coaching and managing. Whether dealing with Hall of Famers like Paul Molitor, Robin Yount and Ryne Sandberg at the major league level, or future stars like Rickey Henderson in rookie ball, I have used Coach Dunn's teachings. Today, I will take these instructional strategies to my new position with the San Francisco Giants, just as I took them to all my stops in professional baseball. The basics remain the basics, and no one covers them as well as Coach Dunn."

Tom Trebelhorn
Major League Manager, Milwaukee Brewers and Chicago Cubs
Major League Coach, Brewers, Cubs and Baltimore Orioles
Minor League Manager, A's, Indians, Pirates, Brewers and Giants organizations
Director of Instruction/Farm Director, Baltimore Orioles

"Coach Dunn is one of the most respected coaches the game of baseball has ever had. His thirst for knowledge about the finer points of the game is legendary. Over his many years as a coach and player, he has attempted to turn over every stone to make himself a better coach, whether it is talking to other coaches, reading books or watching video. Now that he is retired, he has made it his quest to give back to the game by writing what he has learned over many years in the game to help other coaches grow as teachers of the game of baseball."

Lou Pavlovich
Editor, Collegiate Baseball Newspaper

"Jack Dunn has one of the best baseball minds of his generation. In my short time working with Jack, I learned more about the game than I ever thought I would. Many of his ex-players have become successful coaches and are using his ideas to teach their players.

Tom Gorman
Former Major League Pitcher
Pitching Coach, Gonzaga University and Portland State University
High School Pitching Coach

"The success Coach Dunn has had at the high school and college levels is a result of him being able to *teach* the fundamentals and strategies in a manner that will allow individuals and programs to be successful. This book exemplifies coaching at its best."

Roy Love
Associate Professor of Physical Education, Head Baseball Coach and Director of Athletics, Portland State University, 1961-1992

"Jack's energy for the game is as great as it was 30 years ago. He understands how to break the game down like few others—and still have fun while doing it."

Mike Clopton
Head Baseball Coach
Wilson High School

"Even after 13 years as a professional baseball play-by-play announcer, I still search for new knowledge about the game. I had the honor of working with Jack on the development and layout of this book, and I can tell you this—you will not find a better man, nor a more knowledgeable coach, anywhere in baseball. The good news? The knowledge I have gained here will make my broadcasts infinitely better. The bad news? After reading chapters like "The Three-in-One Drill" and "First-and-Third Double Steals," part of me wants to toss broadcasting aside to go coach!"

Rich Burk
TV and Radio Play-By-Play Announcer
Portland Beavers, Pacific Coast League

From The Third Base Coach's Box

By Jack Dunn

FROM THE THIRD BASE COACH'S BOX. Copyright © 2008 by Jack Dunn. All rights reserved. No part of this book may be reproduced or transmitted in any form or by any means, electronic or mechanical, including photocopying, recording, or by any information storage or retrieval system, without written permission from the author/publisher. For more information, contact:

Jack Dunn
jackdunnpsu@comcast.net

Visit Jack Dunn on the Worldwide Web at
http://thejugscompany.com/coaches/thirdbasebox.cfm

The Library of Congress has established a cataloging-in-publication record for this title.

ISBN 978-0-6151-8876-8

FIRST EDITION

Printed in the United States of America.

Back cover painting by Leslie Woods, Sports Artist.

I dedicate this book to
my wife Jean—
a patient, loving wife and mother

and to our three sons
John, Jeff and Jim
through whom
her memory
lives on.

Acknowledgments

I want to express my thanks and appreciation to my assistant coaches and former players for their contributions to this book. Many ideas and techniques that improved our overall approach to teaching the game came via our assistant coaches and players. They brought with them many concepts learned from other coaches and teachers.

Steve Candello, a former assistant coach of mine at Portland State University and now the advertising and marketing manager for the Jugs Pitching Machine Company, is the person responsible for me undertaking this project… I will be forever grateful and indebted.

Hugh Luby, a longtime Pacific Coast League second baseman and minor league manager, was an excellent strategist and shared his knowledge with me during my playing days with the Salem Senators. Hugh was the manager for the Senators. He taught me to think ahead and foresee the consequences of possible tactical moves.

Don Kirsch, the former University of Oregon head baseball coach, taught a course entitled "Baseball Coaching Techniques." This class served as a great opportunity to learn from a very knowledgeable veteran coach.

Art Verment, although not a baseball coach, greatly influenced my coaching career. Art was a World War II veteran who was in the first wave at Iwo Jima, and was in five other South Pacific invasions. Later, he was the head basketball coach at Cleveland High School in Portland, where I coached the junior varsity basketball team. He taught me practice organization, the use of multiple drills, and to have fun while still running a disciplined program.

Bob Freeman, a naval officer in World War II, played professionally in the Chicago Cubs' and New York Giants' farm systems after college. He had a strong baseball background, and was a person from whom I could seek advice and tap his knowledge. Bob was a master teacher.

Roy Love, the former baseball coach and athletic director at Portland State University, served as a confidant for over four decades, and many of the ideas we exchanged appear in this text.

Carolyn Bulkley deserves thanks, not only for her secretarial skills, but for her encouragement and enthusiastic concern for the development of this project.

Rich Burk, the play-by-play announcer for the Portland Beavers of the Pacific Coast League, brought organizational and graphic skills that enabled this material to be presented in the most advantageous manner possible. Rich is a future big-league play-by-play announcer.

Larry Sellers, the former sports information director at Portland State University, is always available for counsel. And he always made me look good in his press releases.

Gil Scharringhausen, a former Pacific Coast League pitcher, brought a wealth of knowledge and a calm approach to teaching our pitchers.

Ted Yeamans was an ex-infielder who studied the power of positive thinking. Thanks for teaching me how to win, and for all your efforts on behalf of our players.

Kelly Smith, a former colleague and now the enthusiastic, knowledgeable coach at Lower Columbia College in Longview, Washington, deserves thanks for his many contributions to Portland State University baseball.

Mike Wantland, who played and coached at Portland State for many years, deserves a great deal of thanks. He is a tireless worker and an outstanding hitting instructor.

Rob Nelson, whose creative mind (he invented Big League Chew) helped Portland State University in countless ways, deserves much credit.

Tom Gorman deserves thanks for his great attitude and effort and for passing on his big-league pitching knowledge to our players.

Jack Humphrey pitched at Oregon State and played in the Astros organization, and was a tireless, dedicated worker at Portland State and for our Watco Electric American Legion team.

Marion Reneau provided incredible support to me during my American Legion years. Thank you for your sponsorship and your genuine concern for our youth.

Periodical literature is a great source of knowledge, and in many specific instances maybe more valuable than a textbook. Coaches will often have an area of offensive or defensive expertise that they have developed to the "nth degree." Because of their excitement for the topic, they will write an article for one of the coaching journals, discussing how their particular idea should be taught, although they may never write a book. It behooves the career coach to read the periodical literature to take advantage of the many superb ideas that are available through these resources. I thank the many anonymous coaches who contributed to my knowledge in this manner.

Mike Clopton played and coached for me and brought outstanding organizational and planning skills. Thanks for your all-out effort.

Leslie Woods painted the illustration on the back cover, for which I am greatly indebted.

Carol Joerg deserves thanks for her support and patience during the completion of this project.

Thank you to my boys, John, Jeff and Jim, for the contributions they have made to my baseball knowledge, and to my life.

And finally, thank you to Jean Dunn, for allowing me to be a "kid" for 39 years.

Contents

Foreword *by Dale Murphy* 1
Introduction *by Dwight Jaynes* 3
Preface 5

Part One: Defense

▶ Defensive Drills and Techniques

Deep Thoughts About Defense 10
Throwing: The Key to Defensive Baseball 15
Throwing Drills: Part One 19
Throwing Drills: Part Two 23
Teaching Throwing Via the Black Stripe Baseball 30
Glove Control Drills 32
Multi-Ground Ball Drill 36
Infield Specialty Drill 38
The Three-In-One Drill 42
New Approaches to the Slow Roller at Third Base 69
Playing the Ball 73
Pop Fly Defense Drills 76
Learning the Drop Step 82
Boot Drills 84
The Double Play via the Free Right Foot 86
Middle Infielders' Bounce Drill 91
Keys to Executing the Rundown 95
Rundown Drills 102
Catchers' Drills 106
Breaks and Leads 108

▶ Defensive Strategy

Defending the First-And-Third Double Steal 112
Defending the Not-So-Common First-and-Third Situation 128
Bunt Defense with a Runner on First 131
Bunt Defense with Runners on First and Second 137
Pickoff at First Base with a Bunt in Order 143

Part Two: Offense

▶ Batting Drills and Techniques
The Toss Drill 154
Enhanced Situation Hitting Drills 160
You *Can* Increase Bat Speed 168
The Defensive Roll 171
Hitting the Curveball: A Few Ideas 173
The Sacrifice Bunt 178
Hit With Your Head 182

▶ Baserunning Drills and Techniques
You Can't Steal First (But You Can Try!) 188
The Box Baserunning Drill 192
Short Hop/Block and Run Drill 195
The Bent Leg Slide 198
The Measured Leadoff 201
Stealing Second Base Using a Moving Lead 204

▶ Offensive Strategy
Hitting Strategies 208
Baserunning Strategies 212
"Think and Grow Rich" 215
The Hit-and-Run 218
First-and-Third Double Steals 222
Spin 'Em and Keep the Infield Honest 234
The Suicide Squeeze 238
The Safety Squeeze 245

Part Three: Organization and Other Thoughts

Practice Organization 250
The Timed Pitching Scrimmage 257
Occupational Hazards 261
Play Smart: Know the Rules 263
Nervousness: Make it Work For You 269
The Game Ball Sponsor Program 273

About the Author 277

From the Third Base Coach's Box

Foreword

I have always said, during my career, and in the years since I retired, that I never had a coach that taught the concepts and fundamentals of baseball better than my high school coach, Jack Dunn. There is no one better than Coach Dunn to guide and counsel young baseball players as to how to play the game of baseball.

This book will give coaches and players of all levels valuable insight into their most important responsibilities. I see major league players make mistakes that should have been taught to them in high school or even Little League. This book applies to all players at any age. The major leaguer and the little leaguer alike will benefit from this great book.

To truly appreciate the game of baseball, one needs to understand the hows and the whys of the techniques and strategies of the game. One concept comes to mind that Coach Dunn taught us in high school that I have continually taught to young players that I have coached—the value of trying to pick runners off the bases. We try to pick runners off of the bases to keep them close to the base, so the odds increase of getting them out at the next base. We do this to shorten their lead. To pick them off is a bonus.

Some are reluctant to spend time and thought on this concept because they don't feel it works. They don't pick guys off. To truly understand the value of a properly executed pickoff play is to understand the underlying reason of why it is attempted. I could go on and on about all that I was taught by Coach Dunn, but that is why you have this book.

As you follow the teachings in this book and impart them to your players, you will see their performance and love for the game increase. You are a teacher and your students are eager to learn, and there is no better textbook around.

Look at this book as a road map written by someone who has been down the road and back many times, and not only understands the roads to take, but why you should take them. Jack Dunn is passionate about the game of baseball and is a great teacher of the game. There isn't a better book on teaching the intricacies, nuances and fundamentals of the great game of baseball than the one you're holding in your hands right now.

— Dale Murphy
Atlanta Braves, Philadelphia Phillies, Colorado Rockies
National League Most Valuable Player, 1982 and 1983
Wilson High School, Portland, Oregon, 1974

Introduction

For decades, Jack Dunn was the gold standard for baseball coaches in Oregon. At Cleveland and Wilson high schools, then at Portland State University, Jack was way ahead of the curve.

He developed players for the next level, he developed young men for successful lives, and he won a lot of games. How did he do it?

I believe the secret to Jack's success—and this is coming from someone who, as a sportswriter and columnist for three decades, has watched a lot of very good coaches—is that he's one of the most organized people I've ever met. The man ran practices the way a great chef prepares a meal—all the ingredients were always in proper proportion and order (with just the appropriate amount of spice, too).

He did it in a manner that allowed his players to enjoy what they were doing, a difficult thing to accomplish when you want your team to be as fundamentally sound as Jack Dunn's always were. But instead of boring and listless repetition day after day, Jack's practices were swift and challenging. Instead of drudgery, they were fun.

I think that was because Jack himself needs to be constantly challenged. This is a coach who was going to be bored himself if he didn't keep his approach lively and fast-paced. He is, even today, constantly seeking new ways to break down complicated baseball situations.

That's why I think it was imperative that Jack Dunn put his approach down on paper for others to see. Baseball coaches need books like this one to remind themselves of the joyful experience the game can be if it's first taught, then played, correctly. This is what Jack always stood for and what he'll be remembered for—his teams played the game the way it was supposed to be played and had fun doing it!

Jack knows the game as well as anyone. He has coached major league players and big-time successful businessmen in a career that earned him a spot in the Oregon Sports Hall of Fame.

And Jack has never stopped studying baseball, breaking it down into the tiny little pieces that, when assembled, make for a wonderfully successful approach to teaching and coaching. And nobody is better than he is at finding, then teaching, those little pieces.

And that's what this book is all about.

— Dwight Jaynes
Executive Editor, Portland Tribune
Former Player for Jack Dunn at Cleveland High School
in Portland, Oregon

Preface

"Choose a job you love, and you'll never work a day in your life." – Confucius

---

My motivation for writing this book was not monetary gain, but to pass my knowledge on to other coaches in hopes of enhancing their teaching skills and, to some degree, improve baseball in general.

This book also satisfied my desire to give something back to the game. Giving something back has become more meaningful to me as I have gotten older.

I would like to help young, aspiring coaches who are seeking ways to improve their knowledge and teaching skills. I admire those coaches who have a real thirst for knowledge and self-improvement, as I did in my youth.

The quest for knowledge is interesting. The more our knowledge of a subject increases, the more we become aware of how much more there is to know. Early in our careers when our knowledge is limited, we are oblivious of how much there is to know. As our experience increases, so does our awareness and our concern for situations and aspects of play that earlier in our careers were meaningless.

Seeking knowledge is like playing "crack the whip," and you are the outside man—you never quite catch up. The more you know, the more you become aware of how much there is to know. Or, as an old Chinese Proverb says, "To know is to know you don't know." I agree wholeheartedly.

During my playing and coaching years, I had the good fortune to come in contact with several outstanding people. Two of these men were particularly influential in my career. Both of them were intelligent, dedicated and innovative thinkers who were years ahead in their understanding of the game of baseball. Needless to say, both were outstanding teachers.

Wade Williams was my first real coach. He was a career teacher and coach at Lincoln High School in Portland, Oregon. Several of his players went on to play professionally. Johnny Pesky, the shortstop for the Boston Red Sox during the Ted Williams era, was the most prominent.

Wade Williams was a "tough taskmaster"! He insisted on perfection and accepted no excuses. Daily practice was a part of his regime. His credo was "Practice, tell 'em and play!"

Not only was I coached by Mr. Williams, but he continued to attend my games and critique my performance as a coach. His instructions improved me as a player and greatly enhanced my coaching skills.

"Take what I give you, improve on it and pass it on." This was Wade Williams' charge to me, and another reason I had for writing this book.

Bernie DeViveiros was the Detroit Tigers' scouting supervisor. I had the good fortune to meet him during my minor league playing days. He was a natural teacher—enthusiastic, dynamic and innovative. His passion for the game is unsurpassed.

"As long as you will listen to me, I will help you," was his message. I listened and was rewarded as a player and as a coach. My relationship with Bernie continued for many years after my playing days were over.

The bent leg slide, double play pivot, defensive roll, "Spin 'Em" and compact throwing arm were some of Bernie's ideas that paid dividends and withstood the test of time.

Bernie said to me, with great emotion, "Jack, it's your responsibility to pass this knowledge on to future generations and to keep it alive. Don't let it die!" This book is an attempt to fulfill that responsibility.

I would like to also thank those coaches who have enhanced my knowledge of the game of baseball. Over the years, I have attended countless clinics and read most textbooks written on the subject, plus thousands of periodical articles. Thank you for sharing your ideas and teaching skills.

Another part of my baseball education came on the field, where many of my colleagues "took me to school"! I thank them for teaching me, even though it was a hard way to learn.

If I have inadvertently failed to acknowledge some sources, I beg your indulgence.

— Jack Dunn, December 2007

Part One:

DEFENSE

Defensive Drills and Techniques

Deep Thoughts About Defense

"I don't like them fellers who drive home two runs and let in three." – Casey Stengel

Defensive Observations

▶ An alert, capable defense makes for a winning team. The ability to make the *routine play consistently* is the hallmark of solid defensive play.

▶ In rare cases, an exceptionally good pitcher is able to win consistently with a mediocre defensive team playing behind him. This is the exception and not the rule.

▶ Good defense will keep a team in most games.

▶ Defense can be taught.

> ***Defense wins!***
> To be a consistent winner, a team must play solid defense. *Defense decides who will win and offense decides by how much.*

▶ In a nine-inning game there will be approximately 27 opportunities to put someone out. The team that makes the most of these opportunities—with the fewest errors—will most likely win the game.

▶ A good hitter who is weak defensively will never knock in the number of runs he lets in (the designated hitter being the obvious exception). Consider playing the solid defensive player ahead of the good hitter who is poor defensively. You may want to play the good hitter early in the game, and if ahead, play the better defensive player later in the game.

▶ By minimizing defensive errors and mistakes, you limit your opponents to only those opportunities they earn.

Build your defense up the middle

▶ **Develop your pitching staff:** Pitching is considered to be 80 to 85 percent of the defensive game. It's cliché because it's true: good pitching beats good hitting.

▶ **Develop your catcher:** A strong, mentally alert catcher is necessary if a team is to be solid defensively. The distinguishing mark of a great receiver is his ability to catch the low ball and balls in the dirt to prevent runners from advancing. Practice catching low-thrown balls often.

Build your defense up the middle:

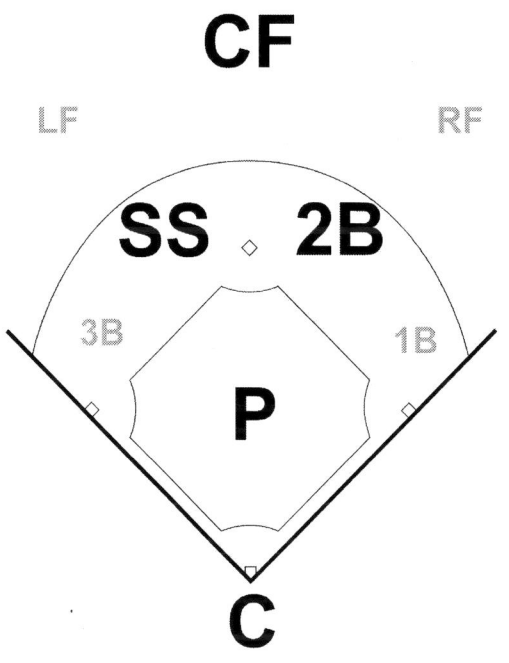

Tenets of Defense

▶ **Develop your shortstop and second baseman:** The majority of batted balls are handled by the infield; of these, most are played by the shortstop and second baseman. Many coaches feel the shortstop should be the team's best athlete and best player because he is involved in more defensive plays than any other team member (except the catcher). An alert, capable middle infield is a primary ingredient for a winning team.

▶ **Develop a center fielder:** The center fielder should be the outfield quarterback—that is, he should take charge of the outfield. Because he must cover the most territory, he must have the ability to *get a jump* on the ball, be fast afoot and possess a strong throwing arm. A solid center fielder complements the team's total defensive scheme. Often, *the outfield corrects the pitchers' mistakes and infielders' errors.*

▶ **Build your team defensively up the middle:** This maximizes the chances of being strong defensively, or at least being as good as your team can be. It is the backbone of team defense!

▶ **Get one out for sure:** Regardless of what happens during the course of a play, *get someone out*. This is particularly true when your team is ahead.

▶ **Make the easy, routine play, make it consistently—and make it under pressure:** If you make the easy plays, the hard plays will take care of themselves. Limit your opponents to what they earn. *Being good is being consistent!*

▶ **Eliminate random throws:** When a player makes a throw where there is little or no chance of making an out, it is considered a random throw. The only result of a random throw is something bad.
  – When a player is trying to throw out a baserunner, the nearer that runner is to home plate, the more certain the player making the throw must be that there is a strong chance of getting an out.
  – *If a throw is to be made to third base, the defensive player should be 90 percent certain he has a play before making a throw.*
  – Don't give your opponents an easy unearned run by throwing the ball away when no play on the baserunner exists. (Catchers take note.)

▶ **Know the priority system of "ball, then base":** If you are catching a throw and you're uncertain whether to leave the base or get the ball, *go get the ball.*

▶ **If you are not involved in a play that is taking place, cover your base**—a subsequent play may develop at your base and you must be there. *The baserunner must come to the base, and if you're not there, there is no play.*

Defensive Strategy

▶ **Count your runs:** Understand which runs are important and which are not. This can be ascertained by counting the number of runners on base plus the batter, and determining what the score would be if they crossed the plate. For example, if you lead 4-0 with a runner on third base, and the runner and batter both scored, the score would still be 4-2 in your favor.

▶ **Concede the run:** If you lead 2-0 with a runner on third base and less than two outs, concede the run at third base (which would make the score 2-1) by playing your infield back and increasing your chances of keeping the batter—the tying run—off base.

▶ **Avoid fanning the flames:** When your team is ahead, don't keep your opponent's rally alive by throwing to home plate (or third base) in an effort to nail a baserunner whose run means nothing even if he does score.

▶ **Keep the double play in order:** Throwing to home plate or third base on a single to the outfield when the run is meaningless allows the batter/runner to advance to second base. This takes the double play opportunity away from the infield, scores another run on a single, and keeps your opponent's rally alive. Keep the double play in order by conceding the run and keeping the batter/runner off second base.

> *Count your runs*
> Determine what the score would be if the batter and all runners scored. By doing so you will know when you can give a run and when you cannot.

▶ **Pay attention to the tying run:** Know which batter or baserunner is the tying or go-ahead run and keep him out of scoring position by throwing to the correct base. Keep the tying or winning run off second base if possible.

▶ **Don't be afraid to give a run:** Concede a run early in the game to get a sure out and prevent your opponents from having a big inning. *If you don't score at least one run, you can't win anyway.*

Infield in or back?

▶ **Know the situation:** The coach has the responsibility of knowing the defensive situations and strategy of play. Tactical errors in judgment, such as playing the infield in when it should be deep, can have disastrous results and can result in unnecessary losses.
  – Counting your runs will make your decision easier.
  – Correct infield depth can mean the difference between winning and losing a ballgame.
  – Playing the infield in to cut off a run turns a .250 hitter into a .500 hitter—it doubles the batter's chance of getting a hit because the infielders have less time to react.
  – Playing the infield back early in the game can be the difference between a big inning or a one-run inning for your opponent.
  – Strategy will vary depending upon the score of the game, the inning (early innings vs. late innings) and the hitter's ability.

> *Correct infield depth can make the difference between winning and losing a ballgame. Know when you should play the infield in, and when you should leave it back!*

▶ **With a runner on third base, play the infield deep…**
… when it's early in the game.
… when ahead by two or more runs.
… when the bases are loaded or if there are runners on first and third with one out—go for the double play unless the runner at third base is the winning run late in the game.
… with runners on second and third base—unless the runner at third base is the winning run. With the infield in, the hitter's chances of getting a hit are doubled, which could score two runs.

▶ **With a runner at third base, play the infield in…**
… to prevent the winning run from scoring.
… when you are behind by a large score.
… with one out and a runner on third base, playing the infield in is a fairly good gamble. If the batter hits safely, the offensive team is apt not to bunt, the chances of a big inning are not too great, and you may prevent a run from scoring.
… in the bottom half of the last inning when the winning run is on third base and there are less than two outs. Also, bring the outfielders into shallow position—this way, no ball can fall in front of them, and they can throw out the runner on third base after catching a fly ball. (A deep fly would score the run even if the ball were caught.)

Specific Situations

How should you play your infield during the following situations?

1. Runners on second and third bases, one out, you are ahead 3-1.
The infield plays deep. The batter is the winning run and the runner on second base is the tying run. Concede the run at third base on a ground ball for the out. Playing deep will increase your chances of keeping the winning run (the batter) off base, and decrease the chances of the tying run scoring.

2. Runners on first and third bases, one out, your team is leading 4-2.
The infield plays deep and tries for the double play. The run at third base means nothing—the tying run is at first base and the winning run is at bat. Keep the tying run off second base if possible, but *get one out for sure*.

3. Bases loaded, first inning, no outs.
The infield plays deep and concedes a run in an effort to get a double play and break the inning. *One run is nothing.* Remember: if you don't score at least one run, you can't win anyway. Give a run in hopes of breaking up a big inning.

4. Runner on third base, one out, your team leading by one run.
Play the infield in. This is a good gamble even though the batter constitutes the go-ahead run. Playing the infield in with one out in this situation is fairly safe. A base hit will put the go-ahead run on base, but the offensive team will usually need two more hits to score and you have the double play in order defensively.

5. Bases loaded, no outs, your team leading by five runs in the last inning.
Play the infield deep. Don't keep the opponent's rally alive by playing the infield in. You are ahead by five runs. Give a run for an out and you win.

6. Last of the ninth inning, score tied, one out, batter triples.
Option #1: Intentionally load the bases, play your infield in and your outfield shallow. (The outfield must be shallow enough to throw the runner out at home or discourage the runner from trying to score. All plays are to home plate.) *Option #2:* You may want to pitch to a particularly weak hitter. If he is retired, walk the following hitter or hitters and then move the infield and outfield back.

Good Luck!

Throwing: the Key to Defensive Baseball

"You spend a good piece of your life gripping a baseball, and in the end it turns out that it was the other way around all the time." – Jim Bouton, Ball Four

The Importance of Throwing

▶ It is the single most important defensive skill.

▶ Fielding errors are typically one-base errors. Throwing errors are often two-base errors (or worse).

▶ If an infielder doesn't field the ball cleanly, the runner gets one base—but if the infielder fields the ball and then overthrows any base, the runner usually gets two bases.

▶ Failure to throw the ball accurately to the relay man or cutoff man results in the runners advancing an extra base.

▶ Inaccurate throws result in a breakdown of the team alignment system.

▶ Successful coaching of throwing uses a variety of word pictures.

> ***Develop this important skill!***
> There is no known method of giving a player a great arm; but, if your players have an understanding of the mechanics of throwing, and drills are practiced daily to implement these mechanics, a coach should come close to developing each player to his fullest throwing potential.

The Grip

▶ A proper grip is the foundation for good throwing.

▶ Grip the ball with the index and middle fingers across the seams where the seams are widest. This grip promotes a four-seam rotation, giving optimum friction, carry, and a true hop.

▶ The thumb should be under the ball, not resting on the side of the ball; the thumb acts as a "runway" or a "launching pad" for the throw.

▶ The ring finger rests against the side of the ball.

▶ The fingertips and thumb should be in contact with the seams.

▶ The grip can be compared to a triangle—the index and middle fingers form the base and the thumb forms the vertex angle.

▶ Spread the index and middle fingers slightly. This will provide a stable axis, helping to eliminate tailing of the ball on long throws. (The proper spread is about the width of your index finger. To obtain the proper width, place the index finger of your non-throwing hand between the index and middle fingers of the throwing hand while gripping the ball.)

▶ Do not grip the ball too tightly or spread the fingers too wide—this will impede flexibility.

▶ Do not "choke" the ball off by burying it too deeply in the hand.

> **Finding the grip quickly:** Conscientious practice while playing catch will enable players to find the seams and establish a correct grip every time.

▶ If hand size does not permit the two-finger grip, allow younger players to grip the ball with three fingers.

Directional Side

▶ The directional side is the glove-side of the body, which includes the shoulder, elbow, hand, hip, knee, and foot. The directional side has two main considerations—the shoulder and the stride.

▶ In the correct throwing position, the directional side is pointed at the target. To determine if the directional side is in correct throwing position, have the player elevate his glove directly from his side (not out front) and extend his arm. The glove should point directly toward the target. The player must be conscious of the front shoulder and feel that he is throwing over it.

▶ The stride gives the player *lateral control* of the throw. Draw a line from the pivot foot to the target, and for a right-handed thrower, the striding foot should land slightly to the left of this line, not on it, when making the throw. Of course, the reverse is true for a left-handed thrower.

▶ The most common fault is stepping across the imaginary line to the target (this is what we mean by "throwing across the body") when making a throw. The stride foot should land in the same relationship to the target on every throw.

▶ To see if a player's stride is correct, have the player stride and hold the position, then elevate the glove and see if it still points at the original target—if it does, the stride is correct.

> **COACHING KEY:**
> *The "Directional Side"—that is, the front shoulder and the stride—should go directly toward the target.*

Release: Vertical Control of Throw

▶ Players must understand that the ball is released off the tips of the index and middle fingers, imparting a backspin rotation upon the ball.

▶ To prevent a slider or screwball effect, the ball must be released with equal pressure on the index and middle fingers.

▶ To achieve maximum rotation on the ball, the wrist must be supple and drive downward as the ball is released.

▶ Vertical control is determined by the release point: too early and the throw is high; too late, and the throw is low.

▶ To find the correct release point, throw your hand at the target.

Arm Action

▶ The correct arm action utilizes the full arm.

▶ The shoulder, elbow, and hand inscribe a circle.

▶ The elbow should be shoulder-high in most cases.

▶ To assure proper arm action, the hand should be on top of the ball, with the fingers on top of the ball (not under it) at the time of release.

▶ Reinforce the following to correct or improve arm action:
 – *Turn the thumb in.* By turning the thumb of the throwing hand slightly inward, the hand and fingers are forced *on top of the ball.*
 – Make a perfect circle with the ball.

Follow Through

To complete the throw, a proper follow-through is necessary. This can be achieved by having the body end up square to the receiver. That is, both shoulders and both hips should be facing directly toward the player receiving the throw.

> *Rhythm: a major key to accurate throws*
>
> Mechanics are no good without throwing rhythm. Do not throw flat-footed.
>
> *For beginners:*
>
> 1. **Catch** the ball in the center of your body.
>
> 2. **Step** toward the target with the left foot (for right-handed players).
>
> 3. **Close** it up by bringing the heel of the right foot forward and alongside the middle of the left foot; **Set** your grip and bring your directional side into alignment during the "close" phase.
>
> 4. **Step** toward the target and throw.
>
> *Tell your players "STEP, CLOSE, STEP" or "STEP, HOP, STEP" to generate throwing rhythm*
>
> *For more advanced players:*
>
> Simultaneously catch the ball and transfer your weight to the pivot foot—right-handed throwers should get to their right foot. Take throwing steps as the catch is made—play through the ball.
>
> *Remember, while the rhythm step is being taken, two important things happen: Players "set their grip" and get their "directional side" into proper throwing position.*

Rules For Playing Catch

▶ Use the same partners every day. The shortstop and second baseman should always be together, as should the first baseman and third baseman.

▶ Knees flexed, weight on balls of feet.

▶ Two hands—thumb to thumb.

▶ Chest-high throws.

▶ Center on the ball.

Warm-up Period

The warm-up period should be approximately 10 minutes once the players are in shape and weather is decent. A longer warm-up period may be necessary earlier in the season.

The Bottom Line

Defensive baseball is predicated upon the ability to play catch, and throwing is the key ingredient. Many coaches overlook the importance of throwing. *Don't do this!* Develop your players' throwing to its fullest capability.

Good Luck!

Throwing Drills: Part One

"Give me six hours to chop down a tree and I will spend the first four sharpening the axe."
– Abraham Lincoln

Once the players understand the basic mechanics of throwing, drills must be incorporated into the practice schedule to implement these mechanics. *Throwing drills should be used daily after the players' arms are completely warmed up.* The following drills are examples of those a coach can use to improve individual and team throwing.

Of course, not all drills should be used at any one practice, so pick and choose those that meet your needs. *Do not tire your players' arms, particularly in the early season.* And remember, as a safety precaution, all throwing should be done in the same direction.

Grip Drill

Purpose: To teach the proper grip of the ball, and to teach players to find the four seams on the ball.

Procedure:
1. Give each player a ball.
2. Players line up side-by-side with their feet in a straddle position along the foul line.
3. Players toss the ball in the air, about head high.
4. Players catch the ball with both hands, take the ball out of their gloves and establish their grip as they do so.
5. Players extend their throwing hand in front of their body for coaches to examine and correct their grip if necessary.

Perfect Circle Drill

Purpose: To teach the correct arm action.

Procedure:
1. Players are paired off at a distance of 20 feet.
2. Players assume a straddle position with their feet.
3. Players grip the ball correctly across the seams and extend their throwing arm shoulder high in front of their bodies.
4. Players throw to their partners using the correct arm action: *Down, around, and over the top.*
5. Feet remain stationary while throwing, and the hand remains on top of the ball.
6. Players should not throw too hard—*make nice soft throws.*

Knee Drill

Purposes:
1. To isolate the upper body by having players throw while down on one knee.
2. To make the player aware of the front shoulder, directional side of the body, and proper arm action.
3. To help players establish the proper release point by throwing the hand toward the target.

Procedure:
1. Squad members are paired off and separated into parallel lines facing each other. The lines are approximately 45 feet apart. Adjust the distance according to maturity and skill.
2. Designate one line as "throwers" and one line as "receivers." Throwers kneel down on one knee. Receivers stand to receive the throw. After five or six throws, reverse the procedure and have the receivers become throwers and the throwers become receivers.
3. Check to be sure that the stride leg is in correct position—for a right-handed thrower, to the left of the imaginary line from the knee to the target.
4. Do not allow throwers to "sit down" on the heel of their down-leg while throwing.
5. On the coach's command "Ready!" each thrower places a baseball into his glove. Hands are together chest-high, resting against the body. On the coach's command "Break!" each thrower breaks his hands apart by removing the ball from his glove and extending his throwing arm shoulder-high to the rear. Fingers must be *on top* of the baseball. The glove arm is extended in front of the body, pointing directly at the receiver. On the coach's command "Throw!" each thrower throws the ball to the receiver. The throwing hand goes directly toward the target, while the glove goes to the heart.
6. To assure correct arm action, have throwers rub the thumb of their throwing hand down their shirt to the belt or thigh area. Players should *turn the thumb in.* Rubbing the thumb down the shirt puts *the hand on top of ball,* which forces correct arm action. The White Sox organization had a good visual for correct arm action. It was, *"Thumb to thigh, then reach for the sky."*
7. This drill can be used daily if limited to five minutes. And by the way, it is an excellent drill to help third basemen develop their throws across the diamond—have the third baseman kneel down in line with first base and throw to first from various distances.

Eyes Closed Drill

Purpose:
To emphasize the basic mechanics of throwing—the directional side (shoulder and stride), release point, and throwing rhythm. This drill will teach players to rely solely upon mechanics and rhythm for throwing accuracy.

Procedure:
1. Line players in single-file between the pitcher's mound and second base in line with home plate.
2. Station a receiver at home plate and give each player a ball.
3. Players throw one at a time to the receiver; each player is instructed to throw with his *eyes closed*—have them look at the target, close their eyes, take their rhythm step, then throw. To be successful, a player must rely upon his directional side (shoulder and stride), the proper release and good throwing rhythm.

4. This drill allows for self-analysis—ask the player why his throw went where it did.
5. Try variations on this drill—catchers can throw to second base with their eyes closed, and middle infielders can make various pivots and throws to first base with their eyes closed. *This should improve confidence.*

Airliner Drill

Purpose: To develop good throwing rhythm and teach players how to get into position to throw by centering on the ball. This is a particularly good drill for outfielders.

Procedure:
1. Players are paired off at a distance of 90 feet. The distance may be shortened or lengthened depending upon skill level and maturity.
2. All players throw in the *same direction!*
3. Players make soft looping throws (not fly balls) to each other. A looping throw enables the receiver to catch the ball with ease and have ample time to get the body into proper position to throw.
4. Throwing rhythm and position to throw are emphasized on the return throw because accuracy is dependent upon both. Again, throws should be looping or arcing, not fly balls.

Rapid-Fire Drive Drill

Purpose:
To develop quick hands and a quick release by learning to carry the throwing hand next to the glove and having the body in position to throw by centering on the ball.

Procedure:
1. Players are paired off at a distance of 45 feet.
2. All players throw in the same direction—one ball per group.
3. Players throw against time—15 seconds. The pair with the most throws in 15 seconds wins.
4. This drill can be used daily—players like competition.

> **COACHING KEYS:**
> – Catch the ball!
> – Get a hold of it!
> – Throw it!
> – In rhythm!

Bounce Drill

Purposes:
1. To develop the technique of imparting proper backspin on the ball and achieving a perfect bounce.
2. To develop the ability to throw *low and on the line.*
3. To stretch out the arm.

This is an excellent outfielder's drill, although it is limited by the condition of the practice field. If it is too rough or too wet, this will make the drill impractical to use.

Procedure:
1. Players are paired off at a distance of 90 feet. The distance may be shortened or lengthened depending upon skill level and maturity.

2. Players bounce the ball back and forth to achieve the longest bounce possible.
3. Partners move apart gradually until they reach a maximum throwing distance of approximately 250 feet for mature players and 150 feet for younger players. The distance maximum can be best adjusted by the coach.

Dead Ball Drill

Purpose:
To reinforce the mechanics of throwing: grip, directional side (shoulder and stride) and rhythm step, and to teach players to pick up a dead ball with their throwing hand.

Procedure:
1. Station players single-file at third base, shortstop, second base and home plate. (The first baseman acts only as a receiver and does not participate in throwing. Players may act as first basemen, but we recommend that the coaches become the receivers. This will give first basemen an opportunity to throw. If you use players at first base, use two to keep the drill moving smoothly.)
2. Place balls at each infield position and in front of home plate—place them in normal fielding positions.
3. The third baseman starts the drill by picking up the ball, taking his rhythm step, and throwing to first base. The shortstop throws next, then the second baseman, followed by those players stationed at home plate.
4. After the first baseman receives a throw, he rolls the ball back to the position from which it came. The thrower places the ball back into its proper fielding position, and goes to the back of the line.
5. Rotate player groups from position to position after each player has thrown two or three times. Rotate those at home plate to third base, third base to shortstop, shortstop to second base and second base to home plate. All players should throw from all positions.

Conclusion

With the proper knowledge of the mechanics of throwing, complemented by good body rhythm, a player's throwing will become more accurate and consistent. This will make his defensive play an asset rather than a liability to the team.

Good Luck!

Throwing Drills: Part Two

"I flailed my arm in a throwing motion before I could even walk." – Willie Stargell

Line Relay Drill

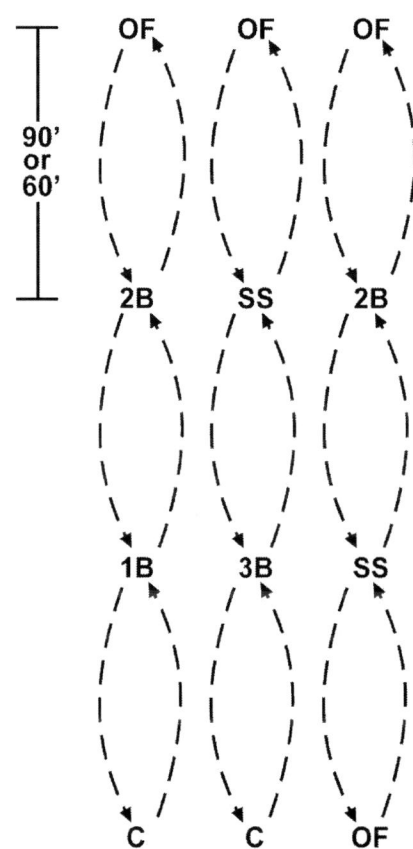

Purposes:
1. To simulate throwing under game conditions.
2. To force the players to throw quickly and accurately while under pressure.
3. To emphasize the proper execution of throwing and relay mechanics.
4. To teach players to turn correctly during a relay throw.

Procedure:
1. Divide the team into groups of four. Groups of three are okay if necessary, but not ideal.
2. Place members of each group about 90 feet apart for adults, or 60 feet apart for little leaguers. This will approximate the throwing distance between bases and is about the distance the relay man is from the outfielder.
3. Place the first player on the foul line, and place the balance of players in that group one-by-one an equal distance apart toward the outfield fence. Groups should be as far apart from each other as practical for safety's sake.
4. Infielders should be in the middle positions (2 & 3) of lines to practice relay moves and throws.
5. Outfielders and catchers should be at end positions (1 & 4).
6. Players at the beginning of each line start with a baseball.
7. Begin the drill on the coach's command. Teams throw the ball down and back a predetermined number of times. If an overthrow occurs or a relay man is missed, the ball must be returned and thrown accurately to the overthrown player before the ball can be advanced.
8. The winning group is the one that can throw the ball quickest to the end of the line and back the designated number of times.

Remember: The relay man should turn to his glove-hand side on accurate throws to him to facilitate making his throw to the next player. *Do not put all the best arms in one line*—it destroys competition.

24 FROM THE THIRD BASE COACH'S BOX

Outfield / Tandem Relay Drill

Purposes:
1. To teach the correct mechanics of the relay throw on extra-base hits.
2. To teach outfielders to throw accurately to the relay man.
3. To teach the Tandem Relay System.

Procedure: This drill (Phase #1 and Phase #2) can be run with both groups throwing at the same time. Or, the groups may alternate—that is, the left field group throws, then the right field group throws (this is the safer of the two mechanics and is easier for the coach to supervise and instruct).

Phase #1:
1. Divide the team into two groups, with half of the outfielders in left field and half in right field. Place several balls on the ground in left-center and right-center fields.
2. An outfielder in left field *runs and picks up* a ball in left-center field and throws it to the relay man (the shortstop), who throws to third base. The second baseman trails the shortstop if the Tandem Relay System is used.
3. Then, an outfielder in right field *runs and picks up* a ball in right-center field and throws it to the relay man (the second baseman), who throws to the catcher at home plate. The first baseman acts as a cutoff man. The shortstop trails the second baseman if the Tandem Relay System is used.

Phase 1 of the Outfield / Tandem Relay Drill:

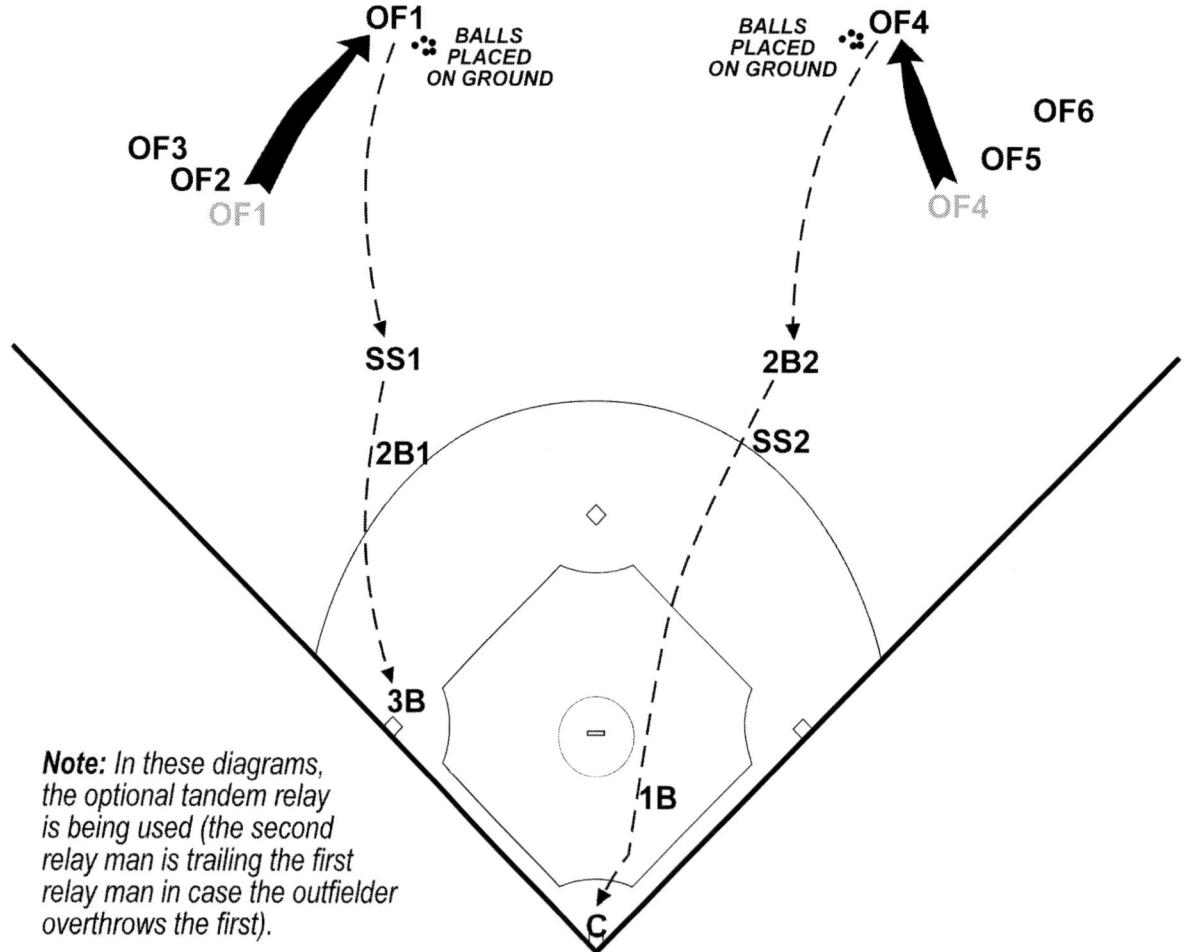

Note: In these diagrams, the optional tandem relay is being used (the second relay man is trailing the first relay man in case the outfielder overthrows the first).

Phase #2:
1. Flip flop the drill by having the right fielder throw to the relay man (the second baseman), who throws to third base.
2. The left fielder throws to the relay man (the shortstop) who throws to the catcher at home plate. The first baseman acts as cutoff man. (The first baseman must be alert for throws coming from right field to third base to avoid being hit by the ball.)
3. Include trailers if the Tandem Relay System is used.

Phase 2 of the Outfield / Tandem Relay Drill:

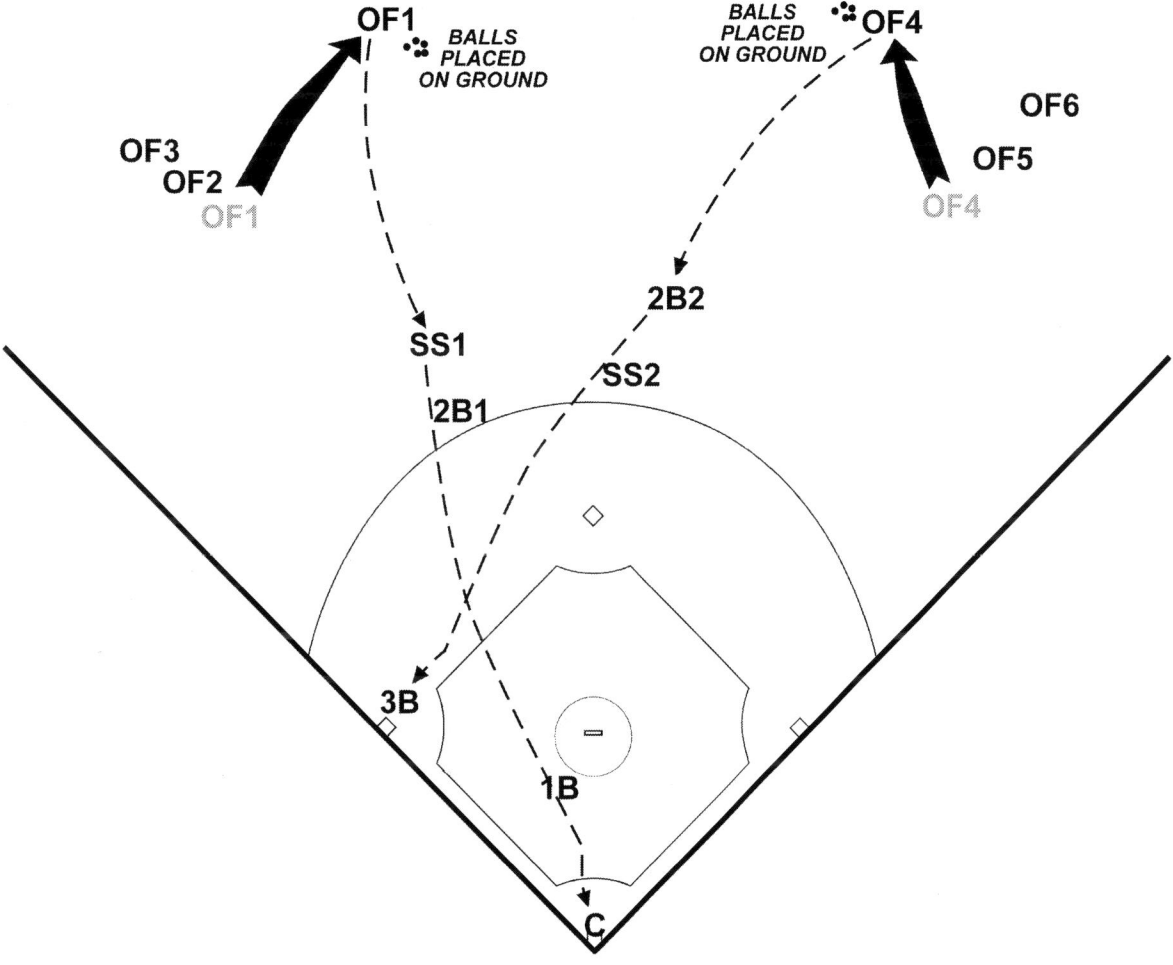

Box Drill

Purpose: To develop quick, accurate throws, and to emphasize proper mechanics and rhythm.

Procedure:
1. Four players form a box—60 feet apart for older players, and 45 feet for little leaguers. Use throw-down bases to simulate a diamond, if needed.
2. Throw the ball around the box/bases clockwise for 30 seconds, then switch groups.
3. Have groups throw in counterclockwise direction for variety.
4. For competition, count the times each group throws the ball around the box in 30 seconds.

Cover Your Bases

Purposes:
1. To emphasize proper throwing techniques.
2. To learn to throw accurately under pressure.
3. To teach infielders to *cover their base*s when they are not directly involved in the play.
4. To teach communication between infielders.
5. To build throwing confidence.

Procedure for variation #1:
1. Divide the team into groups of five. Place the infielders and the catcher on their bases.
2. The catcher has the ball and starts the drill; he may throw to any base he chooses.
3. The shortstop and second baseman should be close to second base. The shortstop covers second base at the start of drill; the second baseman has second base responsibility when the third baseman has the ball, while the shortstop has second base responsibility when the first baseman has the ball. When the catcher has the ball, second base responsibility belongs to the middle infielder last covering the base (other than when the drill first starts). The middle infielders must communicate to determine who has second base responsibility.
4. The player who receives the throw may throw to any base he chooses. The receiver at the next base will do likewise.
5. Players must be alert and *cover their bases* so they will not be hit by the ball or have the ball thrown into the outfield.
6. To make the drill competitive, have players count the number of throws made successfully during a specified time.
7. Every third throw must be across the diamond (1B to 3B, 3B to 1B, C to 2B or 2B to C). That will keep the players from always making the shortest throw.

Procedure for variation #2:
1. All players in their defensive positions.
2. The coach stands near the pitcher's mound and fungoes balls to the outfield—left field first, then center field, then right field.
3. The outfielder fields the ball and throws to the cutoff or relay man, who then throws to the base that has been predetermined by the coach. The coach may elect to practice any of the various defensive alignments, such as: a single with nobody on base; a single with a runner on first base; an extra-base hit with a relay to third base; an extra-base hit with a relay to home; etc.

COACHING KEY:
Young players often do not know whether to go after the ball or stay on the base.

The following "Priority System" should correct this problem.

Priority System:

 # 1 – Ball
 # 2 – Base
 # 3 – Back-up (base, throw)

If a player is uncertain about whether to stay at the base or go get the ball on a slightly errant throw, go get the ball!

This is particularly important for first basemen, but applies to other infielders and the catcher. Many first basemen anchor their foot to the base while the throw sails by a short distance from the base.

When in doubt, go get the ball!

Communication to player is: Ball! Base! Back-up!

4. Once the ball reaches the appropriate base, the infielder that receives the throw may throw the ball to any base he chooses. The receiver at the next base also throws wherever he chooses, and the drill continues (in the same way as variation #1) until stopped by the coach. This forces the infielders to be alert and *cover their bases* so that they will not be hit by the ball or have it thrown into the outfield.

Procedure for variation #3:
1. Use only the infielders.
2. Drill begins similar to conventional infield practice.
3. The coach fungoes a ground ball to the third baseman, who throws to first base; the first baseman throws to the catcher; the catcher throws the ball back to the third baseman.
4. Once an infielder receives the catcher's return throw, he may throw the ball wherever he chooses.
5. Throwing continues (as in other variations) until the coach stops the drill.
6. This drill can be used in conjunction with conventional pregame infield.

Outfield Throwing (Spice Drill)

Purposes:
1. To develop outfielders' throwing accuracy.
2. To emphasize the importance of throwing the ball *low and on the line.*
3. To develop the alignment system.
4. To give the outfielder a feeling of importance.

Procedure:
This drill is divided into three sets:

Set #1—Left Field:
1. All outfielders are in left field in a single-file line.
2. The infielders and catchers are in their positions.
3. The coach fungoes:
    A. A ground ball down the left field line; the outfielder throws to second base, then goes to the back of the line. Outfielders throw one at a time.
    B. A ground ball to left-center field; the outfielder throws to second base, then goes to the back of the line.
    C. A ground ball directly to the outfielder, who throws home, then goes to the back of the line.
    D. A routine fly ball directly to the outfielder, who throws home and goes to the back of the line.

> ### *Inside/Outside Concept:*
>
> To minimize the chances of hitting a baserunner with a thrown ball, this simple concept must be understood.
>
> The "inside/outside concept" means that the thrower and the receiver visualize an imaginary line running between the bases. If the thrower is behind this line, the receiver should receive the throw on the outside of the base.
>
> For example, if the ball is hit to the first baseman behind the baseline (that is, on the "outside"), the shortstop should be on the right field side of the base to receive the throw.
>
> If, on the other hand, the first baseman fields the ball on the infield grass—inside the baseline—then the throw to the shortstop must be inside, with the shortstop tagging second base with his left foot.
>
> This same concept is true for throws at all bases.
>
> **An understanding of the inside/outside concept prevents throwing across, or into, the runner.**

4. The outfielders rotate to center field after the last outfielder throws.
5. After the infielder or catcher receives a throw, the ball may be thrown around the infield in any manner the coach decides. This prevents the infielders from standing around when the initial throw is not made to their base.

Set 2#—Center Field:
1. All outfielders are in center field in a single-file line.
2. The infielders and catchers are in their positions.
3. The coach fungoes:
   A. A ground ball to left-center field; the outfielder throws to third base, then goes to the back of the line.
   B. A ground ball to right-center field; the outfielder throws to third base, then goes to the back of the line.
   C. A ground ball directly to the outfielder, who throws home, then goes to the back of the line.
   D. A routine fly ball to the outfielder, who throws home, then goes to the back of the line.
4. The outfielders rotate to right field after the last outfielder throws.
5. After the infielder or catcher receives the throw, the ball may be thrown around the infield in any manner the coach decides.

Set 3#—Right Field:
1. All outfielders are in right field in a single-file line.
2. The infielders and catchers are in their positions.
3. The coach fungoes:
   A. A ground ball directly to the outfielder, who throws to third, then goes to the back of the line.
   B. A ground ball directly to the outfielder, who throws home, then goes to the back of the line.
   C. A routine fly ball to the outfielder, who throws home, then goes to the back of the line.
4. Infielders should line up throws in whatever manner or alignment system the coach chooses.

Note: Teach your outfielders to *throw at the cutoff/relay man's knees rather than at his chest!* This will result in fewer overthrows and a better and more consistent cutoff and relay system.

Follow the Ball Drill

Purposes:
1. To emphasize the basic mechanics of throwing.
2. To emphasize receiving the throw correctly and being in position to throw.
3. To reinforce the concept of "ball, then base!"
4. To teach players how to cover the base correctly and make a tag correctly.
5. To teach players to hustle.

Set-up:
1. Divide players into four equal groups. Group 1 is stationed at first base, Group 2 at second base, Group 3 at third base and Group 4 at home plate. All players on the team should be involved, regardless of their normal position.

2. One player from each group should be at the base to start the drill. All other players should stand to the side of the base in single file out of the direct line of the throw, waiting their turn to cover the base.
3. After making his throw to the designated base, a player "follows the ball" to that base and goes to the end of that line.

Procedure:
1. The drill begins with the catcher. He throws to second base, and follows his throw there (he approaches second base from the third base side to avoid the throw being made to first base). The catcher then goes to the end of the line at second base.
2. The second baseman receives the throw from the catcher. He then makes a throw to first base and follows the throw there (he approaches first base from the right field side to avoid the throw being made to third base). The second baseman then goes to the end of the line at first base.
3. The first baseman receives the throw from the second baseman. He then makes a throw to third base and follows the throw there (he approaches third base from the left field side to avoid the throw being made to home plate). The first baseman then goes to the end of the line at third base.
4. The third baseman receives the throw from the first baseman. He then makes a throw to home plate and follows the throw there (he approaches the plate from the right side to avoid the throw being made to second base). The third baseman then goes to the end of the line at home plate.
5. The coach should emphasize that players are to *hustle* to the next spot after making their throw.
6. As players become familiar with the drill, the coach should incorporate instruction on how to cover the base and on how to tag the runner—have players fake a tag before throwing to the next base.

Good Luck!

Teaching Throwing Via the Black Stripe Baseball

"Excellence is an art won by training and habituation." – Aristotle

At Portland State University, it was our belief that throwing was the single most important defensive skill.

We were also of the opinion that throwing was one of the most neglected aspects of coaching. Consequently, we spent a great deal of time instructing our players on the mechanics of throwing and used daily drills to implement these mechanics. By doing this, we hoped to develop each player to his fullest throwing potential.

One of the most helpful techniques we found to improve throwing was the striped baseball. Its purpose is rotation analysis (how the baseball is spinning), which reveals many throwing flaws.

Because velocity, accuracy, a true hop, and successful throwing in general are so dependent upon proper rotation, the coach must be able to analyze the rotation of balls thrown by his players, particularly those players who are experiencing throwing difficulties. Analyzing the rotation of the baseball is the best diagnostic technique the coach has to determine how the baseball is being released and thrown.

Many players are guilty of unequal pressure on the index or middle fingers at the time the ball is released. This unequal pressure results in a slider or a screwball type of action on the baseball, neither of which is desirable. Other players are guilty of not gripping the baseball correctly across the seams or not keeping their hand on top of the baseball, which results in a sidearm throw. The sidearm-thrown baseball breaks away from its target, doesn't hop straight to the base, and generally is more inaccurate than the overhand or three-quarter-arm throw.

> ### *Benefits of "The Black Stripe Baseball":*
>
> – It is field-tested and proven.
> – It is an easy method to improve team throwing.
> – It assures a proper grip every time.
> – It helps develop and improve arm action.
> – It enables players to self-analyze their throws.
> – It enables the coach to analyze the throws of a large number of players at one time.
> – It makes playing catch constructive, meaningful, and fun.
> – It gives players and coaches immediate feedback, thus facilitating learning.
>
> **The black stripe will stand out and be clearly visible when proper throwing mechanics are implemented.**

For years, playing catch with individual players and carefully studying the rotation of the baseball was the most satisfactory means of rotation analysis. But now a much more effective technique has been devised to improve throwing—"The Black Stripe Baseball." As you might imagine, it is a baseball with a black stripe drawn around it—or, you may wind a piece of electrician's tape around the baseball. The stripe, which should be about half an inch wide, intersects all four seams in the "four-seam" rotation.

By gripping the baseball with the fingers on each side of the stripe and placing the thumb on the stripe below, a correct grip is assured every time. Players should "make the stripe stand up"— that is, they should make the baseball rotate vertically. If done properly, the black stripe will stand out and will be clearly visible and easy to read, indicating that a proper release, arm action (an overhand throw) and rotation have been achieved. If the baseball is released incorrectly, the stripe will be blurred.

If the arm angle is three-quarters, the black stripe will rotate at a 45-degree angle. The arm angle should be no lower than three-quarters, unless a desperation throw is necessary. But regardless of the arm angle, if the baseball is gripped and released correctly off the fingertips the black stripe will stand out and will be clearly visible. If the baseball is released incorrectly, the black stripe will be blurred.

The black stripe baseball permits easy rotation analysis by individual players while playing catch, and also enables the coach to analyze a large number of players at one time. This immediate feedback greatly facilitates the learning process.

Good Luck!

Glove Control Drills

"If you do the little jobs well, the big ones will tend to take care of themselves." – Dale Carnegie

---

Glove control is critical to good defensive play, and glove control is dependent upon having a glove that fits the player's hand. Too large a glove is difficult to control, while too small a glove often lacks an adequate pocket to receive the ball easily. Physical size is of concern when choosing a properly fitted glove. Unlike clothing, it isn't advisable to buy a large glove that the youngster will grow into. The interim could be a defensive disaster.

A glove is measured from the heel of the palm to the fingertips. Choose carefully!

Keys to receiving the ball:
1. The glove should be in front of the body between the eyes and the ball.
2. The pocket of the glove should be "open to the ball."
3. The hands should be relaxed and should "give" with the impact of the ball in the pocket of the glove. This will absorb the shock.
4. The ball should be caught near the bottom of the webbing of the glove, between the thumb and index finger. This will prevent the ball from stinging the hand or bouncing out of the glove by making direct contact with the hand.

> *Rule of Thumb for Glove Size:*
>
> Gloves are measured from the heel of the palm to the fingertips.
>
> **Youth players:** 9-11 inches
> **High school/Adult players:** 10½-12½ inches

Cup the Hand Drill

Purpose: To teach young players how to correctly place their hand in their glove to form the best possible pocket to receive the ball, and to protect their hand from the impact of the ball.

Procedure:
1. Place players abreast of one another in a straddle position along the back of the infield in the shortstop area.
2. Players are without their gloves, and they "cup" their bare glove hand.
3. Players make a fist with their throwing hand and pound into their cupped, bare glove hand.
4. The coach explains that "cupping" the hand inside their glove will help form a better pocket in their glove, and will protect their hand from the direct impact of the ball, which will sting and is more likely to bounce out of their glove if it makes direct contact with their hand.
5. Players put their gloves on and pound the pockets of their gloves with the fist of their throwing hand to form a pocket.
6. The coach checks to see if each player's hand is placed correctly in the glove and that the proper pocket is being formed.

Pocket Check / Slap Drill

Purpose: To teach players where the ball should be caught in the glove.

Procedure, phase #1:
1. Place players abreast of one another in a straddle position along the back of the infield in the shortstop area. Each player has glove on his hand and a baseball.
2. Players pound the ball into their glove to form a pocket. The coach instructs players to place the ball in the pocket of their glove where they would normally catch the ball.
3. Players extend the glove and ball in front of their body, with the back of the glove facing down. The ball should be in the pocket of the glove facing up.
4. The coach checks to see if the ball is placed correctly in the pocket of the glove. The ball should be held between the thumb and index finger at the bottom of the web.

Procedure, phase #2:
1. Players extend glove and ball in front of their body.
2. The back of the glove is facing up, and the ball in the pocket of glove is facing down.
3. The coach slaps the back of the glove (not too hard) of each player. The ball will be dislodged if it is not held in the pocket of the glove correctly, or not held tightly enough.
4. The coach makes necessary adjustments if the ball is dislodged.

Drop and Catch Drill

Purpose: To teach players what the proper hand action should be within their glove. This is a difficult drill, but it emphasizes and makes players aware of proper hand action in the glove.

Procedure, variation #1:
1. Place players abreast of one another in a straddle position along the back edge of the infield.
2. Players should *not* have their gloves. Each should have a ball in his bare glove hand.
3. Players extend their bare glove hand in front of their body. The back of the hand should be up and shoulder high.
4. Each player drops the ball from the bare hand and attempts to re-catch it before it hits the ground.

Procedure, variation #2:
1. Same as above, except players put gloves on with the ball in the pocket.
2. Players extend their glove and ball in front of their body, with the back of the glove up and the ball facing the ground.
3. The player drops the ball from the glove and attempts to re-catch it before it hits the ground.

Bare Hand Toss Drill

Purpose: To teach players to use both hands when catching the ball, and to develop "soft hands."

Procedure:
1. Pair players up
2. Players face each other approximately six feet apart.

3. Players assume the ready/set fielding position *without gloves on.*
4. Players toss the ball back and forth to each other underhanded.
5. The ball must be caught in the bare glove hand with the throwing hand alongside—*two handed!*

For competition:
1. The first pair to successfully catch 25 tosses wins! One-handed or improper catches do not count.
2. Or, the pair that has the most catches in a prescribed time (15, 20, 30 seconds, etc.) wins.

Glove Toss Drill

Purpose: To teach players the correct glove position when the ball is thrown high (above the waist), or low (below the waist).

Procedure:
1. Pair the players up, and have them face each other approximately six feet apart with their gloves on (the distance players are apart should be such that the player tosses ball to his partner and is unable to lay the ball in his partner's glove).
2. Players assume a ready/set position.
3. Players the toss ball back and forth to each other underhanded. The ball must be caught in the glove with the throwing hand carried alongside—two-handed.
   – **High Ball:** the fingers of the glove should be pointing up, thumb to thumb.
   – **Low Ball:** the fingers of the glove should be pointing down, little finger to little finger.

For competition:
1. The first pair to successfully catch 25 tosses wins! One-handed or improper catches do not count.
2. Or, the pair that has the most catches in a prescribed time (15, 20, 30 seconds, etc.) wins.

Crab Drill

Purpose: To teach infielders to move forward and to stay low when fielding a ground ball.

Procedure:
1. Give each player a ball and have players line up single-file at the shortstop position.
2. One coach should kneel about 20 to 25 feet in front of the players, and another coach should be at first base with a glove.
3. Player tosses his ball to the coach directly in front of him and assumes a ready/set position.
4. The coach gives the command "crab."
5. The player moves forward, feet apart, "fanny" down, and slaps the back of his glove on the ground as he "crabs" forward.
6. The coach rolls the ball to the player, who fields it and throws it to first base. (The player should move forward under control for a short distance, about 10 feet, before the coach tosses the ground ball. Actions should be exaggerated, but controlled.) The coach makes necessary corrections.
7. The player gets the ball back from the first baseman and goes to the end of the line.

GLOVE CONTROL DRILLS 35

One-Hand Glove Control

Purpose: To teach players to open their gloves when fielding ground balls. Many players fail to open their glove enough to allow easy entry for the ball. The glove is closed and there is no place for the ball to go. This drill allows the coach an opportunity to check each player's glove control.

Procedure:
1. Players line up single-file at the shortstop position. Each player has a ball.
2. The coach kneels about 20 to 25 feet in front of the players.
3. The first player in line steps forward and tosses the ball to the coach.
4. The player assumes a ready/set position and places his throwing hand behind his back in a back pocket, or grabs his belt.
5. The coach rolls a ground ball to the player's glove-hand side, observes how the player controls the glove, and makes necessary corrections. The player keeps the ball and returns to the end of line.

Backhand Drill

Purpose: To teach players how to use the glove to backhand the ball correctly.

> **COACHING KEY:**
> On a backhand play, the pocket of the glove should be open to the ball with the glove out in front of the glove-side foot.
>
> A right-handed thrower should backhand ball to his extreme right in front of his left foot, take a short half-step with his right foot to gain rhythm, and come up throwing.

Procedure, phase #1:
1. Players stand abreast in a straddle position along the back of the infield dirt.
2. The coach stands in front of the players and demonstrates the backhand glove position.
3. The players should be in the ready/set position. On the coach's command ("backhand"), players step across their bodies with their glove-side foot and bring the glove to the ground in a backhand position.
4. The glove should be open to the ball with the thumb pointing or touching the ground and the little finger of the glove pointing upward.
5. Right-handed throwers will pivot on their right foot, step across their body with their left foot, and backhand the ball in front of their extended left foot. Left-handed throwers will pivot on their left foot, step across their body with their right foot, and backhand the ball in front of their extended right foot.

Procedure, phase #2:
1. Players form a single-file line at the shortstop position. Each player has a ball.
2. The coach kneels about 20 feet to 25 feet in front of the players.
3. The first player in line tosses his ball to the coach and assumes the ready/set position.
4. The player places his throwing hand behind his back in a back pocket, or grabs his belt.
5. The coach rolls a ground ball to the player's throwing-hand side, and the player backhands the ball regardless of where it is tossed.
6. The coach checks the player's glove position and sees that the pocket is open to receive the ball, then makes the necessary corrections.

Good Luck!

Multi-Ground Ball Drill

"Pop flies, in a sense, are just a diversion for second basemen. Ground balls are his stock in trade."
– Jackie Robinson

The Multi-Ground Ball Drill is a great exercise to give infielders practice at fielding a large number of ground balls within a short period of time. It should be an important part of any team's routine. And as you'll see, precautions *must* be taken to ensure the drill is conducted in a safe manner.

Procedure for Fielders:
1. Place infielders at their defensive positions.
2. Two fielders at each position are desirable, but this is not absolutely necessary.
3. Upon occasion, using outfielders as well as infielders will sharpen everyone's ground ball fielding skills.

How to run the Multi-Ground Ball Drill:

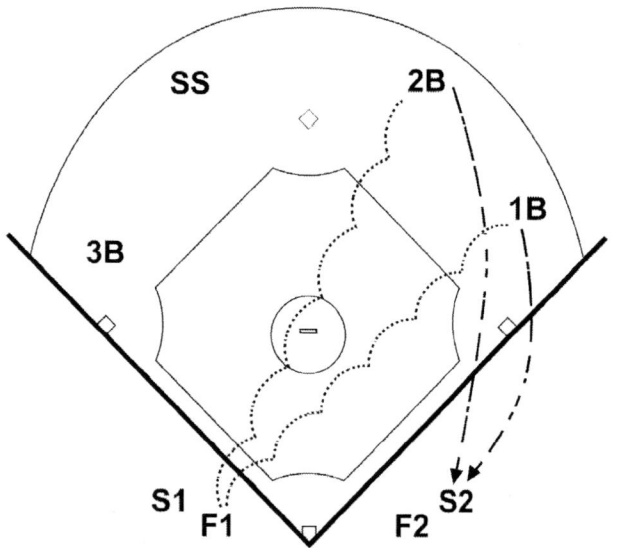

Diagram 1: Fungo Hitter #1 (F1) alternates hitting ground balls to the first baseman and second baseman, who flip easy tosses to the shagger/feeder (S2) stationed on the opposite side of home plate, near Fungo Hitter #2. (Throwing to the opposite shagger/feeder reduces the number of balls crossing the middle of the infield.)

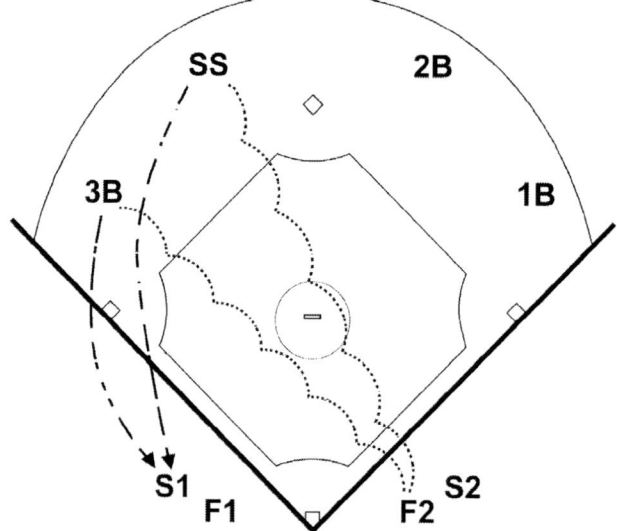

Diagram 2: At the same time Fungo Hitter #1 is hitting ground balls to the first and second basemen, Fungo Hitter #2 (F2) alternates hitting ground balls to the shortstop and third baseman, who flip easy tosses to the shagger/feeder (S1) stationed on the opposite side of home plate, near Fungo Hitter #1. (Note: There can be more than one player at each position.)

Procedure for Fungo Hitters:
1. Use two coaches to act as fungo hitters.
2. Fungo Hitter #1 stands on the third base side of home plate and fungoes ground balls to the second baseman and first baseman.
3. Fungo Hitter #2 stands on the first base side of home plate and fungoes ground balls to the third baseman and shortstop.

Procedure for Shagger/Feeders:
1. Each fungo hitter has a shagger/feeder who receives throws from the infielders after they have fielded the ground ball.
2. Fielders' throws to the shagger/feeders are soft tosses designed only to return the baseball to the fungo hitter.
3. After receiving the fielder's throw, the shagger/fielder gives the ball to the fungo hitter.

> ***Remember... safety first with the Multi-Ground Ball Drill:***
>
> For safety reasons, it is important to take the time necessary to explain thoroughly how the drill is to be executed, and particularly where return throws are to be made. *Remember, return throws to the shagger/feeder are nice, soft tosses.*
>
> When first introducing the Multi-Ground Ball Drill, do so slowly, again for safety reasons! As the players become familiar with the drill, it can be a highly efficient practice and teaching technique and will move rapidly.

Use the Multi-Ground Ball Drill Often

This drill gives the players a maximum number of ground balls in a limited amount of time; consequently, it can be used daily.

Good Luck!

Infield Specialty Drill

"When I throw a ground ball, I expect it to be an out, maybe two." – Warren Spahn

---

This is a great drill to give the infielders intensive practice fielding ground balls. The Infield Specialty Drill can be used during batting practice, as a separate infield drill, or instead of the traditional pregame infield practice.

Procedure:
1. Place a protective screen on the home plate side of second base, and another screen on the home plate side of first base.
2. Place infielders in their defensive positions. Have two coaches, pitchers, or utility players act as receivers at second base and first base behind the protective screens.
3. Select two skilled and alert fungo hitters. Each has only one baseball for safety purposes. (No rapid-fire ground balls.)
4. Fungo hitters hit ground balls to designated fielders only between batting practice pitches.
5. The drill is divided into three sets. Each set usually lasts ten minutes, but the coach can decide the time that best suits the team's needs.

Set 1 of the Infield Specialty Drill:

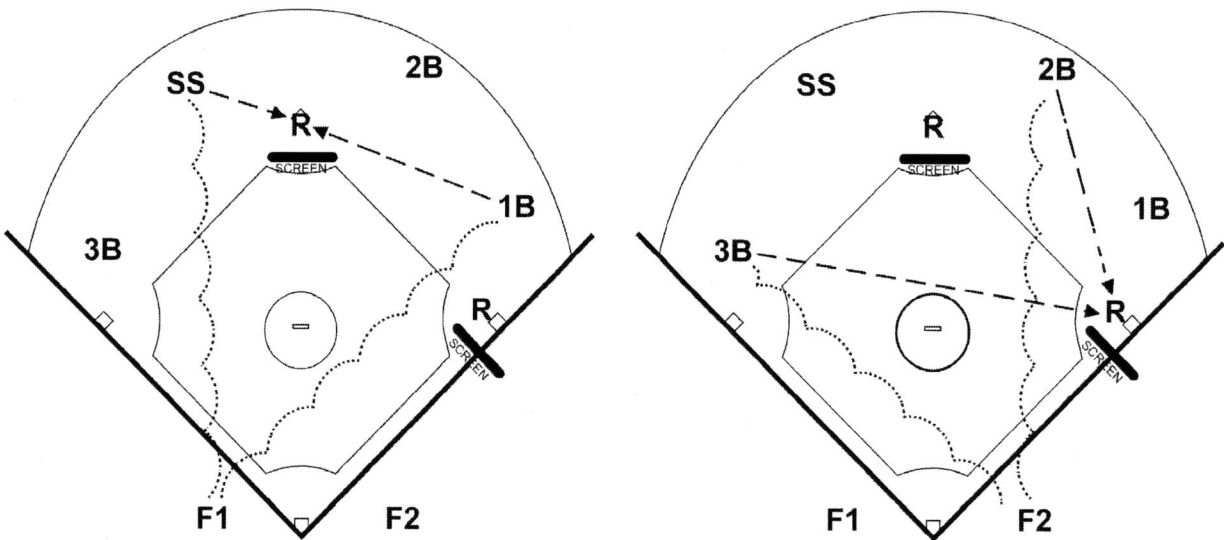

Diagram 1A: Fungo Hitter #1 (F1) alternates hitting ground balls to the shortstop and first baseman, who throw to a receiver stationed at second base. The first baseman must take care to avoid hitting the second baseman with a throw.

Diagram 1B: Fungo Hitter #2 (F2) alternates hitting ground balls to the second baseman and third baseman, who throw to a receiver stationed at first base. The second baseman must stay deep to avoid being hit by the first baseman's throws, and must take care not to hit the first baseman with a throw.

INFIELD SPECIALTY DRILL

Set #1 (See Diagrams 1A & 1B):
1. Fungo Hitter #1 stands on the third base side of home plate, and alternates hitting ground balls to the shortstop and first baseman.
2. The shortstop and first baseman throw to the receiver covering second base.
3. The receiver at second base returns the ball to Fungo Hitter #1.
4. Fungo Hitter #2 stands on the first base side of home plate, and alternates hitting ground balls to the second baseman and third baseman.
5. The second baseman and third baseman throw to the receiver covering first base.
6. The receiver at first base returns the ball to Fungo Hitter #2.

Attention: *Caution must be observed by both the second baseman and first baseman when making throws, so that they don't hit one another with the ball.* The second baseman should be in a deep infield position. The first baseman should field and throw from a moderately deep position. Both players must remain aware of each other's relative fielding position to avoid hitting each other with a throw. Neither player should field poorly fungoed balls that would bring them into the baseline. Here is the rule of thumb while using this drill: "If it's slow, let it go!" This will keep the second baseman out of the way of the first baseman's throw to second base.

Set 2 of the Infield Specialty Drill:

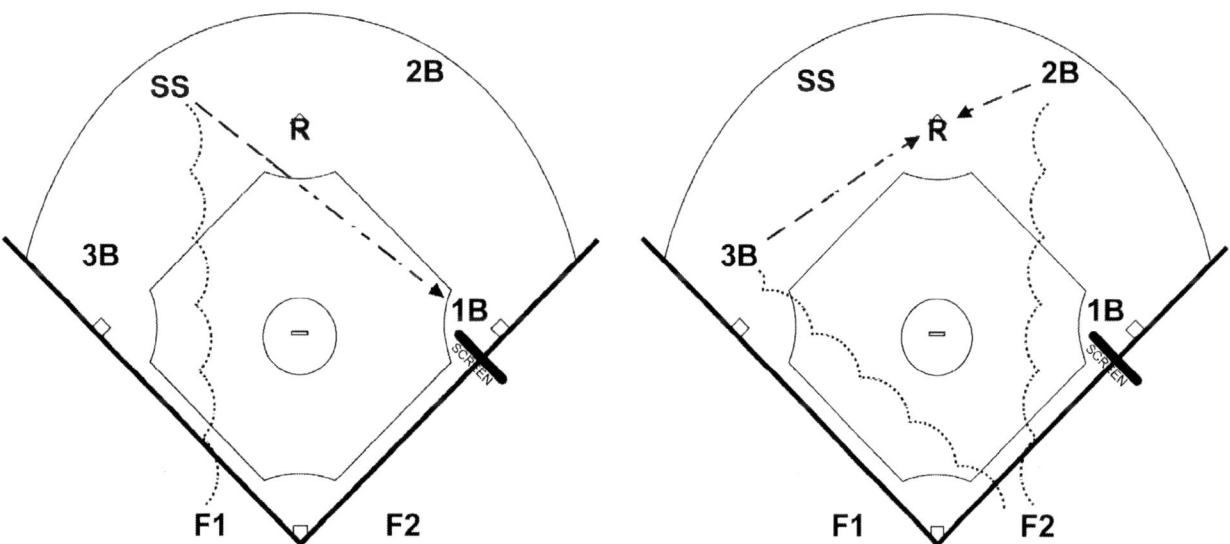

Diagram 2A: Fungo Hitter #1 (F1) hits ground balls to the shortstop, who throws to the first baseman at first base. The shortstop must take care to avoid hitting the receiver at second base with a throw, and must avoid charging ground balls that would bring him into the line of the third baseman's throws to second: "If it's slow, let it go!"

Diagram 2B: Fungo Hitter #2 (F2) alternates hitting ground balls to the second baseman and third baseman, who throw to a receiver stationed at second base. The third baseman must take care not to hit the shortstop with a throw.

Set #2 (See Diagrams 2A & 2B):
1. The setup is the same as Set #1, except for one thing: the coach or utility player does not act as a receiver at first base. Instead, the first baseman receives all throws at first base. The protective screen remains in place on the home plate side of first base to protect the first baseman.
2. Fungo Hitter #1 hits ground balls to the shortstop only.
3. The shortstop fields and throws the ball to first base.
4. Fungo Hitter #2 alternates hitting ground balls to the third baseman and second baseman.
5. The third baseman and second baseman field and throw to the receiver at second base.

Attention: As directed in Set #1 with the first and second basemen, in Set #2 it is the shortstop's responsibility to play deep and out of line of the third baseman's throw to second base. The shortstop should not field poorly fungoed balls that would bring him into the baseline. Again, "If it is slow, let it go!" This will keep the shortstop out of the way of the third baseman's throw to second base.

Set 3 of the Infield Specialty Drill:

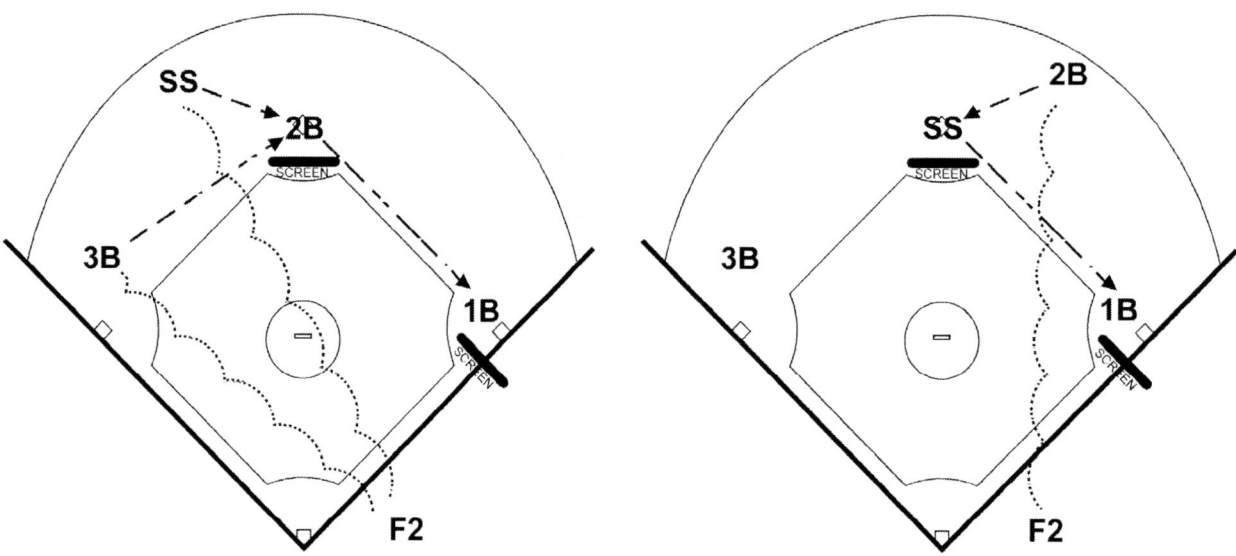

Diagram 3: Fungo Hitter #2 (F2) alternates hitting ground balls to the third baseman, shortstop and second baseman, who start double plays by throwing to second. The second baseman executes the pivot on ground balls to third and short, while the shortstop executes the pivot on ground balls to the second baseman. The first baseman acts only as a receiver and does not field ground balls during this set of the drill.

Set #3—Double Play practice (See Diagram 3):
1. The protective screens remain in place on the home plate side of second base and first base.
2. Use only one fungo hitter. Fungo Hitter #2 (on the first base side) may be the best choice.
3. The fungo hitter alternates hitting ground balls to the third baseman, shortstop and second baseman. The first baseman acts only as a receiver and receives no ground balls during this phase.
4. Infielders field ground balls and start double plays by throwing to second base. The third baseman and shortstop throw to the second baseman, who executes the pivot and throws to first. When the second baseman fields a ground ball, he will throw to the shortstop, who executes the pivot. The protective screen placed on the home plate side of second base protects the middle infielders from batted balls if the drill is used during batting practice.

If Set #3 is *not* used during batting practice:
1. Only one fungo hitter is used, and he hits ground balls from home plate.
2. The fungo hitter hits ground balls to ALL infield positions, and they execute the double play via second base.
3. This drill can be more "rapid-fire" because the risk factor of batting practice is removed, and there are no return throws from the catcher.
4. If the drill is not used as a part of batting practice, you may want to incorporate into Set #3 slow rollers and throws to home plate, similar to a conventional infield practice.

Be Careful

Don't use this drill during batting practice unless fungo hitters are *skilled and alert*. If this drill is used during batting practice, particular attention must be paid to *safety!* Fungo hitters must hit ground balls only between pitches to the batter taking batting practice. This prevents the infielder from being hit by a batted ball while fielding the ground ball being fungoed to him. This drill takes advantage of time often wasted during batting practice.

Use the Infield Specialty Drill Often

This is an excellent drill; just instruct your infielders to be careful not to field the ball if it is in line with another fielder's throw during Sets 1 and 2. Remember: "If it is slow, let it go!" Fungo hitters can alternate hitting ground balls to minimize the possibility of a fielder being hit by an errant throw.

The Infield Specialty Drill gives infielders additional practice at fielding ground balls, making the long throw to first base, and making throws to second base to start the double play. It is a great way to maximize practice time and keep players involved during batting practice.

(Many concepts in this chapter were gleaned from "Some Teaching Tips," an article written by Pat Daugherty in the *American Baseball Coaches Association Clinic Notes* in 1984.)

Good Luck!

The Three-in-One Drill

"Nine-tenths of wisdom is being wise in time." – Theodore Roosevelt

---

It has often been said that "Defense and pitching win games, and offense determines by how much." It behooves coaches to have an efficient and effective method of practicing the defensive game.

The solution: a "master multiple defensive drill" which allows several critical areas to be practiced simultaneously. This has many advantages:

1. More learning will take place if key defensive fundamentals are practiced for *short periods of time* at regular intervals than in longer, more widely spaced practice sessions.
2. By practicing defensive skills for short periods at regular intervals, a transfer of learning to actual game situations will become routine and automatic.
3. It makes maximum use of limited practice time, enabling critical areas of the defensive game to be taught thoroughly.
4. It gives the players a sense of confidence when dealing with defensive situations.
5. It makes difficult defensive situations seem routine.
6. It gives the players a sense of accomplishment and growth.

> ***Maximize the value of your practice time!***
>
> Learn the components of the Three-In-One Drill, and make it a part of your regular practice.
>
> This chapter not only covers the mechanics of the Three-In-One Drill, *it also covers the fundamentals necessary for each player during each portion of the drill.*
>
> **This drill will be one of the most important things you learn from this book!**

When deciding which components of the defensive game play the most important part in developing a solid defensive team, the coach must consider which situations occur most often and then incorporate them into a master multiple defensive drill.

How important is a particular defensive skill or situation to winning? This, then, is the percentage of practice time that should be allocated to practicing this defensive skill and situation.

The coach must take the time to lay a solid foundation for the defensive game. This is done by thoroughly teaching each segment of the drill before continuing onto the next set. It takes time, but it will pay dividends over the course of the season.

As the players become familiar with the drill, not only will it become highly efficient, but the experienced players will help coach the newcomers and/or rookies.

Teach thoroughly what you expect your players to learn, and then *fully expect the players to perform what you have taught.*

The Three-In-One Drill? Or the Twenty-One-In-One Drill?

The *Three-In-One Drill* is an excellent example of a master multiple defensive drill. Yet, it has become a misnomer. Originally, the Three-In-One Drill distilled three parts of the defensive game into one drill. Over the years, though, it has grown to incorporate many more. In fact, the drill as it is detailed here is actually 21 drills in one!

Overview

1. The "Three-In-One Drill" is divided into two parts, and each part is divided into sets. Part I has three sets, and Part II has four sets.
2. All drills within a set are run simultaneously. For example, while the pitchers are working on covering first base, the middle infielders and third baseman are working on the reverse double play.
3. Players should practice each drill a prescribed number of times before moving on to the next drill within that set.
4. Devise your own components or modify those suggested. A drill of this magnitude seems difficult, but once mastered it will become a highly effective method of improving your team's defensive play.

Three-In-One Drill at a glance:

The "Three-In-One Drill" is divided into two parts. Part I has three sets, and Part II has four sets. And within each set are separate drills that are to be run simultaneously:

PART I

Set 1:
-- P/1B/2B work on ground balls to the right side of the infield
-- 2B/SS/3B work on the reverse double play and other unique plays

Set 2:
-- P/3B/1B work on bunt defense with runners on first and second
-- 2B/SS practice double play pivot

Set 3:
-- P/2B/SS work on Count Pickoff Play
-- 1B/3B practice fielding slow rollers and bunts

PART II

Set 1:
-- P/1B/2B/SS work on comebackers to the pitcher
-- C/3B work on catchers' throws to third base on stolen base attempts

Set 2:
-- P/1B/SS practice 3-6-1 double play
-- C/3B work on catchers fielding bunts and throwing to third

Set 3:
-- 1B/2B/3B/SS work on double plays
-- P/C practice pitch-outs, intentional walks and covering the plate on passed balls and wild pitches

Set 4:
-- P/C/1B/2B/SS/3B all work on pickoff plays; the field is divided into three stations and pitchers rotate to practice pickoffs at each base

PART I, SET 1
▶ **P/1B/2B work on ground balls to the right side**
▶ **2B/3B/SS work on unique plays**

In this set, the pitchers and first basemen are practicing their coordination in Drills 1-2, with the second baseman joining them for Drill 3. While Drills 1-3 are taking place, the middle infielders and third baseman are working on the reverse double play and other situations in Drills 4-6.

Drill #1: Pitcher Covering First Base

Procedure

Place a pylon 13 feet from first base toward home plate and approximately four feet from the first base line in fair territory. Line the pitchers up single-file behind the mound, each of them with a baseball. One catcher is stationed 30 feet from home plate up the first base line, 10 feet into foul territory; and another catcher is behind home plate. The first baseman is in his position on the dirt behind first base, and a coach is at home plate prepared to fungo ground balls as detailed below.

The first pitcher steps on the rubber, winds up and delivers the ball to a catcher behind home plate. The coach fungoes the ball to the first baseman. The pitcher must hold his position until the ball is fungoed before breaking to cover first base. The first baseman fields the ball and tosses it to the pitcher covering first base.

After making the putout at first, the pitcher turns to his *glove side* and throws the ball to the catcher positioned up the first base line. Some runners will attempt to score from second base while the pitcher is covering first—turning in this manner teaches the pitcher to be prepared to make a throw to the plate (or elsewhere) after making the putout at first.

The catcher stationed down the first base line returns the ball back to the pitcher who made the play, and the pitcher returns to the end of the line behind the mound. The catcher behind home plate gives the ball he caught from the last pitcher to the coach and the drill continues.

Coaching Points for the Pitcher

1. *The pitcher must break to first base on all balls hit to his left.* He runs in a direct line to the pylon. This is the fastest way to get to first base—a curved or banana route may enable a fast runner to beat the pitcher to the base.
2. The pitcher runs around the pylon and then inside and parallel to the first base foul line. This route—rather than running from the mound directly to first base—keeps the pitcher from running into the base line and perhaps colliding with the runner.
3. The pitcher slows down and begins "breaking down"—getting his body under control by using short choppy steps—when he is three steps from the base. *No Later!* Breaking down establishes lateral movement and facilitates the fielding process.

Drills 1 and 4 of the Three-In-One Drill, running simultaneously:

PITCHER RUNS AROUND PYLON, WHICH IS 13' FROM FIRST BASE AND 4' FROM FOUL LINE

This diagram depicts Drills 1 and 4 (the first drills in the Three-In-One Drill) running simultaneously. The pitchers are working on covering first base on ground balls to the first baseman. The middle infielders are working on the reverse double play.

4. Make eye contact with the first baseman and ask for the ball early when two or three steps from the base, if possible.
5. A one-handed catch is acceptable—it gives greater flexibility and reach. Watch the ball into the glove. *Catch the ball first, then touch the base!* To avoid contact with the runner, tag first base with the right foot on the inside third of the bag.
6. Do not run past the base before receiving the throw! Stop at the base when the ball is fumbled by the first baseman and take the throw like a first baseman. That is, touch the base with the ball of the foot on the throwing-hand side (righthanders touch the base with their right foot, lefthanders with their left foot).

Coaching Points for the First Baseman

1. The first baseman fields the ground ball and moves aggressively toward first base. This does two things: it shortens the distance to the base, making the throw easier, and it helps the first baseman determine if he can make the play unassisted.
2. If the play can be made unassisted, *run the pitcher off.* Never throw the ball if the play can be made unassisted. Slide into the base if it's a close play, or if the possibility of a collision exists.
3. If the play can't be made unassisted, get the ball out of the glove and keep it in the pitcher's view at all times. Give the ball to the pitcher chest-high as soon as possible, usually when he is two or three steps from first base—this enables the pitcher to make the catch, then find the base.
4. Use an underhanded toss if your momentum is going toward first base and you are within 20 feet of the base. The underhanded toss should be made with a stiff wrist, palm up, and the tossing hand should go no higher than the shoulder. The follow-through should be like that of a bowler. *Walk through your toss!* Do not stop your momentum.
5. On balls hit to the right of the first baseman or balls that otherwise take him away from the base, he should throw with a three-quarter arm action. This presents the ball on a more level plane.
6. If time will allow, when a three-quarter arm action is required, the first baseman should wait for the pitcher to get to the base. If time will not allow, throw the ball chest-high slightly in front and toward the pitcher's right side—the throw must be ahead of the pitcher so that he can run into it… a throw directly to the pitcher will be behind him.

Drill #2: The Topped Ball Between the Mound and First

The in-between ground ball between the first baseman and the pitcher is an extremely difficult situation to defend. It will occur in almost every game and is often misplayed at the major league level. *Hard and fast rules are a must!*

Both the pitcher and the first baseman must go after the ball. However, the pitcher must understand that he *cannot field a ball behind the direct line* from his position at the completion of his delivery and first base, or leave his feet to dive for the ball; if he does, first base will be left uncovered.

If the pitcher can field the topped ball with *normal effort*, and run directly to first base, the defense's chances of retiring the batter are at their best.

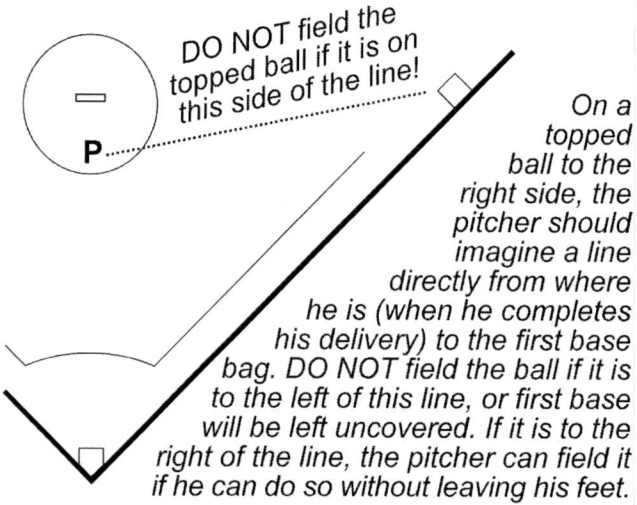

When does a pitcher field the topped ball?

On a topped ball to the right side, the pitcher should imagine a line directly from where he is (when he completes his delivery) to the first base bag. DO NOT field the ball if it is to the left of this line, or first base will be left uncovered. If it is to the right of the line, the pitcher can field it if he can do so without leaving his feet.

Procedure

Remove the pylon from the previous drill. The pitcher steps on the rubber, winds up and delivers the ball to the catcher. The coach fungoes the baseball softly between the pitcher and the first baseman.

Coaching Points for the Pitcher

1. The pitcher breaks on a straight line from the end of his delivery to first base. Field only balls that can be handled easily. *Do not dive or leave your feet*—this would leave first base uncovered.
2. If you can easily field the ball while on a direct line to first base, yell, "I've got it!" This will release the first baseman to go to the base.
3. Run hard toward first base and expect to make the putout unassisted whenever you field a ball while moving in a direct line toward first base.
4. You may field balls to the right (in front of) the direct line to first base. *Call for the ball!* This will release the first baseman to go to the base.

Coaching Points for the First Baseman

1. The first baseman must go after the ball assuming he will have to field it.
2. If the pitcher yells, "I've got it!" the first baseman replies, "Take it!" and returns to first base.
3. If you field the ball, you may have to toss it to the pitcher while he is running to first and looking over his left shoulder. Toss it slightly in front of him to compensate for his forward momentum.

Drill #3: Ground Ball Between the First and Second Basemen

This drill will give the first baseman and second baseman practice in determining who should field ground balls between the two and in making the longer throw to the pitcher covering first base.

Procedure

The pitcher steps on the rubber, winds up and delivers the ball to the catcher behind home plate. The coach fungoes the ball between the first baseman and second baseman, who throw to the pitcher covering first base. The pitcher makes the catch and then throws the ball to the catcher located up the first base line. The pitcher gets the ball back from the catcher and goes to the end of the line.

Coaching Points for the Pitcher

1. On balls to the first baseman's right, the pitcher should break straight to first base and receive the throw like a first baseman. This is the quickest way to get to first base and will allow either the first baseman or second baseman to throw to a stationary target.
2. The pitcher tags the base on the infield side of the base, not on top of the base, and with the ball of the foot, not the side of the foot. Use the right foot if right-handed, the left foot if left-handed.
3. Stride to meet the ball and make the catch only after the ball has been released and you know its location. *Step to the ball after it is released, not before.*

Coaching Points for the First and Second Basemen

1. On ground balls hit between the first baseman and second baseman, the second baseman should yell, "I've got it!" if he can make the play.
2. The first baseman's rule on a ball to his right is: *"If it's hot, give it a shot! If it's slow, let it go!"*

3. Allow the pitcher to get to first base and set up if time permits. Give him a chest-high three-quarter arm throw.

Drill #4: The Reverse Double Play

The "reverse double play" teaches the middle infielders that, with runners on first and second bases, after they have made a force-out at second base and there is no chance of completing the double play at first, a play may exist at third base if the runner there makes too big a turn rounding the base.

The runner from second base often will make an extraordinarily big turn at third under the assumption that the middle infielder will throw to first. Alert teams can often turn this into an easy out, especially if the third base coach is not alert. The runner has his back to the play and cannot see it developing behind him, and when rounding third base, his momentum is going toward the plate and a quick change of direction is often difficult.

Procedure

The shortstop, second baseman, and third baseman are in their positions with a bucket of balls nearby. A coach rolls ground balls to the middle infielders, or each fielder bounces the ball to himself when it's his turn to make the lead throw (see page 91 for the Middle Infielders' Bounce Drill).

The second baseman fields the ground ball (or bounces it to himself) and throws to the shortstop covering second base. (Middle infielders should use and practice their regular double play throws when making feeds to second base…*No sloppy feeds!*) After receiving the feed throw, the shortstop makes a fake throw toward first base and then throws to third base.

> **Timing and Coordination are important:**
>
> While Drills 1-3 are going on, Drills 4-6 happen at the same time. (This use of time is the beauty of the Three-In-One Drill… and it is also where you as the coach must use your time-coordination skills.) In other words, Drills 1 and 4 run concurrently at the beginning of the Set, and you will always do two drills at once.
>
> In this Set, the first basemen and pitchers are involved in Drills 1-3. The shortstops and third basemen are involved in Drills 4-6. The second basemen will work on Drill 4 with the shortstops and third basemen, then join the first basemen and pitchers for Drill 3.

After five repetitions, the procedure is reversed and the shortstop becomes the feeder.

Coaching Points for the Shortstop

1. When the shortstop is the pivot man, he assumes a double play stance at second base and prepares to receive the second baseman's throw. He executes his double play pivot but only *fakes the throw* to first base. (The key to the success of the play is a *legitimate* fake throw. See page 85 for details on the proper way to do this.) On a well-executed fake throw, the third base coach will automatically follow the nonexistent throw to first base, and with the third base coach's attention momentarily diverted from the baserunner, the runner is put in jeopardy and even the smallest turn at third base could result in a putout.
2. After faking the throw to first, the shortstop hops into throwing position and throws to third.

Coaching Points for the Second Baseman

1. When the second baseman is the pivot man, he assumes a double play stance at second base and prepares to receive the shortstop's throw. At this point, he has two options, detailed in points 2 and 3.
2. After receiving the shortstop's throw, he can step on second base and *immediately throw to third.* Because the second baseman is facing third base and the play is in front of him, no fake throw to first base may be necessary against an overly aggressive baserunner or team.
3. Or, he can do as the shortstop is instructed to do—step on the base, make a double play pivot and fake a throw to first base. After making a legitimate fake throw, the second baseman steps with his right foot toward the mound, hops into position and throws the ball to third base.

Coaching Points for the Third Baseman

1. The third baseman assumes a position on the infield side of third base, facing second base. The inside position prevents the baserunner from getting between the ball and the third baseman as the runner attempts to return to third base after rounding the base.
2. Once it is determined the throw is accurate and clear of the runner, the third baseman steps back across the base with the right foot, catches the ball, and applies the tag if the runner slides back into the base, or makes a sweep tag similar to that of a first baseman if the runner returns to the base standing up.
3. Remember, on an inaccurate throw, *leave the base* and get the ball. *No cheap runs!* Ball first, then base!

Drill #5: The Backside Double Play

This is a somewhat unusual play. It occurs when there is a runner on first base and a left-handed pull hitter at bat who hits a ground ball to third base. If the second baseman is playing the hitter to pull, he may be too far from the base to get there in time to turn the double play. In that case, it becomes the shortstop's responsibility to receive the third baseman's throw, make the force-out at second base and complete the double play throw to first.

Procedure

The third baseman and shortstop are involved in this drill. The second baseman is not. The third baseman bounces the ball to himself, fields it and throws to the shortstop covering second base.

Coaching Points for the Shortstop

1. The shortstop covers second base on the third base side of the base, facing the third baseman.
2. He receives the third baseman's throw like a first baseman if a double play is not possible or if there are two outs. The shortstop tags the base with the *ball of the foot* and not the side of the foot. He should wait until the third baseman has thrown the ball and the direction of the ball has been determined before striding. Stride to meet the ball with the foot on the *glove-hand* side. Tag the base with the ball of the opposite foot. (Tagging the base with the *ball of the foot* assures better

contact with the base. The longer the stretch for the ball the more solid the contact with the base will be. Tagging with the side of the foot could result in a loss of contact with the base.)

3. If a double play is possible and the third baseman's throw is accurate, the shortstop can tag second base with his left foot, step to meet the ball with his right foot and then throw to first base to complete the double play. This move is the same as the second baseman's double play pivot via the free right foot (see the chapter detailing this on page 86).

Drill #6: Ball in the Hole Between Shortstop and Third Base

This drill will remind the shortstop and third baseman that a play exists at third base when there is a runner on second and a ball is hit to the shortstop's right (in the hole) and he has no play at first base. When runners are on both first and second base and a force-out at third is possible, this play is especially effective.

Procedure

The shortstop bounces the ball to himself in the hole to his right at medium depth. He makes the catch and throws the ball to the third baseman covering third base. The third baseman plays the base like a first baseman if a force-out exists, or prepares to apply the tag on the runner if the force is not in effect.

****

PART I, SET 2
▶ P/3B work on bunt defense coordination
▶ 2B/SS work on double plays

Two critical areas of the defensive game are covered in this set and practiced simultaneously. The third basemen and pitchers are working on their bunt defense coordination while the middle infielders are working on double play pivots.

Drill #7: Bunt Defense with Runners on First and Second

This drill will teach the pitcher and particularly the third baseman their responsibilities when there are runners on first and second bases and the sacrifice bunt is in order.

Procedure

Station the pitchers at the mound, each of them with a baseball. The third baseman is in a bunt defense position as if there are runners at first and second. The catchers are behind home plate, and a coach is in the batter's box prepared to hit fungoes. The first baseman covers first base to receive either the pitcher or the third baseman's throw if no play is made to third base (this is for drill purposes only—in a normal bunt defense, the second baseman covers first base).

The first pitcher, working from a stretch, delivers the ball to the catcher, and the coach fungoes a simulated bunt toward third base. The third baseman or pitcher fields the ball and throws to third or first base as appropriate.

Coaching Points

For coaching points for the third baseman and pitcher, it is important that you read the chapter entitled "Bunt Defense with Runners on First and Second" on page 137. This details each player's responsibilities in this spot, which is the most difficult defensive situation a third baseman will face.

Drills 7 and 8 of the Three-In-One Drill, running simultaneously:

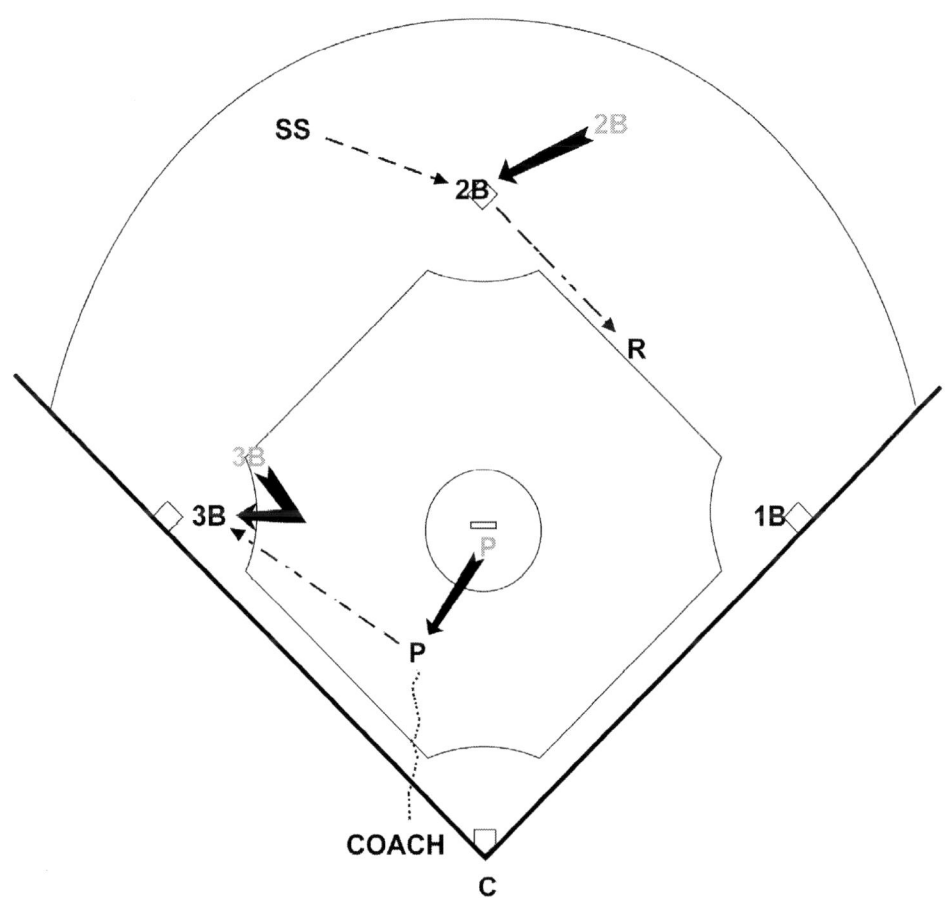

Here, Drills 7 and 8 are run concurrently. The middle infielders are executing the double play bounce drill, with a receiver stationed between first and second to receive the throws. The third baseman and pitcher are working on their bunt defense coordination for the runners-on-first-and-second situation, as the coach fungoes bunts to the third base side.

This diagram happens to show the third baseman retreating to third to receive the pitcher's throw; had the bunt been harder, the third baseman would have charged and thrown to first. See the chapters on the Middle Infielders' Bounce Drill and Bunt Defense with Runners on First and Second for full details on players' fundamentals during this drill.

Drill #8: Shortstop and Second Basemen Double Play Pivot

This drill will help the middle infielders develop their double play feeds and pivots, and will teach them what type of throw to expect depending upon where the ball is hit. This drill runs concurrently with Drill 7.

Procedure

Station one middle infielder at second base to receive throws and execute double play pivots. The other acts as the front man on the double play, bounces the ball to himself and makes feeds to second base. (See the chapter entitled Middle Infielders' Bounce Drill on page 91 for a detailed explanation.)

Station a player or coach approximately halfway between first and second bases to act as a receiver. The middle infielder turning the double play makes a medium-speed throw to this receiver. After making the catch, the receiver returns the ball to the front man on the double play, who then bounces the ball to himself and begins the process over again.

After practicing a prescribed number of feeds, the front man and pivot man should switch roles. The front man/feeder becomes the pivot man and the pivot man becomes the feeder. The second baseman has a greater variety of feeder throws to deal with (on a ball hit directly at him; on a ball hit slightly to his left; on a ball to his extreme left; on a ball toward second base and behind the baseline; and on a ball in front of the baseline), so it is recommended that he execute each of these throws two or three times before switching roles with the shortstop and becoming the pivot man.

Coaching Points

For details on the fundamentals necessary from the shortstop and second baseman during this drill, see the chapters entitled "Middle Infielders' Bounce Drill" on page 91, and "The Double Play via the Free Right Foot" on page 86.

****

PART I, SET 3
- ▶ P/2B/SS practice the count pickoff play
- ▶ 3B/1B work on fielding slow rollers and bunts

Drill #9: The Count Pickoff Play

This drill will teach the pitchers and middle infielders the timing for the "count pickoff play" at second base.

Procedure

Station the pitchers at the mound, each of them with a baseball. The shortstop and second basemen are at their positions. One of the middle infielders signals the pitcher which of them will cover second on the pickoff. The pitcher steps on the rubber, working from a stretch, and at the proper time as detailed below, makes a pickoff throw to the designated middle infielder covering second. Pitchers should alternate pickoff throws to the shortstop and second baseman.

Coaching Points for the Pitcher

1. The pitcher must know which middle infielder has second base responsibility before stepping on the mound.
2. Once the middle infielder gives the verbal sign as detailed below, the pitcher may acknowledge the sign by "brushing down" his pants with his throwing hand.
3. The pitcher steps on the rubber and goes into his stretch. Then, after he comes to the set position, he looks at the middle infielder for the physical sign to begin the play.
4. The pitcher makes a deliberate, exaggerated head turn toward home plate after receiving the middle infielder's sign for the pickoff attempt (the middle infielder will key on the pitcher's head).
5. When the pitcher turns his head back toward home plate, he begins his count (1,001 – 1,002) and then whirls and throws to second base. The pitcher should make a "spin jump," replacing his feet, and then make a firm, waist-high throw over the base. (The pitcher should remember… he does not have to throw to second base. It is legal to make a pickoff move to second without releasing the ball.)
6. The pitcher should realize that he would rather have the pickoff throw be too late rather than too early.

Coaching Points for the Middle Infielders

1. Before the pitcher steps on the mound, the middle infielder who has second base responsibility must let the pitcher know which middle infielder will be covering second. He can do this by getting the pitcher's attention and pointing at himself.
2. Then—also before the pitcher steps on the mound—the same middle infielder gives a verbal sign to the pitcher to alert him of an impending pickoff attempt. Examples include statements like "Not too much straight stuff," or "Nice and easy, now."
3. When the pitcher comes set and looks back at him, the middle infielder who is to cover second gives the pitcher the signal to turn his head and begin his count. The signal can be something like an open mouth or the glove moving on the knee.
4. The infielder *keys on the pitcher's head,* and when the pitcher makes the prescribed exaggerated head-turn toward the plate, the infielder breaks for second to cover the bag for the pickoff attempt.

Drill #10: Slow Rollers to Third, Bunts to First

This drill will give the third baseman practice fielding slow rollers and throwing to first, while the first baseman will work on fielding the bunted ball and throwing to third base. This drill runs concurrently with Drill 9.

Procedure

When the drill begins, the third baseman is in his defensive position, while the first baseman is covering first base. The coach fungoes slow rollers to the third baseman, who fields the ball and throws to first. After several repetitions, they switch roles—the third baseman covers third, while the first baseman fields simulated bunts from the coach and throws to third. The third baseman should assume his sacrifice bunt position with runners on first and second bases and practice returning to third base to receive the first baseman's throw.

Coaching Points

Two chapters illuminate fundamentals for the first and third basemen during this drill. See "New Approaches to the Slow Roller at Third Base" on page 69—this describes the proper way for most third basemen to make this play. And turn to page 137 for "Bunt Defense with Runners on First and Second" for explanations on how the first baseman should field and throw and how the third baseman should return to third.

****
****

PART II, SET 1
- **P/1B/2B/SS work on ground balls back to the mound**
- **C/3B work on catchers' throws to third on a steal attempt with a right-handed hitter at the plate**

Part II of the Three-In-One Drill does not have to be run on the same day as Part I. As the players become more familiar with the drill, it will run more efficiently and take less time to complete. This will make it more practical to run Parts I and II consecutively during the same practice session.

Drill #11: Comebackers

This drill will teach the pitchers to throw accurately to first and second bases when balls are hit back to them—"comebackers," as they are called—and teach the middle infielders to cover second base correctly when receiving the pitcher's throw.

Procedure

Station the pitchers at the mound, each of them with a baseball. The first baseman covers first, and the middle infielders alternate covering second. A catcher is behind home plate to receive the pitch. (After receiving the pitch, the catcher will throw the ball to third as part of Drill 12, as detailed later.)

The first pitcher steps on the mound, delivers the ball to home plate, and prepares to field his position. The coach fungoes a ball to the pitcher, who throws to the first baseman covering first.

After the pitchers have each fielded and thrown to first base several times, they then practice throwing to second, simulating a comebacker with a runner at first. First, the pitcher receives the signal (as he would during a game with a runner at first) from the middle infielder who will be covering second in the event of a comebacker. The pitcher then toes the rubber, works from a stretch (as he would with a runner at first) and throws to the plate. He fields the coach's fungo and throws to the appropriate middle infielder covering second.

If the throw is accurate, the middle infielder executes a double play pivot and throws to first.

Coaching Points for the Pitcher

1. When throwing to first base, the pitcher should field the ball like an infielder, turn to his glove side, take a rhythm step and make a nice, firm throw.
2. When there is a runner on first base and fewer than two outs, the pitcher must know who is covering second before stepping on the rubber to make the pitch. See below for the way the middle infielder will signal this.
3. The pitcher should throw to second base, not to the middle infielder. Allow the middle infielder time to get to the base—if he's late, take another "crow hop" before throwing. Try to make a chest-high throw.
4. If throwing while going up the mound, be sure to follow through, get on top of the ball and be aware of your release point so as not to overthrow second base. "Throw" your throwing hand right at the target.

Coaching Points for the Middle Infielders

1. With a runner at first and fewer than two outs, the middle infielder who will be covering second must let the pitcher know who is covering. He can do this by getting the pitcher's attention and simply pointing to his chest with his index finger. Do this before he steps on the rubber.
2. Middle infielders should "cheat" toward second in this spot—that is, they should play closer to second base if second base is their responsibility. The rule is "three steps in and three steps over."
3. Get one out for sure! If the pitcher makes an inaccurate throw, leave the base and get the ball. Then come back and touch the base. Remember the priority: Ball! Base! Backup!
4. When covering second on this play, the shortstop squares up facing the pitcher *slightly behind second base.* When the second baseman covers second on a comebacker, he squares up facing the pitcher and *straddling second base.* These positions allow the middle infielders to establish lateral movement, increasing their range to catch errant throws from the pitcher. Accurate throws enable the middle infielder to make the putout at second and throw to first using a normal pivot.

Drill #12: Catchers' Throws to Third with a Right-Handed Hitter

This drill will teach the catchers to throw to third base correctly when a right-handed hitter is at bat and a steal of third base is attempted. It runs concurrently with Drill 11.

Procedure

A catcher is stationed behind home plate as part of Drill 11 as detailed earlier. The third baseman covers third. The pitcher who will field the comebacker in Drill 11 toes the rubber and makes his pitch to the plate. As the coach fungoes a ball back to the pitcher, the catcher receives the pitch and throws to third base as if there were an attempted steal of third with a right-handed hitter at bat.

Coaching Points

1. The catcher should never throw over the hitter.
2. The catcher should mentally split home plate in half. If the pitch is on the inside half of the plate, the catcher should throw *behind the hitter*. Use a "cross back step" with the right foot to clear the hitter. If the pitch is on the outside half of the plate, the catcher should throw *in front of the hitter*. He should use his left arm to run the hitter out of the way and protect his throwing arm.
3. The third baseman straddles third base, and after the ball is released and the throw is deemed accurate, he steps across the base with his right foot, catches the ball and applies the tag.

****

PART II, SET 2
▶ P/1B/SS work on the 3-6-1 double play
▶ C/3B work on catchers' throws to third on bunts

Drill #13: The 3-6-1 Double Play

This drill will teach the first baseman to throw to second base accurately; the shortstop to be in the correct position to receive the throw; and the pitcher to cover first and receive the shortstop's throw.

Procedure

Station the pitchers at the mound, each of them with a baseball. The first baseman is at first base as if holding a runner, and the shortstop is in position at double play depth. A pitcher works out of the set position and delivers the baseball to the catcher. The coach, with a baseball in hand, fungoes a ground ball to the first baseman, who throws the ball to the shortstop covering second. The shortstop completes the double play by throwing to the pitcher covering first.

THE THREE-IN-ONE DRILL   57

Drills 13 and 14 of the Three-In-One Drill, running simultaneously:

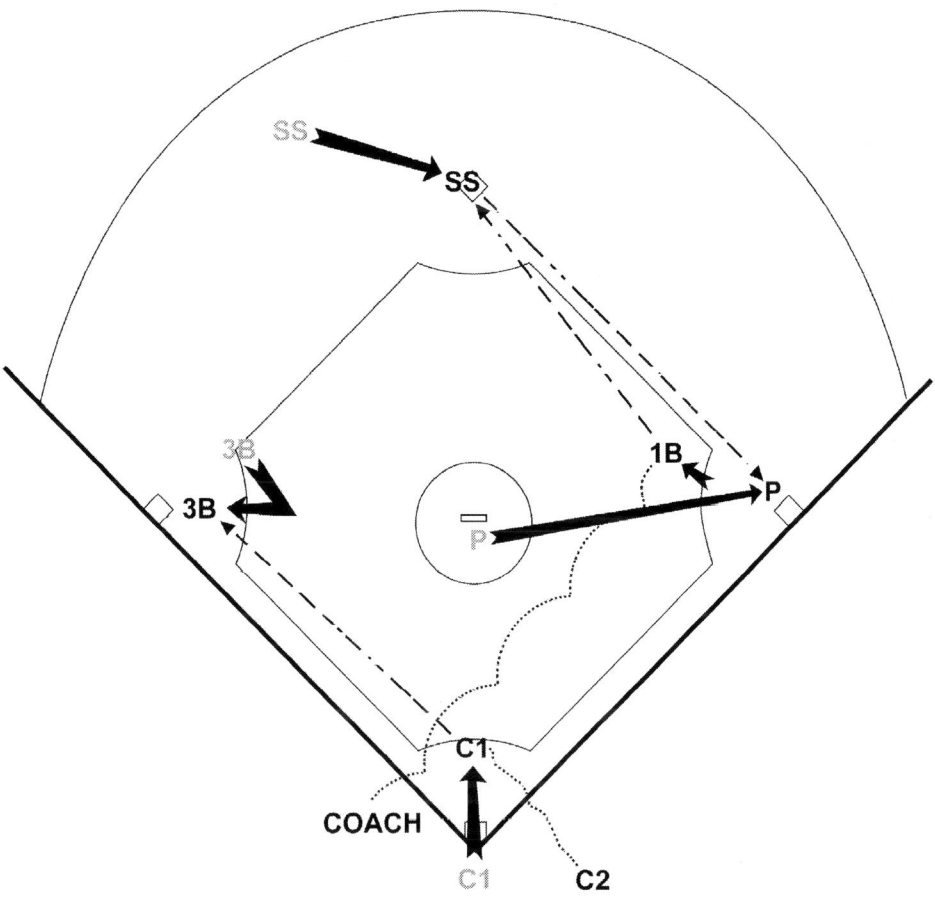

This diagram shows Drills 13 and 14 running at the same time. The pitchers, first baseman and shortstop are working on the 3-6-1 double play. The catchers are practicing fielding bunts and throwing to third.

The coach fungoes a ground ball to first just after the pitcher's pitch crosses the plate. The pitcher runs DIRECTLY to first to cover the bag if necessary. Meanwhile, a second catcher rolls the ball out in front of the plate for the catcher involved in the play to field the bunt and throw to third base.

Coaching Points for the First Baseman

1. The initial throw to the shortstop should be on the infield side of second base to avoid hitting the baserunner. Make a chest-high throw to the shortstop.
2. Don't throw over the baserunner. Left-handed first basemen take a step toward the infield to clear the runner and have an unobstructed throw to second base. Right-handed first basemen use a "cross-back step" to clear the runner and have an unobstructed throw to second (see page 96).

Coaching Points for the Shortstop

1. Give the first baseman an inside target.
2. The left foot is on the third base side of second base, with both hands shoulder-high and body square to the first baseman.
3. Yell "inside!" to give the first baseman a verbal target.
4. Receive the first baseman's throw with hands chest-high and thumb-to-thumb.
5. Take a short step forward with the right foot (the left foot is on the base), make the catch and return the throw to first base.

Coaching Points for the Pitcher

1. Run *directly to first base* and square the body up toward second base.
2. Play the base like a first baseman—stride to meet the ball with the glove-side foot. Delay the stride until the ball has been released and its direction has been determined.
3. Tag the base with the ball of the foot on the throwing-hand side, not with the side of the foot.

Drill #14: Catchers' Throws to Third on Bunts

This drill runs concurrently with Drill 13. It enables the catchers to practice fielding bunts and throwing to third base, simulating the catcher's fielding responsibility in a first-and-second sacrifice bunt situation.

Procedure

A catcher is stationed behind home plate as part of Drill 13 as detailed earlier. The pitcher who will cover first base in Drill 13 toes the rubber and makes his pitch to the plate. As the coach fungoes a ball to the first baseman, another coach or player rolls a ball in front of home plate to simulate a bunt. The catcher moves out front to field the bunt and throws to the third baseman. The third baseman assumes a sacrifice bunt defensive position and stance, and retreats to third base to receive the catcher's throw.

Coaching Points for the Catcher

1. Short bunts often "spin like a top." The baseball must be fielded by placing the mitt in front of the ball and scooping the ball into it with the bare hand. Blocking the baseball with the mitt kills the spin on the ball and forces the catcher to keep his eye on it. The baseball should not be picked up with the bare hand alone.
2. The catcher's chest should be over the ball when picking it up.

Coaching Points for the Third Baseman

1. The third baseman tags the base with the ball of the foot on his throwing-hand side (his right foot), not with the side of the foot. This guarantees solid contact with the base.
2. Stride to meet the ball with the glove-side foot. Delay the stride until the ball has been released and its location and direction have been determined.

PART II, SET 3
▶ **1B/2B/SS/3B work on double plays**
▶ **P/C work on coordination in three key areas**

Drill #15: Double Plays

This drill will give infielders the opportunity to work on double plays as a group. It continues to run while the pitchers and catchers run Drills 16-18.

Procedure

The third baseman, shortstop and second baseman are at their positions. The middle infielders are at double play depth. The first baseman remains at first base to receive throws during the entire drill. The coach fungoes ground balls to the third baseman, shortstop and second baseman, who execute 5-4-3, 6-4-3 and 4-6-3 double plays. The coach should stand in the area outside the right-handed batter's box, slightly up the third base line, clearing the home plate area for the pitchers and catchers to do their work in Drills 16-18, which will run concurrently with this one. This is a rapid-fire drill, but caution must be exercised to avoid injuries. The coach who is hitting ground balls must be aware of the pitchers simultaneously executing their drills, and fungo only when the pitchers are out of the way. This is achieved by hitting only between the pitcher's deliveries.

Coaching Points

Double play fundamentals for the shortstop and second baseman are detailed in the chapters entitled "Middle Infielders' Bounce Drill" on page 91, and "The Double Play via the Free Right Foot" on page 86.

Drill #16: Passed Balls and Wild Pitches

Drills 16-18, involving the pitchers and catchers, all run while the infielders are turning double plays in Drill 15.

This drill will teach pitchers how to cover home plate in the event of a passed ball or wild pitch with a runner on third base. Pitchers will also learn how to help the catcher locate the ball that goes behind home plate toward the backstop. Catchers will learn how to make a shin guard slide and throw to the pitcher covering home plate.

Procedure

Station the pitchers at the mound. They do *not* have a baseball. The catchers are in full gear, taking turns behind home plate. The pitchers take turns working from a stretch and making an *imaginary* pitch to the plate. The catcher is in a receiving position.

The next catcher or a coach stands near home plate, out of the catcher's view, with a baseball in his hand. After the pitch has been made, he rolls the ball toward the backstop. The catcher goes after the ball and throws to the pitcher covering home plate.

Drills 15 and 16 of the Three-In-One Drill, running simultaneously:

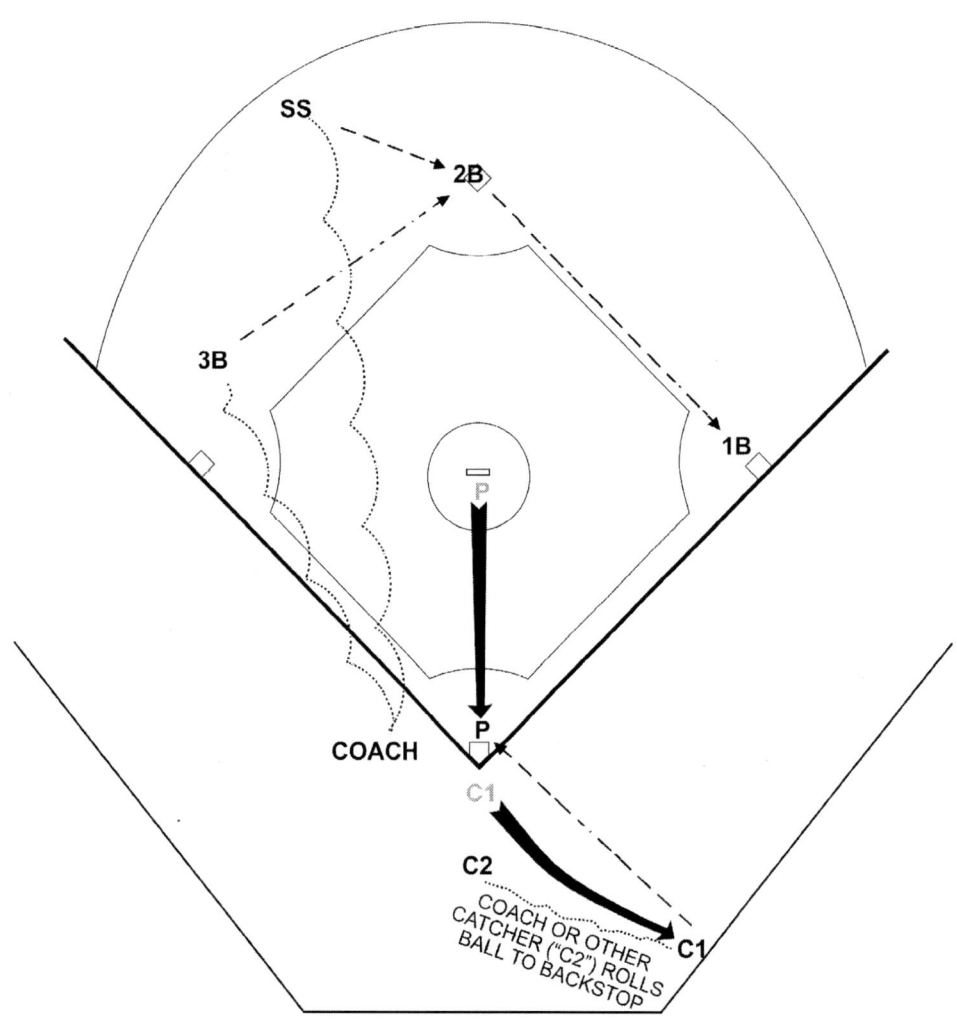

This diagram shows Drills 15 and 16 of the Three-In-One Drill. In Drill 15, the coach fungoes ground balls to the third baseman, shortstop and second baseman, who execute 5-4-3, 6-4-3 and 4-6-3 double plays. (The diagram shows only ground balls to the left side; on a ground ball to the second baseman, the shortstop, obviously, covers second.) In this drill, the first baseman does not field ground balls, but acts only as a receiver.

While Drill 15 is running, the pitchers and catchers work on their coordination in Drills 16-18. This diagram depicts a simulated wild pitch or passed ball from Drill 16 -- the pitcher makes an imaginary pitch, and another coach or the next catcher rolls a ball to the backstop. The pitcher and catcher execute the play as detailed in this chapter.

Coaching Points for the Pitcher

1. As the pitcher runs to cover home plate, he points at the ball to give the catcher a visual clue as to its location and simultaneously yells, "There, there, there!"
2. The pitcher stands in front of home plate (on the fair territory side), facing the catcher. After the catcher tosses the ball and its direction is determined, the pitcher steps across home plate with his left foot, makes the catch and tags the runner attempting to score from third base.
3. Tag the runner with the back of the glove, sweeping the glove in front of home plate. The runner will tag himself out. If time permits, the pitcher should have the baseball in his *bare hand* and then put it back into the glove and make the tag two-handed with the back of the glove. If the hands are split during contact, the ball will not be dropped.

Coaching Points for the Catcher

1. The catcher locates the baseball.
2. He makes a shin guard slide on the right side of the ball, scooping it up and making a quick, compact-arm toss to the pitcher covering home plate.

Drill #17: The Pitch-Out

This drill will teach pitchers how to correctly execute a pitch-out.

Procedure

Station the pitchers at the mound. Each has a baseball. The catchers take turns behind home plate in a receiving position. The pitchers take turns, working from a set position, and making pitch-outs as detailed below. The catcher receives the pitch, shifts into throwing position and fakes a throw to second base.

Coaching Points for the Pitcher

1. The set position should be held longer than normal to disrupt the baserunner's timing when the pitch-out is called.
2. Slide step for a quick delivery to home plate. No high leg kick! Use a knee-to-knee delivery for quickness from the set position, with 80% of the weight on the back leg. Bring the knee of the striding leg to the knee of the back leg when making the delivery.
3. The pitch should be chest-high to the catcher, about three feet outside home plate. Aim for the middle of the opposite batter's box.
4. Don't try to throw "too hard," which negatively impacts accuracy. Give the catcher a ball he can handle easily.

Drill #18: The Intentional Walk

This drill will teach pitchers how to handle the intentional walk.

Procedure

As in the previous drill, the pitchers are at the mound, each with a ball. The catchers take turns behind home plate, each standing as detailed below. The pitchers take turns, working from a set position and making pitches as detailed below.

Coaching Points for the Pitcher

1. Throw medium-speed fastballs at 75% to 80% of normal velocity. Never lob the ball! The pitch should be chest high.
2. Control all baserunners before making the delivery to home plate.

Coaching Points for the Catcher

1. Give the target by standing as far as possible to the side of the catcher's box opposite the hitter. With a right-handed hitter, the target should be made with the right hand extended into the left-handed batter's box. With a left-handed hitter, the target should be made with the catcher's glove extended into the right-handed batter's box.
2. The catcher cannot leave the catcher's box until the pitcher releases the ball.

****

PART II, SET 4
▶ All players work on pitchers' pickoffs to each base

The drills in this set will give pitchers the opportunity to practice and perfect their pickoff moves to all bases, and to use a "compact arm" for quickness on pickoff throws. Infielders will learn proper timing on pickoff attempts, and all players involved will learn the basic pickoff philosophy, which is to control a baserunner's primary lead by "scaring the hell out of him"—an out is a bonus! This philosophy controls the runner's actions and decreases the chances of a wild throw by eliminating desperate, inaccurate pickoffs, and pickoff throws that are too hard.

Pitchers are reminded that it is better for pickoff throws to be late, rather than early. And remember, if there is a breakdown in timing or execution of a pickoff attempt at second base or third base, *do not throw to that base! No play... no throw!*

The pitcher should step off the rubber whenever the timing of a pickoff play breaks down. This sends a message to the baserunner that he must be cautious, achieving the desired result without making a needless, risky throw.

Basic Setup for Drills 19-21

Each pitcher should have a baseball. Three of them work at once: one on the mound, one on the grass by the third base side of the mound, and one on the grass by the first base side of the mound. All other pitchers line up behind the pitcher on the third base side.

Pitchers make three pickoffs at each station, then rotate—third base side to mound to first base side to the end of the line). The middle infielders are in their positions, alternating taking pickoff throws from the pitcher. The first baseman holds an imaginary runner at first base, and the third baseman is at his position. Catchers are stationed behind home plate to work with the pitcher on the mound and the middle infielders.

Drills 19, 20 and 21 of the Three-In-One Drill, running simultaneously:

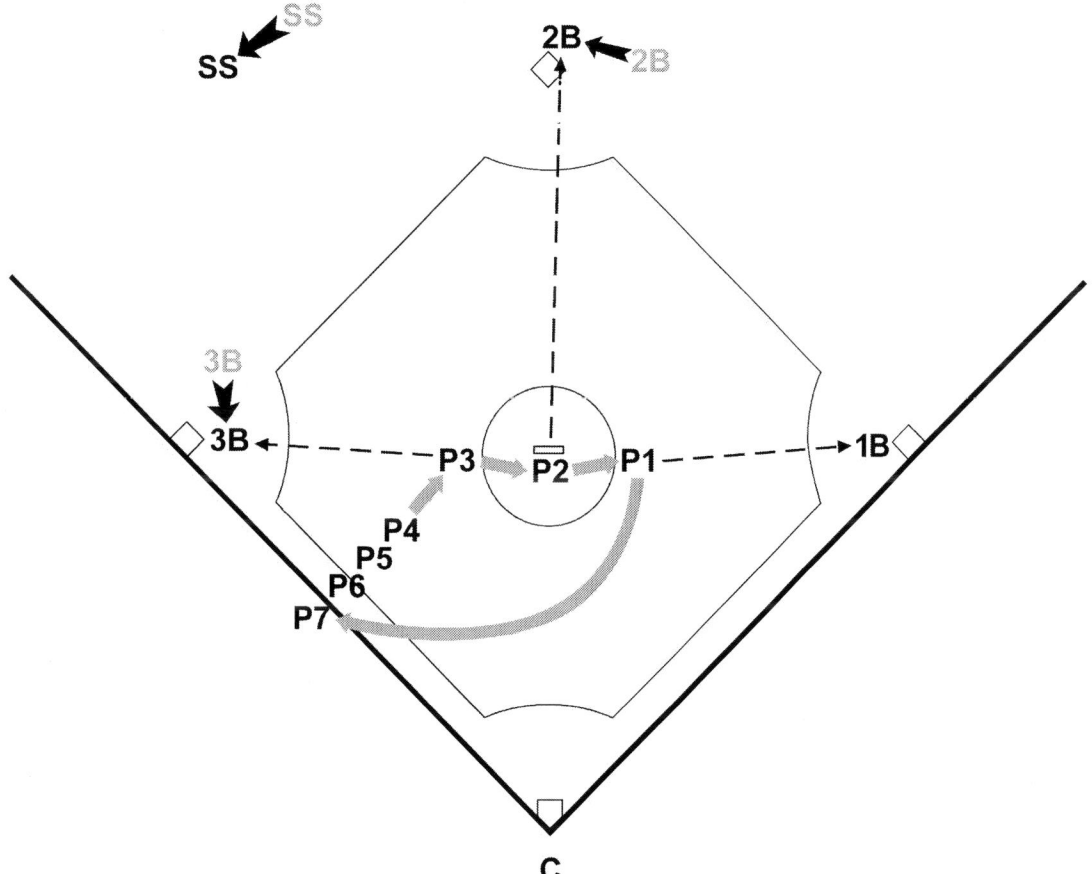

The gray arrows in this diagram depict the rotation of the pitchers in Drills 19-21. For example, "P3" will execute three pickoffs to third base (Drill 20), three pickoffs to second base (Drill 21) and three pickoffs to first base (Drill 19), before returning to the end of the line.

Here the second baseman is covering second, and the shortstop is moving toward the hole to simulate drawing the runner at second farther off the base; on alternating pickoff throws, the shortstop would cover second.

See the description of each drill for details on how pitchers and position players should handle the fundamentals of pickoffs in this portion of the Three-In-One Drill.

Drill #19: Pickoffs to First Base

Procedure

The pitcher on the grass on the first base side of the mound works on his pickoff move to first base.

Coaching Points for the Pitcher

1. Use a "compact arm" for quickness. To do this, keep the hand and fingers on top of the ball, and don't drop the ball below the belt during the pickoff throw.
2. Right-handed pitchers should practice throwing to first base from the following positions (all throws are from the set position): on the way up, on the way down, and at the bottom.
3. For left-handed pitchers to be successful, their arm angle must be three-quarters or lower—overhand arm angle pickoff attempts are very seldom successful.
4. The regular move for a lefthander is very simple and highly effective. The pitcher looks the baserunner in the eye—*eyeball to eyeball!* The pitcher comes to the balance point, turns his head toward home plate, and either picks to first base or delivers to the plate. *All moves of the head should be deliberate and sharp.*
5. The lefthander can also use a "quick step-back" move in a situation where the runner may break on the pitcher's first movement. Ideally, this is used with a 3-2 count and two outs. The pitcher steps quickly back off the rubber and makes a quick sidearm throw to first (although, since he stepped off the rubber, he is now an infielder and does not have to throw). Do not over-use this move… it loses its effectiveness.

> ### *The proper pickoff stance for a first baseman:*
>
> The proper position for the first baseman when holding the runner at first base is to have both feet shoulder-width apart and *pointing toward the pitcher*.
>
> The right foot is next to the inside corner of the base closest to second base. The left foot is parallel to the right foot and pointing toward the mound.
>
> This stance does two things: it enables the first baseman to move laterally for errant throws, and it helps him avoid contact and avoid getting entangled with the runner on bad pickoff attempts.
>
> On the other hand, standing sideways to the pitcher when holding a runner at first base totally commits the first baseman to a perfect throw from the pitcher, costs him lateral movement and guarantees entanglement with the runner on errant throws.
>
> **Ask yourself this: "How often does a pickoff attempt result in a putout?" The answer…** *very seldom,* **when compared to the number of throws that are made to first base. Therefore, it's best to play the throw (with the first baseman in a proper stance) and not the tag (with the first baseman standing sideways).**

Drill #20: Pickoffs to Third Base

This drill will teach the proper mechanics and timing for the pickoff play to third base; reinforce the basic pickoff philosophy of "scaring the hell out of the runner"; reinforce the concept of a "late" pickoff throw rather than an "early" one; and emphasize "no cheap runs" because of a poor pickoff.

Because runners will often break on the pitcher's first movement, this play is especially effective when the bases are loaded, there are two outs and a 3-2 count on the hitter. This scenario leaves the runner at third highly vulnerable to the pickoff play. The pitcher/third baseman pickoff play will also work well against an overly aggressive baserunner who takes a large lead off third base, fakes the steal of home and attempts to distract the pitcher. Overuse of this play will diminish its effectiveness.

Procedure

The third baseman is in a pickoff position—in closer to the base line and slightly behind the base. He puts the sign on and breaks for third base to receive the pitcher's throw. The pitcher working on the third base side of the mound throws a pickoff to third.

Coaching Points for the Third Baseman

1. The third baseman must "cheat" in and over toward third base—how far will depend upon individual quickness and can be determined when practicing this drill. Normally, the third baseman will be even with or slightly back of the base.
2. Faking the runner at third by taking a left-right step toward the hitter will help set up the play. The fake steps condition both the runner and the third base coach to this action, and when the actual pickoff play is on, they concede the first two steps before reacting. This greatly enhances the chances of picking the runner off base.
3. The sign for the pickoff at third base should be both verbal as well as physical to be sure there are no slip-ups resulting in a cheap run scoring. If the third baseman breaks for the bag and the pitcher delivers to home plate, his position is left wide open and the chance for a base hit on a ball hit to the left side of the infield is greatly increased. A good example of a verbal sign is, "Come on righthander," or "Come on lefthander," as the case may be. The physical sign could be the third baseman bringing his glove to his chest and holding it there.
4. With a right-handed pitcher on the mound, throwing from the set position, the third baseman keys on the pitcher's *left foot* and breaks for third base when he lifts it up. With a left-handed pitcher on the mound, the pitcher will take his sign in the windup position. The third baseman keys on the pitcher's head. He breaks toward third base when the pitcher nods his head.
5. The third baseman breaks for a position on the inside/infield side of third base and squares up to the pitcher. This position allows for lateral movement and clearance from the baserunner should the pitcher's throw be off-target. (Straddling the base, on the other hand, increases the chances of the baserunner getting between the third baseman and the ball, resulting in the ball getting away from the third baseman. This can happen even though the pitcher's throw is accurate, if the baserunner comes back in standing up and gets his body between the ball and the fielder.)
6. Ideally, the third baseman should be at the base a second or two before the pitcher releases the ball. When it is determined that the throw is accurate, the third baseman can make the catch, step back across the base with his right foot and make the tag.

Coaching Points for the Right-Handed Pitcher

1. The right-handed pitcher receives the third baseman's verbal or physical sign and replies with a "brush down" on either his shirt or pants with his glove or bare hand.
2. He comes to the set position, then begins his pitching motion, coming to his balance position very deliberately.
3. He steps directly toward third base and makes a three-quarter-arm throw to the base.
4. **Attention!** It is a BALK if the entire free foot breaks the plane of the back edge of the pitcher's rubber and the pitcher throws to any base other than second base or home plate.
5. *Don't overthrow!* That is, don't try to throw too hard, which could result in an inaccurate throw.

Coaching Points for the Left-Handed Pitcher

1. This pickoff attempt differs from the right-handed pitcher's pickoff at third base. The left-handed pitcher's pickoff attempt originates from the windup position, not the stretch.
2. The pitcher receives the third baseman's verbal or physical sign and replies with a "brush down" on either his shirt or pants with his glove or bare hand.
3. The pitcher's left foot is on the rubber and his right foot is farther back to facilitate the throw to third base. The toe of the right foot should be opposite the instep/heel of the left foot. This position makes it easier for the pitcher to open his hips and step directly toward third base. Throwing across the body increases the chance of a wild throw and giving up a cheap run.
4. While standing on the rubber in the windup position and acting as if he were getting the sign from the catcher, the pitcher nods his head—this is the third baseman's key to break for third base. The pitcher's nod must be distinct!
5. The pitcher should watch the third baseman break for the base using his peripheral vision. He then opens up, steps directly toward third base with his free right foot, and makes a sidearm throw as the third baseman approaches the base.
6. *Don't overthrow.* This usually results in an inaccurate, wild throw. No cheap runs!
7. Most runners are picked off third base because they transfer their weight prematurely and are caught with their weight on the wrong foot; therefore, a firm, accurate well-timed throw is the key and is all that is necessary.

Drill #21: The "Flipper Play" Pickoff at Second Base

This pickoff differs in that the pitcher does not look at the middle infielder prior to throwing to second base. He relies solely on the catcher to tell him when to turn and throw.

It's effective because the pitcher doesn't look at second base, but makes what appears to be a "blind" throw. In reality, this is a rather simple pickoff attempt. It can be used any time there is a runner on second base, and it's particularly effective with runners on second and third and two outs. In this spot, the runner at second base is extremely vulnerable because he becomes complacent and careless, with his attention directed more toward the hitter and away from his baserunning responsibilities. And the third base coach tends to direct his attention to the runner at third base, leaving the runner at second on his own.

This drill will teach the pitcher, catcher, and middle infielders the timing necessary to execute this "no look" pickoff play. It will take advantage of the baserunner that expects the pitcher to look back at him before making a pickoff attempt or delivering the ball to home plate.

Procedure

The pitcher in the middle of the drill (the one on the mound) is the one who makes pickoff throws to second. A catcher is in position behind the plate, and the middle infielders are in their positions. Pickoff plays are made as detailed below.

Coaching Points for the Pitcher

1. Before stepping on the rubber, the pitcher first receives the verbal and physical signal from the middle infielder that the "Flipper Play" is on (the pitcher must know which infielder has coverage responsibility at second base). He acknowledges the sign by replying with a "brush down" the shirt or pants with his glove or bare hand.
2. He goes into his set position while looking at the catcher, and does not look back at the runner on second.
3. On the catcher's signal (an upward motion of the right hand on his chest protector—a "flip"), the pitcher makes a spin jump and throws to second base. Pitchers follow their glove—that is, a righthander turns counterclockwise, while a lefthander turns clockwise.
4. Pitchers should remember that they do not have to throw to second base—it is not a balk to fake a pickoff there. Don't throw if there is a breakdown in the timing of the play.

Coaching Points for the Catcher

1. Catchers may initiate the play by using verbal and physical signs. If the play is initiated by one of the middle infielders, the catcher must acknowledge the sign by tugging on his right ear lobe with his right hand.
2. The catcher assumes his catching stance with his open right hand in the middle of his chest protector. He watches the middle infielder break for second base. When he sees the middle infielder is near the base and will beat the baserunner, he makes an upward sweeping motion on his chest protector with his right hand—*a flipping motion*. This is the pitcher's sign to pivot and throw immediately to second base.
3. The catcher must learn to time the "flipping action" to coincide with the middle infielder's arrival at second base. Remember that the pitcher's throw should be late rather than early.
4. If the timing of the play breaks down, the catcher should yell, "Step off!" to the pitcher.

Coaching Points for the Second Baseman

1. The second baseman is the pickoff man with a right-handed hitter at the plate. (Although this play works well with either the shortstop or second baseman, it is slightly more effective when the second baseman is covering.)
2. The second baseman may initiate the play by use of verbal and physical signs. The verbal sign can be, "Come on flipper!" and the physical sign can be a tug of the right ear lobe. If the play is initiated by the catcher with a right-handed hitter at the plate, the second baseman must acknowledge the sign, perhaps by tugging on his right ear lobe.
3. The runner can be "set up" by telling the shortstop to play the hitter to pull—tell him loud enough so that the runner can hear. The shortstop moves away from second base toward third as a decoy.
4. The second baseman takes a position six to eight feet from second base. He begins his fake toward the runner at second base when the pitcher's hands are at the top of his stretch and starting down. The fake is executed by anchoring the right foot and using it as a pivot. Taking a crossover "jab step" with the left foot toward second base and simultaneously pounding the glove will drive the runner back toward the base.
5. After making his initial fake, the second baseman "squares up" to home plate and takes a lateral scoot away from second base. (He must be balanced, have lateral movement, and be ready to

return to second base.) The runner, seeing the second baseman move away from the base, will start to reestablish his lead.
6. The second baseman breaks for the base when he sees the baserunner change direction and begin to reestablish his lead. This timing increases the defense's chances of catching the runner with his weight going toward third base, losing lateral movement and becoming an easy pickoff victim.
7. When the catcher sees the second baseman break for second base, he gives the "flip sign" to the pitcher, who pivots and throws to second. The second baseman covers second base and receives the pitcher's throw by squaring up behind the base (to establish lateral movement) and when it is determined that the throw is accurate, stepping across the base with the left foot, making the catch and applying the tag on the runner.

Coaching Points for the Shortstop

1. The shortstop is the pickoff man with a left-handed hitter at the plate.
2. The shortstop may initiate the play by use of verbal and physical signs when he is the pickoff man, using the same "Come on flipper!" verbal sign and tug-of-the-ear-lobe physical sign detailed in the previous section. And if the play is initiated by the catcher with a left-handed hitter at the plate, the shortstop must acknowledge the sign, perhaps by tugging on his right ear lobe.
3. The shortstop assumes a position approximately six feet behind the baserunner. His right foot is in line with the baserunner's left foot—this gives the shortstop "inside position," which is critical for the success of any pickoff play.
4. The shortstop should begin his fake toward second base when the pitcher is at the top of his stretch and starting down. The fake is executed by anchoring the right foot and making an aggressive "jab step" with the left foot toward second base and simultaneously pounding the glove.
5. After making his initial fake, the shortstop squares up into his normal stance and waits for the baserunner to move away from second base and start to re-establish his lead. When the runner does this, the shortstop breaks for second.
6. When the catcher sees the shortstop break for second base, he gives the "flip sign" to the pitcher, who pivots and throws to second base.
7. The shortstop covers second base and receives the pitcher's throw by squaring up behind the bag (to establish lateral movement). When it is determined that the throw is accurate, he steps across the base with his left foot, making the catch and applying the tag on the runner.

Okay, Take a Deep Breath

You've just been presented with a great deal of information. This drill, when fully learned by your players, will pay dividends all season long. Break it down into its components and learn them one-by-one.

This is just one example of a master multiple defensive drill. Exactly what components should be included in such a drill will be an individual matter. The age, maturity and skill level of the players is of course a prime consideration. The examples that are presented here are advanced and designed for older, more sophisticated players, but should serve as a model.

Good Luck!

New Approaches to the Slow Roller at Third Base

"God watches over drunks and third basemen." – Leo Durocher

The slow roller presents a real fielding challenge for the third baseman. Because the third baseman is charging straight ahead toward home plate, and his momentum is going away from first base, it is extremely difficult for him to make a throw to first which is accurate and has sufficient velocity to beat the batter/runner. For these reasons many third basemen consider it their toughest play.

The slow roller results from a topped ball—often referred to as a swinging bunt—or a drag bunt attempt by the hitter. In either case, it usually creates a do-or-die play for the third baseman.

Traditional Fielding Method

The conventional method of fielding the slow roller to third base was popularized by former Orioles great Brooks Robinson. He said, "The slow-hit ball should be fielded on the run and in front of the right or just outside the right foot. I like to have the ball roll into the palm of my bare hand, while I have my left foot forward. I will then make the throw as I step onto my right foot." (Quoted from *The Complete Baseball Handbook* by Walter Alston and Don Weiskopf, p. 290.) This is a spectacular play, and it looks great when successful.

However, it is difficult to execute at the amateur level, and difficult to teach.

Usually, throws lack velocity and tend to be erratic, due to the fact that the third baseman's momentum is going toward home plate and he is in an awkward position when he makes his throw to first base. One result of this inaccurate tailing throw is the first baseman being pulled off the base and into the foul line on the home plate side of the base. Often, collision or entanglement with the batter/runner results.

A New Concept

There is another way. Salty Parker taught an excellent method of fielding the slow roller when he was the minor league infield instructor for the San Francisco Giants. Parker's method of handling the slow roller at third base does not appear in coaching literature, but deserves serious consideration and thought.

Some advantages of Parker's method are as follows:

– It is easily taught and executed.
– The third's baseman's body is in good throwing position, which allows for greater accuracy and velocity on throws.
– It enables the average third baseman to be successful making this play.
– The third baseman's momentum is toward first base, facilitating his throw there.

The Salty Parker Method

To use this alternate method to fielding the slow roller, the third baseman should:
1. Charge the ball.
2. Approach the ball slightly to the right to get momentum going toward first base.
3. Bring the body under control by breaking down using "chop steps."
4. Field the baseball off the inside of the right foot—the ball of the right foot.
5. Keeping the fanny down when fielding the baseball is an absolute must.
6. Backhand the baseball off the ball of the right foot.
7. The right foot is in front of the left foot when the ball is fielded. This facilitates the throw to first base by allowing the left side of the body to open easily. It also generates momentum toward first base.
8. Once the ball is fielded, come up throwing to save time—do not come up and then throw. The third baseman should field the ball, take his rhythm step and come up throwing in one continuous, almost simultaneous motion.

The greater velocity of the throw using this method compensates for a slightly slower release. (The rule of thumb is that 1½ X miles per hour = feet per second; so, 80 mph = 120 feet per second.) This "backhand method" allows for a high percentage of success, and it builds player confidence because immediate success is possible.

Joe Morgan was a second baseman, but the idea he advocates still applies to this situation. Morgan wrote in his book, *Baseball My Way:* "You want to make sure you catch the ball first, before you try to throw. That is why I don't like to barehand the ball; I want to make sure I catch it. If I miss the runner, I miss him, but at least I haven't missed the ball and given him the certain chance to make it that he wouldn't have had if I had caught the ball cleanly."

Fielding the Slow Roller to the Third Baseman's Left: Bobo's Method

This approach is for a ball that brings the third baseman in and to his left for a ball that needs to be fielded just past the pitcher's mound on the third base side.

If the third baseman gets to the ball quickly and has his body under control, a conventional throw to first base should be made for the putout. *Whenever possible, this is the technique of choice!* However, a large number of slow rollers to the third baseman's left must be fielded one-handed and on the run in the area on the grass between the third baseman and the pitcher's mound.

Running full speed toward first base, the third baseman will often have a difficult time getting his weight under control and his body into throwing position. Because of the difficulty of opening up the left side of his body, the third baseman is forced to throw across his body using a sidearm or submarine throw. The danger with this type of throw is that it often generates enormous ball movement. The ball will often tail away from the first baseman, pulling him off the base, into the baseline and into the runner.

Bobo Brayton, the former Washington State University baseball coach, taught his third basemen (and me) a technique to deal with this particular play:

To use this method of fielding the slow roller *to his left*, the third baseman should:
1. Charge the ball and field it one-handed on the run.
2. Continue running toward first base with his chest open to first base; he is not in a conventional throwing position.
3. Throw the ball overhand while running toward first base.

Using this method, the body and legs will become synchronized almost automatically. A fluid delivery of the ball results. Overhand throws can fool the first baseman only on one plain: vertically. This increases the first baseman's chances of making the catch. Submarine throws, on the other hand, with their ball movement and "tailing" action, tend to fool the first baseman on two plains: vertically and horizontally. This decreases his chances of making the catch.

Drill #1

Purpose: To teach the third baseman the "Salty Parker Method" of fielding the slow roller.

Procedure:
1. Station the first baseman at first base.
2. Place three baseballs on the ground halfway up the third base line, and halfway between the line and the pitcher's mound. The balls should be approximately three feet apart to avoid stepping on them while executing the drill.
3. Line all third basemen one behind the other and even with third base.
4. The baseballs should be fielded in order, starting with the baseball closest to the pitcher's mound and working toward the third base foul line.
5. The third baseman fields the ball using the Salty Parker Method and throws to first base.
6. The coach makes appropriate suggestions and/or corrections.

Drill #2

Purpose: To teach the third baseman the "Salty Parker Method" of fielding the slow roller.

Procedure:
1. Station the first baseman at first base.
2. Line all third basemen one behind the other at third base in their normal position.
3. The coach rolls or fungoes a slow roller to the third baseman.
4. The third baseman fields the ball using the Salty Parker Method and throws to first base.
5. The coach makes appropriate suggestions and/or corrections.

Drill #3

Purpose: To teach "Bobo's Method" of fielding the slow roller hit to the third baseman's left.

Procedure:
1. Station the first baseman at first base.
2. Line all third basemen one behind the other at third base in their normal position.
3. The coach rolls or fungoes slow rollers to the third baseman's left and in on the grass.
4. The third baseman fields the ball using Bobo's Method and throws to first base.
5. The coach makes appropriate suggestions and/or corrections.

Walter Alston summed it up in *The Complete Baseball Handbook:* "The young third baseman should employ the two-hand technique whenever possible and resort to the one-hander only in do-or-die situations."

Good Luck!

Playing the Ball

"Luck is the residue of design." – Branch Rickey

Successful infielders *play the ball*. They move to the ball while reading the hops; they identify the hop they want and then field the ball. They are seldom fooled, and they always seem to get a good hop to field. Yes, it's true: *Good infielders get good hops!* They read the hops of a ground ball like they read the words in a book. And they react accordingly.

Infielders who have difficulties, on the other hand, *allow the ball to play them.* That is, they lay back and wait for the ball to come to them, fielding whatever hop happens to come along. It should be obvious that this method of fielding ground balls leads to inconsistent play. Success is dependent upon chance.

Identifying the Correct Hop

Obviously, the easiest hop to field is the high hop. It is often referred to as the "charity hop," because it is a gift to the defensive player. If the infielder cannot field the ground ball on a high hop, then the short hop becomes the hop of choice, where the ball is fielded close to the ground just after it has bounced and has first started its ascent. The fielder's glove may be touching the ground as the ball is trapped.

See the diagram of the bouncing ball below. #1 indicates the best hop, the high hop; #2 indicates the next-best hop, the short hop:

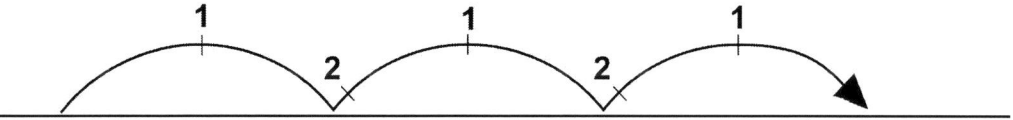

The best place to field a hop is at #1, the apex of the hop. The second-best place to field it is at #2, a very short hop just after it hits the ground.

Short Hop Drill #1

Purpose: To teach infielders to play the ball, move to the ball, read the hop, and field the short hop.

Procedure:
1. The infielders line up single-file on the dirt or hard surface. Each infielder has a baseball.
2. The coach assumes a position approximately 25 feet from the infielders.
3. The infielder tosses the baseball to the coach and assumes a "ready/set" fielding position. He places his throwing hand behind his back and prepares to field the ball one-handed with the glove alone.

4. The coach throws a high bounce—five or six feet high—to the infielder.
5. The infielder moves forward and catches the ball on the short hop only.
6. After making the catch, the infielder keeps the baseball and returns to the end of the line.

Using only the glove hand to field focuses the infielder's attention on the baseball, forcing him to concentrate on reading the hop. One high bounce gives him sufficient time to move forward and field the short hop.

Short Hop Drill #2

Purpose: To teach infielders proper glove control when fielding a short hop.

Procedure:
1. Divide the infielders into pairs and have the two players face each other about six feet apart.
2. The infielders should assume a good defensive position with gloves open and touching the ground in front of their body.
3. Partners throw short hops back and forth to each other. Tosses should be such that they create a short hop for the receiving player and should not be thrown too hard.

High Hop (or Charity Hop) Drill

Purpose: To learn to read the high hop.

Procedure:
1. The infielders line up single-file on the dirt or hard surface. Each infielder has a baseball.
2. The coach assumes a position approximately 25 feet from the infielders.
3. The infielder tosses the baseball to the coach and assumes a ready/set fielding position.
4. The coach throws a moderately high bounce to the infielder.
5. The infielder moves forward and fields the ball on the high hop only. He may use both hands when fielding the ball.
6. After making the catch, the infielder keeps the baseball and returns to the end of the line.

Either Hop Drill

Purpose: To teach infielders to move to a ground ball, read and select the correct hop, and field the ball properly.

Procedure:
1. The infielders line up single-file on the dirt (preferably at the shortstop position) or other hard surface. Each infielder has a baseball.
2. The coach assumes a position approximately 25 feet from the infielders.
3. The infielder tosses the baseball to the coach and assumes a ready/set fielding position.
4. The coach throws a ground ball to the infielder.
5. The infielder moves forward and chooses his hop.
6. After making the catch, the infielder keeps the baseball and returns to the end of the line.
7. The coach reviews how the player read the hop and makes appropriate corrections.

Variation:
1. The coach may move back and fungo ground balls to the infielders.
2. The assistant coach or a player goes to first base to receive throws.
3. The infielders throw to first base after fielding the ground ball.

Wall Drill

Purpose: An easy and excellent way for infielders to practice fielding ground balls.

Procedure when used individually:
1. The infielder throws a baseball against the wall and practices fielding the ball.
2. This is an excellent opportunity for the infielder to practice backhanding the ball.
3. The drill continues until the coach stops it, based on time, number of throws, successful catches, etc.

Procedure when used as a group:
1. Infielders form a single-file line facing the wall.
2. The first infielder in line throws the ball against the wall and then goes to the end of the line.
3. The second infielder in line assumes a ready/set fielding position as the first infielder throws the ball against the wall. The second infielder fields the ball, throws it against the wall, and goes to the end of the line.
4. The drill continues until the coach stops it, based on time, number of throws, successful catches, etc.

The Wall Drill can be made competitive by pairing individuals or groups against each other. The first individual or group to field a prescribed number of ground balls or the most ground balls within a specified time is the winner. (Errors don't count.) Use your imagination!

Summary

Move to the ball and catch it at the *top of the hop*. If this isn't possible, trap the ball on the short hop. *Avoid in-between hops at all costs.*

Good Luck!

Pop Fly Defense Drills

"Gravity is a contributing factor in nearly 73 percent of all accidents involving falling objects."
– Dave Barry

Jim Lefebvre estimated that seventeen percent of all fly balls are base hits. How many of these should have been caught?

Pop flies, for the most part, should be certain outs. Yet far too many routine pop flies drop safely for base hits, as bewildered defensive players look at each other and make the all-too-familiar statements, "I've got it… You take it… I thought you had it!"

One defensive absolute is to *make the routine play, make it consistently, and make it under pressure.* When we consider the number of fly balls hit during a game and season, it behooves us to have an organized system that will maximize our chances of making the routine pop fly a *sure out*.

As important a part of the game as pop fly defense is, many of us are guilty of not having an organized, coordinated system of defense or not practicing this phase of the game enough.

Priority System for Pop Fly / Fly Ball Defense

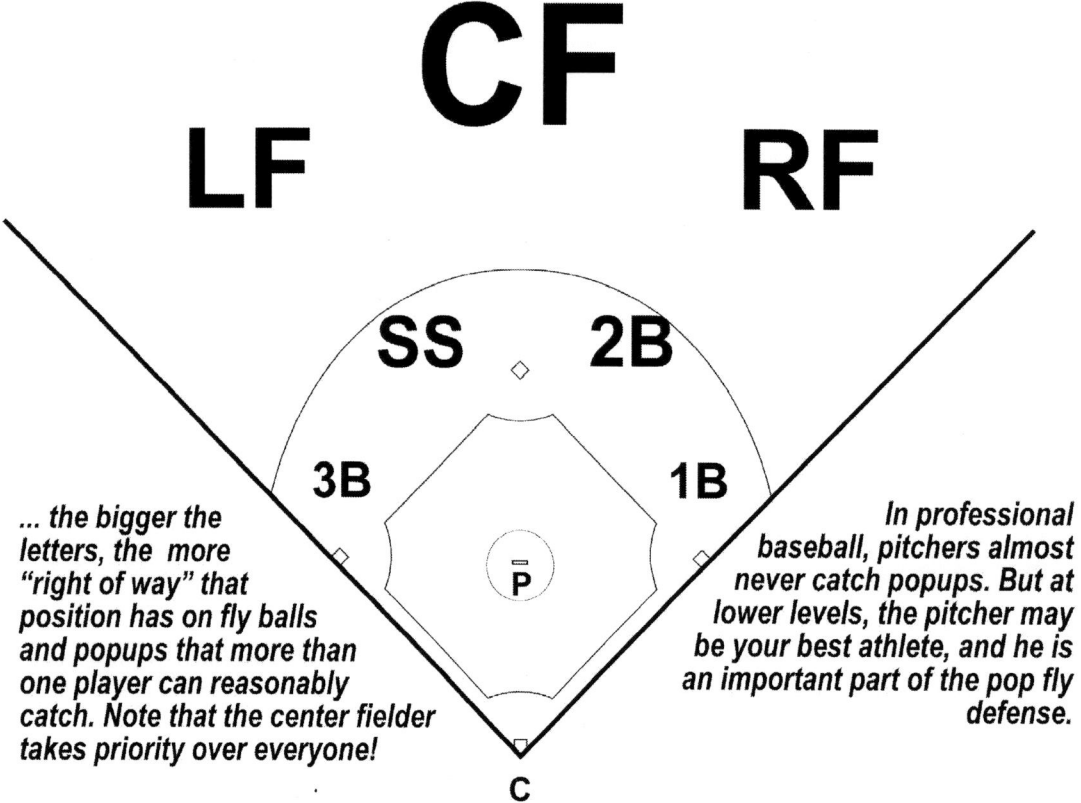

… the bigger the letters, the more "right of way" that position has on fly balls and popups that more than one player can reasonably catch. Note that the center fielder takes priority over everyone!

In professional baseball, pitchers almost never catch popups. But at lower levels, the pitcher may be your best athlete, and he is an important part of the pop fly defense.

▶ Outfielders have *priority* over infielders because they are moving forward and the play is in front of them, while the infielders are moving back. The outfielder is also in better position to throw.

▶ It is the infielder's ball until the outfielder calls him off. Infielders must go aggressively after the ball until called off the play.

▶ The center fielder has priority over the left and right fielders—he is generally the best fielder of the three. If either outfielder can make the catch, priority will depend on the following:

– Which outfielder is in better position to throw?
– Which outfielder has the better throwing arm?
– Which outfielder doesn't have the sun in his eyes?

▶ The shortstop has priority over the third baseman on balls hit behind third base. It is easier for the shortstop to swing behind third base to make the catch than to have the third baseman move straight back.

▶ Likewise, the second baseman has priority over the first baseman on balls hit behind first base. It is easier for the second baseman to swing behind first base to make the catch than to have the first baseman move straight back.

▶ Both the first and third basemen have priority over the catcher when pop flies are hit between them. Balls hit down the baseline are in front of the first baseman and third baseman, and are therefore easier for them to catch. And because of the spin of the ball, pop flies near home plate drift toward the infield.

▶ When a pop fly can be caught by either the shortstop or second baseman, priority will depend upon the following:

– Which infielder is in better position to throw?
– Which infielder has the better throwing arm?
– Which infielder doesn't have the sun in his eyes?

▶ The pitcher must be prepared to make a catch, as he may be the only one who can get to certain popups. And in youth baseball, the pitcher may be your best athlete.

By establishing priorities, players should understand who usually has the "right of way." However, just like in driving an automobile, you do not crash into another player or car simply because you have the right of way.

Basic Principles for Pop Flies and Fly Balls

▶ Wait for the ball to begin its *downward flight* before calling for it! Don't call for the ball too soon—this causes the majority of problems when attempting to catch pop flies.

▶ Run to the spot where the ball will drop. Don't drift with the ball.

▶ An infielder can wave his arms while calling for the ball if he is under the ball and can make an easy catch.

▶ Check the wind during the game by throwing grass in the air… the ball will drift with the wind.

▶ Regardless of how obvious it is as to who will make the catch, the player making the catch should call three times to be sure he is heard. *"Mine! Mine! Mine!"* or *"Ball! Ball! Ball!"* is a good way to call for it. "I've got it" is more cumbersome, but is widely used and is an acceptable method of verbalizing.

▶ The player who does not have priority and must yield to another fielder should reassure the fielder making the catch by hollering, *"Take it! Take it! Take it!"* at least three times.

▶ Including the fielder's first name *("Take it Bob! Take it Bob! Take it Bob!")* further enhances this reassurance and prevents the fielder who is making the catch from hearing footsteps.

Holler Drill

Purpose: To teach players to call for the ball correctly and at the proper time, and to teach players to reply correctly if they are to yield the right of way.

Procedure:
1. Position two lines of fielders single-file approximately 50 feet apart. The first player in each line assumes a ready/set position preparing to catch a fly ball. Players go to the end of the line after completing the play.
2. Use a pitching machine to throw fly balls between the two lines. Adjust the machine to shoot the ball slightly to one side or the other.
3. Players practice making the call at the correct time—when the ball starts its downward flight—and using the correct verbalization.
4. The player who yields to the fielder making the catch also practices correct verbalization, yelling *"Take it! Take it! Take it!"*

Outfield Holler Drill

Purposes:
1. To teach outfielders to call for the ball correctly and at the proper time.
2. To teach outfielders to reply correctly if they are to yield the right of way.
3. To teach outfielders the outfield phase of the Priority System.
4. To teach outfielders to communicate with each other.

Procedure:
1. Station outfielders in left, center, and right field. (Place two fielders at each position if possible—this speeds up the drill.)

2. The coach stands on the outfield grass behind second base and throws or fungoes fly balls between outfielders, first between left field and center field, then between center field and right field.
3. Outfielders practice making the call at the correct time—when the ball starts its downward flight—and using the correct verbalization.
4. The outfielder who yields to the fielder making the catch also practices correct verbalization, yelling "*Take it! Take it! Take it!*"

Infield Holler Drill

Purposes:
1. To teach infielders to call for the ball correctly and at the proper time.
2. To teach infielders to reply correctly if they are to yield the right of way.
3. To teach infielders the infield phase of the Priority System.
4. To teach infielders to communicate with each other.
5. To emphasize the 3B/C, 1B/C, and SS/2B coordination for catching a pop fly on the infield.

Procedure:
1. This drill can be practiced in conjunction with the *Outfield Holler Drill,* if enough coaches are available.
2. Station all infielders and catchers in their positions.
3. The coach stands at home plate and either throws, fungoes, or uses a pitching machine to send pop fly balls to the infield area only—no fly balls on the outfield grass.
4. Send pop flies between the catcher and third baseman and catcher and first baseman, both in fair and foul territory.
5. Send pop flies between the shortstop and second baseman.
6. The coach should reinforce calling for the ball at the correct time, using the correct verbal reply, and the Priority System.

Triangle Drill

Purpose: To teach both the infield and outfield phases of the Priority System for catching fly balls, and to develop coordination between infielders and outfielders when pursuing a fly ball.

Procedure:
1. Station infielders and outfielders at their positions. Use two second basemen and two shortstops.
2. Three coaches are stationed on the field as fungo hitters. *Coaches may choose to throw fly balls during this drill for greater accuracy and more fielding opportunities.*
   – **Fungo Hitter/Thrower #1** is stationed halfway between home plate and third base, and approximately ten feet into fair territory.
   – **Fungo Hitter/Thrower #2** is stationed halfway between the pitcher's mound and second base.
   – **Fungo Hitter/Thrower #3** is stationed halfway between home plate and first base, and approximately ten feet into fair territory.
3. Fungo Hitter/Thrower #1 sends fly balls to triangle #1—that is, the area behind third base and in shallow left field, between the third baseman, shortstop and left fielder.

4. Fungo Hitter/Thrower #2 sends fly balls to triangle #2—that is, to shallow center field behind second base, between the shortstop, second baseman and center fielder.
5. Fungo Hitter/Thrower #3 sends fly balls to triangle #3—that is, the area behind first base and in shallow right field, between the first baseman, second baseman and right fielder.

The Triangle Drill:

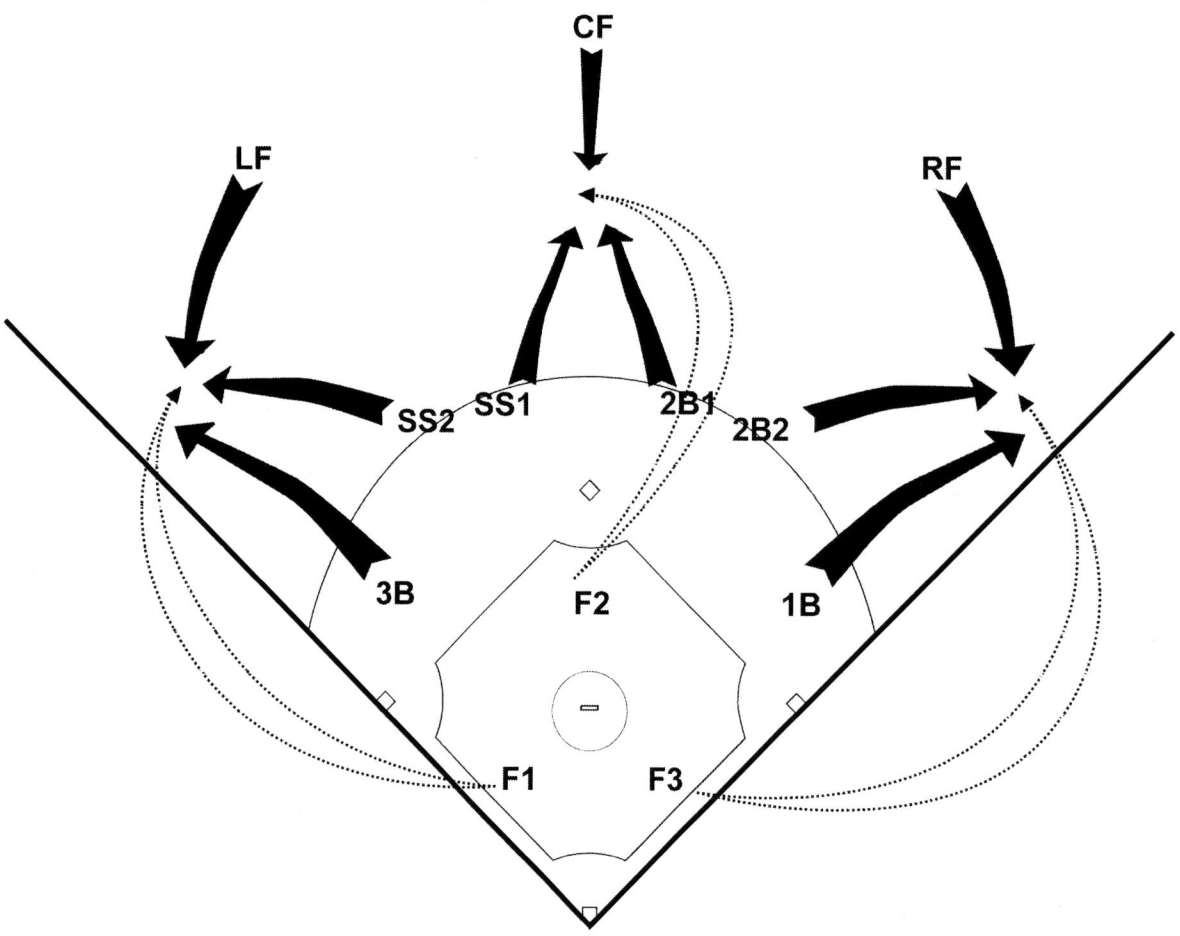

Pop Fly Priority Drill

Purpose: To practice as a team the basic mechanics, correct verbalization, and Priority System for catching pop fly balls.

Procedure:
1. Place players in their defensive positions.
2. Use a pitching machine or fungo baseballs to various areas of the playing field. Be sure the pitcher is out of the way when the ball is fungoed.
3. The coach should reinforce the following: calling for the ball correctly and at the right time (on its downward flight); a correct response by the player who must yield the right of way; and observing and understanding the Priority System.

Other Considerations

▶ **To avoid collision:** Know and honor the Priority System. ... Don't call for the ball too late—make the call for the ball before it's halfway down! ... If you are the fielder to yield the right of way, move at a right angle to avoid a collision. ... The pitcher or another nearby fielder should make the call if a collision is imminent.

▶ **Understand the trajectory of the ball:** Outfielders should understand that balls hit to left field or right field curve toward the foul line—a right-handed hitter will slice balls to right field and hook balls to left field, and a left-handed hitter will slice balls to left field and hook balls to right field. Catchers should understand that when a ball is popped up near home plate, the spin of the ball is such that it comes back toward the infield—the catcher must compensate for this "drift" and adjust his fielding position accordingly.

▶ **When going after a pop fly or fly ball:** Run on your toes to keep your head and eyes still. Don't run with your glove extended—this will slow you down; get under the ball as quickly as possible.

▶ **Playing the sun:** Practice using good sunglasses; learn to shade the sun with the glove or bare hand; don't line up the batter, the ball, and the sun—adjust the defensive position slightly so all three are not lined up.

Make 'Em Earn It

With proper and adequate practice of the Priority System, routine pop flies become sure outs and you limit your opponents to only those runs they earn.

Good Luck!

Learning the Drop Step

"The beginning is the most important part of the work." – Plato

---

The key to successfully catching fly balls hit directly over or slightly to the side of a fielder is determined to a large degree by the fielder's initial step. This first step is critical in achieving the correct angle of pursuit to the baseball. To teach the fielder the proper footwork for going back on a fly ball hit over his head, the fielder must be taught the "drop step."

> **COACHING KEY:**
> *A fielder can recover from too deep a drop step, but never from too shallow a drop step. A drop step that is too shallow results in a poor angle of pursuit to the ball.*

All successful outfielders have this skill in their repertoire, but many infielders have never been taught this technique and have unnecessary difficulty going back on fly balls hit over their head.

The following drills should help teach the drop step correctly.

Drop Step Dry

Purpose: To teach proper footwork for going back on fly balls, and to assure that the drop step is deep enough.

Procedure:
1. The drill is executed without baseballs.
2. Fielders start the drill with their right foot (their pivot foot) on the foul line (when drop-stepping left) or any long straight line the coach chooses.
3. On the command "Drop!" the fielders drop-step straight back ninety degrees with their left foot and hold this position. The left foot should land on or next to the foul line directly behind them.
4. The coach should evaluate each fielder's drop step while he is in the hold position and make necessary corrections.
5. Reverse the drill and have players drop-step in the opposite direction (to the right).

Footwork when Drop-Stepping Left:

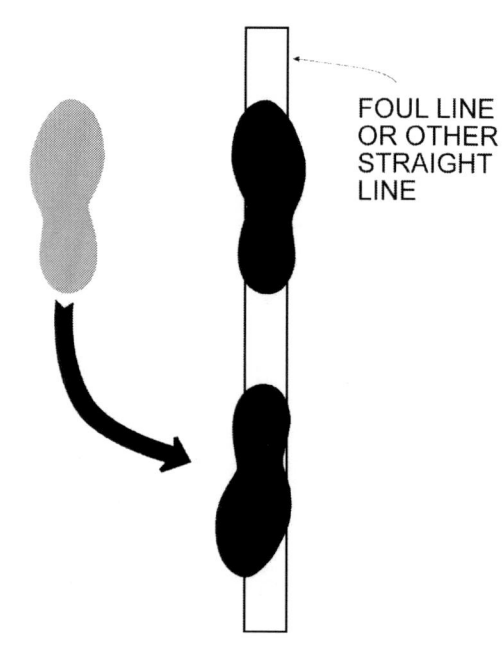

Drop Step Live

Purpose: To teach fielders the proper footwork for going back on fly balls, and to assure that the drop step is deep enough.

Procedure:
1. Fielders form a single-file line in front of the coach. Each fielder has a baseball.
2. The coach is 20 to 25 feet in front of the players, facing them.
3. The first fielder in line steps out and away from the line, tosses his baseball to the coach, and assumes the ready position.
4. On the command "Drop!" the fielder drop-steps straight back with his left foot and holds this position. The drop step should be ninety degrees straight back.
5. On the command "Go!" the fielder runs straight back, looking at the coach over his shoulder.
6. The coach throws a looping fly ball over the fielder's left side. The fielder makes the catch, keeps the baseball, and returns to the end of the line.
7. After all fielders have drop-stepped left, reverse the drill and have all fielders drop-step right..

Wrong Way Drill

Purpose: To teach the fielder to recover from a wrong initial step (turning the wrong way) when attempting to field a fly ball hit over his head.

Procedure:
1. Begin by using steps 1 through 5 of the Drop Step Live drill above.
2. As the fielder is running back (see step 5 above), on the command "Head!" the fielder turns his head around to the opposite shoulder and the coach throws a looping fly ball to the opposite side of the fielder's initial step.
3. The fielder continues around to make the catch.
4. After all fielders have drop-stepped left, reverse the drill and have all fielders drop-step right.

> **COACHING KEYS:**
>
> *The Wrong Way Drill teaches the fielders not to backpedal or get their legs tied up by opening their body to the ball when they have initially turned the wrong way. By continuing around, the fielder maintains his body rhythm and a smooth, coordinated approach to the ball.*
>
> *The one-handed catch is acceptable, and should be encouraged on balls the fielder must reach out to catch. The one-handed catch increases the fielder's reach and enables him to maintain better body balance than is possible using the two-handed method.*

Good Luck!

Boot Drills

"Do not fear mistakes. You will know failure. Continue to reach out." – Benjamin Franklin

---

Even the best infielders mishandle (or "boot") balls occasionally. Good fielders have the ability to recover quickly and correctly, giving them the best chance to record an out in spite of their initial miscue.

When a ball is mishandled, the key is to pick it up quickly and with good form. An infielder's absolutes for picking up the ball are as follows:

▶ **Keep the chest over the ball** when reaching down to pick the ball up. This helps the infielder keep his eyes on the ball, and helps prevent "head-pulling" or looking away before the ball is actually grasped. The chest-over-the-ball position puts the ball in the most advantageous position to be picked up.

▶ **Pick the ball up bare-handed**—never pick the ball up with the glove hand. Picking it up bare-handed is faster, because the ball is already in the throwing hand and does not have to be transferred.

▶ **Use the full hand when picking the ball up,** and adjust the throwing grip as the ball and body are brought into throwing position.

▶ **Push the ball into the ground** when picking it up to assure that a firm grip is established. This also prevents swiping or grabbing, which often results in totally missing the ball. Remind your fielders: *Don't look at the runner—look at the ball!*

Recovery and Throw Drill

Purpose: To teach infielders to react in a correct and positive manner after mishandling a ground ball. Responding quickly and correctly greatly increases the fielder's chances of throwing the runner out at first base.

Procedure:
1. Station the infielders in their positions, and have the first baseman at first base to receive throws from the other infielders.
2. The coach stands at home plate and fungoes ground balls to infielders.
3. The infielder will intentionally mishandle the ground ball fungoed to him by the coach. That is, he fields the ball and then simulates an error by tossing the ball onto the ground in front of his body.
4. The infielder proceeds to pick the ball up correctly and throw to first base.

Fake Throw Drill

Purpose: To teach infielders that after mishandling a ground ball with a runner or runners on base, if no play exists, to *fake a throw*. The fake throw creates the possibility of luring an overly aggressive baserunner into making too big a turn at one of the bases.

Procedure:
1. Station the infielders in their positions.
2. The coach stands at home plate and fungoes ground balls to infielders.
3. The infielder will intentionally mishandle the ground ball fungoed to him by the coach. That is, he fields the ball and then simulates an error by tossing the ball onto the ground in front of his body.
4. The infielder will then quickly pick the ball up and fake a throw. Be certain players observe the "absolutes" for picking up the ball as mentioned at the outset of this chapter.

Making the fake throw:

It is imperative that infielders learn to make a legitimate fake throw. Too often, a fake throw is made too quickly and does not allow the runner enough time to react to the fake…*let the runner take the bait!*

The following points must be followed if a fake throw is to be effective:

Full arm action: The arm must make a complete circle—bring the ball all the way down to the hip at the completion of the arm action (and remember to hang onto the ball).

Stride foot: Step out with the stride foot as if making a real throw.

Pivot foot: Bring the pivot foot into throwing position by stepping forward and bringing it under the body—the infielder is now ready to throw.

Keep an eye out: Look for an overly aggressive baserunner and throw him out.

But remember: no random throws… *No play, No throw!*

Thinking Positive

These are very fine *hustle drills*. They are designed to develop quickness, defensive aggressiveness, and a positive attitude by teaching the infielders that they have other fielding responsibilities after mishandling the ball. Infielders will realize that there isn't time for pouting and other negative reactions after a miscue, because they have further defensive responsibilities before the play is completed.

Good Luck!

The Double Play via the Free Right Foot

"If baseball is a game of inches generally speaking, then it follows that it is specifically a game of split-seconds for second basemen. There is no position on a baseball team which places such a high premium on timing." – Bobby Richardson

Often referred to as the "pitcher's best friend," the double play is the most spectacular play in baseball. When his team is on defense, six-to-four-to-three is music to the coach's ears.

The double play can snuff out a rally, break up an opponent's big inning, and permit playing the infield deep in crucial situations. It is a vital component of a solid defensive team. The ability to consistently turn the double play when it presents itself means winning games and achieving a winning season.

Webster defines "pivot" as *"A point on which something turns; a person or thing on or around which something turns or depends; a central point."* In a baseball context, the second baseman is this central point, and the double play depends largely upon how skillfully he executes this pivot. Team success is directly related to the second baseman's ability to make the double play, because those double plays involving him are the most difficult to complete.

Keys to the Second Baseman Turning the Double Play

▶ **Be there in time:** The most important factor in making the double play is getting to the base before the ball arrives. In order to do so, the second baseman will have to "cheat"—that is, he must move a step or two closer to home plate and a step or two nearer second base whenever the possibility of a double play exists. How far the second baseman cheats in and over toward second base will depend upon individual quickness and agility and will vary from player to player.

Regardless of the number of moves the second baseman may possess, if he is late, he will have difficulty using any of them except merely catching the ball and stepping on the base. A late arrival to the base also increases the chances of a bad throw, because the second baseman presents a moving target. In addition, the second baseman will have difficulty moving laterally while striding toward the base—a perfect throw to him is necessary if he is late.

▶ **Get one out for sure:** The second baseman's primary responsibility is to make the putout at second base, not to throw the runner out at first. An inexperienced second baseman tends to become overly concerned about getting the additional out at first base. This eagerness usually results in no one being put out. Missing the runner at first is of little consequence when compared to the catastrophic effects of the baserunners being safe at both first and second bases.

▶ **Maintain lateral movement and body balance:** As the second baseman approaches the base, his last two or three steps should be short "chop steps." These steps, similar to those used by a defensive halfback in football, enable the second baseman to bring his body weight under control. With his weight under control, he is able to move laterally and increase his fielding range in the event there is a bad throw.

> **COACHING KEY:**
> *Draw a circle with a six-foot radius around second base. When the second baseman reaches this circle, he breaks down (using chop steps) and establishes his lateral movement.*

▶ **Generate throwing rhythm:** *Don't throw flat-footed.* Transferring the weight to the right foot just as the ball hits the glove can generate throwing rhythm. This can be done by taking a step with the right foot in the direction of the throw. This step and weight transfer will place the second baseman in rhythm and position to throw, which will result in a more accurate and powerful throw to first base. Second basemen should be told, "Get to your right leg" for rhythm and power. This will prevent them from throwing flat-footed.

▶ **Step directly toward first base:** The second baseman must step directly toward first base with his left foot while completing his double play throw. If a line were to be drawn from his pivot foot to first base, the striding foot would be placed down slightly to the left of this line. Failure to step directly toward the base results in the pivot man throwing across his body. This means maximum throwing speed cannot be achieved and accuracy is impaired. A premature transfer of the weight to the striding foot or stepping too far to the left of the imaginary line to first base should also be avoided—this causes the throw to be made almost entirely with the arm. A weak, inaccurate throw invariably results.

▶ **Stay out of the baseline:** Many pivot men use footwork which results in their being in the baseline after making the throw. Granted, at times, this is unavoidable, but being in the baseline too often results in getting dumped and possibly injured. It also forces the second baseman to decide whether or not to throw at the baserunner. Inexperienced second basemen try to throw around the runner, losing all chance for the putout at first. We tell our second basemen that first base does not move and it is the runner's responsibility to slide. This has serious implications, because the runner can easily be injured—however, the second baseman cannot be intimidated by the baserunner. It is the coach's responsibility—more accurately, his duty—to be certain that all runners know they must slide or get out of the way when going into second base in this situation.

▶ **Use a compact arm:** It takes a runner approximately 3.5 to 4.5 seconds to run to first base, so it is easy to understand why the second baseman cannot afford to waste a fraction of a second in getting his throw away. One way to achieve quickness is by using a compact arm when throwing. The compact arm means that when the ball is caught in the glove, the glove and the ball are pushed as far to the throwing side as possible. *Simply stated, the elbow leads the way going back and up. The hand is kept on top of the ball, and the ball does not drop below the belt.* The wrist is above the ball, not under it—arm rhythm results from dropping the wrist and making a small circle with the ball (counterclockwise for a righthander). Now contrast this method with that of a full arm extension with the wrist under the ball—obviously, this is slower, more cumbersome, and inaccurate. The compact arm means quickness.

▶ **Keep the throwing hand near the glove, thumb to thumb:** To facilitate quickness, the throwing hand should be carried alongside the glove. The ball can be removed more quickly than would be possible if the glove and ball were brought to the throwing hand. Quickness is a must. *Don't play one-handed!*

▶ **Use a simple pivot:** For the inexperienced second baseman, the fact that he must use different footwork for different kinds of throws confuses him. The more complicated the footwork, the more difficult it will be to teach. Too many moves result in indecision on the second baseman's part, and often becomes more of a problem than too few moves. This confusion and indecision places additional pressure on the second baseman. Teach a simple method.

▶ **Know where the ball is:** Many problems result from the second baseman starting his pivot before he knows where the throw he is receiving will be. This premature commitment by the second baseman destroys his lateral movement, fielding range, and requires that a perfect throw be made to him. The second baseman must not move until the throw has been made. He should wait until he knows where the ball is before he begins his pivot.

The Free Right Foot Method

We have taught this method of pivoting to our second basemen for years and feel that it offers the following advantages:

1. It is easy to teach.
2. It is a simple method of pivoting.
3. The second baseman is out of the baseline when throwing.
4. He is always in position to throw.
5. Confidence is built quickly because success occurs early.
6. Good throwing rhythm and body balance are promoted.
7. Indecision as to footwork is eliminated.
8. Good lateral range is assured.

The Free Right Foot method literally means that the foot is free. That is, the initial step is always taken with the right foot, and the base is always tagged with the left foot.

▶ **Tagging the Base:** Upon arriving at the base, the second baseman tags the base with his left foot. The toe of the right foot is directly opposite the middle of the left foot, no farther back, as lateral movement would be impaired. The weight is on the balls of the feet, the knees are flexed, feet are shoulder-width apart, and the glove and bare hand are chest high, with fingers pointing up and hands thumb-to-thumb. This ready position enables the second baseman to move quickly and will give him maximum fielding range.

▶ **The pivot:** A second baseman's initial step as he receives the throw should always be with his right foot. The precise footwork that he will use depends upon the position of the throw. Three kinds of throws confront him: a perfect throw; a throw to his right; and a throw to his left. The second baseman should not start his pivot until he knows where the throw is; the ball will tell him where to step.

▶ **Pivoting on a perfect throw:** When the throw is made directly over the base, the second baseman may use either of two methods in executing his pivot. Experience and practice will help him decide which move is more comfortable:

The Rocker Step: The left foot is in contact with the base as the ball is caught by the second baseman. He steps back with his right foot, transfers his weight to this foot, and then strides toward first base with his left foot and throws. The rocker step is one of the most common double play pivots, and has proved to be effective at all levels of play.

Step across the base: Instead of using the Rocker Step, the second baseman steps across the base with his right foot as he catches the ball. The catch is made just before the right foot hits the ground. He plants his right foot, strides directly toward first base with his left foot, and throws. Stepping across the base on the perfect throw is by far the better of the two pivots for the following reasons: the second baseman goes to meet the ball and gets the pivot started sooner; the rhythm step is started before the ball is received; and the second baseman is out of the baseline to the inside of the diamond, making it more difficult to be taken out on the play.

▶ **Pivoting on the throw to the right:** On a throw to the left field side of second base, the execution is rather simple. The second baseman steps to his right to make the catch, simultaneously shifting his weight to this foot. He strides toward first base with his left foot and throws. The base is tagged with the left foot by dragging it along the right field side of the base—if necessary, the entire width of the base should be utilized, assuring maximum fielding range to the outfield side of the base. Be sure if the throw is extremely wide to the right that the second basemen leaves the base, catches the ball and touches second base with the left foot for one sure out. Remember, it's "ball, then base"—*get one out for sure.*

> ### Grade the velocity of ground balls:
>
> Many coaches grade the velocity of ground balls 1, 2, 3, or x, y, z—or whatever method communicates. The purpose is to help the infielder gauge the chance of completing a double play.
>
> – A "1" ground ball is a slow roller. There is no chance for a double play, just make the out where the ball takes you.
> – A "2" ground ball is a normal ground ball. A double play is possible if the ball is handled smoothly.
> – A "3" ground ball is a smash—just execute and you have two outs.

▶ **The throw to the left:** The second baseman steps across the base with his right foot at approximately 45 degrees (the exact angle will depend upon how far the ball is thrown to his left). As the ball is caught, the weight is shifted to the right foot, the left foot steps toward first base, and the throw is completed.

▶ **The late arrival to the base:** The late arrival to the base results in the throw being received on the right field side of the base. The key here is that lateral movement must be maintained. As mentioned previously, this can be done by using chop steps—with the body weight under control, the second baseman will be able to shift laterally for the throw. When the ball is caught, the second baseman continues on, stepping on top of the base with his left foot. He steps over the base with his right foot, plants it, and strides toward first base with his left foot, completing the throw.

▶ **Getting out of the runner's way:** After stepping across the base with his right foot and completing his throw to first base, the second baseman steps with his right foot directly toward the mound, and swings his left foot behind his right, thus avoiding the sliding runner.

▶ **Slow rollers**: The second baseman must move to the third base side of second base and receive the throw like a first baseman if no chance for a double play exists, or there are two outs and the ball is hit slowly to the left side of the infield.

▶ **Arm angle**: To improve body balance and throwing rhythm, drop the throwing arm angle to 45 degrees when stepping across the base and making the throw to first. This arm angle is more compatible with the body momentum generated from stepping across second base, and it allows for a more fluid throwing rhythm.

Developing the Free Right Foot

The Free Right Foot method of pivoting is in no way intended to keep the second baseman from developing his own style. As he becomes experienced and proficient, he should make adjustments in his pivoting, and ideally his own style will evolve.

The Free Right Foot method has proven to be an effective way of executing the double play, but like other methods, it must be practiced. Remember, the only way to develop an infielder's ability to make the double play pivot is to practice, practice, practice.

Being good is being consistent. Make the routine play, make it consistently and make it under pressure!

Good Luck!

Middle Infielders' Bounce Drill

"Turning a double play is baseball's ballet." – Dave Anderson, New York Times

Middle infielders need ample opportunities to practice and perfect their double play coordination. The Middle Infielders' Bounce Drill gives them an easy way to practice a large number of *feeds* (throws to second base) and *pivots* in a short period of time.

Shortstops and second basemen will learn what type of throw to make to start the double play, depending upon where they field the ball, and they'll also learn what type of throw to expect when they are the pivot man, based upon where the ball was fielded. And when the pivot man knows what type of throw to expect, the number of mishandled balls will be diminished.

The Bounce Drill doesn't take up much space, and because of this it is an excellent rainy day drill that can be conducted on the gym floor or any hard-top surface. In this case, use a throw-down base that will not slip.

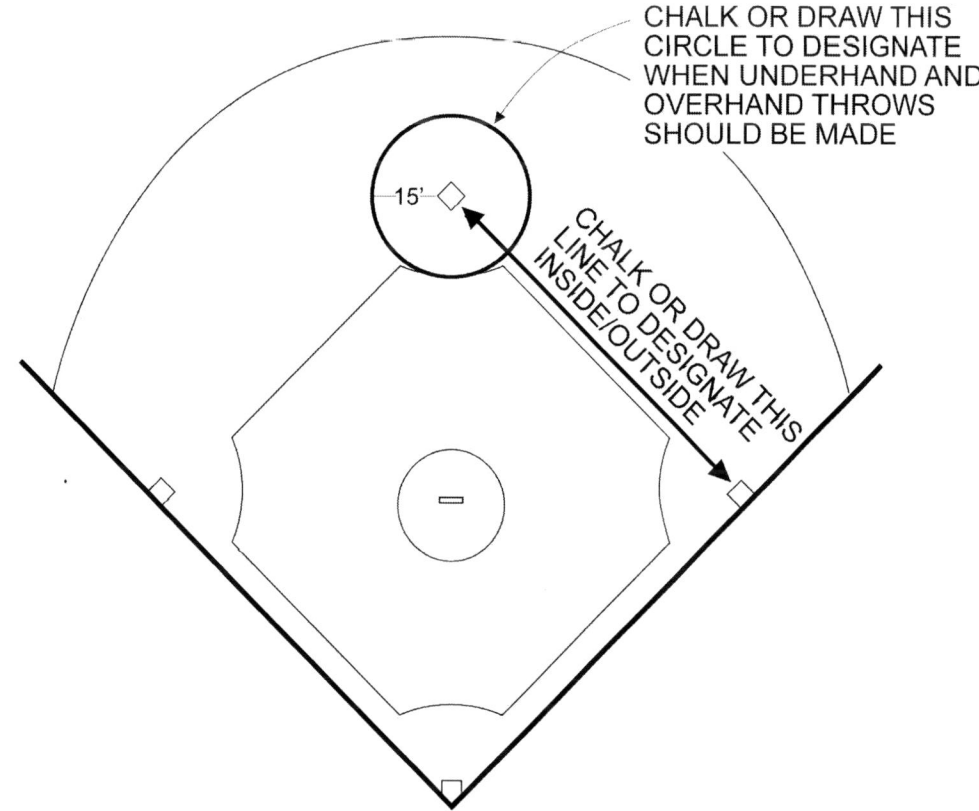

Setting Up

1. Use a throw-down base for use on the gym floor or other hard surface in the event of inclement weather.
2. Give each middle infielder a baseball.
3. The middle infielder, acting as the "feeder," bounces the ball to himself and then throws the ball to second base to start the simulated double play.
4. The middle infielder acting as the pivot man receives the throw from the feeder and executes the appropriate pivot depending upon the location of the throw to him.
5. Draw an imaginary line between first and second base if on a hard surface, or a real line between first and second base if on dirt. Use this line as a reference for inside and outside positions.
6. Draw a circle fifteen feet from second base to help middle infielders determine when it's appropriate to use an underhanded toss to second base.
7. Middle infielders change from feeder to pivot man after a prescribed number of throws.

The Second Baseman (as the feeder)

As the *feeder* or *front man* on the double play, the second baseman fields and makes throws from five different areas or positions:

On a ball hit directly to him:
1. He bounces the ball to himself to simulate the ball hit directly to him.
2. His feet remain stationary after fielding the ball.
3. He turns his body toward second base by pivoting on the balls of his feet. This method helps prevent the second baseman from pulling off the ball and having it go under his glove.
4. His left knee is bent or may touch the ground as the ball is brought into throwing position.
5. The throw to second base should be a chest- or face-high throw.
6. The throw should be made using a three-quarter or sidearm motion. This arm angle tends to fool the fielder only laterally on errant throws.

On a ball hit slightly to his left:
1. He bounces the baseball slightly to his left.
2. He fields the ball and pivots his body toward second base by drop-stepping with the right foot and simultaneously making a "jump turn" to bring his body into correct throwing alignment.
3. The throw should be chest- or face-high and over the base.
4. The throw should be made using three-quarter or sidearm motion.

On a ball hit to his extreme left:
1. He bounces the baseball to his left.
2. He reaches out to field the ball and pivots to his left so that his back is toward the infield.
3. He follows his glove, making a counter-clockwise turn toward the outfield.
4. He takes a short half-step with his right foot after making the catch to facilitate body balance for the turn and throw to second.
5. Because of the distance, the throw should be made using an overhand or three-quarter motion.
6. The throw should be chest- or face-high to second base.

On a ball hit to his right and toward second base:
1. He bounces the baseball to his right.
2. Draw an imaginary line from first base to second base. If the ball is fielded behind the line (on the outfield side) and within 15 or 20 feet of second base, use an *underhanded* toss.
3. The essentials of an underhanded toss:
   – Use a stiff wrist; the hand goes no higher than the shoulder.
   – Walk through the throw as if bowling.
   – Get the glove out of the way so that the ball is visible; show the ball to the shortstop.
   – The closer the fielder is to the base, the softer the toss.
   – The toss should be over the base at the shortstop's chest or face.

On a ball hit toward him and in front of the baseline:
1. He bounces the baseball in front and toward the baseline.
2. Draw a line from first base to second base, or imagine the line if drawing one isn't possible. If the ball is fielded on or in front of the baseline, use a *backhanded* toss to second base.
3. The essentials of an backhanded toss:
   – Use a stiff-wristed backhand flip with the forearm parallel to the ground.
   – An open-palm should be facing the shortstop after the flip.
   – Follow through with the body after making the throw.
   – The toss should be to the first base side of second base if it originates from the infield side of the imaginary line from first base to second base.
   – The toss should be over the base at the shortstop's chest or face.

The Second Baseman (as the pivot man)

When acting as the pivot man, the second baseman receives throws from the shortstop and executes those pivots recommended by the coach. See the previous chapter—The Double Play Via the Free Right Foot—which details the keys to the second baseman turning the double play.

The Shortstop (as the feeder)

As the feeder or front man on the double play, the shortstop fields and makes throws from four different areas or positions:

On a ball hit directly to him:
1. He bounces the ball to himself to simulate the ball hit directly to him.
2. He fields the ball with his right foot slightly forward to facilitate opening the hips.
3. He makes the throw from where the ball is fielded.
4. The throw should be made using three-quarter or sidearm motion.

On a ball hit to his right:
1. He bounces the ball to his right.
2. He moves to his right to get in front of the ball.
3. If possible, the ball is fielded with his right foot slightly forward to facilitate opening the hips.
4. He makes the throw from where the ball is fielded.
5. The throw should be made using three-quarter or sidearm motion.

On a ball hit to his left:
1. He bounces the ball to his left and toward second base.
2. He uses an underhanded toss if moving toward and close enough to second base.
3. The essentials of an underhanded toss:
   – Use a stiff wrist; the hand goes no higher than the shoulder.
   – Walk through the throw as if bowling.
   – Get the glove out of the way so that the ball is visible; show the ball to the second baseman.
   – The closer the fielder is to the base, the softer the toss.
   – The toss should be over the base at the second baseman's chest or face.

On a ball hit behind second base:
1. He bounces the ball to his left and behind the base.
2. He fields the ball with his momentum going behind second base.
3. He uses a backhand toss to second base with his forearm parallel to the ground. Aim the throw to the third base side of the base to compensate for body momentum.

The Shortstop (as the pivot man)

The shortstop has two basic pivots he must execute:

For throws directly over or to the outfield side of second base:
1. Step toward the ball with the left foot.
2. Drag the right foot across the left rear corner of second base.
3. Step with the left foot and throw to first base.

For throws to the inside of second base:
1. Step to make the catch with the right foot.
2. Drag the left foot across the right rear corner of second base or step on top of second base with the left foot.
3. Step toward first base with the left foot and throw to first.

Another Variation

When introducing this drill, the coach can become the pivot man at second base to receive throws from the shortstop and second baseman. In so doing, he can analyze the type of throw he is receiving, the fielder's mechanics, and make necessary suggestions and corrections. This assures that the players practice correctly and that they thoroughly understand double play mechanics.

Let's Turn Two

The Middle Infielders' Bounce Drill is an excellent exercise that can be practiced daily and requires limited space to implement.

Good Luck!

Keys to Executing the Rundown

"Career highlights? I had two. I got an intentional walk from Sandy Koufax and I got out of a rundown against the Mets." – Bob Uecker

---

To complement the total defensive package and to be truly solid defensively, a team must have a well-organized *rundown* system to cope with a baserunner trapped off base.

Being trapped off base occurs as a result of careless baserunning, a well-executed pickoff play, a runner intentionally getting picked off base, or a baserunner stopping between first and second bases and inviting a rundown situation. (The latter two examples are common to first-and-third double steal situations when the offensive team hopes to score the runner from third base while the defense is preoccupied with the rundown between first and second bases.)

Although most young baseball players have played "hot box" in the backyard, a coordinated defensive plan is still essential. Rundown situations occur so often during the course of a season and successfully defending the first-and-third double steal is so dependent upon a team's rundown skills, a plan must be in place to cope with the trapped runner, thus stifling the opponent's offense and adding another component to the defense's total scheme.

Remember: A plan is better than no plan.

Rundown Absolutes

▶ **Run full-speed at the trapped runner:** this forces the runner to commit himself—if he stands still, he will be tagged out, and if he turns and runs full speed toward the next base, he can be thrown out. Running full speed at the runner enables the defense to set the tempo of the rundown. On the other hand, tentative infielders allow the runner to set the tempo. They react to whatever the runner does, resulting in numerous throws and a greater chance for error allowing the runner to escape the "pickle." Your fielders should think, *"Run right over him!"*

▶ **Throws:** Fielders should hold the ball in a high throwing position with the arm cocked. No fake throws! Make nice, light "dart-like" throws that are shoulder-high.

▶ **Positioning:** Both the chaser and the receiver should be on the same side of the runner. If you are the receiver, move to the chaser's throwing-hand side—this will prevent throwing over or across the runner, meaning the runner can't visually or physically block the flight of the ball.

Moving Inside for a Clear Throw:

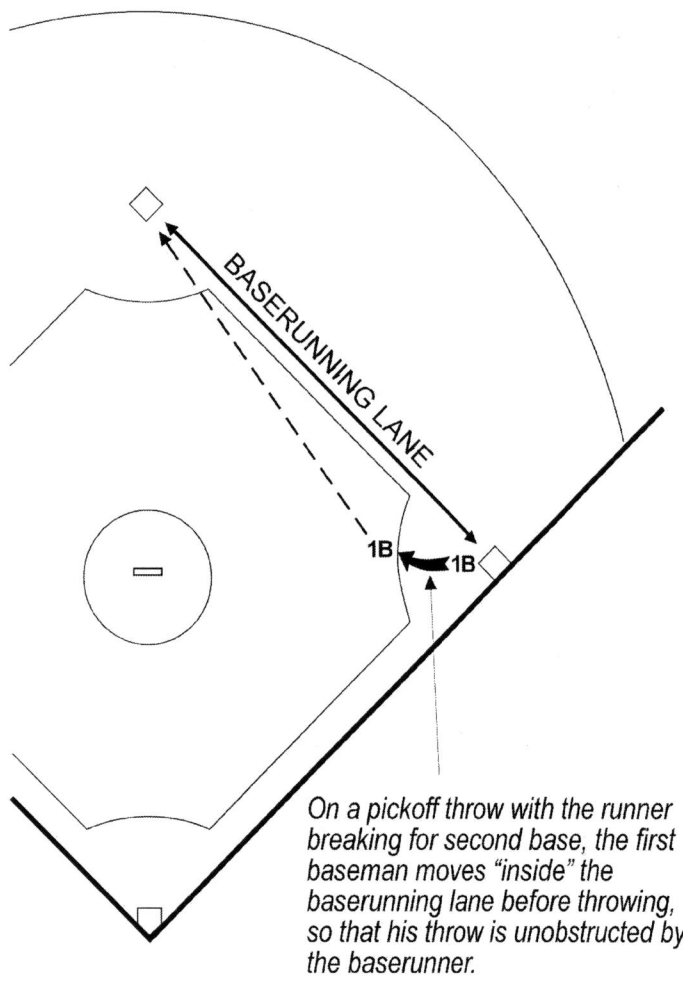

On a pickoff throw with the runner breaking for second base, the first baseman moves "inside" the baserunning lane before throwing, so that his throw is unobstructed by the baserunner.

▶ **After a pickoff:** Initial throws after a runner is picked off by the pitcher should be to the "inside" of the base to which the runner is advancing. And when the pitcher picks off a runner and the runner breaks full speed for the next base, the fielder receiving the pickoff throw should step to meet the ball, and if right-handed, make a "cross-back step" with his right foot (the cross-back step clears the fielder of the runner and allows for an unobstructed open path for the throw to the base).

▶ **Get out of the way:** Once the chaser makes his throw, he should be alert to get out of the runner's way. If the runner runs into the fielder without the ball, the umpire may call obstruction, in which case the runner will be awarded the base to which he was advancing.

▶ **Inside or outside?** All rundowns away from home plate should be on the inside of the diamond. All rundowns toward home plate should be toward the outside of the diamond, with two exceptions: the initial throw after a pickoff by the pitcher with the runner advancing full-speed toward the next base; or, if the first baseman is left-handed.

▶ **Make the throw too soon rather than too late:** Whenever the baserunner breaks full speed for the next base, throw the ball when the runner is 30 feet from the base.

▶ **Rotation:** There are various rotation systems to assure that the chaser is able to get out of the trapped baserunner's way after he makes his throw, and to assure that all bases are covered. One of the simplest methods teaches that after the chaser makes his throw, if he is over halfway to the base in front of him, he continues on to that base, rotating to the right side of the runner; or, if he is less than halfway to the base in front of him, he should hold his ground or return to the base behind him.

▶ **Move 'em back:** When possible, drive the runner back to his original base!

> **COACHING KEY:**
> The chaser should follow his throw and cover the base in front of him. Rotation should be to the right side of the runner.

EXECUTING THE RUNDOWN   97

The Double Rotation System

The Double Rotation System on a pickoff to first base resulting in a rundown (with a runner on first and the other bases empty):

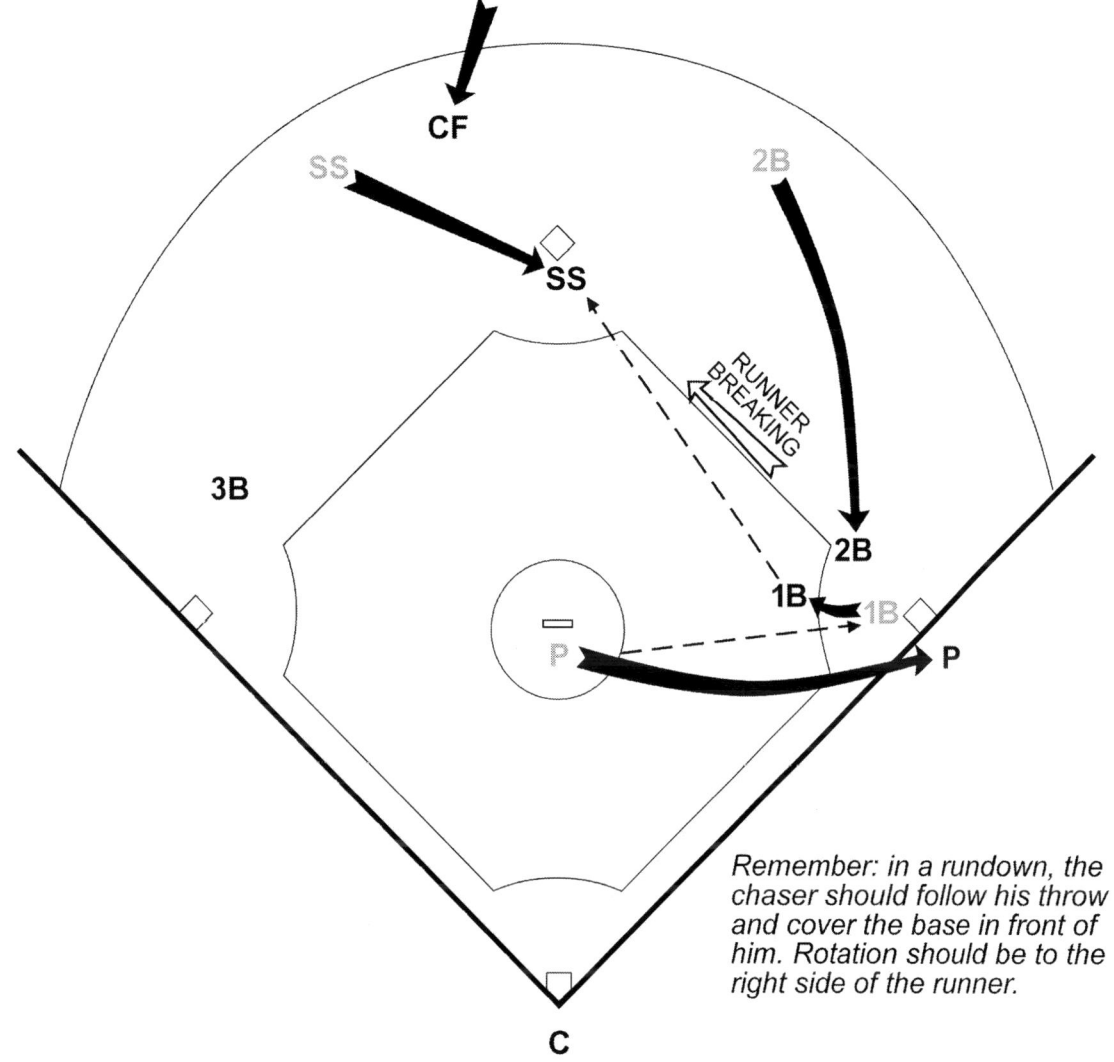

Remember: in a rundown, the chaser should follow his throw and cover the base in front of him. Rotation should be to the right side of the runner.

Here the first baseman is throwing to second after the pickoff because the runner is breaking for second -- if the runner gets hung up in a rundown, the first baseman would chase him.

When the pitcher picks a runner off of first base and a rundown ensues between first and second, players have the following responsibilities:
1. The pitcher backs up first base.
2. The first baseman becomes the chaser; or, if the runner breaks full-speed to second base, the first baseman makes the initial throw to the inside of the diamond to the shortstop.
3. The shortstop covers second base and prepares to receive the first baseman's throw; if the runner breaks at full speed, the shortstop should be on the infield side of second base.
4. The second baseman covers first and assumes a position about 15 feet in front of the base.
5. The center fielder backs up second base on the left field side of the base in a direct line with first.

The Double Rotation System on a pickoff to second base resulting in a rundown (with a runner on second and the other bases empty):

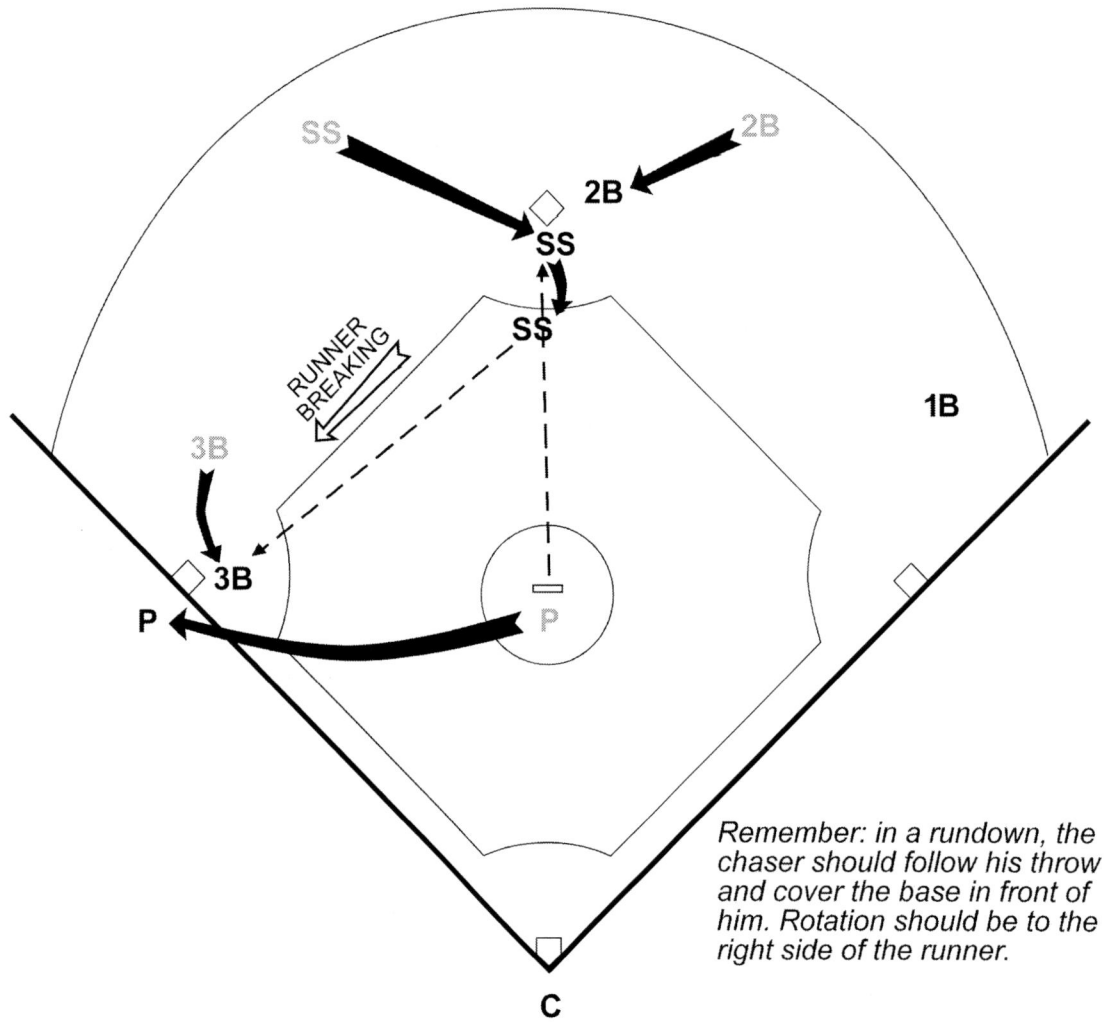

Remember: in a rundown, the chaser should follow his throw and cover the base in front of him. Rotation should be to the right side of the runner.

This diagram happens to show a pickoff play where the shortstop is covering second base, although it could just as easily be the second baseman. Here the shortstop is throwing to third because the runner is breaking for third -- if the runner gets hung up in a rundown, the shortstop would chase him.

When the pitcher picks a runner off of second base and a rundown ensues between second and third, players have the following responsibilities:
1. The pitcher backs up third base.
2. The shortstop or second baseman receives the pickoff throw from the pitcher and becomes the chaser; or, if the runner breaks full-speed to third base, the player receiving the pickoff throw from the pitcher makes the initial throw to the inside of the diamond to the third baseman.
3. The third baseman covers third base and prepares to receive the middle infielder's throw; if the runner breaks at full speed, the third baseman should be set up on the inside of third base.

The Double Rotation System on a pickoff to third base resulting in a rundown (with a runner on third and the other bases empty):

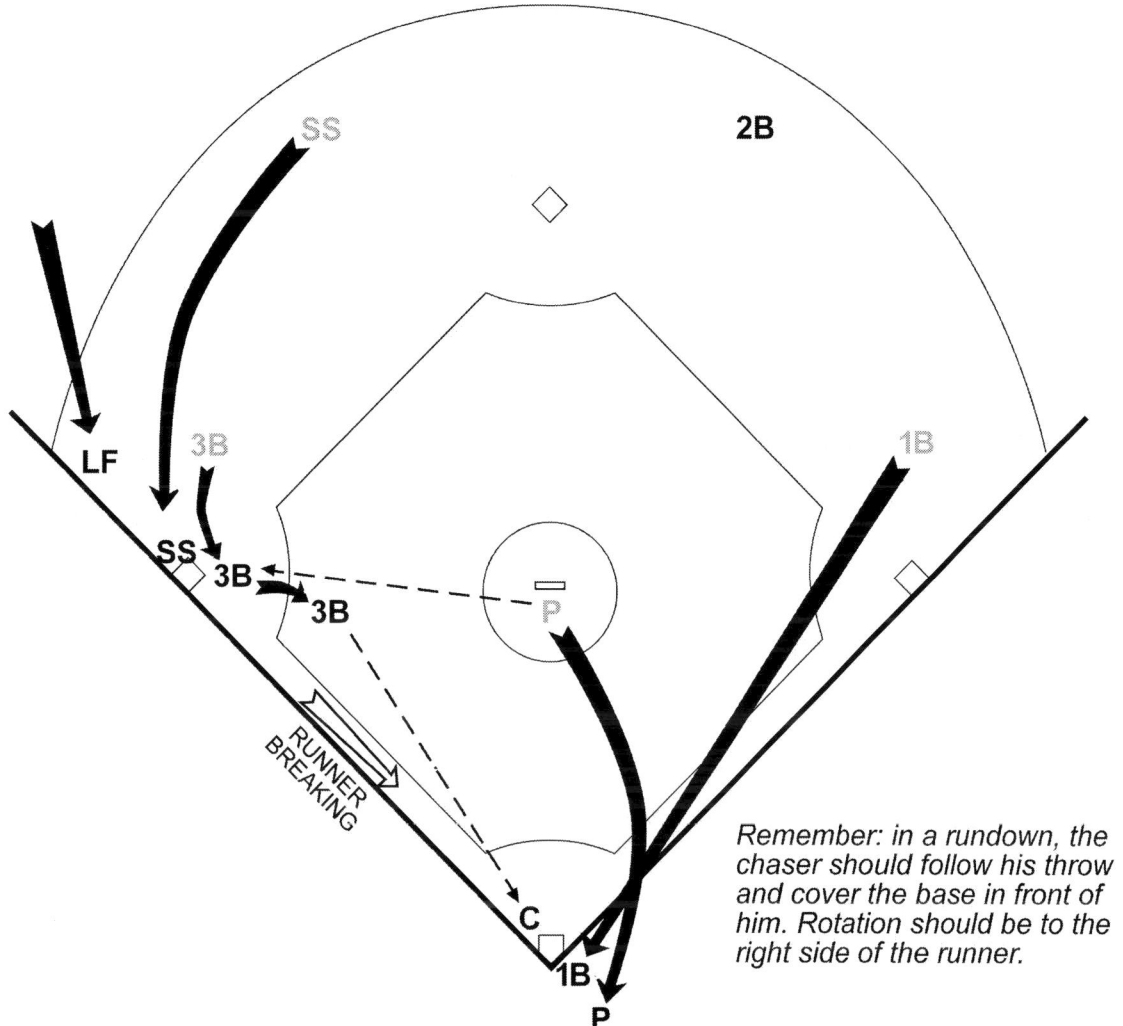

Remember: in a rundown, the chaser should follow his throw and cover the base in front of him. Rotation should be to the right side of the runner.

Here the third baseman is throwing to the plate after the pickoff because the runner is breaking for home -- if the runner gets hung up in a rundown, the third baseman would chase him, although he would throw to the plate early so that the runner would be chased away from home.

When the pitcher picks a runner off of third base and a rundown ensues between third base and home plate, players have the following responsibilities:
1. The pitcher backs up home plate.
2. The third baseman receives the pickoff throw from the pitcher and becomes the chaser; or, if the runner breaks full-speed to home plate, the third baseman makes the initial throw to the inside of the diamond to the catcher (in this case, the third baseman makes a "cross-back step" to the inside of the diamond to create an unobstructed throw to the catcher).
3. The catcher covers home plate and prepares to receive the third baseman's throw. He sets up in front of home plate to receive the throw if the runner breaks full-speed.
4. The shortstop covers third base.
5. The first baseman backs up home plate, and the left fielder backs up third base.

Keys for the Receiver

▶ **Positioning:** Get on the same side of the runner as the chaser, approximately five feet in front of the base. The glove and throwing hand should be held shoulder high and in position to receive the ball.

▶ **Calling for the ball:** It is the responsibility of the receiver to determine when the throw will be made. He should ask for the ball by stepping forward aggressively and simultaneously yelling *"now!"* Ask for the ball when the runner is about thirty feet away and running full speed toward you. *It's better to ask for the ball too soon rather than too late.* By the time the runner stops and changes directions, the receiver will be running full speed at him and should be able to easily tag the runner out.

▶ **Guarding against contact:** The possibility of physical contact exists in most rundown situations. To protect against a contact play, the ball should be firmly held in the throwing hand and then placed in the glove. In the event that contact forces the fielder's hands to split, the ball *will not be dropped* and the runner will be out.

▶ **Applying the tag:** Tag the runner with the back of the glove and protect the baseball (catchers pay attention). Or, if you are able to overtake the baserunner and no contact is involved, apply the tag with the ball held in your bare hand.

Exception to the Rule

There is an exception to the rule that the chaser should run hard at a trapped baserunner. This exception occurs when: 1) there are runners on first and third bases and fewer than two outs; and 2) the offensive team attempts a double steal, and the runner on first base breaks for second base and is trapped. In this case, the runner on third base often does not break for home plate on the catcher's throw to second base, but hopes to score at an opportune moment during the rundown between first and second bases.

In this situation (with fewer than two outs), many coaches tell their players to "walk" the trapped baserunner back to first base. The rationale for this "walking defense" is that it makes it difficult for the runner on third base to know when to make his break for home plate.

The defense is hoping to entice the runner at third base to commit himself. If the runner reaches the "point of no return," he can be caught off base and thrown out.

Some coaches, on the other hand, do not use this "walking defense," but tell their players to run hard at the runner in all situations. You be the judge! Choose the defense that you are more comfortable with and that meets your needs and personnel.

For a look at this in greater detail, see the chapter on defending the first-and-third double steal (page 112).

Drill to determine when to ask for the ball

1. Place pylons, ball bags or other markers between the bases 30 feet apart—so, if you are practicing rundowns between first and second base, one marker should be 30 feet off first, and another should be 30 feet before second base. These will serve as reference points. They should be far enough from the baselines so players won't trip over them, but close enough so they can be seen and serve as reference points.
2. Do not run the baserunner past the last marker!
3. Ask for the ball by yelling "Now!" when the runner reaches the marker closest to the base to which the runner is advancing.
4. The markers will give the chasers a mental picture of when the ball should be thrown, and help the receivers recognize at what distance they must ask for the ball.

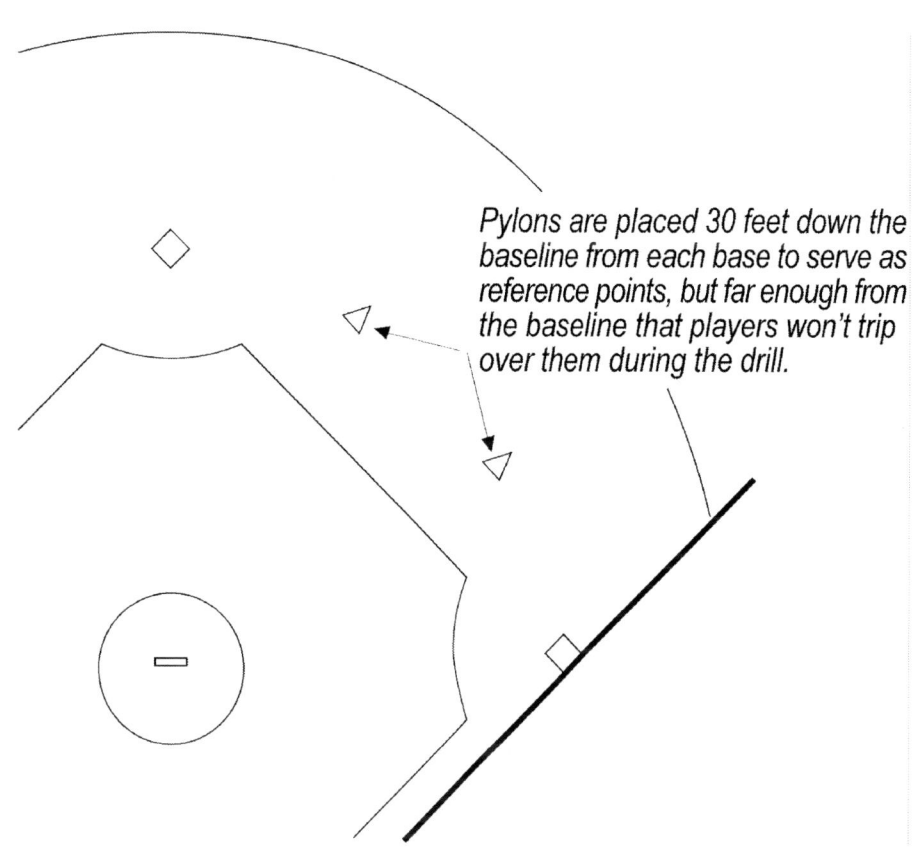

Pylons are placed 30 feet down the baseline from each base to serve as reference points, but far enough from the baseline that players won't trip over them during the drill.

Good Luck!

Rundown Drills

"Ignorant men don't know what good they hold in their hands until they've flung it away."
– Sophocles

Two Man Drill

Purpose: To teach the chaser the stiff-wristed "dart toss" throw, and to teach the receiver how to ask for the ball by having him simultaneously step forward and yell "Now!"

Procedure:
1. Divide the team into pairs.
2. Have players face each other 15 feet apart.
3. One player in a pair has a baseball and is the chaser; the other is the receiver.
4. The chaser holds the ball in the throwing position, and on the receiver's command ("Now!") makes a soft shoulder-high "dart toss" to the receiver.
5. The receiver holds his glove shoulder-high and simultaneously takes a step forward and yells the command.
6. Players reverse position—the receiver becomes the chaser and the chaser becomes the receiver. The drill continues back and forth until the coach says to stop.

Four Man Drill

Purposes:
1. To teach the chaser to run at the trapped baserunner full-speed; to keep his arm up, cocked and in position to throw; to make light shoulder-high dart-tosses; and to rotate to the right after making the throw.
2. To teach the receiver to have his hands up, ready to receive the ball; and to move aggressively forward toward the runner while simultaneously yelling, "Now!"

Procedure:
1. Form two lines facing each other 60 feet apart. Two players in each line.
2. Place a pylon or other marker at 30 feet, halfway between the two lines.
3. The front man in one of the lines has the ball and is the chaser; the front man in the opposite line is the receiver.
4. The chaser runs full speed toward the receiver, holding the baseball correctly, and making a dart-toss to the receiver upon the receiver's command.
5. The chaser rotates to his right after the throw and goes to the end of the line.
6. The receiver has his hands up in receiving position, moves forward aggressively, and calls for the ball by saying "Now!" as the chaser reaches the pylon.
7. The receiver becomes the chaser after receiving the throw, and the drill continues until the coach stops it.

Rundown Simulation Drill

Purposes: To teach the chaser to run full-speed with arm in throwing position and make accurate chest-high dart-tosses to the receiver; and to teach the receiver to ask for the ball at the appropriate time while simultaneously stepping forward.

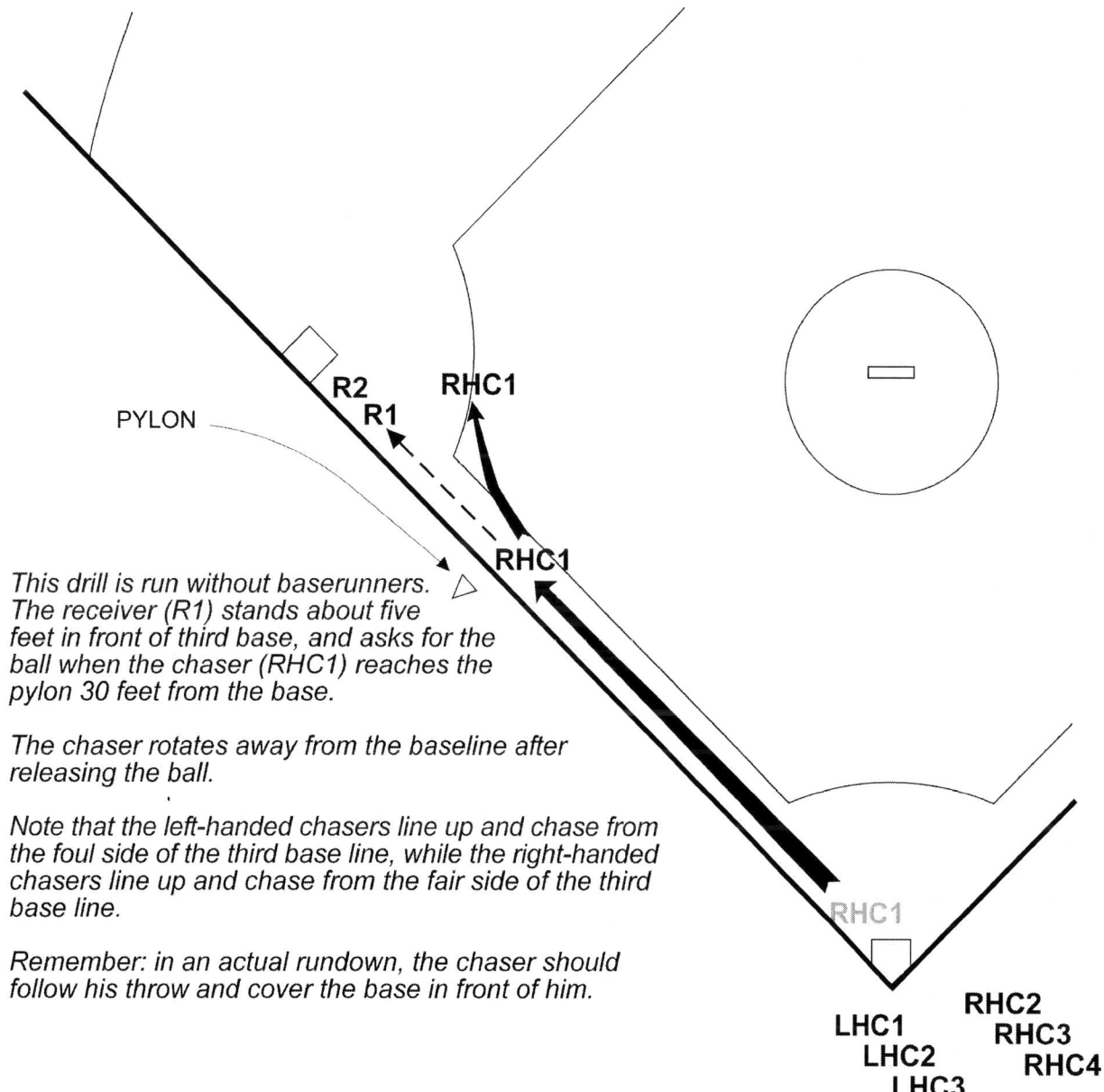

This drill is run without baserunners. The receiver (R1) stands about five feet in front of third base, and asks for the ball when the chaser (RHC1) reaches the pylon 30 feet from the base.

The chaser rotates away from the baseline after releasing the ball.

Note that the left-handed chasers line up and chase from the foul side of the third base line, while the right-handed chasers line up and chase from the fair side of the third base line.

Remember: in an actual rundown, the chaser should follow his throw and cover the base in front of him.

Procedure:
1. Place two infielders at third base. They will take turns acting as receivers. The receiver should be approximately five feet in front of third base.
2. Place a pylon 30 feet from third, on the foul line toward home plate, to act as a "release point."
3. The chasers line up at home plate facing third base. Each has a baseball. Lefthanders line up on the left side of the foul line, while righthanders line up on the right side of the foul line. The chasers are approximately three feet to their side of the foul line.

4. The first chaser holds the ball in the throwing position and runs full speed toward third base.
5. The receiver asks for the ball when the chaser reaches the pylon; the receiver's hands are held shoulder-high in receiving position as he steps forward and yells "Now!"
6. The chaser makes a soft dart-toss to the receiver and rotates right.
7. The receiver simulates a tag and flips the ball back to the chaser, who returns to home plate at the end of the line.
8. The second chaser and second receiver wait until after the first chaser has gotten the ball back before taking their turn.
9. Be sure to rotate new receivers into the drill after a prescribed number of times, usually six to ten, so that all players have been both chasers and receivers.

Circle Rundown Drill

Purpose: To practice proper mechanics of the rundown situation. This drill is an extension of the Rundown Simulation Drill.

Procedure:
1. Place a receiver at third, second, and first bases.
2. Place a pylon thirty feet from each base to act as a release point.
3. Line up players at home plate to act as chasers; each chaser should have a baseball.
4. The first chaser runs full-speed toward third base with the baseball in throwing position.
5. The receiver at third keys on the pylon, making an aggressive step forward and saying "Now!" when the chaser reaches the pylon.
6. The chaser throws to the receiver on command.
7. The receiver returns the ball to the chaser, who continues on to second base and then first base, repeating proper rundown mechanics at each base.
8. The chaser and receiver should rotate after a prescribed number of rundowns so that all players practice chaser and receiver skills.

Live Rundown Drill

Purposes:
1. To teach infielders to properly execute rundown mechanics in a game-like situation.
2. To give infielders practice in defending the rundown situation between first and second bases.
3. To give infielders practice in defending the rundown situation between third base and home plate.

Set-up:
1. Two rundown situations are practiced at one time.
2. Station the catcher behind home plate and an infielder at each position; two players will be needed at shortstop.
3. Place pitchers at the mound area. Each of them has a baseball.
4. Outfielders will act as runners at first or third base.
5. Place two pylons as reference/release points at thirty-foot intervals between first and second bases, and two pylons at thirty-foot intervals between third base and home plate. These pylons should be far enough from the baselines so players won't trip over them, but close enough so they can be seen and serve as reference points.

Rundown between first and second bases:
This portion of the drill involves a pitcher, the first baseman, the second baseman and a shortstop.
1. The pitcher steps on the mound, picks a runner off first base, and the rundown begins between first and second base.
2. Players handle the rundown as indicated in the last chapter under the "Double Rotation System" heading pertaining to the situation when a runner is picked off first.

Rundown between third base and home plate:
This portion of the drill involves a pitcher, the catcher, the third baseman, and a shortstop.
3. After the previous pitcher completes his pickoff to first base as indicated above, another pitcher steps on the mound, picks a runner off third base, and the rundown begins between third and home.
4. Players handle the rundown as indicated in the last chapter under the "Double Rotation System" heading pertaining to the situation when a runner is picked off third.
5. Alternate shortstops so they can practice rundowns between first and second bases and rundowns between third base and home plate. Likewise, pitchers should alternate between pickoffs at first and third bases.

Two Runners on the Same Base

Often, during a rundown, the defense will find that two baserunners occupy the same base. The baserunner closer to home plate is safe; the back runner is out if tagged with the ball. Tag both runners! Then tell the front runner (who is safe and entitled to the base), "You are out!" If he falls for your trick and steps off the base, tag him again—you've got a double play!

Good Luck!

Catchers' Drills

"A catcher must want to catch." – Bill Dickey

A good catcher is a key ingredient of a solid defense. As we have discussed, the best defenses are solid up the middle, and nowhere is this more important than behind the plate. Here are some drills to improve the catcher's fielding.

Dead Ball Drill

Purpose: To teach the catcher to field bunts correctly and throw accurately to the appropriate base.

Procedure:
1. Place three balls approximately 10 to 15 feet from home plate—one down the third base line, one directly in front of home plate, and one down the first base line.
2. Station the catcher behind home plate in a catching position and a first baseman or second baseman at first base.
3. On the coach's command ("Go!"), the catcher fields the first ball and makes a throw to first base. Balls should be fielded in this order: third base line, front of home plate, then first base line.
4. The catcher blocks all balls with his glove—no barehand fielding. Push the ball into the glove—this will stop the spin of the ball.
5. **Ball on the third base line:** The catcher approaches the ball on the third base line in either of two ways: from the infield side, he does a counter-clockwise reverse pivot and throws to first base; or, from the foul line side of the ball, he fields it, does a clockwise turn and throws to first base.
6. **Ball in front of home plate:** The catcher fields the ball, crow hops, and throws to first base.
7. **Ball on the first base line:** The catcher fields the ball and throws to first base using a "cross-back step"—he drops his right foot behind his left foot toward the infield. This helps him avoid throwing down the line and hitting the runner.

Rolling Bunt Drill

Purpose: To learn to field the rolling bunt correctly and to throw accurately to all bases.

Procedure:
1. Place three catchers at home plate (catching gear is optional). Station one catcher in the right-hand batter's box; he throws to third base. Station the second catcher in the left-hand batter's box; he throws to first base. And station the third catcher behind home plate; he throws to second base.
2. Place an infielder at each base.
3. The coach stands behind the catcher and acts as a tosser—he tosses or rolls the ball in front of the catchers one at a time.
4. The catcher fields the ball by blocking it with his glove and pushing it into his glove; this will stop the roll and kill the spin of the ball.
5. The catcher throws to the appropriate base and rotates clockwise to the next position.

Framing Drill

Purpose: To teach catchers to properly frame pitches, increasing the number of called strikes.

Procedure:
1. The catcher assumes a receiving position without a glove—the drill is done barehanded so that the coach can observe the catcher's hand action.
2. The coach assumes a kneeling or squatting position approximately 10 feet in front of home plate.
3. The coach tosses a ball (use JUGS "Softie Baseballs") to different locations in the strike zone.
4. The catcher's hand action is always toward the strike zone as the ball is being caught. On a high pitch, the hand action is *palm down*; on a low pitch, *palm up*; on an inside pitch (to a right-handed hitter), the hand action is *palm in* toward home plate; on an outside pitch, the hand action is *in*, but the ball has to be backhanded and the thumb is down.

Blocking Drill

Purpose: To teach the catcher to block balls in the dirt and keep the ball in front.

Procedure:
1. The catcher is in full equipment (the mask is optional if the ground or gym floor isn't too hard and JUGS Softie or Lite-Flite balls are being used).
2. The catcher assumes a squat, and the coach throws balls in the dirt in front of the catcher.
3. To block the ball, the catcher drops to both knees and places his mitt between knees. To keep the ball in front, his chest should be square to the ball, his head and chin should be down and his shoulders should be "cupped."
4. Variation: use the same procedure as above, but the catcher must keep his hands behind his back without a mitt, using only his chest protector to block the ball.

Pop Fly Drill

Purposes: To teach the catcher how to catch pop flies correctly and to understand the trajectory of the ball on its downward flight.

Procedure:
1. The coach stands at home plate and fungoes balls in the air behind and just in front of home plate.
2. The catcher assumes a squat, and reacts to the pop fly depending upon its location and trajectory.
3. Pop flies behind home plate will come back toward the infield as they descend. They should be caught like an outfielder with the glove up. The catcher should be facing the stands with his back toward the infield, and he should allow the ball to reach its peak and come back to him. Catch the ball chest- or face-high to compensate for its arc back toward the infield.
4. Pop flies in front of home plate will drift toward the mound as they descend. When possible, the catcher should get "past the ball" and turn to make the catch facing the stands with his back to the infield—once he gets past it, the ball will come to him. To compensate for the descending curve of the ball when making a catch facing the infield, play the ball to "hit you on the nose."

Good Luck!

Breaks and Leads

"You have to keep running. I always believed I was going to be safe." – Rickey Henderson

---

Breaks and Leads is an outstanding multiple drill that combines the teaching of both *base stealing techniques* and *defensive skills* to be used against those attempting to steal. It also allows the coach to time three key elements of the game—pitchers' times to the plate; catchers' times when throwing to second base; and baserunners' times when stealing second.

How to run "Breaks and Leads"

Positioning:
Pitchers should stand to the third base side of the mound (out of the way of the catcher's throws), and one pitcher at a time will take the mound for a period of time or a designated number of pickoffs and pitches, as decided by the coach. The catchers should be at home plate in full gear, while the first basemen, second basemen and shortstops are at their positions (the first basemen will be stationed at the bag as they would when holding a runner on). Third basemen and outfielders are the baserunners who work on their breaks and leads, but be sure all position players get a chance to spend time as baserunners to hone this aspect of their game.

For reasons of safety, there is no actual runner on first base. Instead, players line up behind first base along the right field foul line. Space four "throw down" bases about four feet apart on the foul line, so that four players can practice breaks and leads at one time.

Equipment necessary
1. Protective screens: place one protective screen behind second base to protect runners from errant throws from the catcher. Place another protective screen behind first base to protect runners from errant pickoff throws from the pitcher.
2. Four throw-down bases: place them along the right field foul line about four feet apart, with the first one about 10 feet past first base.

Execution:
The pitcher works out of a stretch, while the baserunners take their leads from their throw-down bases behind first base. The pitcher may make one or more pickoff throws to the first baseman, at which time the baserunners work on getting back to the bag. When the pitcher works to home plate, the runners break for second. (They don't actually run to second, of course, since they're stationed well past the imaginary line between first and second bases. Instead, they run to a point even with second base, where they're guarded by the protective screen.)

The catcher, after receiving the pitch, fires a throw to second base. The shortstop and second baseman alternate covering the bag. The coach uses the opportunity to time the pitchers to home plate, the catchers' throws to second, and the baserunners' steal attempts, as directed later in the chapter.

BREAKS AND LEADS

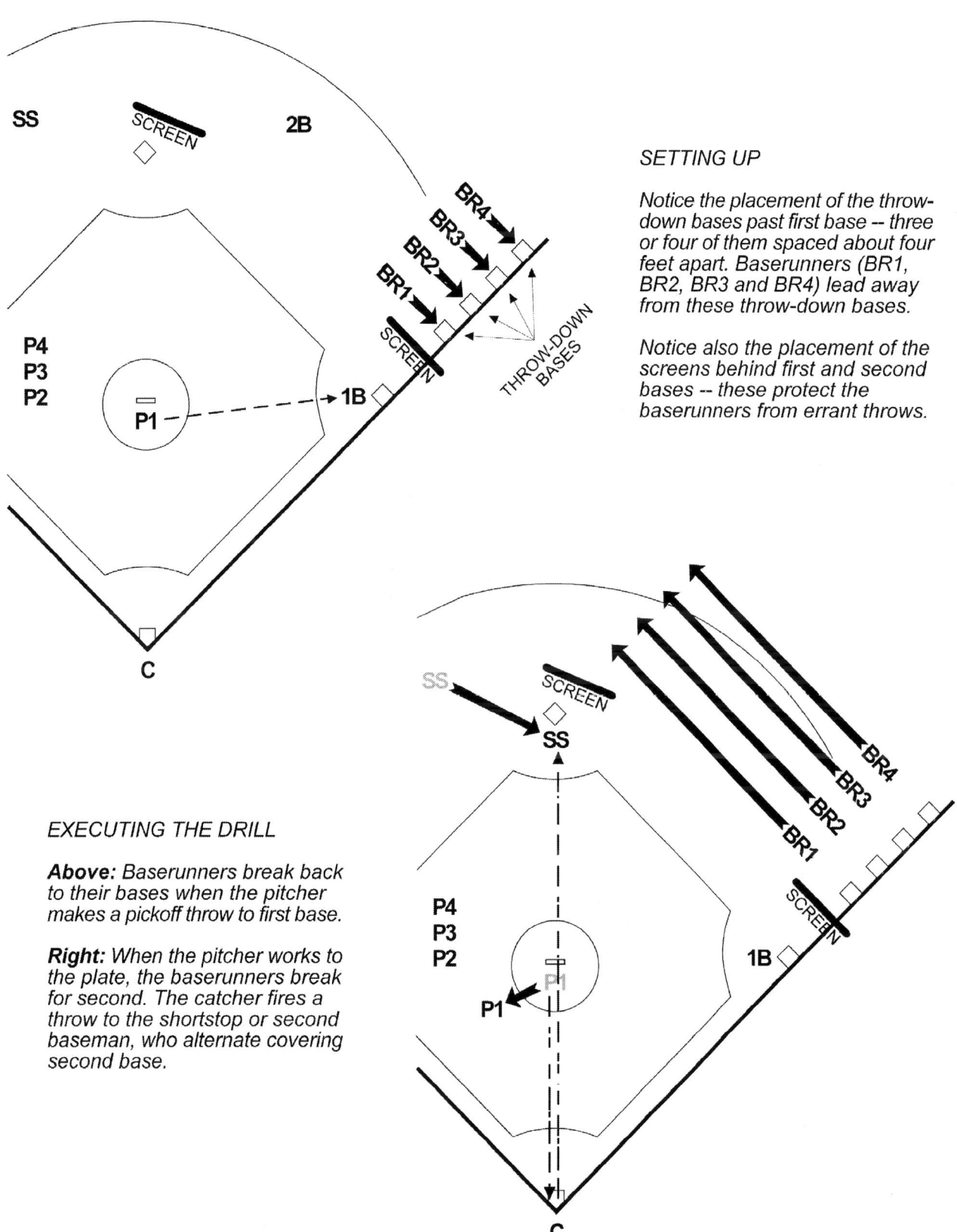

SETTING UP

Notice the placement of the throw-down bases past first base -- three or four of them spaced about four feet apart. Baserunners (BR1, BR2, BR3 and BR4) lead away from these throw-down bases.

Notice also the placement of the screens behind first and second bases -- these protect the baserunners from errant throws.

EXECUTING THE DRILL

Above: *Baserunners break back to their bases when the pitcher makes a pickoff throw to first base.*

Right: *When the pitcher works to the plate, the baserunners break for second. The catcher fires a throw to the shortstop or second baseman, who alternate covering second base.*

Player goals during the drill

Pitcher:
1. The pitcher works from a stretch as if holding a runner on first base.
2. He can try to pick the runner off first base, or he can work to the plate.
3. The pitcher works on varying the time between pitches to keep the runner guessing.
4. The pitcher works on quickness to home plate. He should be timed from the start of his first movement until the ball hits the catcher's glove.
   – 1.6 seconds = poor
   – 1.4 seconds = good
   – 1.3 seconds = excellent

Catcher:
1. The catcher sets up behind home plate in full gear.
2. He receives the pitch and throws to second base.
3. He works on proper shifting and footwork to improve quickness and release time, and he works on accuracy on throws to second base.
4. A coach with a stopwatch times the catcher's throws. Start the watch the instant the ball is caught by the catcher, and stop it when it is caught at second base. The ideal time is 2.0 seconds or less.

First baseman:
1. The first baseman is stationed at first to receive pickoff throws and apply the tag correctly.
2. He assumes the correct position and stance for holding the runner at first base (see page 64).

Middle infielders (shortstop and second baseman):
1. The middle infielders alternate covering second base and backing up the throw.
2. They focus on learning how far they need to "cheat" toward second base to be there in time to receive the catcher's throw.
3. They also work on correctly covering the bag, receiving the catcher's throw and applying the tag.

Baserunners:
1. Baserunners work on how to lead off first base correctly; how to return to first after a pickoff attempt; how to read the pitcher's moves; how to make the correct initial step when breaking for second base; and how to "look in" when attempting to steal as the ball enters the impact zone (see page 220 for the "Look-In Drill").
2. Runners break for second base as the pitcher delivers home. (They're actually leading from the throw-down bases and running to a point even with second base.)
3. Runners do not slide, but instead run behind a protective screen at second base.
4. Runners should be timed:
   – 3.4 seconds = very fast
   – 3.4 to 3.6 seconds = alert to steal
   – 3.6 to 3.8 seconds = questionable
   – 3.8 to 4.0 seconds = hit-and-run
   – 4.0 seconds or more = forget stealing

Good Luck!

Defensive Strategy

Defending the First-and-Third Double Steal

"Good defense in baseball is like good umpiring. It's there, you expect it, but you don't really appreciate it. But when it isn't there, then you notice it." – Doug DeCinces

---

A major component of a solid defensive team is its ability to deal with the first-and-third double steal situation. At the youth, high school, and (to a lesser degree) college levels of play, it is almost automatic that the runner at first base will attempt a steal of second base when there are runners on first and third. *This is especially true when there are two outs and a weak hitter is at bat.*

The rationale for stealing in the two-out situation is that the offense's chances of scoring a run by a defensive mistake are greater than the hitter's chances of getting a base hit. This is logically a good gamble. The disadvantage? If the play is unsuccessful, the offense will start the next inning with the weak hitter leading off.

> *Philosophy / General Rules:*
>
> **Throw through to second base if:**
> - The runner stealing second base is the tying or winning run.
> - Your team is far ahead. Do not play on a meaningless run. Throw the runner out stealing from first base and break the back of the inning.
>
> **Concede second base if:**
> - The winning run is at third base.
> - There are two outs and a very poor hitter is at bat.
> - Your catcher has a weak arm.
> - Your middle infielders have weak arms, have inaccurate arms, or tend to get rattled.

Because the first-and-third double steal situation occurs so often, practice time must be allotted to develop a defensive strategy to cope with it during a game. Once the defensive scheme is introduced and understood, it must be practiced regularly so that the defensive team can react calmly and confidently when the situation presents itself in a game.

Types of Defenses

There are many options to defend the standard first-and-third double steal. The following list will meet most team's needs. If learned thoroughly and practiced regularly, these defenses will provide the tools necessary to thwart the first-and-third double steal, or at least limit its effectiveness.

Defense #1: Throw through to second base
Defense #2: Cut by the pitcher
Defense #3: Full arm fake by the catcher
Defense #4: "Third base right now"
Defense #5: Cut by the second baseman in the halfway position
Defense #6: Direct throw to the shortstop or second baseman

Defense #1, the throw through to second base, is the primary tactic. The others are secondary defensive plays that should be part of every team's repertoire—they make scoring a cheap run much more difficult. And for those teams not physically strong enough to throw through to second base effectively, the secondary defenses may be the most effective way to defend the first-and-third double steal situation.

In addition to the above defenses for a *standard* first-and-third double steal, the defense must be able to defend against the first-and-third "forced balk" (or "early break"), the first-and-third delayed steal, and the first-and-third "intentional pickoff" (or "long lead").

Defense #1: Throw through to second base

The throw through to second base is the basic defense against the first-and-third double steal. It is also the hallmark of a solid defensive team. In this strategy, players have these responsibilities:

Pitcher's responsibilities

During this defense, the pitcher delivers the pitch and then steps aside to give the catcher an unobstructed view of second base. As the throw passes the pitcher, he must *fake* cutting the catcher's throw by slapping his glove. The pitcher then challenges the runner at third base by pretending to have the ball and jumping into position to throw, as if he were going to throw to third base. The fake cut is essential to the success of the play. If the runner on third base stops and transfers his weight back toward third base or loses momentum, his chances of scoring are greatly diminished.

The pitcher must also be alert to cover home plate for a possible rundown there.

Catcher's responsibilities

The catcher receives the pitch, looks the runner back at third base, and throws through to second base. The lower the catcher's throw as it passes the pitcher, the longer the runner at third base must wait to be certain the ball will not be cut off by the pitcher.

The catcher must read the runner at third base. If the runner is walking toward home plate, do not throw to second base. Instead, use a full-arm fake to second base to lure the runner farther down the line, or throw immediately to third base. The throw to third base must be on the inside of the base (on the fair territory side of the base), not directly to the base where the runner is likely to be hit by the ball. For details on the Inside/Outside Concept, see page 27. If the runner's chest is open (facing you), he is preparing to run on the throw to second base.

The catcher must also read the third baseman. If his hands are in the air, throw to third base on the inside of the diamond. If the third baseman has his hands in the air and the runner is moving down the baseline toward you, use a full-arm fake to second base first.

If the catcher throws through to second base, after releasing the throw, he must move in front of the plate to be in position to receive a return throw.

First Baseman's responsibilities

The first baseman must let the catcher know that the runner on first base is stealing by yelling, "There he goes!"

Do not trail the runner with none or one out: If the first baseman trails the runner to second base in this situation, the runner's chances of scoring from third base are greatly increased. This is particularly true if the first baseman makes the tag up the baseline near second base—the first baseman will then have to make a long and accurate throw to home plate from a difficult position, often with his momentum going toward second base and away from home plate.

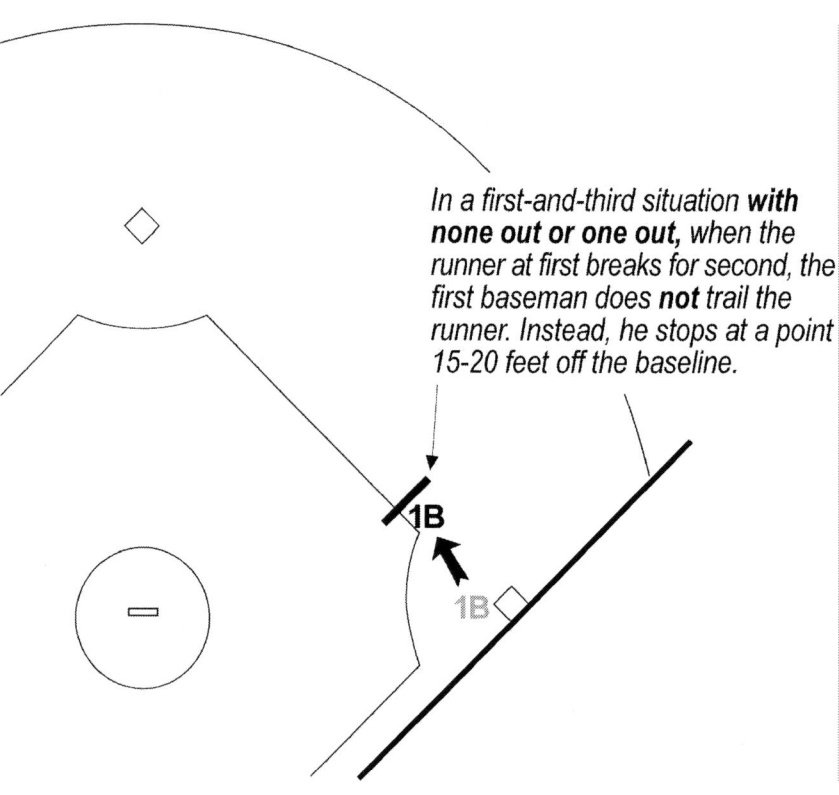

In a first-and-third situation **with none out or one out,** when the runner at first breaks for second, the first baseman does **not** trail the runner. Instead, he stops at a point 15-20 feet off the baseline.

So, with none out or one out, if the runner breaking from first base is caught in a rundown, the first baseman does not trail, but instead remains just off first base (15 to 20 feet), awaiting the runner to be driven back to him. Then, when the runner is close enough to the first baseman that a quick tag and putout can be made, the first baseman takes a step forward and simultaneously asks for the ball from the pursuing infielder by saying "Now!" He then makes the tag for the out and freezes the runner at third base. (The worst-case result of not trailing the runner would be to have the runner return to first base safely, and the same situation would present itself all over again.)

With two outs, the first baseman should trail the runner, and if a rundown ensues, disregard the runner on third base and make the tag on the runner between first and second, ending the inning before the runner on third base can score.

If a rundown between third base and home plate occurs, the first baseman should be prepared to cover home plate.

He should run the pitcher out, if necessary. The first baseman has priority.

Responsibilities of the shortstop and second baseman:

It is the responsibility of the middle infielders to cover second base and receive the catcher's throw. They should "cheat" toward second base and protect their position first, then cover the base. When covering second base, the fielder should stand in front of the bag to stay clear of the baserunner.

If the runner on third base attempts to score when the catcher throws through, the infielder covering second should move quickly forward to the ball. His body should be completely under control and in position to throw *before* throwing the ball back to the catcher. The fielder should not look at the runner when making the return throw to the catcher—it may cause him to panic unnecessarily.

If the runner on third base does not break for home plate, then of course apply the tag on the runner coming into second base.

> ### *Let the math go to work:*
>
> With the runner at third breaking for home plate, there's no need for panic from the middle infielder receiving the throw from the catcher. The formula *x miles per hour times 1½ = y feet per second* provides an idea of how fast the ball travels and how quickly the runner's advantage disappears.
>
> So, if the fielder throws 80 mph, *80 times 1½ = 120 feet per second*. Middle infielders should maintain their poise and allow the math to work for them.

The middle infielder who is not assigned the responsibility of covering second becomes the backup man. The backup man should cheat toward second base, protect his position first, and then back up second base.

Rundown between first and second bases: If the runner on third base does not attempt to score on the catcher's throw to second base and a rundown occurs between first and second with none out or one out, the middle infielder has two options.

First, he can run hard at the baserunner. If the chaser (the middle infielder) runs hard at the trapped baserunner, two things happen: as the chaser gets closer to first base, the length of his throw to home plate is shortened; and the rundown distance is shortened, limiting the area the runner has to avoid being tagged out.

Or, the middle infielder can use a "walking defense"—that is, he can walk toward the runner at first. The chaser should hold the ball in his throwing hand and elevate it in the air, and simply walk toward the baserunner, forcing him to commit to returning to first base. At the same time, the chaser watches the runner on third base for a possible break for home plate—if the runner breaks, the middle infielder "releases" and throws him out; or, if the runner on third base reaches "the point of no return," the middle infielder releases and runs at him, then throws to the appropriate base for the out.

One admonition: when the middle infielder releases and runs toward the runner at third base, he must have his body under complete control and be in position to throw before making the actual throw. He should not throw on the run.

Third baseman's responsibilities

The third baseman should protect his position first, and then cover third base. He should walk toward the hitter, under control, to shorten the distance to third base.

The third baseman should break for third base after the ball has passed the hitter. Then assume a position on the inside of third base, with the right foot on the infield side of the base. This position gives the catcher a clear target, diminishing the chance of hitting the runner with the throw.

When the runner on first base breaks for second base and the catcher looks at third base, the third baseman should hold both hands in the air if the runner on third base has too big a lead (25 feet or more) and can be picked off.

If the catcher throws through to second base and the runner on third attempts to score, the third baseman should yell, "Home, home!" "Four, four!" or "There he goes!"

With none out or one out during a rundown between first and second bases, it is the third baseman's responsibility to alert the rest of the infield if the runner on third breaks for the plate or gets too far off third base. If the runner on third is "creeping" down the third base line, yell "Release!" when the runner reaches the "point of no return" (see below). If the runner on third base breaks for home after the rundown has begun between first and second, the third baseman should yell, "There he goes!" "Four, four!" or "Home, home!"

The Point of No Return

The "point of no return" is a position approximately 25 to 30 feet down the third base line, where the baserunner is too far off third base to return to the base safely. This distance will vary slightly depending on the individual runner's quickness.

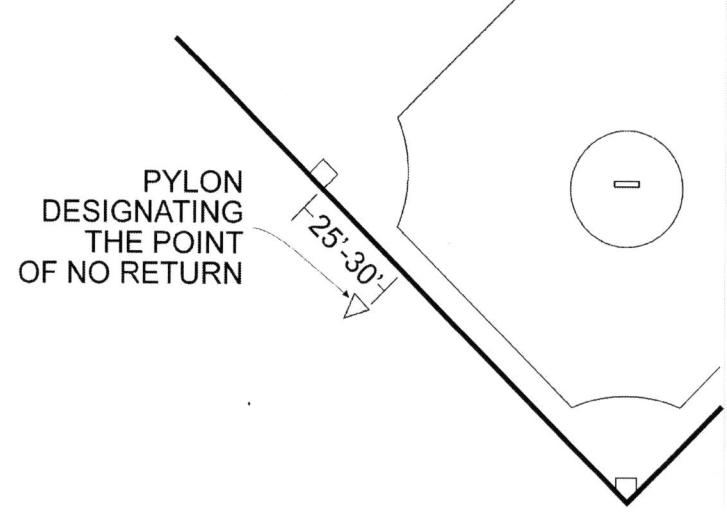

During a rundown between first and second with none out or one out, when the runner at third base begins to creep down the line, the defense must know this point of no return. Once there, if the defense reacts properly, the runner will be, in baseball parlance, hung out to dry. In this case, the defense can now focus its attention upon him.

A mental picture of the point of no return must be implanted in the minds of all infielders. During practice, place a pylon or other marker 25-30 feet down the line (and somewhat off the line so that it won't be tripped over). In a game, of course, there is no pylon to serve as a reference point. If necessary, players can use a distinguishing mark on the grandstand to serve this purpose.

Once the runner on third base reaches the point of no return, either the third baseman or the middle infielder acting as the backup man should yell "Release!" This will allow the middle infielder involved in the rundown between first and second bases to release from that rundown and direct his attention toward the runner trapped off third.

If the runner on third base makes an all-out break for home plate, the defense should yell "Home, home!" or "Four, four!"

Rundowns

To successfully defend the first-and-third double steal, a team must have a well-planned defensive system to deal effectively with rundown situations. For basics on handling rundowns, see the earlier chapters *Executing the Rundown* and *Rundown Drills.* These fundamentals must be practiced regularly before they can be integrated into the first-and-third defensive scheme.

The defense should beware: when there are two outs and a rundown occurs between first and second bases, the runner on first is coached to *stop*, get caught in a rundown and avoid being tagged out for as long a time as possible. This tactic is designed to give the runner on third base sufficient time to reach home plate before the third out of the inning can be made. In this scenario—when there are *two outs* and the runner on third base does not break for home plate on the catcher's throw to second base—the middle infielders and first baseman should focus their attention on the runner trapped between first and second bases and make a total commitment to tag him for the third out before the runner on third base can score.

Defense #2: The Cut by the Pitcher

This defensive tactic is used when the runner on third base represents an important run. The defense concedes second base to the runner stealing from first and directs its attention to the runner at third base, hoping to catch him too far off base or breaking prematurely for home plate.

This play is often thought of as being amateurish or "bush-league," but it can be extremely effective if used against overly zealous runners who do not wait until the ball clears the pitcher's head before breaking for home plate.

▶ **The catcher:** The catcher steps out in front of home plate and gives the defense the sign for the "cut by the pitcher" play. When the catcher receives the pitch, he does *not* look at the runner on third base. Instead, he throws the ball hard and head high-to the pitcher. To be effective, the throw must look like it is going to second base.

▶ **The pitcher:** Once the catcher gives the sign for the "cut by the pitcher" play, it is absolutely imperative that the pitcher "reply" to the catcher to let him know that he understands that he must cut the ball off. A simple "brush down" on his pants with his glove will tell the catcher that the pitcher is aware of the play and of his defensive responsibilities. If the pitcher does not reply, this could result in the pitcher side-stepping or ducking the catcher's throw and a run scoring. *No reply—no play!*

The pitcher cuts the catcher's throw off and turns immediately toward third base. If the runner is breaking toward home plate, or is caught off third base and attempts to get back, the pitcher should throw him out. If the runner is hung up between third and home, the pitcher should run at him from the home plate side, forcing him back toward third base, and then tag or throw him out.

If the runner on third base is a very important run and is *not* fooled by the cut and caught off base, the pitcher should turn and make a full-arm fake toward second base, then turn and check the runner at third base again. To be effective, the pitcher needs to "sell" the fake and make it seem real. For details, see the box on *making the fake throw* on page 85.

▶ **The first baseman:** The first baseman yells "there he goes!" to alert the catcher that the runner on first is breaking for second. This is particularly important when a left-handed batter is up because he tends to block the catcher's view. As in Defense #1, the first baseman should trail the runner only with two out. With none out or one out, he waits in the first base area approximately 15 feet off the base.

▶ **The second baseman:** The second baseman should break to second base when the catcher receives the ball, in the event the catcher overthrows the pitcher. He should be alert for a possible rundown between first and second, but because this defensive scheme concedes second base, a rundown is unlikely.

▶ **The shortstop:** If the runner is picked off third base, the shortstop should break to third for a possible rundown. Or, the shortstop can break to second base if a rundown occurs there.

▶ **The third baseman:** The third baseman covers third once the ball has passed the impact zone at home plate. He should assume a position on the infield side of third base, not behind the base—this prevents the baserunner from getting between the ball and the third baseman if the pitcher throws to third base on a pickoff attempt.

Defense #3: The Full Arm Fake by the Catcher

This play concedes second base and is designed to pick the runner off third base. It may be used any time the coach deems appropriate, but is often used when the winning or go-ahead run is on third base late in the game. It is particularly effective against an undisciplined, anxious, or overly aggressive runner who does not wait until the ball passes the pitcher before breaking for home plate.

▶ **The catcher:** The catcher steps out in front of home plate and gives the defensive team the sign for the "full arm fake" defense. He then receives the pitch, does *not* look the runner back at third base, and makes a *realistic* full-arm fake to second. After faking the throw to second, the catcher looks at the third baseman—if the third baseman has both arms in the air, the catcher throws immediately to third base on the inside of the base to avoid hitting the baserunner. If the runner is breaking toward home plate when the catcher looks at third base, he should not throw the ball—instead, run at the baserunner and get him in a rundown.

▶ **The pitcher:** If the runner is picked off third base, the pitcher should back up home plate for a possible rundown.

▶ **The third baseman:** The third baseman should cover third base after the catcher receives the pitch—if the runner can be picked off, he should let the catcher know by raising both arms in the air. Assume a position inside the base—the right foot should be along the inside edge of the base, decreasing the chance of hitting the runner on a throw to third. It also diminishes the chances of the runner blocking the third baseman's view.

The third baseman should trail the runner if he prematurely breaks for home plate. If a rundown ensues, it will take less time to make the putout, and with less than two out, it may prevent the runner on first base from advancing.

▶ **The shortstop:** Covers third base if the runner is picked off and a rundown occurs.

▶ **The second baseman:** The second baseman covers second base after the catcher receives the ball, then moves into the seal position if the runner stops between first and second bases.

Defense #4: "Third base right now"

This play is designed to catch the baserunner off third base that has taken too long a secondary lead, has transferred his body weight and is leaning toward home plate, or is overly aggressive. Often, the baserunner is anticipating the catcher's throw to second base and is caught flat-footed. This play concedes second base and is often used when the runner on third represents the winning run.

▶ **The catcher:** The catcher steps in front of home plate and gives the defensive team the sign for the "third base right now" defense. After receiving the pitch, he throws without hesitation to third base. The throw must be on the inside of third base to avoid hitting the baserunner. Don't overthrow—be accurate!

▶ **The pitcher:** After the pitcher delivers the pitch, he must be prepared to back up home plate if the baserunner is picked off third and a rundown results.

▶ **The third baseman:** Breaks to third base after the catcher receives the pitch. He assumes an inside-the-base position with his right foot along the inside edge of third base, receives the catcher's throw and makes the tag. Of course, in the event of an inaccurate throw by the catcher, the third baseman leaves the base to get the ball. The priority is *"ball, then base!"* No cheap runs!

▶ **The shortstop:** Protects his position until the ball passes the hitter, then breaks toward third base for a possible rundown.

▶ **The second baseman:** Protects his position until the ball passes the hitter, then covers second base.

▶ **The first baseman:** Stays alert to cover home plate in the event of a rundown between home and third base.

Defense #5: Cut by Second Baseman in the Halfway Position

This play concedes second base and is designed to dupe the runner at third base into thinking the catcher's throw will go all the way through to second base. However, the second baseman assumes a position halfway between the pitcher's mound and second base, cuts off the catcher's throw and returns the ball back to home plate for the out if the runner at third should attempt to score.

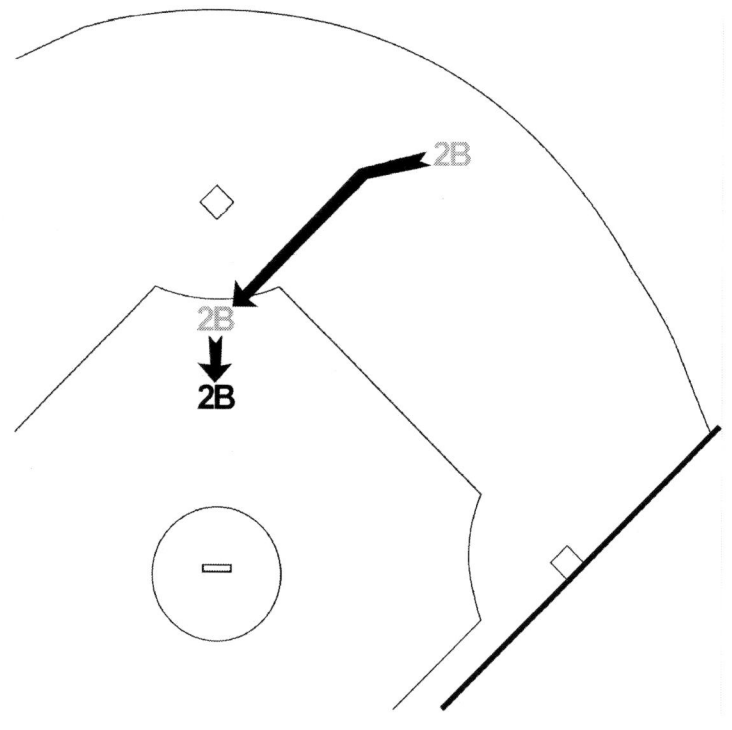

As the middle infielders scramble to get to their defensive assignments, two defensive positions are left unprotected. As a consequence, this defense is vulnerable to exploitation by the hit-and-run (or most ground balls). So it is imperative that the pitch-out be used in conjunction with this defensive scheme.

▶ **The catcher:** Steps in front of home plate and gives the defensive team the sign for the "cut by the second baseman in the halfway position" defense. He gives the pitcher the pitch-out sign, and after receiving the pitch-out as the runner on first base breaks for second base, he looks at the runner on third and then throws directly to the second baseman in the "halfway" position. If the runner on third base is breaking for home plate when the catcher looks at him, the catcher should execute a full-arm fake toward second base and then start the rundown of the trapped runner from third.

▶ **The pitcher:** Delivers the pitch-out, then steps aside to give the catcher an unobstructed view of the second baseman. He does not fake cutting the catcher's throw, as this may prevent the runner on third base from breaking to home plate.

▶ **The second baseman:** Cheats toward second base and evacuates his position as the pitcher starts his delivery to home plate. (He does not need to protect his position because the pitcher will deliver a pitch-out.) He angles over and runs to a point approximately 20 feet in front of second base, in a direct line with home plate, then moves forward, bringing his body under control and establishes lateral movement preparing for the return thrown to the catcher. When he receives the ball, he will be approximately halfway between the mound and second base. He cuts off the throw and returns it to the catcher for the out. The second baseman must have his body under complete control and be in position to throw before releasing the ball back to the catcher. If the runner stops between home and third base, run at him from the home plate side, forcing him back toward third base, then tag or throw him out.

▶ **The shortstop:** Covers second base in the event the catcher makes an errant throw to the second baseman. (Again, because of the pitch-out, he needn't protect his position before breaking to second base.)

▶ **The third baseman:** Assumes an inside-the-base position in the event catcher throws there, then trails the runner as he breaks for home plate for a possible rundown.

▶ **The first baseman:** Stays alert to cover home plate for a possible rundown.

Defense #6: Direct Throw to Shortstop or Second Baseman

This defensive play concedes second base and is designed to throw the runner breaking from third base out at home plate. The runner at third may be fooled into thinking the catcher's throw will go through to second base—as soon as he sees the ball pass the pitcher and that it will not be cut off, most runners will break for home plate. Under game pressure, it is very difficult for the runner at third base to tell that the throw isn't going to second base.

Whichever middle infielder has responsibility at second base breaks straight toward home plate as the runner on first base breaks toward second. The catcher throws the ball directly to this middle infielder, who cuts off the throw and relays it back to the catcher for the out.

Note: Having the catcher throw directly to the second baseman is more deceptive than having him throw to the shortstop—the throw from the catcher to the second baseman passes behind the pitcher, and is more likely to appear to the runner at third to be a legitimate throw to second base. On the other hand, when the catcher throws to the shortstop, the ball passes between the pitcher and the runner at third, making it easier to read. The coach may opt to have the second basemen receive all throws from the catcher and totally eliminate the shortstop when this play is used.

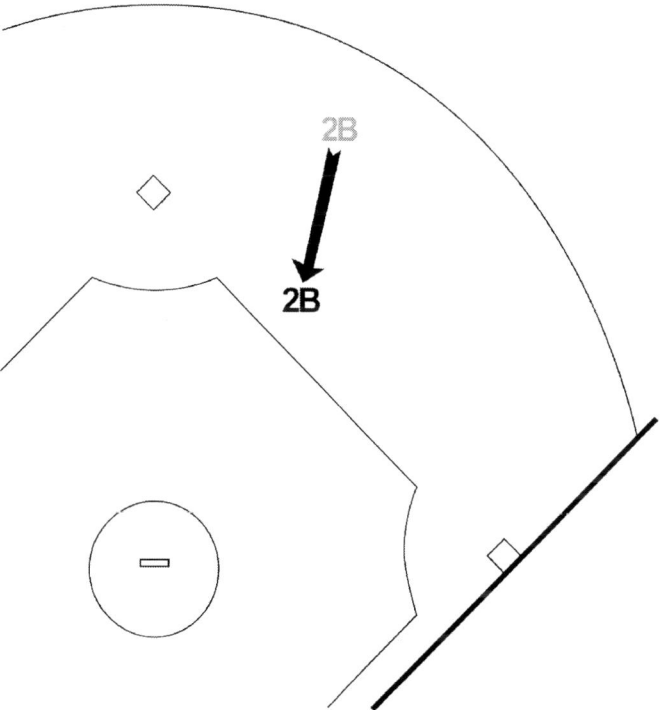

Here, the second baseman has broken directly in for a direct throw from the catcher. The shortstop can also be used on this play, although it may be more deceptive to the runner at third if the catcher's throw is to the second baseman.

▶ **The catcher:** The catcher receives the pitch as the runner on first base breaks toward second. He looks at the runner on third base and then throws the ball directly to the shortstop or second baseman, whichever one has second base responsibility. *This play demands that the catcher throw accurately—an errant throw would be disastrous.* He receives the middle infielder's return throw to home plate and tags the runner out. If the runner on third base is breaking for home plate when the catcher looks at him, the catcher should execute a full-arm fake toward second base, then start the rundown of the trapped runner from third.

▶ **The pitcher:** After delivering the pitch, the pitcher does *not* fake cutting the catcher's throw off. He is alert to backup home plate should a rundown occur there.

▶ **The middle infielder:** The middle infielder designated as the catcher's target breaks *directly toward home plate*. (Taking two steps toward second base before breaking directly toward home plate may add realism to the play, but it is optional.) The middle infielder receives the catcher's throw and relays it back to the catcher, who applies the tag for the out on the runner breaking from third base.

The infielder must move aggressively toward home plate, yet be under complete control when approaching the catcher's throw. Establish lateral movement by changing from a "speed step" to a "jab step." This will allow lateral movement to the ball should the catcher's throw be off line. Receive the catcher's throw with the body in position to throw and under control. *Don't throw on the run!*

▶ **The third baseman:** The third baseman covers third base on the inside of the base. He trails the runner as the runner breaks for home plate in the event of a rundown.

▶ **The first baseman:** Stays alert to cover home plate for a possible rundown.

About Secondary First-and-Third Defenses

The above secondary defenses (Defense #2 through Defense #6) are all designed to catch the runner off third base, and they concede second base to the runner who is breaking from first. Sometimes the runner from first will stop short of second base and invite the defense to play on him if the runner on third is not picked off base. It should be predetermined by the coach and relayed to the defense whether to ignore the runner going to second base or not.

Normally, one of these secondary defenses is chosen because the runner on third base is overly aggressive, the run on first base is meaningless, or the defense lacks the skill or physical maturity necessary to successfully defend the play. In these cases, it may be wise to ignore the runner advancing to second base even though he deliberately stops short of second base and allows himself to be caught in a rundown.

If, after failing to pick the runner off third, the defense decides to take the runner's challenge and engage in a rundown between first and second, the second baseman should get to the "seal position" if possible. The seal position is a point in the baseline between first and second base, and is as far from second base toward first as the stopping baserunner's location permits. The seal position restricts the area the trapped baserunner has to work in and elude the defense—the smaller the area the runner has, the quicker the defense can make the putout. The first baseman must not trail the runner breaking from first unless there are two out.

Defending Other First-and-Third Ploys

There are several first-and-third double steal plays that present themselves during the course of a season other than the straight double steal discussed in the defenses earlier in this chapter. A solid defensive team is prepared to cope with these double steal variations.

Defending the "Forced Balk" or "Early Break"

This play occurs when the runner on first base breaks for second as the pitcher goes into his stretch. The success of this play is predicated upon the element of surprise—it is designed to startle the pitcher and cause him to commit a balk, allowing the runner on third to score. When this happens, players have the responsibilities detailed here.

▶ **The pitcher:** To offset the element of surprise, the pitcher *must look at the runner on first base* as he goes into his stretch. This eliminates the effectiveness of this play, as the pitcher will not be startled. When the runner on first base breaks early for second, the pitcher should *calmly* step back off the rubber, turn clockwise toward third base and *freeze* the runner there—if the runner at third is caught off base, throw him out. If the runner at third is close to the base and there is no play, check the runner going to second. Again, this is a *clockwise* turn toward second base.

To repeat, pitchers must know to "step off, check third, check second," while turning clockwise. If the runner breaking for second base stops between first and second, the second baseman will be in the "seal position," and the pitcher should throw the ball to him. If, on the other hand, the runner breaking for second runs *past* the second baseman, throw the ball to the shortstop covering second base.

If the runner at third is an important run and you do not wish to play on the runner from first base, execute a full-arm fake toward second base, then turn and check the runner at third for a possible play there (see page 85 for details on proper execution of a full-arm fake).

It is a good idea *not* to run at the runner if he stops between first and second base. Either full-arm fake toward second, or throw the ball to one of the middle infielders, preferably the second baseman in the seal position.

▶ **The first baseman:** The first baseman must yell, *"step off" AND NOT "there he goes"* when the runner on first base breaks early for second base. ("Step off" reminds the pitcher of what he must do defensively in this situation, and it's less likely to startle the pitcher, causing him to balk, in the event he has failed to watch the runner at first base while going into his stretch position.) The first baseman should be alert for a possible rundown. As discussed before, with none out or one out, he should not trail the runner, but with two outs, trail the runner for a quick putout before the runner at third can score.

▶ **The shortstop:** Should cover second base and stay alert for either the runner at third base breaking for home or a rundown between first and second.

▶ **The second baseman:** Get to the seal position and be alert for a possible rundown between first and second bases.

▶ **Third baseman:** Cover third base and stay alert for a throw from the pitcher, especially if the pitcher executes a full-arm fake toward second base. Stay alert for a rundown between home plate and third base.

▶ **The catcher:** Cover home plate for a possible tag play. Stay alert for a possible rundown between home and third.

Defending the Delayed Steal

The intent of the delayed steal is to catch the middle infielders napping instead of covering second base. The "delayed steal" literally means that the runner on first base delays his break for second until the pitch has been delivered.

There are a number of variations on the delayed steal, but all are designed to catch the middle infielders flat-footed, resulting in no one covering second base. Often, when middle infielders see that the runner on first base does not break for second when the pitcher makes his first move, they "relax" and direct their attention to the hitter and away from the runner. Consequently, when the runner on first breaks for second after a slight delay, no one moves to cover the base. Even if the catcher is alert, he has no one to receive his throw—he either must hold the ball and concede second base, or if he chooses to throw, risk throwing the ball into center field.

> ### *Compare strategies:*
>
> After reading this chapter and the next one ("Defending the Not-So-Common First-and-Third Situation"), move to page 222 and read "First-and-Third Double Steals," which details an offensive team's options in this situation. Then return to this chapter and the next one and read them again. This will further build your understanding.
>
> Solid baseball teams can exploit the first-and-third situation while on offense and thwart it while on defense. This is not coincidence—if a team understands how to run the play on offense, they will also have an idea what an opponent is trying to do.

Even if a late-arriving middle infielder gets to the catcher's throw, he will have his momentum going away from home plate, making a return throw to the plate difficult at best. This is particularly true when a left-handed hitter is at bat and the shortstop has second base coverage. If the shortstop is late in covering second base and makes the catch on the run, his momentum will carry him past the base toward right field, making it virtually impossible to throw out a runner breaking from third base.

The middle infielders and the catcher are the keys to successfully defending against the delayed steal. Each must do his job to avoid being caught by surprise when the runner on first base makes his delayed break to second. They must *anticipate* that the runner on first base may break for second on every pitch.

Exactly when the runner breaks for second base depends upon the type of delayed steal the offensive team chooses to run. Common variations include: the runner on first breaking for second as the ball crosses the front edge of home plate; the runner on first breaking for second as the catcher is about to throw the ball back to the pitcher; and the runner on first breaking for second after taking three or four sideways shuffle-steps on the pitcher's delivery to home plate. These and all other delayed steal variations are designed to catch the middle infielders and catcher off-guard.

It stands to reason that if a baserunner has difficulty stealing second base on a normal break, it should be virtually impossible to steal second if he delays his break until after the pitcher has delivered the ball, or after the catcher has received the pitch. If each player stays alert and does his job, the delayed steal can be neutralized.

To combat the delayed steal, players have the following responsibilities:

▶ **The catcher:** The catcher must be alert on every pitch, and must shift into throwing position on every pitch. He must glance at the runner on third base when making a throw to second, and he must be especially alert with a left-handed hitter at bat, because his view of the runner is obscured. After receiving a pitch, he must not be lazy and lob the ball back to the pitcher from his knees—instead, fire the ball quickly back to the pitcher to disrupt the timing of the runner at first base should he choose to break for second on the catcher's throw back to the pitcher.

▶ **The middle infielder:** When first base is occupied, particularly in the first-and-third situation, the infielder assigned to cover second on a steal attempt must go to the bag after the catcher receives the ball on every pitch—otherwise, there is no one to receive the catcher's throw. Covering second after every pitch will do more to dissuade the use of the delayed steal than any other single tactic. The middle infielder must move in front of second base and be prepared to receive the catcher's throw. Moreover, he must stay alert for a possible delayed steal as the catcher receives the pitch—no dirt-kicking or looking down at the ground after the ball crosses home plate.

▶ **The first baseman:** It is the first baseman's responsibility to let the catcher and middle infielders know when the runner breaks for second base. He should be prepared for a possible rundown between first and second.

▶ **The third baseman:** Covers third base on the inside of the bag in the event the catcher throws there. The third baseman should hold his arms in the air if the runner at third has too big a lead and can be picked off. And he yells "Home! Home!" or "Four! Four!" if the runner on third breaks for the plate on the catcher's throw to second. He must stay alert for a possible rundown between home and third.

▶ **The pitcher:** The pitcher must be alert to the situation. If the runner on first base runs the delayed steal on the catcher's throw back to the mound, the pitcher should turn toward third and freeze the runner there, or throw him out if he is too far off base. After freezing the runner at third base, the pitcher should throw the ball to the middle infielder covering second base, or to the second baseman in the seal position. Then, he should be prepared for a rundown between first and second or between home and third.

Defending the "Intentional Pickoff" or "Long Lead"

On this play, the runner at first base deliberately invites the pitcher to pick him off by taking an extraordinarily long primary lead, or invites a pickoff attempt by the catcher by taking an exceptionally long secondary lead. In either case, if the ball is thrown to the first baseman, the runner on first will break for second, hoping to get the first baseman to make the long throw to second base and enabling the runner on third to score.

The defense must decide in advance whether or not to play on the runner breaking from first base or to concede second base. *Know which runner to play on before the play develops.*

▶ **The catcher:** If the runner at first is picked off by the pitcher, the catcher should hold his position and be alert for a play on the runner trying to score from third. If the runner at first base takes an exceptionally long secondary lead, inviting a pickoff after the catcher receives the pitch, the catcher should check the runner at third before throwing to the first baseman. (The catcher will have time because the runner at first wants to be picked off.)

▶ **The pitcher:** The pitcher should take his stretch while looking at the runner on first base, so as not to be caught by surprise—this helps the pitcher stay mentally alert and aware of the situation. If the runner on first takes an exceptionally long primary lead, inviting a pickoff, the pitcher should do the following:

1) Step off the rubber, preventing a balk and making the pitcher an infielder free to move in any manner or direction.

2) Check the runner at third base. If there is no play there, the pitcher may: A) make a full-arm fake toward the runner at first base, then check the runner at third again to see if he has taken too big a lead or is breaking toward home plate (be alert to the possibility that the runner on first may break for second when the full-arm fake is made; if so, check the runner at third base, make a clockwise turn, and throw the ball to second base); B) throw the ball to the first baseman; C) throw the ball to the second baseman in the seal position; or D) throw the ball to the shortstop covering second base.

▶ **The first baseman:** During this play, the first baseman should do the following:

1) If the runner at first base takes an extraordinarily long primary lead inviting a pickoff, *move off the base and next to the runner*—this shortens his lead, puts you closer to him for a possible quick tag and may confuse him and disrupt the play's timing. Tell the pitcher to "Step off!" If the pitcher throws the ball to the first baseman, he should check the runner at third, and if he is breaking for the plate, throw him out.

2) If the runner at third base is the potential winning run late in the game, concede second base—make a full-arm fake toward second and then check the runner at third again. If the runner at third base is at the point of no return, run at him from the home plate side until he commits to home or third base, then throw him out or tag him out if he stands still.

3) If the runner at third base is of no consequence, throw the ball to the shortstop covering second base. The throw should be on the inside of the base to avoid visual interference or hitting the runner with the ball.

4) Trail the runner to second base if there are two outs, and tag the runner out before the runner on third base can score.

▶ **The shortstop:** Cover second base and prepare to receive a throw from the first baseman and participate in a possible rundown between first and second base. Back up third base if a rundown develops there.

▶ **The second baseman:** When the second baseman determines that the runner at first base has an extraordinarily long lead, he should go immediately to the seal position—run directly into the baseline between first and second bases. Then, cover second base if a rundown involving the first baseman and shortstop develops between first and second bases.

▶ **The third baseman:** Cover third base and stay alert for a possible play there. Expect a throw from the pitcher or first baseman, especially if either has made a full-arm fake toward the runner on first base. Be alert for a possible rundown should the runner break from third base and be trapped between home and third.

A Final Word on First-and-Third

As you can tell from the length of this chapter and the amount of information herein, handling the first-and-third situation is an extremely important part of a team's defensive arsenal. Responding properly to the opponent's tactic is imperative, and learning the proper response takes a great deal of practice.

It is the coach's responsibility to predetermine which baserunner the defense should focus on, and point at the runner that has priority.

Good Luck!

Defending the Not-So-Common First-and-Third Situation

"Catching a fly ball is a pleasure, but knowing what to do with it after you catch it is a business."
– Tommy Henrich

Defending the Foul Pop Fly Behind Home Plate

When a foul pop fly is hit behind home plate with runners on first and third and fewer than two outs, both runners may tag up, and the runner on first may break for second after the catcher makes the grab. *If there is no cutoff man for the catcher's throw to second, the runner on third will score easily.*

Defending this play depends on the shortstop and second baseman recognizing the situation and responding correctly—one of them must be in the cutoff position when the pop fly is caught. The cutoff position is about halfway between the catcher and second base (if the cutoff man can get that far in time), in a direct line between the catcher and second base. Each player's defensive responsibilities are as follows:

▶ **The pitcher:** Covers home plate and prepares to receive a throw from either the catcher or cutoff man in the event that the runner on third base tags up and breaks for home plate.

▶ **The catcher:** Makes the catch of the foul pop fly and looks at the runner at third base—if the runner breaks for the plate, the catcher throws the ball to the pitcher covering home. If the runner at third is not attempting to score, the catcher throws the ball to the cutoff man. Do not throw to third base if the runner on third has tagged up and has taken an extraordinarily long walking lead—well-coached runners will invite a throw, then break for the plate on the catcher's throw to third, and will beat the third baseman's return throw to home plate.

▶ **Middle infielders:** The location of the pop fly determines which middle infielder will be the cutoff man. The cutoff position is approximately even with the mound and in a direct line between the catcher and second base. Divide the infield in half by drawing an imaginary line from second base through home plate to the backstop—the shortstop is the cutoff man when the foul pop fly is caught on the shortstop's side of the imaginary line, and the second baseman is the cutoff man when it is on his side. The middle infielder who is not the cutoff man covers second base.

The cutoff man receives the catcher's throw, looks at the runner at third base, and throws either to home plate or second base depending on what the runner at third base does.

Defending the Foul Popup with Runners on First and Third:

On this play, the catcher has caught a foul popup near the backstop on the first-base side. After checking the runner at third, the catcher has thrown to the second baseman, who has positioned himself as a cutoff man near the mound, between the catcher and second base. (If the popup were on the third-base side, the shortstop would be the cutoff man and the second baseman would cover second.)

The middle infielder acting as the cutoff man prevents the opponent from either taking second base easily or stealing an easy run.

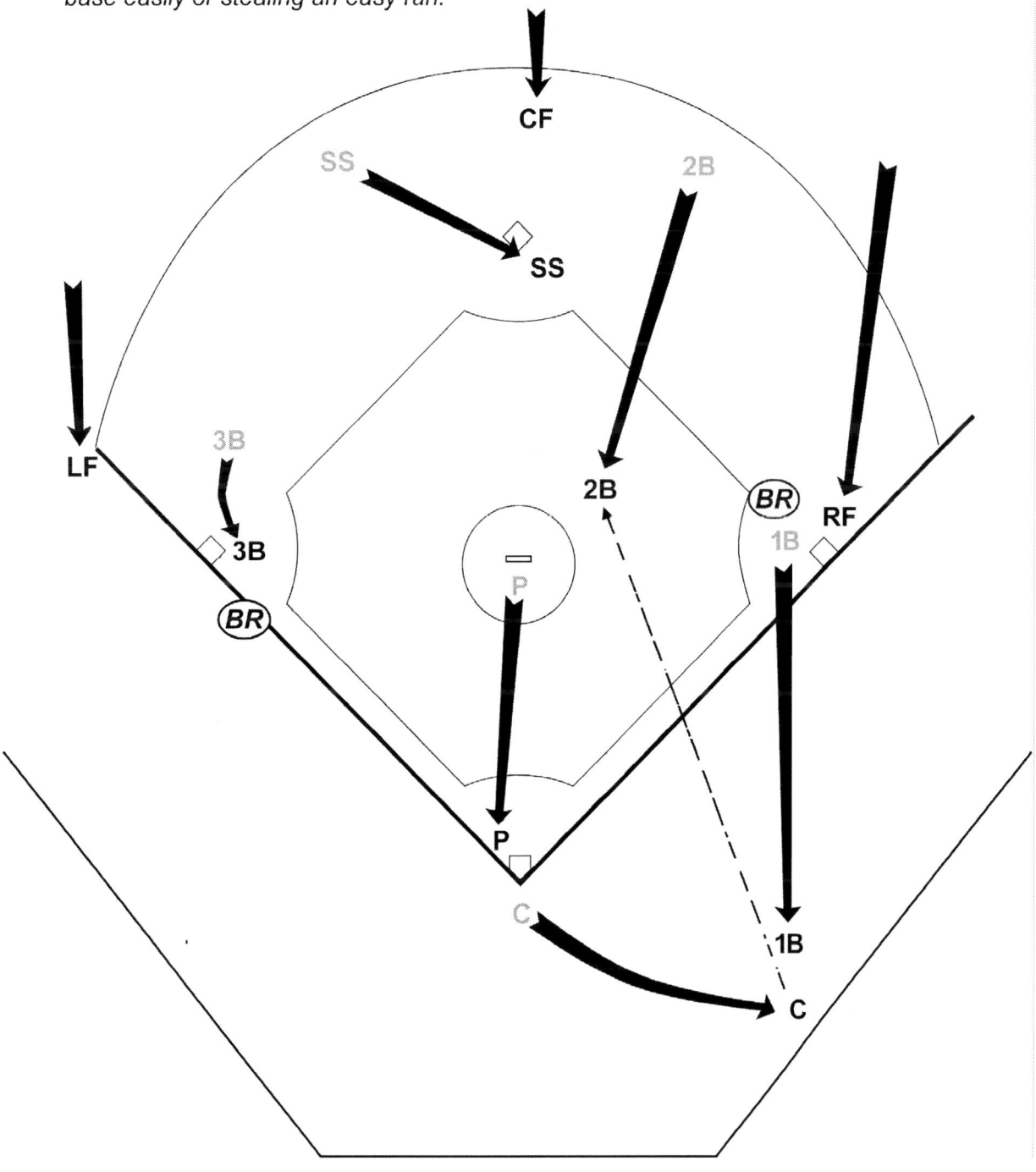

- ▶ **The first baseman:** Goes after the foul popup (if it's on the first base side) and returns to first base for a possible rundown.

- ▶ **The third baseman:** Covers third base and is alert for a possible play there.

- ▶ **The left fielder:** Backs up third base.

- ▶ **The center fielder:** Backs up second base.

- ▶ **The right fielder:** Covers or backs up first base.

Defending the Walk/Strikeout and Passed Ball or Wild Pitch with a Runner at Second

Now let's say, with a runner on second base, the batter either strikes out or draws a walk, and the final pitch heads to the backstop on a wild pitch or passed ball. Of course, the runner on second base advances to third. But what if the batter/runner, after hustling down to touch first, without hesitation breaks hard for second base? Your team must be ready to deal with this play.

Once the runner on second base advances to third and the batter/runner reaches first, a first-and-third situation exists that is comparable to the previous foul popup situation.

When the batter/runner touches first base and breaks for second, the runner on third will score easily if the catcher picks the ball up at the backstop and throws to second with no cutoff man in proper position.

The middle infielders must recognize this situation and respond accordingly—one of them runs to the cutoff position and the other to second base.

The same individual defensive rules and responsibilities apply to this situation as discussed in the previous section.

The middle infielders must be alert and anticipate the situation before it happens. The distance of the backstop from home plate is a major factor in successfully defending these situations—the farther the backstop is from home plate, the longer the catcher's throw will be to the cutoff man.

Good Luck!

Bunt Defense with a Runner on First

"I had a grip on the ball, but not a good grip." – Yankees closer Mariano Rivera, whose hurried and ill-advised throw to second on a sacrifice bunt went awry, helping the Arizona Diamondbacks win Game Seven of the 2001 World Series

---

Solid defensive baseball demands that a team be able to successfully defend against the sacrifice bunt. To be successful here, all members of the defensive team must understand the following:

– The basic philosophy of the defense, which is this: *take the sure out.*
– Their individual area of fielding responsibility.
– Who has the "right of way" (that is, the priority) when attempting to field the bunt.

Tenets of Bunt Defense

1. Take no chances on the lead runner, particularly early in the game.
2. Never gamble on the lead runner and fail to make the out; this could result in a big inning.
3. If in doubt, *take the sure out*—that is, put out the batter/runner going to first base.
4. Throw to first base after fielding the bunted ball if:
   – You do not get to the ball quickly.
   – You bobble the ball, even slightly.
   – You can't get the ball out of your glove quickly.
   – You hesitate for any reason, mentally or otherwise.
5. Before attempting to throw the runner out at second base, the fielder must consider the following:
   – How fast is the runner? (Know this ahead of time.)
   – How hard has the ball been bunted?
   – Where has the ball been bunted—right at you?
   – Was the ball fielded cleanly?

> **COACHING KEY:**
> *In the early innings, get the sure out:*
>
> – *Innings 1-6 in a 9-inning game*
> – *Innings 1-4 in a 7-inning game*
>
> **Don't gamble on the front man and miss.**

The sacrifice bunt is misplayed 20 to 25 percent of the time at the amateur level, usually because the defense wants to throw the runner out at second at all costs. The offense increases its chances of scoring by only about two percent if the sacrifice is successful. The defense should take the sure out and get the batter. *Take the sure out and over the course of the season you will be "money ahead."*

It is advisable for the coach to diagram the defensive bunt situations prior to taking the field. This enables the players to form mental pictures of their individual defensive responsibilities. Use of the chalkboard helps the players see how their part is related to the whole defensive picture, and with this understanding, they are less likely to forget their assignments or play them incorrectly.

Basic Coverage Assignments on a Sacrifice Bunt with a Runner on First Base:

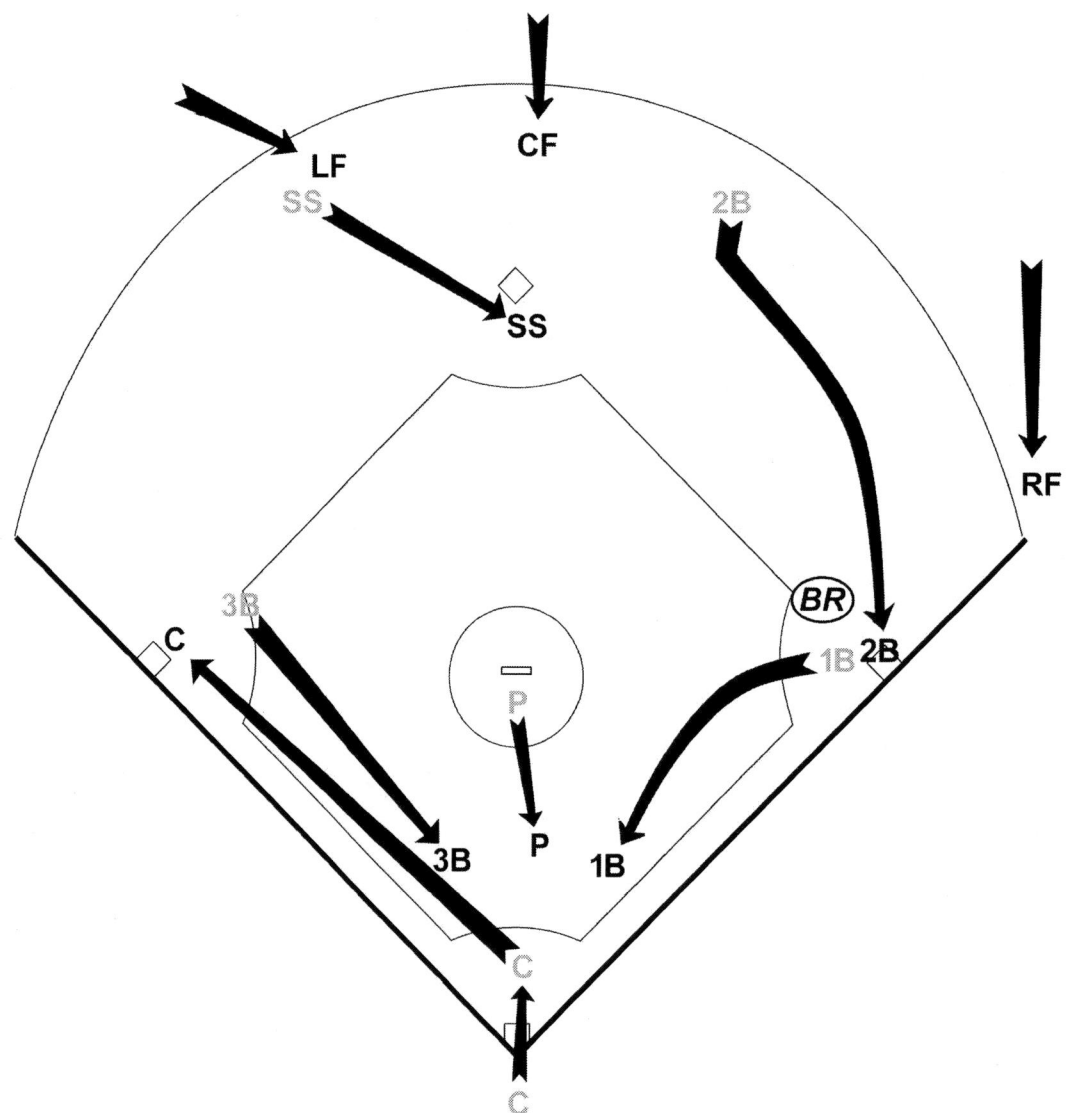

Players Must Know Their Responsibilities

The third baseman, pitcher and first baseman are each responsible for one-third of the diamond and the catcher is responsible for the area in front of home plate. The second baseman covers first base, the shortstop covers second, and the outfielders back up the bases.

Because the play is in front of the catcher, most teams rely on him to make the call as to where the throw should be made. However, the most effective method is having each defensive player be responsible for making his own decision as to where the ball should be thrown. This decision is based on a thorough understanding of the bunt defense philosophy.

The Catcher

1. With the play in front of him, the catcher may assume the responsibility of directing the play by calling out where the ball should be thrown.
2. He is also responsible for fielding bunts in front of the plate. Because short bunts are often spinning like a top, these balls should not be fielded barehanded, but rather by placing the mitt in front of the ball and scooping the ball into it. This should kill the spin.
3. The catcher is also responsible for covering third base when the third baseman fields the bunt. Of the catcher's fielding duties, failure to cover third base in this situation is the most common mistake. The catcher and third baseman must have a prearranged signal to remind the catcher that he has third base coverage if the third baseman fields the bunt.

General Coverage Territories:

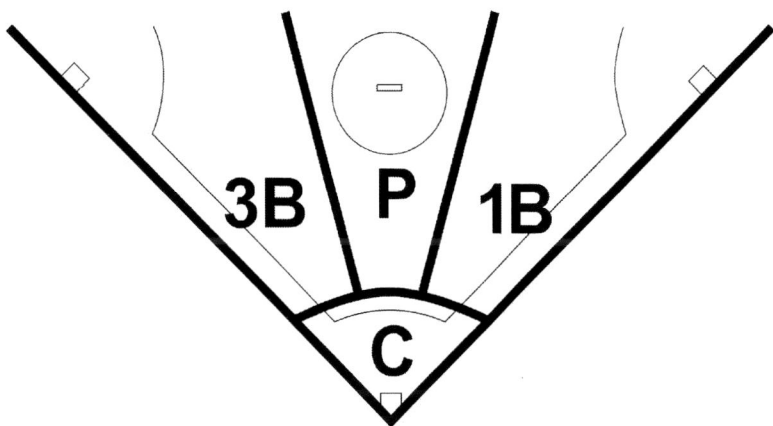

Note: this diagram shows GENERAL coverage territories. However, the third baseman has no base-coverage responsibilities, and should field all balls that he can reasonably get to.

Make 'em tip their hand:

There are several things a pitcher can do to find out if the batter intends to bunt.

Make him wait: Once he comes to the set position, the pitcher can make the batter wait—over-anxious hitters will often tip off their intentions.

Step off: After a short pause, the pitcher can step off the rubber quickly. The hitter will often misinterpret this movement as the beginning of the pitcher's delivery, and will commit himself.

Throw to first base: An attempted pickoff at first will often dupe the hitter into committing his intentions to bunt.

Pitch out: This is a very accurate way to find out if the hitter intends to bunt, but it has the disadvantage of putting the pitcher behind in the count.

The Pitcher

1. The pitcher is responsible for the center third of the diamond. He has priority over the first baseman.
2. He should hold the runner tight to first base, and upon delivery of the ball, charge straight forward and slightly to his left.
3. The pitcher should remember to stay low when fielding the bunt—bend the knees, drop the fanny to create a low center of gravity, and look the ball into the glove.
4. The pitcher must remember that if he bobbles the ball, his only play is first base.
5. When he is certain a bunt is coming, in most cases, the pitcher should throw high fastballs—these pitches are more likely to be popped up. However, the curveball, although easier to bunt into the ground, is often effective as an element of surprise and should not be eliminated in this situation. It also tends to make the runner at first base vulnerable to the pickoff play.

The First Baseman

1. The first baseman is responsible for the right-side one-third of the diamond.
2. He is responsible for holding the baserunner close to first base before charging into the diamond to field the bunt.
3. When charging, he should take two steps directly toward the mound at a 45-degree angle, then move toward the hitter. His initial step should be with his left foot. The approach is somewhat like an arc, placing the first baseman in the center of his fielding territory, rather than to the foul line side as is common with those first basemen who charge directly in.
4. In a sacrifice bunt situation, the first baseman should have a sign with the pitcher telling him when and when not to throw over to first base. (The pitcher should allow the first baseman to break toward the plate before starting his delivery. It is the pitcher's responsibility to watch the runner and step off the rubber if the runner breaks for second.)
5. After his initial steps, the first baseman should bring his weight under control and establish lateral movement by using the chop-step method of footwork.
6. Do not over-charge, and be sure the hitter intends to bunt.
7. Read the barrel of the bat to help determine the direction of the bunt—if the barrel is facing you, it is likely to be your ball; if the barrel is facing away, the ball will likely be bunted elsewhere.
8. If the ball is bunted hard, make the play at second base.
9. In the event the ball is obviously going to be fielded by the pitcher or third baseman, the first baseman should return to the base and take the throw himself. However, if the second baseman is at the base, *kneel down so as not to interfere with the play* and let the second baseman take the throw and make the putout.

Taking an Arc Route:

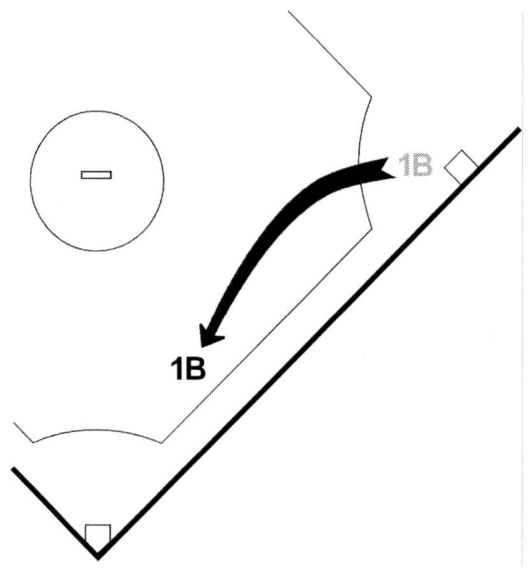

Breaking Down

When charging to field a bunt, a player's first three or four steps should be stride steps (that is, "speed steps"). As the hitter turns to bunt, the fielder must "break down" and prepare to field the ball.

Breaking down means the feet are moving in short, chop steps, not in long strides. This footwork is similar to that used by a defensive halfback in football—it establishes lateral movement and greater fielding range.

Most fielders employ a stride method that frequently results in a tragedy—the hard bunt often goes past the fielder because he has lost his lateral movement. If the ball happens to pass by him just as his striding foot hits the ground, it is almost impossible for him to get the glove on the ground to field the ball. Hard bunts, even slightly to the side, are usually base hits or misplayed.

Do not over-charge and be sure to use the chop-step method of footwork.

The Second Baseman

1. On a sacrifice bunt, it is the second baseman's responsibility to cover first base. It is necessary for him to cheat in that direction—that is, he must move in toward the baseline and over a few steps nearer first. This position enables him to get to first base in time to receive the throw.
2. The second baseman should not leave his position until the ball is actually bunted. His first two steps are directly toward the hitter—this protects his position against a hard push-bunt or slash bunt (fake bunt and swing) between the pitcher and the first baseman.
3. His approach to the base is from the right field side in an arcing manner. This method enables the second baseman to approach the ball in a straight line, not at an angle. It also facilitates finding the base, and permits better lateral movement should the throw go astray.
4. When receiving the throw, the second baseman's left foot should be in contact with the inside of the base. After the putout is made, the second baseman should immediately charge into the diamond toward second base—this will discourage the runner from trying to advance to third, and may catch a careless runner who is making too big a turn at second. (Some teams employ a mandatory throw to second after a putout is made at first base. This is intended to nail the careless runner who makes too big a turn, but this can result in a "random throw," which is unsound.)
5. In the event the first baseman returns to the bag in time, the second baseman should back up the throw. If, however, the second baseman thinks the first baseman can't get back in due time, he must yell loud and clear "I have it, I have it!" to let the first baseman know that he has the base. The second baseman must take charge and be vocal in this situation.

The Third Baseman

1. With the bunt in order, the third baseman's position can be either five or six steps in front of the base (approximately 20 feet), or in as far as the back of the dirt cutout of the pitcher's mound. The exact position is dictated by how certain it is that the bunt is on. *Don't be too close too soon.*
2. The third baseman should watch the barrel of the bat and the hitter's hands as they move up the bat. This will reveal the hitter's intent.
3. He should assume a trackman's stance; that is, one foot should be placed in front of the other. This enables him to start quickly.
4. As the pitcher delivers the ball, the third baseman should move forward rapidly toward the hitter. After three or four steps, he establishes lateral movement by employing the chop-step method of footwork.
5. It is important for the third baseman not to charge too soon, so that he is not too close to the hitter and unable to protect his position against a hard bunt or a fake-bunt-and-hit.

Right of way / Priority system

Just as in driving an automobile, the sacrifice bunt defense has its "right of way" rules, which indicate who shall yield whenever there is the possibility of a collision between defensive players. In other words it's a *priority system.*

The defensive players must know and keep in mind the following rules:

-- **The third baseman:** Has priority over everyone—the pitcher, catcher, and first baseman.
-- **The catcher:** Has priority over the pitcher and first baseman.
-- **The pitcher:** Has priority over the first baseman.
-- **The first baseman:** Has priority over no one.
-- **The second baseman:** Has priority over the first baseman when receiving the throw at first base. He must yell, *"I have it"* to avoid confusion and interference.

6. Once he fields the bunt and makes the throw to first base, he must be prepared to return to third base immediately in the event the catcher forgets to cover the base.
7. If someone else fields the bunt, he should return to third base to prevent the runner from advancing an additional base.

The Shortstop

1. The shortstop should move into double-play depth, placing him closer to second base. He has second base responsibility whenever the hitter shows bunt.
2. Before leaving his position to cover second base, the shortstop must be certain that the hitter intends to bunt—moving to the base prior to the pitcher's delivery makes the left side of the infield susceptible to the fake-bunt-and-hit.
3. When covering second base, the shortstop should assume a position on the inside (or home plate side) of the base. This position makes it possible for him to stretch for the throw like a first baseman, and it also prevents the runner from interfering with the throw.

The Outfielders

1. The outfielders have duties which, when successfully executed, complete the defensive picture.
2. The right fielder backs up first base and the center fielder backs up second base.
3. The left fielder backs up second base on attempted putouts there from the right side of the infield, and backs up third base on attempted putouts at that base should the runner try to advance.

Quick Reference Chart

Player	Areas of responsibility when fielding a bunt	When fielding a bunt, has priority or "right of way" over…	Mechanics
3B:	Left side and front	… all other fielders	Twenty feet in front of base… trackman's stance… read bat… short chop-steps
C:	Short front, alert to cover third base	… the pitcher and first baseman	Block ball with glove
P:	Center and slightly left	… the first baseman	High fastballs…read bat…short chop steps
1B:	The right side	… no one	Toward mound 45°… read bat… short chop-steps
2B:	Covers first base	… the first baseman (when covering first)	Cheat… first two steps toward hitter… right field side approach to 1B
SS:	Covers second base		In front of second base… play like a first baseman

Good Luck!

Bunt Defense with Runners on First and Second

"The problem in defense is how far you can go without destroying from within what you are trying to defend from without." – Dwight D. Eisenhower

---

This is one of the most difficult situations to defend at all levels of baseball. It ranks along with the first-and-third double steal situation in degree of difficulty.

Many coaches have reconciled themselves to the fact that the only safe method of defense is to retire the runner at first base. Getting "one out for sure" in this situation is a must; however, if the defense is played correctly, the runner attempting to advance from second to third base can be put out a percentage of the time, preventing needless runs from scoring. By conceding the runners second and third base in this situation, the defense is faced with additional problems:

1. With runners on second and third, the defense now has to decide whether to play a deep or shallow infield. Playing deep automatically concedes a run if the ball is hit on the ground, particularly to shortstop or second base.
2. Playing the infield in doubles the hitter's chances of getting a base hit and scoring two runs.
3. Walking the hitter to set up the double play is also an option, not without its own risks.

Other coaches have used bizarre defenses, which are only effective as elements of surprise, or if used in isolated instances. Most of these defenses cannot be relied upon game after game.

An inability to defend the bunt successfully can lead to many runs for the opponent. This could make the difference between a winning and losing season.

Players Must Know Their Responsibilities

– **The catcher** covers the area in front of home plate.
– **The pitcher** covers the area from the mound to the third base line.
– **The first baseman** covers the area from the first-base line to the mound.
– **The second baseman** covers first base.
– **The shortstop** covers second base.
– **The third baseman** protects against the hard bunt, and then covers third base.
– **The outfielders** back up the bases.

Basic Coverage on a Sacrifice Bunt with Runners on First and Second Bases:

Note: the basic coverage on this play has the third baseman covering third. However, the third baseman's judgment is critical -- if the hitter lays down a bunt that the third baseman feels is too hard for the pitcher to make a play on, he must vacate third base, charge the ball and get the out at first.

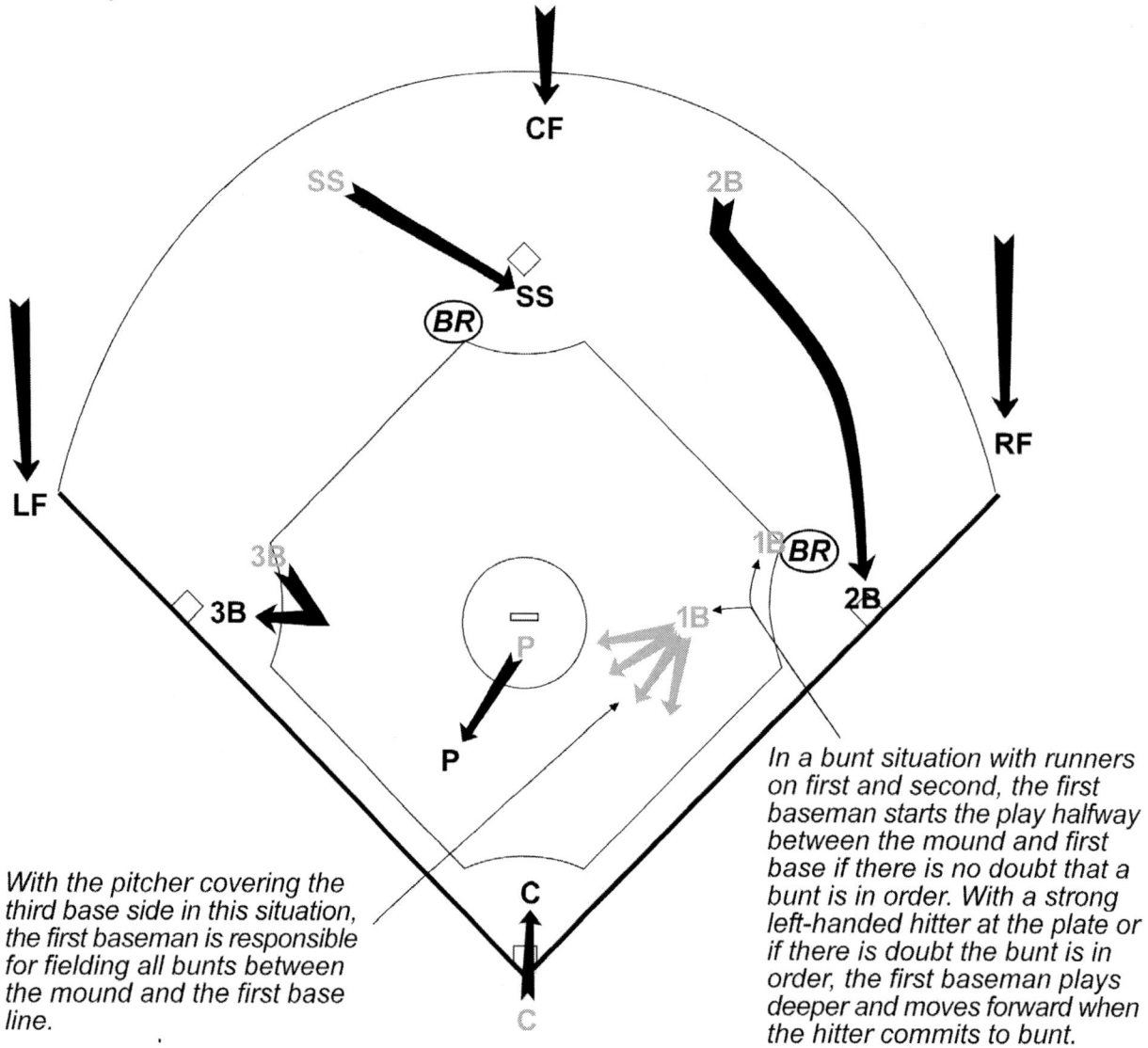

With the pitcher covering the third base side in this situation, the first baseman is responsible for fielding all bunts between the mound and the first base line.

In a bunt situation with runners on first and second, the first baseman starts the play halfway between the mound and first base if there is no doubt that a bunt is in order. With a strong left-handed hitter at the plate or if there is doubt the bunt is in order, the first baseman plays deeper and moves forward when the hitter commits to bunt.

The Catcher

1. The catcher is responsible for the area in front of home plate. He must be alert for the force-out at third base whenever he fields the bunt.
2. He must direct the defense verbally.
3. The catcher does *not* cover third base when the third baseman fields the ball.
4. The catcher and shortstop must realize the possibility of a pickoff exists at second base anytime the hitter misses the ball or takes a pitch. The catcher must be in position to throw each time.

5. A prearranged pickoff play originating from a pitch-out is an excellent play because many runners take a crossover step before the ball is bunted. However, throwing to second when the runner is caught too far off base can be dangerous—an alert runner may advance to third while the throw is made behind him. If the runner is too far off base, the catcher should run directly at the runner and force him to commit to one base or the other, and when he does, throw him out.
6. The catcher and second baseman should have a prearranged pickoff play at first base originating with a pitch-out, with the second baseman sneaking in behind the runner at first to receive the throw and make the tag. This can be quite effective because the runner at first is not held tightly to the base and the first baseman plays in front of the runner. Beware: this play has inherent danger—an alert runner on second may move to third while the throw is made behind him to first.

The Pitcher

1. When a bunt is in order, the pitcher should rely primarily upon the high fastball.
2. In order to get a force-out at third base, it is imperative that the pitcher hold the runner close to second base. The pitcher can help this cause by stepping off the rubber whenever the runner has too big a lead (a movement which tends to intimidate the runner).
3. By not delivering to the plate until the runner has transferred his weight toward second base, or is leaning or moving in the direction of second base, the chances of the baserunner being thrown out at third base are greatly enhanced.
4. A pickoff from the pitcher to the shortstop or second baseman will also keep the runner honest.
5. Once the pitch is made, the pitcher holds his position for a split-second and then runs directly toward the third base line. This places him about halfway between home and third base.
6. As soon as the pitcher is certain he can field the ball, he yells out, "I've got it!" This helps the third baseman make his decision to return to third base if he knows the pitcher can make the play.
7. Upon fielding the ball, the right-handed pitcher turns in a counterclockwise direction toward third base, while the left-hander turns clockwise—that is, the pitcher *follows his glove.* When fielding the bunt the pitcher must be sure to bend his knees and lower his center of gravity by keeping his "fanny" low to the ground, before attempting to field the ball. Do not attempt to field the ball standing up—*field low and come up throwing, rather than coming up and then throwing!*
8. Use a sidearm or three-quarter-arm throw—this way, the receiver can only be fooled on one plane—*horizontally*, if the throw is slightly errant.
9. If the third baseman calls for the ball, the pitcher must allow him to make the play and get out of the way—continue into foul territory.

The First Baseman

1. When the first baseman is certain that the hitter intends to bunt, his position is halfway between first base and the mound.
2. If the first baseman is unsure about the bunt, or a strong left-handed hitter is at bat, he should play on the edge of the grass and creep forward as the hitter turns to bunt.
3. The first baseman is responsible for all bunts between the first base foul line and the mound.
4. The first baseman should assume a trackman's stance, which will facilitate his start. He should use the chop-step footwork to maintain his lateral movement as the ball is bunted.
5. Hard bunts that are fielded cleanly should be thrown to third base with a sidearm/three-quarter throw—*come up throwing.* Slowly hit or bobbled balls should be thrown to first base.

The Second Baseman

1. The second baseman's main responsibility in this situation is to cover first base.
2. He must cheat toward first, but must also protect his position against the slap bunt or batted balls by taking two steps directly toward the batter before evacuating his position.
3. When receiving the throw, the second baseman's left foot should be in contact with the inside of the base.
4. The pickoff at first is an always-present defensive counter. The runner is lulled into a sense of security because he isn't held tightly to the base, and the base coach is often watching the hitter and not the second baseman. On a pickoff attempt, the second baseman approaches first in an arcing manner, from the outfield side. He stands behind the base, facing the catcher, to maintain lateral movement should the throw be inaccurate. When he determines the throw is accurate, he steps across the base with his left foot, receives the catcher's throw and makes the tag.
5. Beware: an alert runner at second base may try to advance to third on a pickoff to first base.

The Shortstop

1. The shortstop's primary job is to hold the runner close to second base. If he fails to do this, there is very little chance that the defense will succeed. It is not necessary for the runner to be driven back to the base, although this would be ideal. Merely getting the runner to move, lean, or transfer his weight toward second base will decrease his chances of reaching third safely.
2. The shortstop plays behind the runner and off his left shoulder. The shortstop's right foot should be in line with the

---

Advanced Pitcher-Shortstop Timing Method to Keep the Runner Close

Remember, the goal of the defense is to dupe the runner into breaking back to second base as the pitch is made so that it is more likely he will be put out at third base on the bunt. Often, a shortstop's fake is of little value if the defense gives the runner time to regain his lead.

The defense must coordinate the timing between the pitcher and shortstop so that the shortstop's attempt to drive the runner back toward second is synchronized with the pitcher's delivery to the plate.

This can be achieved through a system of signs given by the shortstop. Before toeing the rubber, the pitcher looks at the shortstop, who touches his left arm with his throwing hand. A touch to the wrist means "no looks," to the elbow means "one look," and to the shoulder means "two looks."

(To confuse the defense, the shortstop may touch his arm in several places. The shortstop and pitcher should predetermine which touch is the one that counts—the first, second or third touch.)

If the signal indicates "no looks," the pitcher comes to his set position, waits an instant, and makes his pitch without looking back. (Use this "no look" option less often, simply as something to keep the runner guessing.) If the signal indicates "one look," the pitcher comes set, looks back at the runner, then looks to home plate and makes his pitch. And if the signal indicates "two looks," the pitcher turns his head twice toward the runner, and after the second time looks to the plate and makes his pitch.

The advantage to all this? The shortstop will know the exact time the pitcher will make his pitch to the plate, and he can coordinate his fake (that his, his jab step and glove slap) to occur at the same time.

This method achieves two goals: it drives the runner back to second as the pitch is made, making it more likely he can be put out at third base on the bunt; and it ensures the pitcher doesn't become a "one-looker"—a pitcher who always looks once back to second before making his pitch, a common mistake that makes a steal of third a concern.

runner's left foot—this places him in an excellent position to harass the runner, who must remain constantly aware of the shortstop's presence. From this position, the pickoff play can be used effectively, whereas playing outside the runner makes a pickoff play from the pitcher virtually impossible.

3. When attempting to hold the runner at second base, the shortstop must not fake too soon. Faking too soon allows the runner time to regain his balance and lead, making the fake of little value.
4. As the pitcher comes set, the harassment and faking should begin. An effective method of getting the runner to lean or transfer his weight toward second is to have the shortstop play immediately behind the runner, with the shortstop's right foot in line with the runner's left foot. Using an anchored right foot and simultaneously stomping his left foot, slapping his glove and yelling "Back, back!" will force the runner to react. The pitcher should deliver the ball at this time.
5. A similar method involving more timing is to place the shortstop six to eight feet behind the runner (again, with the shortstop's right foot in line with the runner's left foot). The shortstop should take a left-right step directly toward the runner, then simultaneously make a hard jab step toward second base with his left foot, slap his glove and yell "Back, back!" This enhances the pitcher/shortstop pickoff play because the runner and base coach become conditioned to the shortstop's movement and will concede the shortstop's first two steps. Consequently, they are often slow to respond in the event a pickoff is attempted.
6. In either method, if the runner at second has too big a lead or has his weight leaning toward third, the shortstop flashes an open glove with his arm extended. *This is an automatic pickoff sign to the pitcher.* The shortstop then continues to second base to receive the pickoff throw from the pitcher.
7. As the pitch is made, the shortstop moves down the line to protect his position against a batted ball. He uses a shuffle-type footwork, similar to that employed in basketball defense, to maintain lateral movement. When a bunt is missed or a pitch is taken, the shortstop covers second, using an inside position. The probability of a force-out at second is almost nonexistent, but the possibility of a pickoff from the catcher exists every time the ball passes the hitter.

The Third Baseman

With runners on first and second base and the bunt in order, the third baseman is faced with his most difficult defensive situation.

1. He assumes a trackman's stance and a position on the edge of the grass a few feet from the line. The threat of a steal is ever-present, so the third baseman must be careful not to creep too far forward or charge in as the hitter squares around to bunt. The third baseman should have the feeling that *he would like to go in but must stay back,* and he must be prepared to field any ball that is bunted too hard for the pitcher to field.
2. Because so much judgment is involved in this coordination with the pitcher, the chance of making a mistake is great. The third baseman must understand that if he makes a mistake in judgment, *it must be in favor of first base and the sure out.* That is, if he is uncertain whether the pitcher can field the bunt, or if he is caught too far out of position, he should not return to third base, but should field the ball himself and retire the runner at first.
3. The third baseman must have a mental picture of the area where the pitcher can't make the play to third base, or would have difficulty throwing the runner out at first base. This is the area down the third base line close to the foul line. If the ball is bunted here, the third baseman should run the pitcher off and make the play to first base.

> ### *Field the bunt? Or return to third?*
>
> In a bunt situation with runners on first and second, the third baseman has three basic considerations: the fielding ability of the pitcher; where the ball is bunted; and how hard the ball is bunted.
>
> In the event the pitcher is able to field the bunt, the third baseman covers third base.
>
> Once the ball is bunted, the third baseman takes one or two steps forward and makes his decision.
>
> When the third baseman is certain the pitcher will field the ball, he pivots on his right foot toward the third base line and crosses over with his left leg, making a turn, which is somewhat less than 180 degrees. He returns to the base looking over his right shoulder, then assumes a position in front of the base, awaiting the throw like a first baseman. He must be sure he tags the base correctly with the ball of his foot, not with the side of his foot.
>
> Another method is to pivot on his right foot, making a full 180-degree turn, then running directly to the inside of third base. There the third baseman executes a reverse pivot on his left foot, swings his right foot back and around and prepares to receive the throw.
>
> Of the two methods, the former allows the third baseman to watch the play develop as he returns to the base. Consequently, he is less likely to be caught by surprise when the throw arrives, and the pitcher and first baseman tend to be more confident in throwing to third base.
>
> Proper coordination between the pitcher and third baseman is essential. Almost as important is pitcher/shortstop timing to prevent the runner from getting too large a lead off second base.
>
> **Drills that emphasize this phase of the defense should be practiced regularly.** *During practice, have the pitcher and third baseman switch positions so that they understand each other's defensive problems.*

The Outfielders

The outfielders back up the bases: the right fielder backs up first base; the centerfielder backs up second base; and the left fielder backs up third base.

Bunt Defense with a Runner on Second Base

With a runner on second base and the bunt in order, team defensive responsibilities remain the same. The exception, of course, is that the third baseman must tag the runner at third base rather than force him out.

The Bottom Line

When possible, attempt to throw out the runner at third base. But remember: *get one out for sure!*

Good Luck!

Pickoff at First Base With a Bunt In Order

"Subtlety set a trap and caught itself." – Latin proverb

Momentum plays a critical part in athletics. A sack, pass interception, or fumble recovery in football, or a blocked shot, forced turnover, or a stolen pass that results in a lay-up in basketball—these can have meaningful psychological implications for both teams as momentum swings occur during the course of a game.

In baseball, the pickoff play, when successful, is a great momentum stopper. It crushes the offense and ignites the defense. Just ask the Colorado Rockies—they lost Game Two of the 2007 World Series when star Matt Holliday was picked off first base by Jonathan Papelbon, for the final out *in the eighth inning of a 2-1 game.* Moreover, Todd Helton, who had a higher career batting average than any active National Leaguer, was left standing at home plate. Who knows—if Helton gets a chance to swing, the outcome of that game, and possibly the series, could have been different.

As it was, the Boston Red Sox won the game, 2-1, and went on to a series sweep. It was a huge swing in momentum.

It is important to remember that the basic philosophy for all pickoff plays is to *scare the hell out of the baserunner,* taking away his aggressiveness and controlling his actions. Actually picking him off is a plus.

The pickoff play can be successful even if no throw is made. The runner knows the defense's intent, even when no throw is attempted. Fear of the pickoff tends to intimidate the baserunner, making him more cautious… and this is done with no risk to the defense.

With this philosophy in mind, if there is a breakdown in timing or no play exists, there should be no throw. Players should remember this tenet: *No play, no throw!*

Rushing or forcing the pickoff throw results in an increased number of inaccurate throws, some of which end up in the outfield, advancing the runner or runners at least one base. *Therefore, it is preferable to have a pickoff throw be late instead of early.*

And the closer the runner is to home plate, the more certain the pickoff attempt must be—*lest a run is scored on a wild throw.*

An Ideal Time for a Pickoff

The sacrifice bunt situation with a runner at first base is often an ideal time to attempt a pickoff. This is particularly true when a careless or overly aggressive runner is on base.

As the batter turns to bunt the ball and the pitch is delivered, many baserunners put themselves in jeopardy of being picked off base by:

— Being too far off base, the result of an overly aggressive secondary lead.

— Taking a crossover step toward second base before the ball is actually bunted, resulting in a loss of lateral movement and the ability to return to the base quickly.

— Transferring their weight onto their right leg and doing a "toe dance" in anticipation of the ball being bunted. In this case, the runner has lost lateral movement and is often suspended in "no man's land" if the pitch isn't bunted.

If these or other baserunning errors are observed, a pickoff attempt is appropriate.

Overview

This play is designed to lull the runner at first base into a sense of complacency, setting a trap and then picking him off base. Players have the following general responsibilities:

1. The first baseman charges the batter early to increase the runner's leadoff and his sense of security.
2. The pitcher throws a pitch-out.
3. The second baseman sneaks behind the runner, covers first base, and receives the catcher's pickoff throw.
4. The catcher receives the pitch-out and throws the ball to the second baseman, who is covering first base.
5. The third baseman charges hard to add realism to the play.
6. The shortstop covers second base as in a normal bunt defense.

There are two slightly different methods to use this play—try both to see which meets your needs, or develop your own pitcher/first baseman timing and coordination scheme.

By the way, don't use this play indiscriminately—it will lose its effectiveness.

The Pickoff at First Base in a Bunt Situation:

Note: the timing of this play is critical -- the first baseman must begin his charge at the proper time. See Method #1 and Method #2 for options.

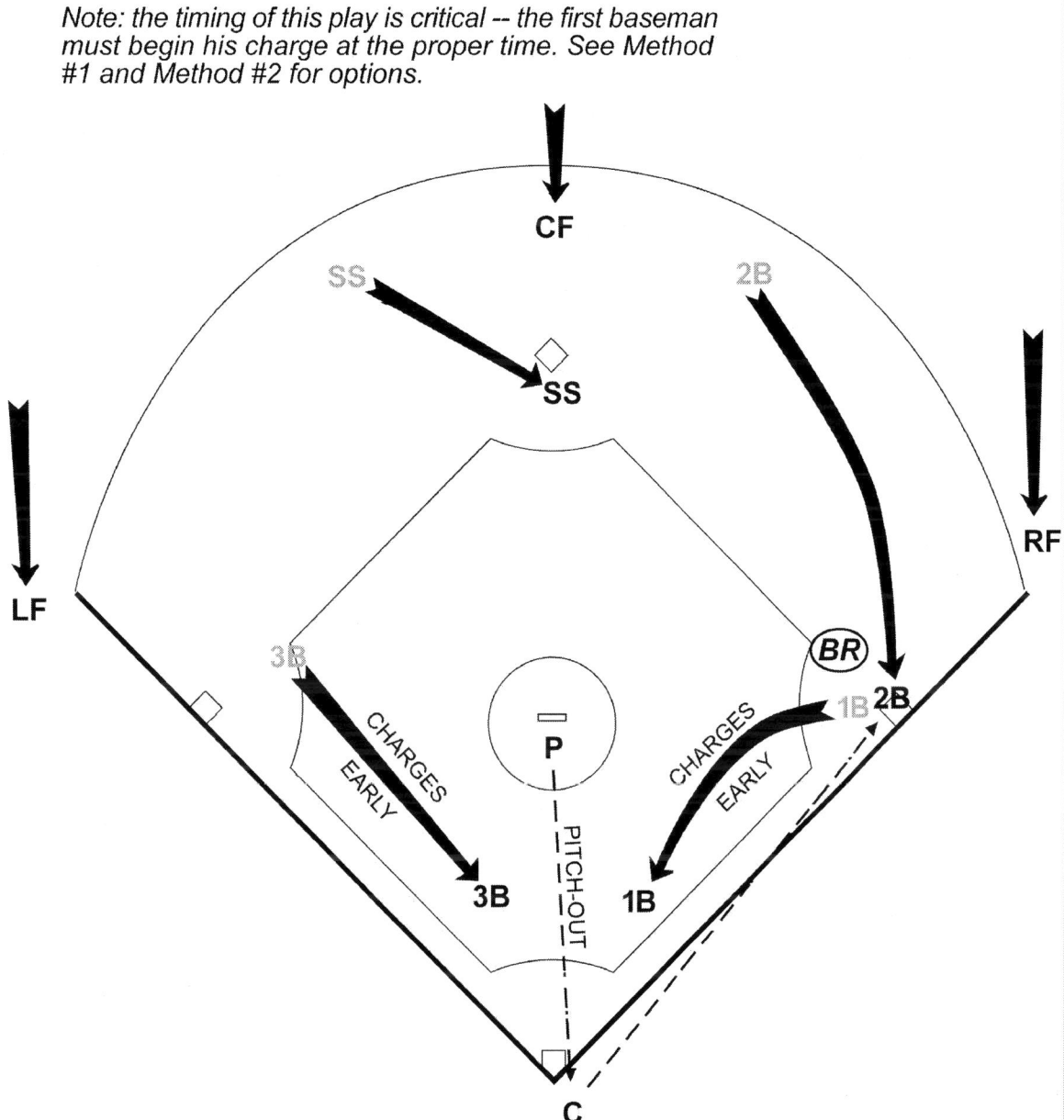

Method #1

The pitcher:
1. The pitcher goes into his stretch position, watching the runner at first base and the first baseman.
2. He does not hold at the bottom of his stretch; his hands simply hit at the belt, pause and change direction upward. Be careful: if the pitcher fails to change direction with his hands when going into the set position, the umpire might call a balk.
3. He does *not* throw to first base while a pickoff play is on. He delivers a pitch-out to home plate.
4. If the runner breaks early (when the first baseman evacuates), he steps off the rubber and makes the appropriate play—he throws to second, or if the runner stops between bases he runs at him.

5. He moves forward toward the batter after the pitch is made to add realism to the play and field the bunt if a poor pitch-out is made.

The catcher:
1. Calls for the pitch-out and throws to first base, where the second baseman receives the throw and makes the tag. Remember: *no play, no throw!*
2. He must be alert to field a bunt in the event of a poor pitch-out, and cover third base if the third baseman fields the bunt.

The first baseman:
1. The first baseman breaks toward the batter when the pitcher reaches the top of the stretch and his hands start down.
2. He must be sure the pitcher does not throw to first base.
3. He must be alert to field a bunt in the event of a poor pitch-out.

The second baseman:
1. The second baseman cheats towards first base and breaks to first when the pitcher starts his delivery to the plate.
2. He covers first base and maintains lateral movement by having both feet astride the base and on the right field side of the base.
3. He should step across the base with the left foot only after the throw has been released and it has been determined that the throw is accurate, and then apply the tag.

The shortstop:
1. The shortstop watches the runner at first and yells "Step off!" if the runner breaks early.
2. He covers second base on the inside of the diamond.

The third baseman:
1. The third baseman charges early to add realism to the play.
2. He must be alert to field a bunt if there is a poor pitch-out, and he returns to third if no play exists.

The outfielders:
1. The right fielder backs up first base.
2. The center fielder backs up second base.
3. The left fielder backs up third base.

Method #2

All responsibilities are the same as Method #1, except that the coordination and timing of the break by the pitcher and first baseman are slightly different.

The pitcher:
1. The pitcher comes to a complete set position and watches the runner at first base.
2. He nods or drops his head to start the first baseman's break toward the batter.
3. He delivers a pitch-out after the first baseman has taken three steps toward home plate… *left, right, left—then pitch.*

The first baseman:
1. The first baseman focuses on the pitcher's head.
2. He breaks toward the batter when the pitcher nods or drops his head.

With Runners on First and Second Bases

The pitch-out and pickoff play at first base will work equally well with runners on first and second base and the bunt in order; however, it is always dangerous to throw behind the lead runner—an alert runner at second base may advance to third base when a pickoff throw is made to first. Gauge the alertness and baserunning ability of the runner on second base, and have the shortstop fake a pickoff, driving the runner back to second base. Also, in this case, the third baseman must hold his ground, lest the runner on second steal third behind him.

****

Fake Pickoff and Go (with Bunt in Order)

The logical corollary to the pitch-out and pickoff play at first base with the bunt in order is the *fake pickoff play*. Once your opponent knows that your team has the pitch-out and pickoff play in its arsenal, the fake pickoff play can be used to your advantage to thwart an attempt to bunt the runner from first to second.

To be most effective, the fake pickoff play should be used sparingly and be reserved for late in the game when one run is crucial. Overuse will diminish its effectiveness.

Purpose

The fake pickoff is used to decrease the baserunner's chances of successfully advancing to second base when a sacrifice bunt is attempted. When it works, this play will dupe the baserunner at first base *and* the first base coach into thinking that a pickoff attempt will be made at first base, driving him back to the bag and making the force-out at second base more likely.

Similar to the pitch-out and pickoff play, there are two methods that may be used. The disadvantage of Method #1 is that if the pitcher fails to change direction with his hands when going into the set position the umpire might call a balk. The disadvantage of Method #2 is that the pitcher must assume an additional defensive responsibility. This added burden could adversely impact the proper execution of the play.

Try both methods and see which meets your needs, or develop your own pitcher/first baseman timing and coordination scheme!

The Fake Pickoff and Go with a Bunt in Order:

Note: On this play, the pitcher does NOT throw a pitchout, but instead throws a pitch down the middle. As in the pickoff at first with a bunt in order, timing is important. See Method #1 and Method #2 for options.

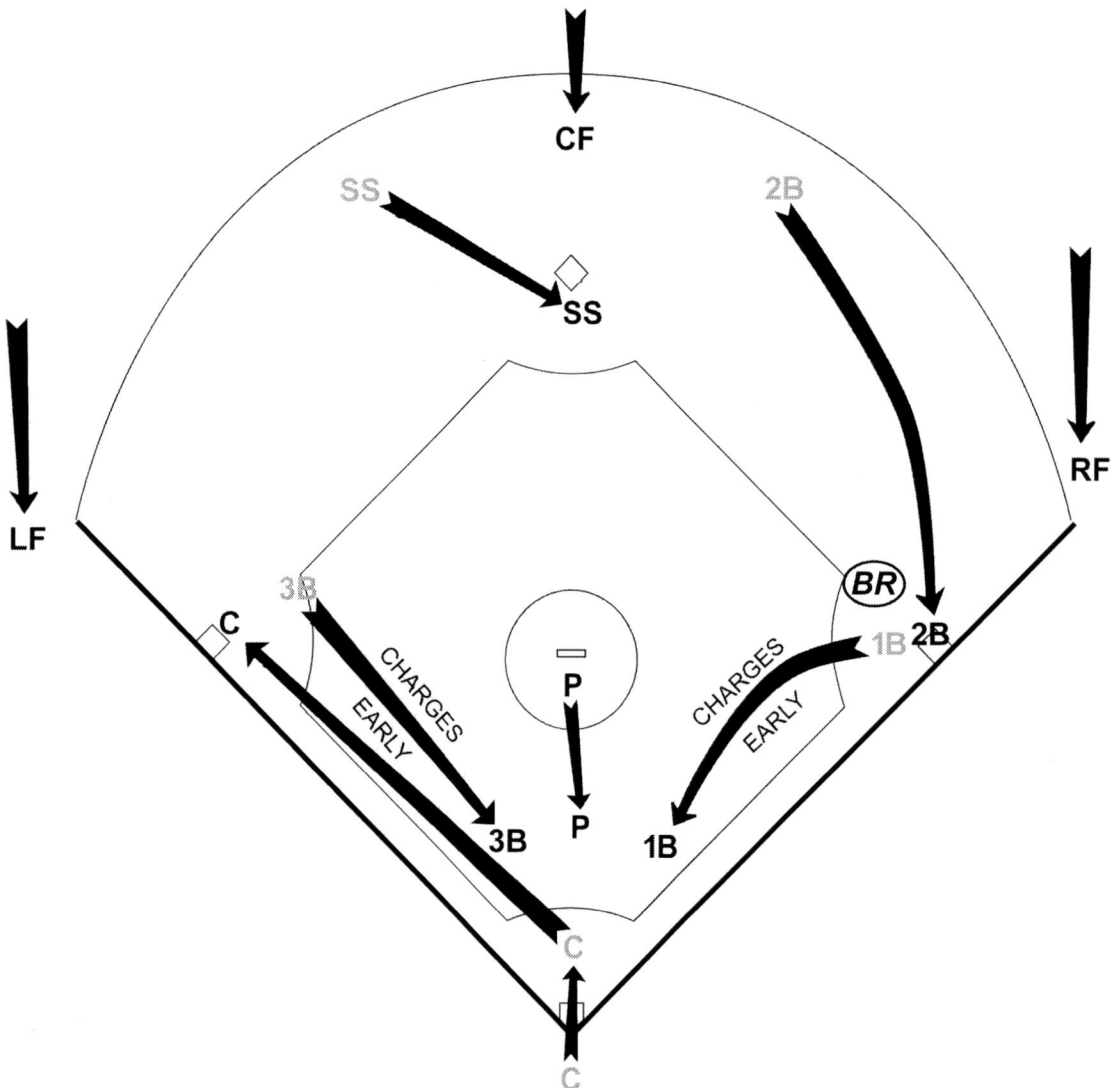

Method # 1

The pitcher:
1. The pitcher goes into his stretch position watching the runner at first base and the first baseman.
2. He does not hold at the bottom of his stretch; his hands simply hit at the belt, pause and change direction upward. Be careful: if the pitcher fails to change direction with his hands when going into the set position the umpire might call a balk.
3. He does *not* throw to first while a fake pickoff is on. He throws a pitch down the middle.
4. If the runner breaks early (when the first baseman evacuates), he steps off the rubber and makes the appropriate play—he throws to second, or if the runner stops between bases he runs at him.
5. He moves forward toward the batter after the pitch to field the bunt and make the play to second.

The catcher:
1. The catcher calls for the pitch down the middle of home plate.
2. He must be alert to field the bunt and make the play to second base, and he must be alert to cover third base if the third baseman fields the bunt.

The first baseman:
1. The first baseman breaks toward the batter when the pitcher reaches the top of the stretch and his hands start down.
2. He must be sure the pitcher does not throw to first base.
3. He must be alert to field a bunt and make the play to second base.

The second baseman:
1. The second baseman cheats towards first base and breaks to first when the pitcher starts his delivery to the plate.
2. He yells, "I've got him," hoping to drive the runner back to first base.
3. He covers first base to receive a throw in the event a play is made there.

The shortstop:
1. The shortstop watches the runner at first base and yells "Step off!" to the pitcher if the runner breaks early.
2. He covers second base on the inside of the diamond so that the baserunner does not interfere with the throw.
3. He receives the throw for the out, playing the base like a first baseman.

The third baseman:
1. The third baseman charges early to add realism to the play and be closer to the bunter.
2. He must be alert to field the bunt and make a play at second base.
3. He returns to third base if the ball is not bunted to him.

The outfielders:
1. The right fielder backs up first base.
2. The center fielder backs up second base.
3. The left fielder backs up third base.

Method #2

All responsibilities are the same as in Method #1, except that the coordination and timing of the break by the pitcher and first baseman are slightly different.

The pitcher:
1. The pitcher comes to a complete set position and watches the runner at first base.
2. He nods or drops his head to start the first baseman's break toward the batter.
3. He delivers the pitch after the first baseman has taken three steps toward home plate… *left, right, left—then pitch.*
4. He throws a pitch down the middle of home plate, then breaks toward the batter and prepares to field the bunt and make a play to second base.

The first baseman:
1. The first baseman focuses on the pitcher's head.
2. He breaks toward the batter when the pitcher nods or drops his head.
3. He is alert to field the bunt and make a play at second base.

Run 'Em Back-to-Back

The fake pickoff play simulates the pickoff at first base, and if executed correctly, it will compel the runner to scurry back to first base, shorten his lead, or transfer his weight back toward the base, making the force-out at second base highly probable.

The *pitch-out and pickoff play* and the *fake pickoff and go* play can be run back-to-back. If one doesn't work, the other might.

Good Luck!

Part Two:

OFFENSE

Batting Drills and Techniques

The Toss Drill

"A baseball swing is a very finely tuned instrument. It is repetition, and more repetition, then a little more after that." – Reggie Jackson

---

The "Toss Drill" is one of the most widely used drills to teach hitting—a very simple yet highly efficient teaching and training tool. It should be in every team and coach's repertoire. The Toss Drill:

– Increases the number of hitting opportunities (swings) that each player has during practice.
– Serves as a warm-up prior to taking live batting practice.
– Helps to perfect the hitting swing (muscle memory).
– Teaches the hitter to keep his head down and eye on the ball.
– Helps develop hand/eye coordination.
– Teaches hitting down on the ball (*tomahawk* hitting).
– Is great for indoor use or other areas with limited space.
– Allows players to practice by themselves (with use of a JUGS Toss Machine).

And those are just a few reasons why the Toss Drill is such an important teaching tool. The creative coach can easily adapt the Toss Drill to teach and practice other critical aspects of hitting.

Equipment Needed

Bucket of balls: JUGS Lite-Flite Balls and JUGS Poly Bulldog Balls are ideal for indoor and outdoor use—among other things, they add a dimension of safety to the Toss Drill. Balls that rebound off the fence, wall, or other surfaces are of no consequence—they present no safety hazard for the tosser, hitter, or bystander. Conventional baseballs can also be used for the Toss Drill, but caution must be used when choosing a hitting surface to prevent rebounding baseballs from striking the tosser, hitter, or bystanders. *Be alert!* Do not hit into a fence post or cross-member on the fence. JUGS Lite-Flite Balls and JUGS Poly Bulldog Balls are available at www.jugsbaseball.com.

Hitting screen: A hitting screen, such as the JUGS Instant Screen, is necessary. (The JUGS Instant Screen pops open and closes in seconds, and fits in the trunk of any car. There is no assembly required, which makes it perfect to travel to all games or practices. It can be used anywhere.) A screen eliminates most of the worry about rebounding balls. Both conventional balls and safety balls can be used effectively with the JUGS Instant Screen.

Throw-down home plate: A throw-down home plate gives the hitter and tosser a common reference point. If a conventional throw-down home plate is unavailable, use a glove, towel, or ball bag.

Baseball or Softball Bat: Be sure that the hitter has a bat he can control—one that is neither too long nor too heavy. Bat control is one of the vital components of successful hitting. A plastic bat, JUGS Lite-Flite Balls, and the Toss Drill are an excellent combination for beginners to learn the basics of hitting.

Basic Positioning for the Toss Drill:

In the Toss Drill, the Batter ("B") stands 6'-8' away from a screen or batting cage netting, ready to drive the ball straight into the netting. The Tosser ("T") kneels down either at a 45-degree angle 8'-10' away from the Batter (Diagram 1) or 6'-8' away on the opposite side of home plate just off his front knee (Diagram 2). The positioning in Diagram 2 is safer for younger players.

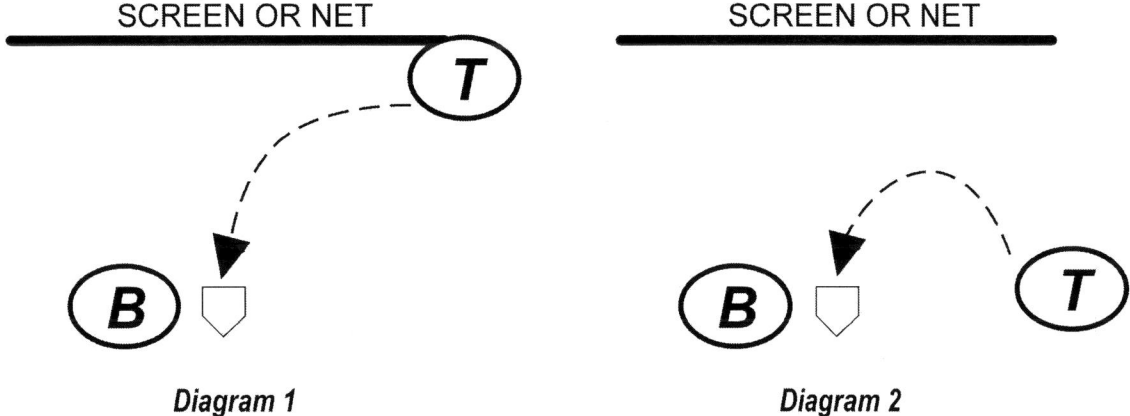

Mechanics of the Toss Drill

Divide players into groups of two—one will be the hitter and one will be the tosser. The hitter and tosser should change positions after a prescribed number of swings—10 to 15 depending upon age and physical maturity.

The effectiveness of the Toss Drill depends to a large degree upon how well the tosser does his job. It is incumbent upon the tosser to prepare the hitter for the pitch, rather than tossing the ball in a haphazard or rapid-fire method. The hitter must have enough time to *load* and then *explode* into each pitch.

The tosser should kneel down on one knee approximately 8 to 10 feet from the hitter. A right-handed tosser is on the right knee, a left-handed tosser on the left knee. For safety reasons, the tosser may assume one of two positions: in front of the hitter at approximately a 45-degree angle and off to the side (this delivers the ball from a more realistic direction); or at a right angle to the hitter just off his front leg (this assures maximum safety for younger players).

The trajectory of the toss should not be flat, but rather a soft, looping arc. The ball should be tossed in front of the hitter so that contact is made in front of home plate.

To prepare the hitter to swing, the tosser must:

- *Present the ball to the hitter* by holding the ball in his "extended arm." The ball should be clearly visible to the hitter. At this point, the hitter assumes his batting stance.

- *Drop his arm and the ball*, at which point the hitter rotates his body into hitting position, or "loads."

- *Pause slightly*, allowing the hitter time to load (rotate the body and bring the bat into the "launching" position.)

- *Toss the ball*—a nice, soft flip in front of the hitter. Balls are tossed over the front edge of the plate so that contact is made in the "power zone."

The hitter, meanwhile, assumes his batting stance when the tosser extends his arm; *loads* (rotates his body and bat into the launching position) when the tosser drops his arm; and *explodes* into the pitch, driving it into the portable screen or other netting. The hitter should focus on driving the ball into the net on a line using proper mechanics. He should take 10 to 15 swings before rotating, depending upon age and physical maturity. *Too many swings without rest is counterproductive as fatigue will set in and the swing is adversely affected.*

These drills are not only for practice sessions or pregame batting practice; if space permits, they can be used as a warm-up before actually going to bat in a game. Going to bat "cold"—that is, standing around for a few innings in cold weather without taking several practice swings—greatly limits the hitter's chances for success when he comes to bat. The Toss Drill can alleviate this problem—so, if possible, set up a "Toss Drill station" for game-time use.

Variations of the Toss Drill

The following drills can be used to increase the number of swings each player gets during practice, and to correct various hitting faults. *When using the Toss Drill as a warm-up prior to actually hitting in a game, the regular Toss Drill detailed on the previous page will suffice.*

The majority of drills presented here are equally effective whether the ball is delivered by a tosser, or by a machine such as the JUGS Toss Machine.

Kneeling Drill: This drill prevents the hitter from upper-cutting by forcing him to hit down on the ball—excellent for hitters who drag the bat through the strike zone. The emphasis is on hand quickness and hitting down on the ball, and is also a solid drill to combat head-pulling.

The hitter should kneel on his back leg, with his front leg extended. He tries to drive the ball into the net on a line; his bat will hit the ground if he uppercuts.

A great idea for self-practice

Consider getting a JUGS Toss Machine, from the JUGS Company of Tualatin, Ore. (www.jugsbaseball.com). A JUGS Toss Machine is the perfect tool for the Toss Drill, whether baseball or softball. Weighing only 13 pounds, it holds up to fourteen baseballs and ten softballs, and automatically tosses a ball every five seconds.

It is ideal for back yards, gyms, basements, or garages, and it comes with an internal rechargeable battery, providing over six hours of practice time. The major advantage of the JUGS Toss Machine is that it enables players to take batting practice by themselves. *This is something to think about!*

Head Control Drill: This drill teaches the hitter to combat head-pulling and to keep his head down and still. The hitter should place a fielder's glove on his head, pocket-side down. He assumes a normal batting stance and drives the ball into the net, concentrating on keeping the head down and still—the glove will fall off if the head is pulled or jerked.

Glove Under Front Arm Drill: This drill teaches the hitter to keep the front arm close to the body and the front elbow pointing toward the ground, preventing uppercutting and allowing the bat head to come through quickly and correctly. The hitter should place a batting glove, towel or cap underneath the front arm, and then swing as usual. If the swing is done correctly, the glove will not drop to the ground; a quick, compact swing is the result.

Spaced Hands Drill: This drill gives the hitter better bat control and allows the hitter to feel how each hand functions when swinging correctly. The hitter assumes a normal stance and grips the bat with both hands, but the hands are spaced about 3 inches apart. The hitter should emphasize driving the top hand over, and "backhanding" with the bottom hand.

Balance Position Drill: This drill teaches the hitter weight control and prevents lunging. The hitter learns to *step to hit*, not *step and then hit.* In the Balance Position Drill, the hitter assumes a position similar to a pitcher's balance position, with the weight entirely on the back leg, and either the front foot off the ground or the toe of the front foot resting lightly on the ground. The hitter waits as long as possible and gets the ball with the bat. If the hitter goes after the ball prematurely, it will be virtually impossible to make solid contact.

Front Foot Drill: This drill corrects uppercutting and emphasizes hitting down on the ball. The hitter stands with all weight on the front foot, and the back foot is off the ground. The hitter must hit down on the ball from this stance.

One-Handed Top Hand Drill: This drill teaches the hitter the proper action of the top hand and how it brings the club head of the bat through the strike zone. The hitter assumes a normal stance and grips the bat with the top hand only, similar to a tennis grip, then drives the ball into the net, emphasizing a quick, downward stroke.

One-Handed Bottom Hand Drill: This drill teaches the hitter the proper action of the bottom hand. Again, the hitter assumes a typical stance, but this time grips the bat with only the bottom hand on the bat, and drives the ball into the net with a quick downward stroke and backhanding action. Emphasis should be on the lead elbow pointing toward the ground and not flying open in the air. The hitter can also focus on throwing the "pinky finger" at the pitcher's feet. This helps create proper hand action.

Throwing the Club Head Drill: This drill teaches the hitter to throw the club head of the bat through the strike zone, developing a quick, compact swing. From the hitter's usual stance, the bat is gripped with the bottom hand in the normal manner. The hitter then places the top hand open and flat against the bat and "throws the club head" at the ball during the swing. The lead arm elbow should be pointing toward the ground and the bottom hand should be "backhanding" to assure a proper swing.

Cross-Handed Drill: This is another drill that teaches the hitter the concept of rapidly throwing the club head of the bat through the strike zone. In a normal stance, the hitter grips the bat cross-handed—that is, with the bottom hand on top and the top hand on the bottom—and drives the ball into the net.

Tomahawk Drill: This drill teaches the hitter to hit down on the high pitch. The hitter assumes a normal stance, and the tosser flips the ball to the top of the strike zone. The hitter should hit the ball with a downward swing, similar to that used by a tennis player, and the hands should be below the ball when swinging.

Opposite Field Drill: This drill teaches the hitter the proper point of contact and proper hand action when hitting to the opposite field. With the hitter in a normal stance, the tosser flips the ball toward the hitter's front hip. The hitter focuses on hitting the inside part of the ball. The ball must pass the hitter's hands to be hit to the opposite field—if the club head is in front of the hands, the ball will be pulled or missed completely.

Positioning for the Backdoor Hitting Drill:

In this variation of the Toss Drill, the Tosser ("T") is positioned directly behind the hitter in the normal catcher's position. As in the normal Toss Drill, the Batter ("B") drives the ball straight into the netting.

SCREEN OR NET

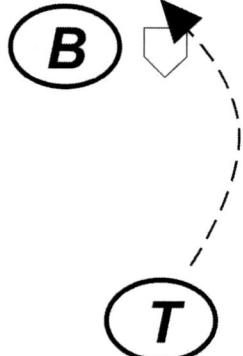

Load and Explode Drill: This drill teaches the hitter to be back and ready to hit (that is, "loaded"), then explode into the pitch with a quick compact swing and proper weight transfer. The tosser should give the hitter a six-second interval between pitches, so that the hitter must be ready for the next delivery. The hitter assumes a normal stance, then must get the hands into the launching position and cock the hips prior to the ball being delivered (the load phase of the drill). The hitter is then ready to "explode" into the ball, driving it into the center of the net. The rhythm is *one, load; two, explode!*

Backdoor Hitting Drill: This drill teaches the hitter to hit the breaking ball to the opposite field, and to keep the head down to track the ball. Eye contact with the ball should be stressed. (This is also a good hit-and-run drill.) With the hitter in a normal stance, the tosser flips the ball over the plate *from directly behind the hitter*, in the catcher's normal position. The hitter drives ball into the opposite field and into the net.

The Toss Game

Each spring, players are faced with the problem of making the transition from winter sports activities back to baseball. Two major adjustments are necessary; one is mental and one is physical. *Mentally,* the players must begin "thinking baseball" again after several weeks of winter sports. *Physically*, the players must become accustomed again to the size of the ball (compared to a basketball, the baseball looks like an aspirin), the velocity of the ball, and their reaction to it. These adjustments take time.

A valuable way to help players make the transition back to baseball is the Toss Game. As a drill, the Toss Game has many advantages. It is a fun, efficient way to play an early season intrasquad game, before pitchers are ready to throw. It gets the players "thinking baseball," and it enables a large number of players to be involved in a relatively short period of time. It creates a degree of pressure and competition, and keeps the defense on their toes because hitters get just one swing. It helps younger players adjust to a faster tempo. It doesn't disrupt the normal practice schedule because the game can be played quickly, and it is an excellent activity to end practice on an "up" beat.

How to play:

- Field two teams of seven players. Pitchers are not necessary, and catchers are optional.
- Team A is at bat for 6, 7, or 9 innings.
- Team B comes to bat *after team A has completed all of its designated innings*. The bases are cleared after every third out and a new inning begins *for the team already at bat* (unless they've completed their designated number of innings). This eliminates the time it takes to change sides.
- The tosser (or a JUGS Toss Machine) sets up along the first base foul line for right-handed hitters, and along the third base foul line for left-handed hitters. The tosser (or machine) flips baseballs as in the regular Toss Drill, but the hitter, instead of driving the ball into a net or screen, puts the ball in play as in an actual game.
- If using a machine to toss balls, adjust it occasionally so that all balls are not pulled or hit to one particular area of the field.
- Each hitter gets one pitch per time at bat. Foul balls, swings-and-misses, and taking the pitch (not swinging) are outs.
- *No bunting. No stealing bases.* This is a hitting drill.

Consider concluding practice each day with the Toss Game. This will add competition—your "teams" can play a five-game series against each other every week. A word of admonition, though: be sure arms and legs are in shape!

Good Luck!

Enhanced Situation Hitting Drills

"I find my greatest pleasure, and so my reward, in the work that precedes what the world calls success." – Thomas Edison

---

"Situation Hitting Drills" are an excellent way to develop a team's baserunning skills, defense, and hitting strategy, under near game-like conditions. These drills are designed to: emphasize base-running mechanics and strategy; emphasize team defense and communication (e.g., alignments, cut-offs, relays, pitchers backing up the correct base, etc.); build offensive strategy by having the hitter execute whatever play the coach wishes to employ; teach the players to respond to game situations and game pressure automatically on both offense and defense; and teach the team's offensive and defensive signals.

Before using any of the Situation Hitting Drills, it is advisable that the baserunning, defensive, and hitting aspects and strategies necessary for a particular drill be taught in advance. Teaching in advance maximizes the effectiveness and efficiency of the drill.

Getting Set Up

▶ **The defense:** Put a defensive team in the field. Players may be substituted individually, or if team numbers permit, as a group. An infielder and outfielder should be at each position, and catchers should be in full gear (or the drill can be run without catchers). One pitcher stands behind the batting practice pitcher or the pitching machine and backs up whatever base the play dictates. Extra pitchers form a line in foul territory between home plate and first base awaiting their turn.

▶ **The offense:** Designate four to six players to be the offensive players. Each bats one at a time. After hitting a fair ball, the batter reacts to the play, as do the baserunners, as they would in an actual game situation. Place baserunners on the appropriate bases to create the situations you wish to practice.

▶ **Also:** To allow the maximum offensive and defensive opportunities, use a pitching machine or have a coach throw batting practice. All plays and/or situations must be played to their completion. After a predetermined number of outs, plays or time, switch your offensive and defensive players.

Use first and third base coaches to help with baserunning fundamentals and strategy. As players increase their knowledge, eliminate base coaches to force baserunners to rely on their own knowledge.

Coaches should stop play whenever appropriate to make necessary corrections.

****

RUNNERS ON FIRST-AND-THIRD DRILL

This is the best of the Situation Hitting Drills. It will create baserunning and defensive situations that occur the most often during a game, while also providing excellent batting practice opportunities under game conditions.

The drill begins with runners at first and third bases and a hitter at home plate. If possible, there should be extra baserunners waiting in foul territory at both first and third bases—this will speed up the drill. Regardless of how far the baserunners or batter may have advanced during the course of the play, each player must return to the designated station (the runner on first base becomes a runner at third base, the runner at third base goes to the hitting station, and the hitter becomes a runner at first base).

> **COACHING KEY:**
>
> **Always** run the First-And-Third Situation Hitting Drill as a **one-out situation.**
>
> This drill can be a simple hitting and defensive drill, or a sophisticated game-like drill that incorporates both offensive and defensive signs and strategy.

Once the players understand their offensive responsibilities, the coach may choose to incorporate the hit-and-run, safety and suicide squeezes and other aspects of the offensive game into the drill. The coach should give the appropriate sign for each play. Not only will the players practice proper execution of a particular play under game-like conditions, but they will familiarize themselves with receiving and understanding the team's signs.

The Runner at First Base (1st & 3rd, One Out)

With runners on first and third and one out, the runner at first base has these responsibilities:

▶ **Leading off:** Work on primary and secondary leads.

▶ **Read the ball off the bat**: Watch the ball from the pitcher's hand (or pitching machine) to the impact zone. Remember, on a line drive, the runner *freezes*. On a ground ball, the runner *goes*.

▶ **Get off as far as you can:** On all fly balls, shallow or deep, get as far off the base as you can and still get back safely. On a deep fly ball, if the runner passes second base and the ball is caught, the runner should *be sure to retouch second base* when returning to first base. If in doubt, play all fly balls as if they are fair balls.

▶ **Avoid the tag:** On a ground ball that is hit in the baseline between first and second bases, never allow the second baseman to tag you out and throw to first base for an easy double play. Get hung up! This is your best chance to avoid the double play and allow the runner on third base to score.

> **Know the rules to go from first to third:**
>
> When determining whether to advance from first to third on a hit to the outfield, the fundamental philosophy for the runner on first base is this: if there are no outs, take no chances in trying to advance to third; if there is one out and at least a 50/50 chance of being safe at third base, *go for it*. This drill is primarily a one-out drill, so the one-out philosophy will prevail.
>
> Factors to consider when deciding whether to attempt an advance to third base: the outfielder's throwing ability; the playing field conditions (is it wet?); the depth of the outfielders; where the outfielder fields the ball; and how hard the ball is hit.

▶ **On a fly ball to left field:** On a routine fly ball to left field with the runner on third base tagging and a play at the plate, the runner on first base tags up and breaks for second when the outfielder releases the ball. The runner at first should "read white"—that is, see the ball leave the outfielder's hand before advancing to second base. By tagging up and advancing on the outfielder's throw to home plate, the runner from first base can force the defense to cut off the throw, allowing the run to score, or advance into scoring position should the throw go through to the plate. An average runner, if he breaks for second base at the right time, can beat the outfielder's throw to the cut-off man and the third baseman's return throw to second base. This play is almost exclusively a left field play—if a fly ball is hit other than to left field its chances for success are diminished.

▶ **Tag up on foul fly balls:** On all foul fly balls, tag up and be ready to advance.

The Runner at Third Base (1st & 3rd, One Out)

▶ **Execute a proper leadoff and return to third base:** the primary lead for the runner at third base is as far as the third baseman plays from the base. The runner should use a walking lead for the secondary lead. And remember: go down the line in foul territory, and back in fair territory.

▶ **Read the ball off the bat:** Watch the ball from the pitcher's hand to the impact zone and be ready to react. *Anticipate!* Use the location of the pitch as a key to react quickly and correctly to the batted ball. A high pitch usually means a fly ball; a low pitch typically will result in a ground ball.

▶ **Know your two options:** In this situation, with runners on first and third and one out, the runner on third does one of two things when the ball is hit, and nothing else. On any ball hit in the air, be it a line drive or a fly ball, he tags up. (He should tag with the left foot on all fair fly balls, and tag with the right foot on foul fly balls down the left field line). Or, on any ball hit on the ground, he attempts to score.

▶ **Score on a ground ball:** The runner on third base should attempt to score on ground balls to the infield with a runner on first base. If the defense goes for a double play and fails, the runner will score. Or, the runner at third may prevent a double play by forcing the defense to go after him.

▶ **If you're dead,** *get hung up*: If the runner attempting to score from third base is obviously out, he should get in a rundown to allow the runner from first base to advance to third and, if possible, the batter/runner to advance to second.

The Hitter (1st & 3rd, One Out)

▶ The hitter should focus on the proper way of leaving the batter's box, crossing first base and rounding first base as explained in the chapter titled "You Can't Steal First (But You Can Try!)," which begins on page 188. His initial step should always be with his rear foot; he should "nod the base" and then break down; he should look right after crossing first; and on a clean hit to the outfield, he should round first base aggressively, making the ball stop his progress.

The Infield Defense (1st & 3rd, One Out)

▶ The defense should practice playing the first-and-third, one-out situation two different ways: at double-play depth, and at the halfway position.

▶ At double-play depth, the infield is back and attempts to complete the double play, preventing the run from scoring. The infield should be played back during most of the drill.

▶ At the halfway position, the middle infielders play at medium depth (halfway between the deep position and the baseline). The first baseman and the third baseman play even with the base. On a hard-hit ball, the middle infielders go for the double play via second base. On a ball hit slowly, the middle infielders throw the runner out at home plate.

****
RUNNER ON SECOND DRILL

This drill is designed to teach the runner at second base to react correctly to ground balls and fly balls when he is the only runner on base and there are fewer than two outs.

The Runner on Second Base

▶ **Primary lead:** The runner on second base should take a primary lead only as far as is certain he can get back safely. The lead should be established as the pitcher goes into his stretch. The runner should look only at the pitcher, not at the infielders. Build your lead as the pitcher delivers the ball.

▶ **Secondary lead:** The runner on second should take two or three shuffle steps sideways as the pitch is delivered—no cross-over steps until advancing toward third base. (Crossing of the legs prematurely results in a loss of lateral mobility and makes the baserunner vulnerable to being picked off, or being doubled up on a line drive.)

▶ **On ground balls:** *The runner on second should advance to third base if:* the ball gets past the pitcher and is to the shortstop's left (be sure the ball gets *past* the pitcher); the ball is topped, or is a slow roller that brings the third baseman in toward home plate; the ball is a slow roller to the shortstop that brings him into the baseline or farther; the ball takes the third baseman deep into the hole; the ball takes the shortstop into the hole toward third base ("read white" and advance on his throw to first base); the ball forces the third baseman to backhand the ball behind third base (again, "read white" and advance on the third baseman's throw to first base). **Attention:** If the baserunner makes a mistake and advances when he shouldn't, he should get in a rundown to allow the batter/runner time to advance to second base... no damage done!

▶ **On fly balls:** The baserunner at second base can do one of two things on a fly ball—he can either "tag up" or "hang out"; which one he chooses can impact the outcome of the game. The number of outs dictates in large part how the runner at second base will react on a fly ball to the outfield. These fly balls are often hit deep and the baserunner is uncertain whether they will be caught or not.

The strategy for the runner at second base remains the same whether other bases are occupied or not.

With no outs, tag up—if the fly ball drops in, the runner will at least be at third base with nobody out if he is unable to score. Conversely, if the baserunner "hangs out" and does not tag up and the ball is caught, the offensive team now has a runner on second base with one out and has lost the third-base-with-one-out situation, greatly decreasing their chances of scoring a run. Tag up on all routine fly balls. *Fake* a break to third base to draw a throw, or advance if possible.

> ### *The number of outs dictates priority:*
>
> The baserunner at second base must understand which base has priority when a fly ball is hit to the outfield with less than two outs.
>
> The Priority System (going to third base vs. scoring a run) depends upon the number of outs: with no outs, getting to third base is the priority, and the runner should tag up. With one out, scoring a run has priority, and the runner should remember, *if in doubt, hang out.*
>
> **Run the drill with no outs and then with one out to expose the baserunner to both situations.**

With one out, "hang out"—that is, the runner should go as far off second base as he knows he can get back safely *on fly balls he is uncertain will be caught.* By hanging out, the baserunner greatly enhances his chances of scoring should the ball drop safely. If the ball is caught, the runner returns to second base. The offensive team now has a runner on second base and two outs.

On the other hand, if the baserunner tags up instead of hanging out and the ball drops in safely, his team may lose a scoring opportunity... third base vs. a run. In other words, with one out, scoring a run should have priority over third base on fly balls that the baserunner is uncertain will be caught.

Remember: If in doubt with one out, hang out!

Exception to the rule—shallow fly balls: Regardless of the number of outs, the runner on second base should "hang out" on all shallow fly balls in front of the outfielders. The rationale is this: the runner will not be able to advance after the catch because the outfielders will be too close to the infield. Hanging out gives the runner a chance to advance should the ball drop safely.

The Hitter

▶ With no outs and less than two strikes, the batter should attempt to hit the ball to the right side of the infield to advance the runner to third base. (With two strikes, just make contact and put the ball in play.)

****
RUNNER ON THIRD BASE ONLY DRILL

This drill is designed to: give the hitters practice driving in runs; give the runner at third base practice using correct baserunning techniques; and give the defense practice throwing the runner out at home plate. Run this drill mostly as a one-out situation.

The Hitter

▶ **Read the defense:** If the infield is playing back, the defense is conceding the run. A ground ball to the shortstop or second baseman will score a run. Reading the defense will take the pressure off the hitter if the infield is playing back. The hitter should "concede power for contact" with a runner on third base and less than two outs, and simply get the ball in play. Use a compact swing and don't swing for the fences.

▶ **Have an RBI contest:** Here's a great drill—have the hitters count the number of times they drive home the runner from third. This will create competition and force the hitters to concentrate.

The Runner at Third Base

▶ **Primary lead:** The runner should remember: down in foul, back in fair. He should go down the line in foul territory about one foot off the foul line; if he is hit with a batted ball while in foul territory, he is not out. And he should come back to the bag after the pitch in fair territory to block the catcher's view of third base. The length of the lead off third base is determined by how far the third baseman plays from the base—the runner can be the same distance from the base as the third baseman. If the third baseman stands on the base, lead off as though you were leading off first base.

▶ **Secondary lead when the pitcher is in the windup:** After taking the primary lead, the runner is ready for the secondary or walking lead, which is a four-step sequence: cross over with the left leg, then take a step with the right leg, followed by left and right steps. Steps one and two are "momentum steps," and steps three and four are "timing steps." The runner is walking directly toward the hitter in foul territory during this sequence. If done correctly, the weight will land on the right foot as the ball enters the "impact zone." The right foot is the "accelerator" or "brake."

▶ **Secondary lead when the pitcher works from the stretch:** This will probably result in a two-step secondary lead, eliminating the momentum steps. Before taking a secondary lead, the runner should be sure the pitcher throws to home plate and doesn't have a pickoff move to third base. Begin the lead when the pitcher's throwing arm is even with his body, a split-second before his stride foot hits the ground. This will eliminate the pickoff possibility. The secondary lead will have to be done quickly to insure proper timing and a large-enough lead.

▶ **When the ball is hit:** The runner on third base does one of two things—and nothing else—when the ball is hit. He either *tags up* (on any ball hit in the air, be it a line drive or high fly) or *goes* (attempts to score on a ground ball unless told otherwise by the coach beforehand). If the runner will obviously be thrown out at home plate, he should get into a rundown. This will allow the batter/runner to advance into scoring position while the rundown is taking place.

***

WINNING RUN ON THIRD BASE DRILL

This situation occurs when the runner on third base represents the winning run in the last inning of the game with no outs or one out. This scenario is rarely if ever practiced, and when it presents itself in a game is unfamiliar and intimidating to the defense.

The Defense

▶ **The infield plays in:** The infield should play in, *on the edge of the grass*, to prevent the runner from scoring, or else the game is over.

▶ **The outfielders are in a short outfield position:** The outfielders must assume a position that is shallow enough to enable them to throw the runner out at home plate should he attempt to score. Deep fly balls will score the runner anyway, so playing in a shallow position may enable the outfielder to catch a line drive that otherwise would be a base hit, and it will prevent the runner from scoring on short fly balls.

The Hitter

▶ The hitter's main concern is getting the ball in play. With the infield up close, his chances of getting a hit are doubled. So, the hitter should "concede power for contact" and use a compact swing.

***

RUNNER ON SECOND BASE WITH TWO OUTS DRILL

This drill will teach the batter/runner to advance aggressively to second base, forcing the defense to decide whether to cut the throw off and allow the runner from second base to score, or play on the runner attempting to score. If the play is made on the runner attempting to score from second base and he is safe, the batter/runner will have advanced to second base and will be in scoring position.

If the throw from the outfield is cut off and a play is made on the batter/runner advancing toward second base, he must be extremely careful not to be tagged out before the baserunner attempting to score from second base has crossed home plate. The batter/runner should "get hung up" (that is, get in a rundown) if there is any doubt that the baserunner has not crossed home plate. This will allow the run to count before the third out is made. In effect, the offense has conceded an out for a run.

A great way to practice:

Situation Hitting is an excellent way to practice defensive and offensive situations under game-like conditions. Rather than taking batting practice with everyone standing around except the batter, multiple aspects of the game can be taught and practiced simultaneously.

Procedure

As in the other Situation Hitting Drills, place a full team in the field. For this drill, make sure there is a catcher in full gear behind the plate. Have a batting practice pitcher (perhaps an assistant coach) or pitching machine on the mound throwing strikes. The pitcher participating in the drill (not the batting practice pitcher) stands behind the mound and practices backing up home plate.

The situation is this: there is a runner on second base with two outs. In this drill only, the infield permits all ground balls and line drives to go through to the outfield—they make no attempt to field the ball. The runner on second base must attempt to score on all hits to the outfield. After the ball has passed the infield, infielders assume the proper defensive alignment position, and/or cover the proper base. The hitter advances to second base to force a cutoff, and gets hung up if necessary with two outs to allow the runner from second base to score. For further details on this play, see page 215.

Place a pylon 20 feet from home plate on the third base foul line. The runner coming home from second base *stops here* to avoid contact with the catcher; the pylon acts as a barrier and the runner is not to go beyond this point. The catcher receives the outfielder's throws and simulates a play at home plate. This drill gives the catcher practice receiving the outfielders' throws and having the feeling of a baserunner "bearing down" on him.

Good Luck!

You *Can* Increase Bat Speed

"If I were again beginning my studies, I would follow the advice of Plato and start with mathematics." – Galileo

---

Contrary to popular belief, it *is* possible to increase a hitter's bat speed. In this chapter, I'll present some ideas to you, and then provide some drills.

Choose a Lighter Bat

Swinging a lighter bat will increase a player's "swing speed," and therefore, the amount of force with which the ball is hit. Too heavy a bat, one that adversely affects the swing speed, will have the opposite effect.

There is a law of physics that applies in this situation. It's called *kinetic energy*, and is stated as follows:

K.E.= ½MV^2

K.E. = Kinetic Energy or Force
M = Mass or Weight of Bat
V = Velocity or Swing-Speed

Because the velocity in this formula is "squared" (the number is multiplied by itself), the easiest way to increase force—or how hard you hit the ball—is to increase velocity, or swing the bat faster. So choose a lighter bat.

The faster you swing the bat, while under control, the harder you will hit the ball.

Grip the Bat Correctly

Grip the bat in a natural, relaxed manner, laying the bat across the hands where the fingers begin and the palm ends. The grip may be slightly diagonal with the bat lying from the base of the index finger across the palm of the hand.

Placing the bat too much into the fingers will result in a weak or less-secure grip. Burying the bat too deeply in the palms will reduce or destroy flexibility. Use your fingers as you would in gripping a bicycle handlebar grip.

Grip the bat firmly, but not too tightly. "Don't squeeze sawdust out of the end of the bat" was a saying told to hitters who gripped the bat too tightly. When a hitter grips the bat too tightly, the hands become tense and rigid, thus impeding a smooth and flexible swing. Tenseness in the hands can radiate throughout the body, further destroying flexibility and swing speed.

To counteract too rigid a grip, try gripping the bat only with your middle, ring, and little fingers, with your thumbs and index fingers resting lightly around the bat. This grip makes it difficult to form a fist, and should result in a more relaxed grip. The thumbs and index fingers will automatically tighten on the bat as contact is made.

A correct grip will improve your flexibility, wrist action and swing speed.

Hold the Bat at the Proper Angle

Your bat should be held at a 45-degree angle, near the launching position, while in your stance. This allows for a relaxed, tension-free stance and beginning of the swing. The weight of the club head of the bat will help propel the bat through the impact zone, thus maximizing your swing speed. A flat bat means you must "lug" the weight of the club head through the impact zone. A vertical bat position should also be avoided for similar reasons.

You should always begin your swing as close to the "launching position" as possible to avoid lengthening your swing.

Improve Your Strength

There is a very strong correlation between strength and success in hitting. A strenuous physical fitness program that incorporates strength training and flexibility exercises will permit you to develop to your full potential.

Any strength program must be under the supervision of an exercise physiologist or certified trainer. This is especially true if the athletes involved are teenagers or younger. A professional who understands child growth and development must administer any strength program.

DRILLS TO INCREASE BAT SPEED

There are many drills that can be used to enhance players' swing speed. Some of them have already been covered in the chapter titled "The Toss Drill." See these drills from that chapter:

– Glove Under Front Arm Drill (page 157)
– Throwing the Club Head Drill (page 157)
– One-Handed Bottom Hand Drill (page 157)
– One-Handed Top Hand Drill (page 157)
– Cross-Handed Drill (page 158)

What follows are just a few more of the many drills that can be used to increase bat speed.

Fence Drill: This drill will increase swing speed by developing a compact swing. The hitter assumes his batting stance facing a fence, and then swings the bat—if the hitting arc is too long, the bat will hit the fence. For correct distance from the fence, place the knob of the bat at your navel with the club head of the bat (parallel to the ground) touching the fence. You may need to step back a half-step to start, then work forward as your swing becomes more compact. A compact, short-arc swing should be completed without hitting the fence.

Twist Bat Drill: This drill will determine if a hitter is gripping the bat too tightly. The hitter takes a normal batting stance, and the coach goes behind the hitter, grabs the club end of the bat, and twists it. If the player's grip is too tight, the bat will not rotate in the player's hands.

Weighted Bat Drill: This drill will strengthen the muscles used in the swing. Players should swing a *slightly weighted* bat 50 times a day. The bat should be light enough to allow for a normal, fluid swing—too heavy a bat can lead to an improper swing.

Screen Throw: This drill is simple, yet effective. The hitter practices exploding with the hands by throwing a bat into a screen.

Tennis Ball Drill: Another simple, yet effective tool you can use if you have chain-link fencing. Use *tennis balls* for this drill. Players do the Toss Drill in the normal fashion (see page 154), with the goal of *driving the tennis ball through the chain-link fence*. (If hit with enough force, the ball *will* go through the fence.) This helps players focus on generating bat speed.

Good Luck!

The Defensive Roll

"Some people give their bodies to science. I give mine to baseball." – Ron Hunt, who was hit by a pitch 50 times in 1971, setting the modern major league single-season record.

A great deal has been written about the art of hitting, but one critical dimension of this art is continually neglected by the literature. Little (if any) time is devoted to the aspect of fear. Yet this is a common commodity at all levels of play.

Take for example the left-handed hitter who jokingly—and quite suddenly—becomes ill and would like out of the lineup when he discovers a hard-throwing southpaw warming up in the bullpen. Or a right-handed hitter who likewise develops some malady when he discovers a hard-throwing, cross-firing right-hander cranking up. These players are of course joking, but these remarks nonetheless represent apprehension.

And it stands to reason: when we consider that a pitched ball travels at speeds of 70, 80, or 90-plus miles an hour; and that many games are played in the late afternoon darkness with shadows creeping across the field, or are played at night on poorly lit fields, it is no wonder hitters are apprehensive!

However, if a hitter is to be successful, he must learn to overcome this apprehension. No one wants to be hit by a pitched ball, but it is an occupational hazard. Therefore, it is important that the players understand how to get out of the way of the ball properly and give themselves maximum defensive protection.

To combat fear at Portland State University, we taught "The Defensive Roll." This method was introduced to me in the early 1950s by Bernie DeViveiros, the scouting supervisor for the Detroit Tigers and one of baseball's outstanding teachers.

In this method, the hitter literally rolls away from the pitch on knockdown pitches; that is, he turns in the direction of the catcher with his back to the ball. He simultaneously drops to one knee, extends his bat, and ducks his head.

And on close pitches, the hitter simply rolls his upper body away from the pitch.

The Defensive Roll affords many advantages:

- By rolling away from the ball, the face and elbows are protected.
- By rolling away from the ball on close pitches, the bat is moved away from the strike zone and unnecessary foul balls are avoided.
- By rolling away from the ball on a breaking ball, when fooled, the hitter is able to recover and still make good contact. (Compare this to being fooled by a breaking ball and stepping in the bucket where no recovery is possible.)
- By rolling away from the ball, the head is well-protected and blows will be glancing.

We break the Defensive Roll down into three teaching keys: 1) Pivot; 2) Knee and 3) Duck. Once the components are mastered, the entire movement is put together and executed rapidly in one simultaneous action.

In the *Pivot* phase, the hitter spins on the balls of his feet so that at the completion of the pivot, his feet are in a striding position and he is facing the catcher.

The *Knee* involves dropping to the ground on the knee of what was formerly the front or striding leg.

Finally, the final key, *Duck*, has one critical aspect—the bat must be extended backwards and the arms inside the upright knee. This assures that the elbows will be protected. The head should be below the shoulders so that if the hitter is struck in the back, the ball will glance over his head.

The Defensive Roll instills confidence in hitters because they have an effective way to protect themselves. Consequently, they become better and more aggressive hitters.

Good Luck!

Hitting the Curveball: A Few Ideas

"Hitting is timing. Pitching is upsetting timing." – Warren Spahn

---

Dear Mom,

"I'll be home soon. They're starting to curve me."

This is the sad lament of many an aspiring player. The curveball—affectionately known as the drop, swerve, deuce, jug, hook, and a myriad of other names—has been responsible for the demise of many hitters. It is most effective when a right-handed pitcher is facing a right-handed hitter, or a left-handed pitcher is facing a left-handed hitter.

> **COACHING KEY:**
>
> *To learn to hit the curveball correctly and consistently, the hitter must understand that the curveball is an "off-speed" pitch and that off-speed pitches should be hit to the opposite field.*
>
> **Remember: "Off-speed, off-field!"**

The average curveball is thrown 15 miles per hour slower than the same pitcher's fastball. This change of speed is probably more of a problem to the hitter than the actual break or curve of the ball. To compensate for this change of velocity, the hitter must learn to "wait" on the curveball. And hitting the curveball to the opposite field is one method of teaching the hitter to wait on the pitch. Thinking "opposite field" makes the hitter wait on the curve and improves his chances of hitting the ball solidly.

(Note: "Opposite field" does *not* mean down the foul line—*this is a common misconception.* Rather, the opposite field for the right-handed hitter vs. a right-handed pitcher means the area from the shortstop's left to the right field foul line; the opposite field for the left-handed hitter vs. a left-handed pitcher means the area from the second baseman's right to the left field foul line.)

The location of the pitch will determine where in this area the ball should be hit; *pull only those curveballs that are hung high and inside.* Attempting to pull a good curveball results in two major problems. The first of these is *lunging*—a failure to recognize that the curveball is an off-speed pitch gets the hitter out on his front foot. And the second problem is *pulling away from the pitch*, which is often a manifestation of fear of being hit by the ball, or trying to pull the ball.

The correct point of contact to hit the curveball to the opposite field should be on the *inside half of the baseball when the ball is over the plate.* The barrel of the bat should be behind the hands upon contact. Also, upon contact, the back of the bottom hand should be facing skyward. This prevents pulling the ball—think "wristwatch to the sky."

To help keep his weight back, the hitter should begin the "Defensive Roll" (see the previous chapter on this topic) by rolling the front shoulder inward when the pitch is recognized as a curveball. *The hitter's first move should be a weight shift back!* The Defensive Roll helps keep the hitter's front side and front shoulder closed as long as possible.

Even if the hitter strides too soon, he should remember: *Don't commit your weight!* Keep your weight and hands back. To help keep your weight back, hit the ball the way it is breaking—if it is breaking away from you, hit it to the opposite field; if it is breaking into you, hit it back through the pitcher's box. Again, the only curveballs that should be pulled are those that are hung high and inside.

Considerations

Look for the fastball: Look for the fastball and react to the curve. *Don't guess curveball.* If you do, they'll throw the fastball right by you, and you could also be hit with the pitch.

What type of curveball does the pitcher have? Is it a "round-house curve"—that is, a big sweeping flat curve that fools the hitter on one plane, horizontally or laterally? *Take this pitch if it starts on the outside half of the plate*—it will be out of the strike zone. Or is it a sharp down-and-out curve? This pitch will fool the hitter on two planes, vertically as well as horizontally. *If this pitch starts low or away, take it!*

Can the pitcher control his curveball? Look for the fastball on the first pitch, and *take* the curveball. Too many hitters swing at curveballs out of the strike zone on the first pitch and are then behind in the count. Now they are vulnerable for a diet of curveballs.

After a curve misses to go to a 1-0 count: If the first pitch is a curveball for a ball, lay for the fastball on the next pitch— 99% of catchers and/or coaches will call for a fastball in an attempt to even the count.

Does the pitcher tip off his pitches? That is, does he give any visual checks or tip off the fact that he is throwing a curveball? Possible clues include changing his arm angle, adjusting his grip in the glove, or an abnormal twisting or curling of the wrist. While in the dugout and on deck, hitters should study this.

Watch for patterns: While on deck and in the dugout, hitters should study the catcher and his calls. Is there a pattern—say, fastball, curveball, fastball? Does the pitcher throw his curve only when he is ahead in the count? Only with two strikes?

Move up: Move forward in the batter's box and hit the curve before it breaks. It may be helpful, but beware—moving up makes the pitcher's fastball more effective.

Where RIGHT-HANDED HITTERS Should Hit Most Curveballs from RIGHT-HANDED PITCHERS:

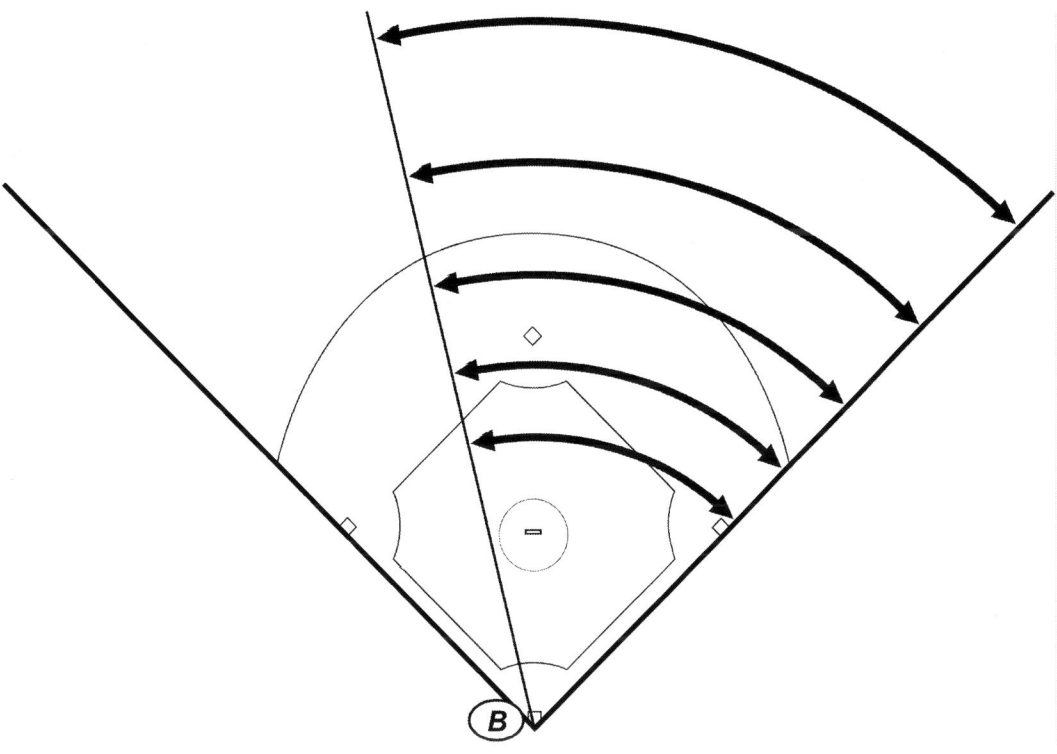

Where LEFT-HANDED HITTERS Should Hit Most Curveballs from LEFT-HANDED PITCHERS:

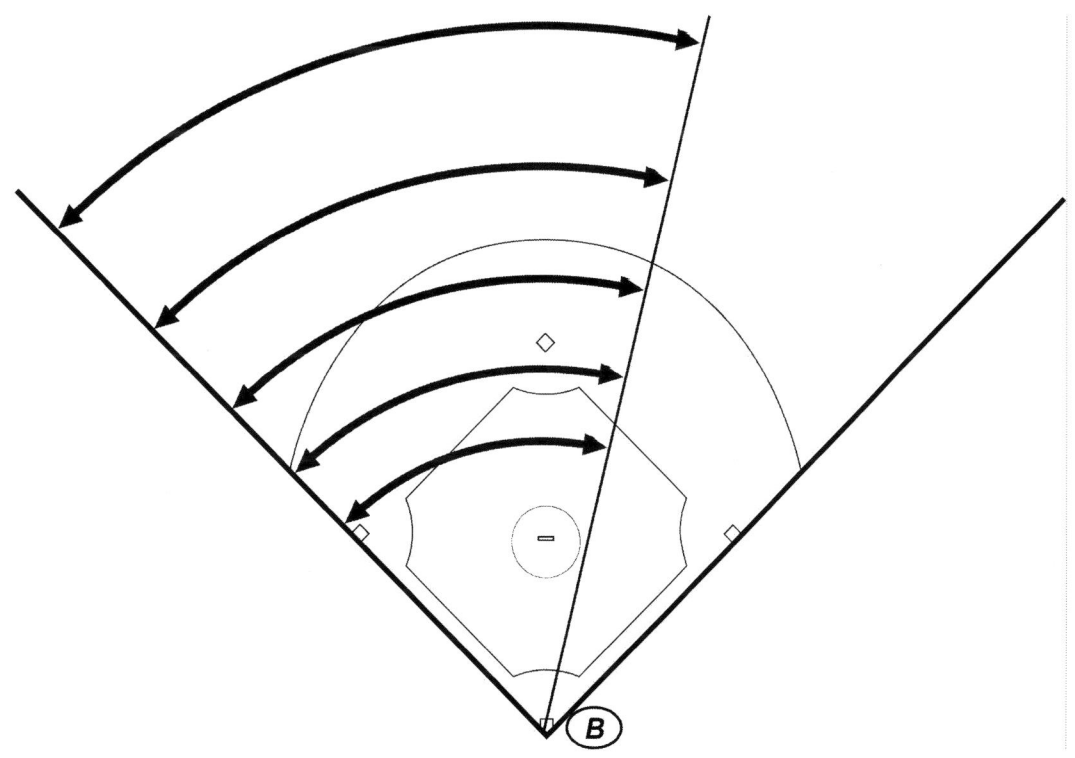

Curveball Hitting Drills

These drills will aid the hitter in learning how to hit the curveball and learning where the point of contact with the baseball should be made. Set a pitching machine, such as a JUGS Pitching Machine (www.jugsbaseball.com) to throw curveballs waist-high on the outside half of the plate. The machine should be set to simulate a righthander's curve to right-handed hitters, and a lefthander's curve to left-handed hitters. Players should focus on hitting the ball to the opposite field, and they should exaggerate their "shoulder roll" during drills.

Bunt Drill: The hitter should bunt the ball to the opposite field five times.

Spin 'Em Drill: The hitter should "slap bunt" or "slash" the ball to the opposite field five times. (See the separate chapter, "Spin 'Em: A Weapon to Keep the Infield Honest" on page 234 for an explanation of the slap bunt.)

Lob Drill: In this drill, the pitching machine should be set to throw slow, looping curveballs down the middle of home plate. The hitter assumes an extraordinarily wide stance and does not stride. He *waits* on the pitch, allowing the ball to come to him before swinging the bat. When the swing is taken, the hitter should be sure to unlock the hips by rotating the back heel upward and out—*squash the bug*.

Regular Curveball Hitting Drill: The hitter takes his normal stance and uses his usual stride. The pitching machine should be set to throw curveballs waist-high and on the outside third of home plate. The hitter hits the curveball to the opposite field, waiting on the ball by keeping his weight back and his front shoulder closed. Remember, to keep weight back, roll the front shoulder inward when the pitch is recognized as a curveball. Look for a fastball and react to the curve. The hitter should focus on keeping the back of his bottom hand facing skyward—again, think "wristwatch to the sky"—when the bat makes contact with the ball. This prevents pulling the outside pitch.

Pylon Curveball Drill: Set the pitching machine to throw waist-high curveballs on the outside third of home plate, and place a pylon between second and third bases, 20 feet away from second base (for right-handed hitters). Then, space three or four additional pylons (or other markers such as a ball bag) in a direct line from the initial pylon toward home plate to form a line of demarcation. Hitters should attempt to hit all pitches to the right of this line of demarcation. *Reverse the drill for left-handed hitters:* put the line of pylons on the opposite side of the field (heading toward the second baseman's position), and left-handed hitters should attempt to hit all pitches to the *left* of this line of demarcation—that is, to the second baseman's right.

> **COACHING KEY:**
>
> *Tell right-handed hitters on curveballs breaking away from them to "Hit the ball to the shortstop's left." Left-handed hitters, on curveballs breaking away from them, should "Hit the ball to the second baseman's right."*
>
> **The Pylon Curveball Drill will help your players visualize this.**

Opposite Side Drill: This is the Regular Curveball Drill, but with a twist—in this drill, players have the curveball breaking into them. In other words, use the pitching machine to simulate a lefthander's curveball to the right-handed hitters, and a righthander's curve to the left-handed hitters. *In this drill, the hitter should attempt to drive the curveball back through the pitcher's box, and in all probability, the ball will be pulled. If the hitter is being jammed, the hitter should attempt to pull the ball.*

A Few More Thoughts

There is an old baseball adage that says, "Don't curve the old ballplayer." The rationale here is that you don't get to be an old ballplayer unless you can hit the curveball. Also, the curveball is a slower pitch and allows for more reaction time, which benefits the older player.

The old ballplayer has learned to *wait* on the curveball, to hit the ball the way it is breaking, which in most cases means the opposite field, and pull only those pitches that are hung in the upper inside quadrant of the strike zone (high and inside).

The curveball breaking away from the hitter is where the majority of problems occur—that is, a curve from a right-handed pitcher to a right-handed hitter, and a curve from a left-handed pitcher to a left-handed hitter.

Curveballs breaking into the hitter (a right-handed pitcher to a left-handed hitter, and vice-versa) present fewer problems, as the fear factor for the most part has been removed. Following the pitch is easier because the ball is coming into the hitter. Curveballs breaking into the hitter should be hit "back through the box" (up the middle), but in all probability will be pulled.

My old coach told me, *"If all else fails… use an ironing board to hit with!"*

Good Luck!

The Sacrifice Bunt

Learning how to bunt and hit-and-run and turning two is more important than knowing where to find the little red light at the dugout camera." – Ryne Sandberg

---

The sacrifice bunt is a viable part of any team's offensive game and can be the difference between winning and losing.

When we consider that most hitters are reluctant to lay down a sacrifice bunt, and that the sacrifice bunt is usually used late in the game when pressure is at its greatest and the game is on the line, it's no wonder most sacrifice bunt attempts fail.

It has been estimated that 20 to 25 percent of all sacrifice bunts are misplayed by the defense. *So, why not sacrifice bunt more often?*

Tenets of Successful Sacrifice Bunting

"Up front, out front, and in front": That's what coaches should get across to their players. They should be *up front* in the batter's box, with their back foot even with the middle of home plate—this increases the chances of the ball going into fair territory. The bat should be extended *out front*—that is, to consistently bunt the ball into fair territory with good placement, the bat must be extended "out in front" of the hitter's body and home plate. And the bat must be *in front* of the hitter's line of sight—between the ball and the hitter's eyes. *You must see your work!*

Strategy and Mental Considerations: When laying down a sacrifice bunt, players should remember these things:

- Bunt only strikes.
- Give yourself up—at no time attempt to make a base hit out of the bunt.
- Don't bunt in motion. *Bunt the ball first, then run!* See the ball down.
- Bunt the ball in the area halfway to the mound and three feet from the foul line. Don't work the foul lines.
- Assume the bunting stance when the pitcher lifts his front foot to deliver from the stretch.
- With a runner on first base, bunt down the first base line.
- With runners on first and second bases, bunt hard toward the third baseman. If the third baseman fields the ball, his only play is to first base.

Mechanics

Stance: The bunter should place the back foot even with the "break" of home plate—that is, even with the middle of home plate. This will make it easier to bunt a fair ball. Pivot on the balls of the feet, with both feet pointing at the pitcher. The knees and arms are slightly flexed, and the bunter is close enough to the plate to be able to reach the outside pitch.

> **COACHING KEY:**
>
> *Remember: when bunting, the fingers of the top hand do NOT go around the bat. Instead, the thumb and index finger of the top hand form a "V" where the bat rests.* **The bat must be gripped properly so the fingers cannot be smashed with a pitched ball.**

Grip: The bunter should hold the bat firmly with the bottom hand two or three inches up from the knob. Slide the top hand to the trademark (if you let go with the bottom hand, the bat should balance there). Hold the top hand near the trademark with the thumb and index finger forming a "V"—this is the standard grip. Point the index finger of the top hand up the back of the bat to aid bat control. This is a very effective method of bunting, but not too common.

Bat position: The club head of the bat should be slightly elevated above the hands—too much elevation causes a loss of plate coverage. Carry the bat at the top of the strike zone and bunt only balls below this level. Any pitch above the bat is a ball. Remember, smart pitchers throw high fastballs trying to make the hitter pop-up the bunt. *Catch the ball on the bat*—don't jab at it! Never let the club head of the bat drop below the hands—if you do, it's an automatic pop fly. Low pitches are bunted by lowering the body. This is done by bending the back knee, not by dropping the club head. Remember: hold the bat in front of your body (or the plate) so that contact is made in front of your eyes: *Ball! Bat! Eyes!*

Where to Bunt

Runner on first base: With a runner on first base, the ball should be bunted toward first base between the area about three feet from the foul line and halfway to the mound. The bat is parallel to the third base line, with the knob of the bat pointing at the third baseman. Right-handed hitters should bunt the inside half of ball, while left-handed hitters should bunt the outside half of the ball.

General Target Area for a Sacrifice Bunt with a Runner on First Only:

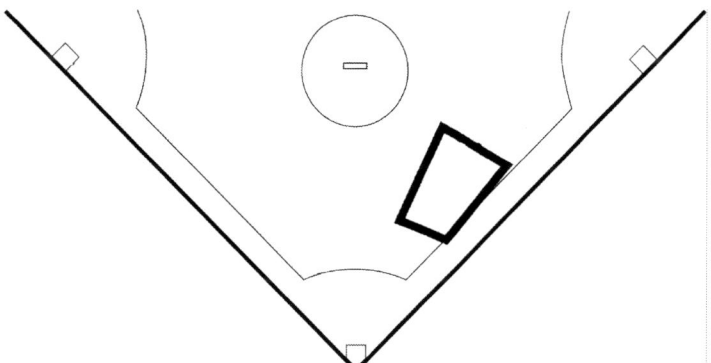

Bunting on the "weak side": Right-handed batters often have more difficulty bunting to third base than first base, while left-handed batters have more difficulty bunting to the first base side. A method to facilitate bunting to the batter's weak side is to bring the rear foot forward so that it is slightly forward of the front foot. The toe of the front foot is about opposite the middle of the now-forward rear foot. This position makes it easier to create the bat angle necessary to bunt to the weak side.

Runners on First and Second Bases: In this situation, the ball should be bunted hard toward the third baseman on the infield grass. The bat is parallel to the first base line, and the club head points at the first baseman. Right-handed hitters should bunt the outside half of the ball, while left-handed hitters should bunt the inside half of the ball. The hitter should assume his stance early and then read the shortstop. If he evacuates his position to cover third base, then execute a "slap bunt." (See the chapter titled "Spin 'Em: A Weapon to Keep the Infield Honest" on page 234.) Bunt to the first base side if the first baseman plays extraordinarily deep, if he's a poor fielder or has a weak arm.

General Target Area for a Sacrifice Bunt with a Runner on Second:

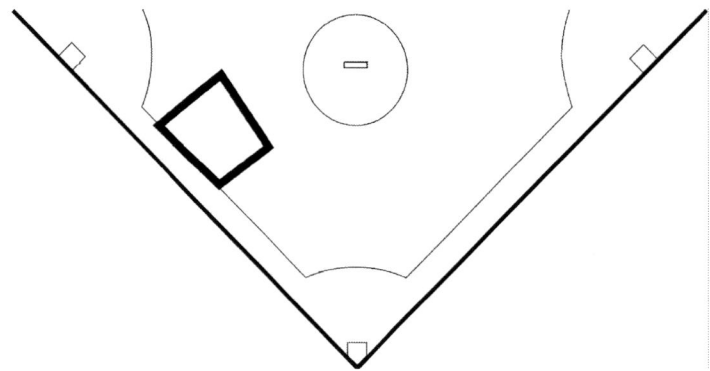

Bernie's Notes on Bunting:

One of the game's all-time great teachers, Bernie DeVivieros was a noted expert on sliding (see page 198), and he also had strong opinions on bunting. He once wrote the instructions below to me. (You'll notice a couple of areas where Bernie's thoughts don't match my own from earlier in this chapter. As with anything else, pick and choose what's right for you!)

Grip: Hold the bat firmly with the bottom hand off the knob. Slide the top hand to the trademark, with the first index finger along the back, thumb on top. The second, third and fourth fingers ride along the bottom of the bat, with the knuckles bent. (Note: The fingers are not around the bat so that they cannot be smashed with a pitched ball. Quite a few noted pitchers have been injured in this manner.) Practice sliding the hand up the bat until you have mastered this action. Remember, slide the hand to the trademark so you have balance of the bat. (Let go of the bottom hand and you will note that the bat will balance there and keep the grip firm at all times.) Have the bat always at an angle of 45 degrees, in both hands, when ready to bunt.

Bottom Elbow: Have the bottom elbow jammed in the lower area of the waist. The elbow can slide along in this area, in or back-and-forth, to reach the ball. The bottom elbow must never come up—if it does, the top end will drop down and you will pop the ball in the air or foul it.

Angle of the Bat: The angle of the bat (big end up) remains slightly forward of the bottom hand. The top end of the bat always comes down on the ball to make it bounce. The bat is never in a level position at any time, except when the ball is bunted waist-high. The big end of the bat continues down for all low pitches, and the bottom elbow never leaves its position, but slides along to reach or goes back for the inside pitch. On all high pitches, the big end goes up, with a little forward angle, to make the ball come down and make it bounce. The bottom elbow always remains close to the side, but never comes out. *That is the secret of it all!*

Stance: Use a square stance to the plate. Never turn around and face the pitcher—it's a dead giveaway. Keep the bunt a secret as long as possible. A very slight shoulder turn can be used if so desired, it's hard to keep away from that. Do it slow for better rhythm. The front foot never moves. It stays even with the plate. You can stay back, if so desired, but it is harder to bunt outside pitches and the hard slider. They are hard to reach. Always look for the high fastball when bunting, a curve or a change-up is a mistake. The back foot can move to any position, in, out, or back as the ball is approaching; it helps to kill (deaden) the ball. A slow move straight back, towards the catcher as the ball is coming, is the best for any type of sacrifice; again, it helps to kill the ball.

Where to bunt: Bunt on top of the ball and *make it bounce* on all sacrifice bunts. It is best to bunt down the first base line at all times—keep the high angle of the bat, but turn the angle in that direction and stay on top of the ball and make it bounce! The pitcher is well trained on handling bunts in all situations, so do not let him handle the ball if possible. The first baseman generally is a big, slow man who will not throw the ball to third base with a man on first and second as the throw is too long. Very few first basemen will make the play. Have you ever seen one do it? It's hard to bunt down the third base side to make the third baseman field the ball. If it is too hard, he can go for the double play. Watch out here. It's an old tradition to go down the third base side and has lost more games than you can count. Take note. Most clubs are now going down the first base side. I have proved it to them. Play the percentage.

The suicide squeeze: Just step back with the pitch and bunt it anywhere. Stay on top and *make it bounce*. Any bouncing bunt will hang in the air so it gives more time to get the run in. Any bunted ball on the ground, or Astroturf, is too fast and the play could be lost. Again, down the first base side is best. Work hard on this. Practice is the only way.

Bunting for a base hit (right-handed batters): When attempting to bunt for a base hit, a right-handed hitter moves his back foot away from the plate, drops the bat on the ball and takes off, with the ball going down the third base line. Another option is a *push bunt*, where a right-handed hitter does the same back step (making it look like a third-base bunt), but comes out of it quickly and pushes the ball hard to the second baseman. This move brings the pitcher over to the third base side and leaves the first base side open. You make him think you are going down the third base side. It's a bluff!

Bunting for a base hit (left-handed batters): For a base-hit bunt down the third base line, a left-handed hitter's front foot steps first toward the right field foul line as the pitch is coming, with the angle of the bat high and slightly back, and with the right elbow stuck in the right side. He places the bat on the ball and makes it bounce, and with a crossover step is in full running speed. On a drag bunt up the first base line, he does the same thing, but carries the bat a little lower, looking for a low pitch; and with a hard thrust of the left hand, he drags the ball hard past the pitcher and makes the second baseman field the ball. *This is the Mickey Mantle style.* Do not leave too soon or step toward the pitcher, and do not try to drag high pitches.

Bunting is required skill. *Practice and practice.* Never sacrifice in motion. Give yourself up in the sacrifice hit…again—*practice and practice.*

Signed, Bernie DeViveiros, D.S. (Doctor of Sliding).

Good Luck!

Hit With Your Head

"He can, who thinks he can, and he can't, who thinks he can't." – Henry Ford

---

If you were to ask the average hitter what he is thinking while at bat and the pitcher is delivering the ball, his answer surely would be, "I'm going to hit this pitch if it's in there!" This negative mental approach is common to many hitters and leads to indecisiveness and usually a late swing. It limits the hitter's aggressiveness at the plate and greatly decreases his chances of getting a base hit.

A negative mental approach is the result of two factors:

1) Coach's instruction: For generations, coaches have yelled, "Get a good pitch to hit," "Make sure it's a strike," and "Don't swing at any bad ones."

2) The hitter's fear of being hit by the baseball. This fear overrides all other aspects of hitting and must be overcome if any degree of success is to be achieved.

When a hitter thinks something along the lines of, "I'm going to hit this pitch if it's in there," his mind now must analyze the pitch, send a message to the body to *get ready*, and then tell the body to *swing the bat*. Too much valuable time has been consumed and the end-result is often a swing and a miss or a pop fly, which results from a late swing.

It takes a fifth of a second for the ball to travel from the pitcher to the catcher. It has been estimated that the baseball is in the contact zone for only one fiftieth of a second. *That's not much time.*

A Positive Mental Approach

Because the mind triggers the body into action, the hitter must start with a positive approach to the task of hitting the baseball. A simple adjustment in thinking will dramatically improve a hitter's chances for success. As the pitcher begins his windup, the hitter says to himself, *"I'm going to hit this pitch!"*

The hitter is now physically (bat in launching position) and mentally ("I'm going to hit this pitch") ready to hit. No valuable time is lost when the pitch is to his liking and he decides

Fear = Negative Thinking

A negative mental approach to hitting is not only the result of the coach's admonition to "get a good ball to hit," but also to the player's fear of being hit by the ball. This fear results in the hitter making certain the pitch is not going to hit him rather than getting mentally and physically ready to swing the bat. It leads to a slow, late swing often accompanied by "stepping in the bucket."

No one wants to be hit by the ball. This is normal. All hitters are fearful to varying degrees. So it behooves us as coaches to teach our hitters how to protect themselves—that is, how to get out of the way of the pitch. Teaching hitters the "Defensive Roll" will give them a simple and effective method to protect themselves, and will make them more aggressive at bat. For details on the Defensive Roll, see page 171.

to swing the bat. And if the pitch is a ball, the hitter simply "takes" the pitch. This thought process will dramatically improve the hitter's success.

When using this positive mental approach, the "gun is cocked" and it is just a matter of pulling the trigger—quick, aggressive and decisive. Conversely, when using the negative mental approach, the gun must be cocked *before* the trigger can be pulled. It's slow, time-consuming and indecisive.

Dr. Norman Vincent Peale wrote a book entitled *The Power of Positive Thinking*. In this text, Dr. Peale stated, "People become really quite remarkable when they start thinking that they can do things. When they believe in themselves they have the first secret of success."

Look for a Fastball

To prevent the pitcher from throwing the fastball by the hitter, the hitter must be mentally set to hit the fastball. The hitter can make an adjustment from a fastball to a slower pitch such as a curveball or changeup; however, it is extremely difficult, if not impossible, to look for an off-speed pitch and then react to the fastball.

As a general rule, a curveball will be 15 mph slower than the fastball and a changeup will be 20 mph slower than the fastball. These slower velocities allow the hitter enough time to adjust from the expected fastball to the slower curveball or change up.

The hitter *must not guess* what the pitch will be! Look fastball, then adjust to the curveball or changeup. Guess hitting—such as looking for a curveball or changeup—could result in the hitter being unable to pull the trigger on a fastball, or unable to get out of the way of a fastball up and in. Always look fastball.

Off-Speed Pitches

The pitcher's job is to disrupt the hitter's timing. This is done by changing speeds on his pitches. Curveballs, changeups, and split-fingered fastballs are examples of "off-speed pitches."

Remember, speeds are relative. A pitcher with a mediocre fastball may appear to have above-average velocity on his fastball after giving the hitter a diet of off-speed pitches. *Smart pitchers understand this concept.*

When mentally set to hit the fastball, the hitter must have a way to compensate for off-speed pitches should the pitcher choose to throw them. To compensate for a change in velocity of up to 20 mph, the hitter must understand this concept: *Off Speed = Off Field*. By thinking "off field," the hitter is forced to wait on the pitch, allowing it to get to home plate before swinging at it.

Remember, "off field" does not mean hitting the ball down the opposite-field foul line. Rather, it means right-handed hitters should hit the ball to the shortstop's left, and left-handed hitters should hit the ball to the second baseman's right. How far to the shortstop's left or the second baseman's right the ball will be hit will be determined by the location of the pitch and its velocity.

Because the majority of curveballs thrown to right-handed hitters break away from them, the concept of hitting the ball to the shortstop's left is an invaluable teaching concept.

Off Speed = Off Field is the hitter's counter to the pitcher's attempt to disrupt his timing.

Adjust from the Outside

The hitter should mentally look for a fastball away from him on the outside part of home plate. From there (the outside), the hitter can adjust to a pitch on the inside; but he cannot adjust to the outside if he looks inside first and pulls off the pitch.

This mental approach, "I can adjust from there, but not to there" has several advantages: the front side of the hitter's body stays closed, maximizing his power; it becomes easier for the hitter to make good contact and to hit to all fields; it prevents pulling off the ball, dissipating power and hitting routine ground balls to the pull side; it makes it easier to hit off-speed pitches; and it makes it easier to hit pitches on the outside part of the plate.

The hitter should look for a fastball on the *outside* part of home plate. If the pitch is on the inside half of home plate, the hitter can adjust. Any other approach will result in the hitter only being successful on inside pitches.

Do Your Homework

The hitter should study the pitcher prior to his at-bat, both while in the dugout and on deck. These are a few things a smart hitter can look for while awaiting his turn at bat:

- Does he tip off any of his pitches?
- Does he noticeably adjust the ball in his glove for the curveball? The change up? The split-finger fastball?
- What about his "arm angle?" Does it change when he throws a curveball or change up?
- What pitch does he throw when he is behind in the count?
- What pitch does he throw when he is ahead in the count?
- Can he throw his curveball for a strike? (If not, lay off the curve until there are two strikes.)
- If he throws a curve for a ball on his first pitch to a hitter, does he always come back with a fastball to even the count?

Stand Away from Home Plate

Many hitters are afraid that they cannot reach pitches that are thrown on the outside part of home plate. As a consequence, they "crowd the plate"—that is, they stand too close to it.

Don't do this. The closer the hitter stands to home plate, the faster he makes the pitcher. This is because the hitter must hit the ball farther out in front of home plate to keep from being hit on the handle of the bat. The contact point is critical. If the baseball is contacted too far in front of home plate, the ball will be hit foul. If contact is made too late, the ball will be hit on the handle of the bat.

The closer the hitter stands to home plate, the quicker he must be with his bat. There is also a tendency by hitters who stand too close to home plate to pull off the ball, or "step in the bucket" in an attempt to keep from getting jammed by the pitch. This often leads to head-pulling and being pull-conscious instead of hitting to all fields.

By moving away from home plate the hitter gains many advantages:

- The hitter has more time to react to the pitch.
- The majority of pitches are hit when the ball is over the plate and the bat is roughly at a right angle to the ball. This exposes the maximum hitting surface of the bat to the baseball.
- The point of contact is greater and more forgiving. The ball can be hit solidly from a larger arc. As a result, timing is less critical.
- It is more difficult for the pitcher to jam the hitter, as the inside pitch is a ball.
- It helps hitters who have a slower bat.
- It enhances a hitter's chances of hitting to all fields, and using the entire field to hit in is the hallmark of all high-average batters.

Remember, though, that the hitter must have plate coverage. He cannot stand so far away that he can't get to the pitch on the outside edge.

Ted Williams said a hitter should stand "approximately 10 inches to a foot" away from home plate. The following methods can be used to gauge the proper distance.

1. Have the hitter tap the outside corner of the plate with his bat—if he can do this, outside coverage is guaranteed.
2. Have the hitter assume his stance in the batter's box and then extend his bat, at arms length, belt high out over the plate. Then drop the bat over the plate to check its coverage.
3. Have the coach hold the club head of the bat while the hitter walks behind home plate and checks how much of the plate is covered.
4. Have the hitter place his bat on the ground with the club head on the outside edge of home plate and the handle of the bat extending into the batter's box. Where the end of the bat lies is an indicator as to how far the hitter should be from home plate.

Finally, how deep in the box should a hitter stand? An excellent starting point is to have the hitter align his belt buckle with the center of home plate—this is called the "Belt Buckle Theory." With experience he may adjust from this position. Professional players stand deeper in the box.

Know the Strike Zone

The strike zone is the area from the hitter's armpits to the top of his knees and is the width of the plate, 17 inches wide. The strike zone will vary from age group to age group and according to the individual umpire's ability, but for the most part a pitch in this area is a strike.

A hitter can learn the strike zone by swinging only at strikes during batting practice. Also, ask the umpire if he would have called the pitch you just swung at a strike—this will help define your strike zone, and his.

Another way to learn the strike zone is to stand in the batter's box in the bullpen while a pitcher is warming up and watch pitches without swinging. Try to identify balls, strikes and those pitches that are "your pitch." Ask the bullpen catcher for his opinion (ball or strike) on borderline pitches.

Know Your Pitch

Each hitter should know the pitch he can hit solidly. Look only for your pitch on your first strike and jump on it whenever it comes. Don't swing if you are fooled. With two strikes, on the other hand, protect the plate—swing at anything close. In this spot, the hitter should *concede power for contact*—gain bat control by choking up slightly on the bat and using a compact swing.

Do Think

There is an old baseball adage that says, "Don't think… You'll hurt the team." This may be true in certain instances, but when it comes to batting, "hitting with your head" can greatly enhance the hitter's chances for success.

As my old coach said, *"Use your head… It's the little things that count!"*

Good Luck!

Baserunning Drills and Techniques

You Can't Steal First (But You Can Try!)

"The only thing he has to do to steal more is to hit more singles." – Maury Wills, on how a player could raise his number of stolen bases

---

Once a batter hits a fair ball, he becomes a baserunner. The batter/runner has two possible approaches to first base. The approach he chooses depends upon where the ball is hit.

1) On a ground ball to the infield, he runs straight to first base to try to beat the infielder's throw.

2) On a ball hit to the outfield, the batter/runner rounds first base and is in position to advance another base or bases should the opportunity present itself.

Running to First Base on a Ground Ball to the Infield

Because most infield ground balls result in extremely close plays at first base, the batter/runner must get down the first base line as quickly and efficiently as possible to improve his chances of being safe. Many plays at first base are so close they are referred to as "bang-bang" plays. When teaching the fundamentals of running from home to first the following points should be emphasized:

▶ **A quick start is key:** Being safe or out at first base on a ground ball to the infield can often be traced to a good or bad start out of the batter's box. A quick start is the result of a good follow-through after hitting the ball. A good follow-through transfers the body weight onto the hitter's front foot, which allows the *first step to be with the rear foot.*

▶ **Initial step out of the batter's box:** A right-handed hitter's initial step should be taken with the right foot; a left-handed hitter's with the left foot. The shortest distance between two points is a straight line, so the hitter's initial step out of the batter's box should be directly toward first base.

Some left-handed hitters are guilty of taking their initial step directly toward the pitcher's mound—this wastes time and increases the distance the hitter must run to first base. (This malady rarely, if ever, plagues the right-handed hitter.) Be sure that your left-handed hitters step directly toward first base when taking their initial step out of the batter's box.

The hitter leaves the batter's box with an aggressive driving half-step with his *rear foot*. The second step can be near full-stride, and as momentum is gained the full running stride can be achieved. The batter/runner must now *focus on first base* and not run watching the ball, which is a major baserunning fault of many players. This is an absolute no-no—not only is the player's speed diminished, but the chance of not stepping on first base is greatly increased.

▶ **A quick glance is okay:** When balls are hit directly to the shortstop, second baseman or first baseman, the batter/runner can easily see the ball by using his peripheral vision. No turning of the head is necessary. However, on balls hit to the shortstop's right (toward third base), a *quick* glance to find the ball may be necessary. This enables the batter/runner to alter his approach to first base should the ball go through to the outfield.

A quick glance means a quick turning of the head, chin to left shoulder, which should be all that is necessary to locate the ball. This quick glance will have little or no negative impact on the runner's speed to first base. The quick glance should be taken on the third or fourth step out of the batter's box. It is easier for the batter/runner to look quickly when his right foot is forward and the left foot is back during the running process—this usually occurs on the right-handed batter's third step and the left-handed batter's second step out of the batter's box.

It is not necessary to take a quick look at balls that are topped (swinging bunts) or other slowly hit balls to the left side of the infield. And remember: *No staring allowed.*

▶ **The running lane:** The batter/runner must remain inside the three-foot-wide running lane while going the final 45 feet down the first base line. If he is running outside this lane (either toward the foul side or, more commonly, in fair territory) and, in the umpire's judgment, interferes with a throw to first base, he will be called out. (Exception: The batter/runner may go outside these lines to avoid a fielder attempting to field a batted ball.) The batter/runner is considered outside this three-foot lane if either or both feet are outside the lines. This situation usually occurs when the ball is fielded in the area in front of home plate and the subsequent throw is made to first base. Be sure your players understand this rule, both offensively and defensively.

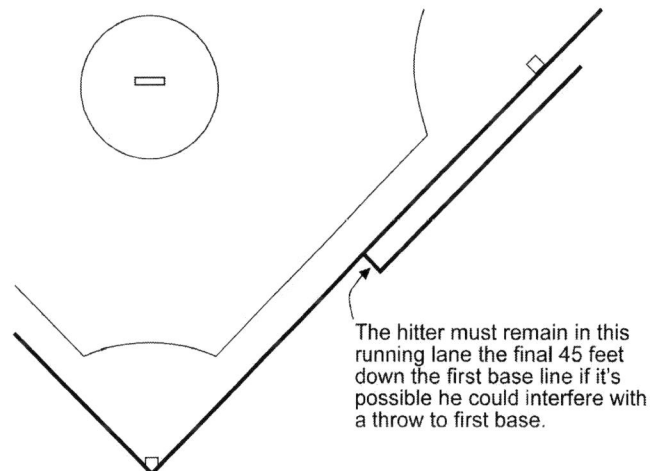

The Running Lane:

The hitter must remain in this running lane the final 45 feet down the first base line if it's possible he could interfere with a throw to first base.

Crossing First Base

▶ **Touch the base:** This is the number-one rule in baserunning. Regardless of how obvious it is that the runner is out, *step on the base.* Also, the player should step in the middle of the base—although stepping on the front edge of the base may be a nanosecond faster, the chance of injury is greater.

▶ **Run to a point beyond first base:** This forces the runner to cross first base at full speed. Young players often "run to the base," and as a consequence have a tendency to slow-up prior to reaching the base, a costly mistake. The rule of thumb should be to *run to a point five or six steps beyond first base.* Be sure to *run* across the base—don't jump or leap into the base, which is slower. And run straight through the base—don't veer right or left when crossing first base, as it increases the distance to the bag.

▶ **"Nod the base":** When crossing first base, the batter/runner should "nod the base"—that is, step on first base and simultaneously bend at the waist. This is comparable to a sprinter "breaking the tape." It may get the player a safe call on a close play at first base.

▶ **Break down:** After crossing first base, the batter/runner should "break down"—that is, change from stride steps (which provide more speed) to short chop steps (which establish lateral control). This allows for a quick change of direction if the ball is overthrown at first base. Begin breaking down on the *third step* past first base.

▶ **Look Right:** After crossing first base and bringing the body under control (with chop steps), the batter/runner should *look to the right* to see if the ball has been overthrown. A runner is able to react quicker by seeing the ball's location himself, rather than waiting for the base coach's instructions.

▶ **Returning to first base:** The batter/runner may turn either left or right when returning to first base without liability of being tagged out, provided he does not attempt to run to second base. Any "fake" toward second also puts the batter/runner in jeopardy of being out. Turning right, toward the foul line, after crossing first base is much safer and probably should be taught to younger players. Be sure your players understand this rule, both offensively and defensively.

Rounding First Base on a Hit to the Outfield

Once the batter determines that the ball is going into the outfield, he must round first base. The purpose of rounding first base is to enable the batter/runner to run a nearly straight line to second base should the opportunity present itself.

Not rounding first base or making too wide a turn increases the distance to second and the time it takes to get there. This lessens the runner's chances of being safe should he attempt to advance.

There are two methods a player can use to properly round first base on a hit into the outfield. Both of these methods are designed to minimize the distance the batter/runner must run to second base while allowing him to run at full speed. Avoid making wide, sweeping turns around the bases:

Method 1: *When the hitter is immediately certain it's a clean hit to the outfield, he runs to the outside corner of the running lane as his first point of reference, then runs to a point approximately 10-12 feet in front of first base and halfway between the coach's box and the foul line (during drills, the coach can place a pylon here as a reference point). This flat circle puts him in a straight line toward second base.*

Method 2: *When he is uncertain a ball will get through the infield, the hitter runs straight to first. Once the ball gets through, he rounds first base by making a small circle, placing him in a straight line toward second base.*

The Two Methods of Rounding First Base:

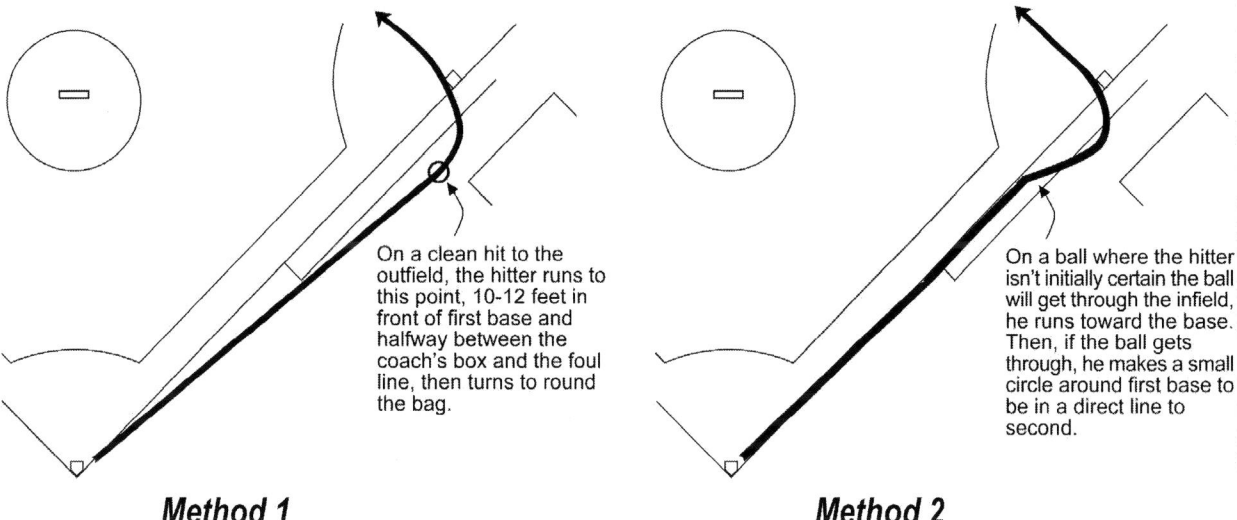

On a clean hit to the outfield, the hitter runs to this point, 10-12 feet in front of first base and halfway between the coach's box and the foul line, then turns to round the bag.

Method 1

On a ball where the hitter isn't initially certain the ball will get through the infield, he runs toward the base. Then, if the ball gets through, he makes a small circle around first base to be in a direct line to second.

Method 2

▶ **Touching First Base:** Touch first base on the inside half of the base with the left foot. (But don't break stride to touch the base with the left foot—step on the base with the right foot if necessary.)

▶ **Upon Rounding First Base:** *Make the ball stop you*—turn first base aggressively, ready to advance if the outfielder bobbles the ball. Make the turn at first base as though every base hit is a possible double. Round first base in an aggressive, challenging manner until the ball is fielded cleanly. If the ball is hit to right field, more caution must be exercised, because the right fielder may throw behind the runner if he takes too big a turn.

▶ **Return to first base watching the outfielder's throw back into the infield:** This will enable the runner to advance in the event the outfielder's throw is bad or the ball is misplayed by an infielder. If the ball is hit to left field or center field, turn counterclockwise toward the infield. If the ball is hit to right-center field or right field, turn clockwise toward the outfield. In either case, keep your eyes on the ball as you return to first base. Be ready to advance if possible.

Good Luck!

The Box Baserunning Drill

"Hitting the ball was easy. Running around the bases was the tough part." – Mickey Mantle

---

The *Box Baserunning Drill* is a superb drill—it can be used daily to reinforce correct baserunning mechanics, and to prepare the body for practice by increasing body temperature, blood flow, and flexibility.

Purposes:
1. To teach players the correct mechanics of running from home plate to first base after hitting a ground ball to the infield.
2. To teach players to use the correct initial step out of the batter's box.
3. To improve the batter/runner's chances of being safe at first base on a close play.
4. To improve the batter/runner's chances of advancing another base on an overthrow at first base.
5. To prepare players' bodies for practice by increasing body temperature, blood flow, and flexibility.

First, Learn the Mini-Drills

To maximize the drill's effectiveness, each component must be taught separately and thoroughly before they can be blended into one comprehensive and highly efficient multiple drill. *These four Mini-Drills should be learned first, and in the order listed:*

▶ **Initial Step Drill:** Assemble all the players at home plate. Then, one at a time, have each player swing (without a bat) at an imaginary ball and then run 15 feet toward first base. Check to see that their initial step is correct (with the rear foot) and that the left-handed hitter's initial step is not only with the rear foot, but is directly toward first base. Stepping toward the mound is a common mistake, and it increases the distance the player has to run to first base.

▶ **"Nod the Base" Drill:** Players line up single-file approximately 30 feet from first base. One at a time, they *walk* to first base, step on the base and simultaneously *bend at the waist*—thus "nodding the base." When players are able to nod the base correctly, have them repeat the drill by running half speed, and then full speed. Once the drill is mastered, move on.

▶ **Breakdown Drill:** Players line up single-file approximately 30 feet from first base. One at a time, players run across first base, nod the base and then "break down." After crossing first base (two or three strides), players should change their foot action from stride steps (speed steps) to chop steps. This establishes lateral control and the ability to quickly change directions. Body control should be established while still on the dirt area of the infield behind first base.

▶ **Look Right Drill:** Players line up approximately 30 feet from first base. One at a time they run across first base, nod the base, break down and look right. "Looking right" enables the runner to see if there is an overthrow of first base, and the player is able to react quicker if he finds the ball for himself in the event of an errant throw. To simulate a wild throw, the coach should take a bucket of balls to a position near first base, and as each player "looks right," the coach tosses a ball into foul territory and the runner advances to second base. The coach should check each runner's mechanics (primarily breaking down and looking right) and the player's reaction to the simulated overthrow. To create an element of surprise, don't toss the ball every time, only occasionally.

Now You're Ready

Once players have mastered each of the Mini-Drills above, you're ready to introduce the full Box Baserunning Drill.

The Box Baserunning Drill:

The team is divided into four groups, and groups are stationed at each base. One player in each group is the "batter." When the coach makes an imaginary pitch, the first batter in each group takes an imaginary swing (without a bat) and runs to the next base (four players do this at once -- one from each base).

Players work on their initial step, nodding the base, breaking down and looking right. Then they go to the back of the line at the base they just crossed.

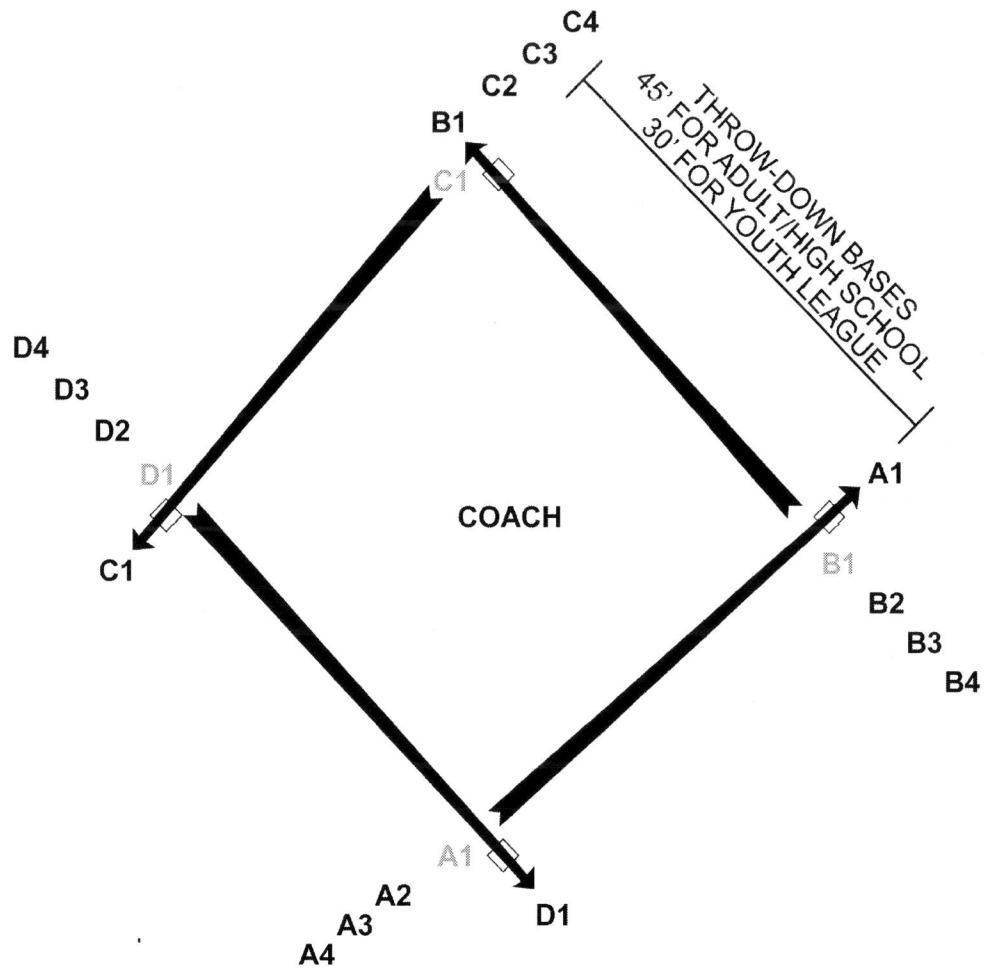

Procedure:
1. Place four "throw-down" bases in a square, spaced 45 feet apart for adult play and 30 feet apart for little league play.
2. Divide the squad into four groups and place one group at each base.
3. The coach stands in the middle of the box and acts as a pitcher. He has no baseball, but makes imaginary pitches.
4. The first player in each line uses his base as a home plate, and assumes a batting stance (*without* a bat). Four players should be doing this at the same time—one at each base.
5. The coach winds up and pretends to deliver a pitch to one of the players (it doesn't matter which).
6. All "batters" take an imaginary swing at the pitch and run to their first base (the base to their right.)
7. Players practice their initial step out of the batter's box (with their rear foot); nodding first base; stepping on the base; breaking down after crossing the base; and looking to the right for a possible overthrow.
8. Players go to the end of the line at the next base after completing their run.
9. The drill continues until all players have run at all bases—approximately five minutes, or as long as the coach desires.

Variation:
Another variation of the Box Baserunning Drill can be used to teach players to bring their bodies into running position by using strong leg action, and to help develop a quicker initial step and reaction time. Everything is the same as in the regular drill, except players assume a "push up" position on the ground in front of their base. On the coach's command ("Ready… Go!"), players drive their legs hard, bringing their bodies into running position. They then run to their first base, nod the base, break down and look right.

The Box Baserunning Drill Pays Dividends

This drill can be used daily, and it is an excellent way to teach and reinforce baserunning skills, while simultaneously warming up players' bodies in preparation for practice.

The Box Baserunning Drill will pay dividends in the number of times players will be able to advance to second base on overthrows of first. More importantly, the Box Baserunning Drill will lay the foundation for an alert, aggressive style of baserunning.

Good Luck!

Short Hop/Block and Run Drill

"He stopped everything behind the plate and hit everything in front of it." – Mel Ott on Yogi Berra

This is both an offensive and defensive drill. While the catchers are practicing blocking pitches thrown in the dirt, the baserunners are practicing proper mechanics for advancing a base when the catcher blocks a ball in the dirt and does not field it cleanly.

Purposes

For the defense:
1. To teach the catcher to fall to both knees, keep his head down and keep the ball in front of him when blocking pitches thrown in the dirt.
2. To teach the catcher to react quickly on pitches thrown in the dirt that are not fielded cleanly, preventing the baserunner from advancing a base.

For the offense:
1. To teach the runner to take a proper secondary lead, the distance of which depends on individual quickness; the player should take two sideways shuffle steps and a secondary lead of 18-25 feet.
2. To teach the runner to return to first base correctly after taking his secondary lead. He should cross over and immediately return to first if there is a pickoff throw by the catcher. If no play is made by the catcher, the runner should cross over and square up—he is now in position to advance if a bad throw is made back to the pitcher.
3. To teach the baserunner to take an extra shuffle step when the pitch is in the dirt.
4. To teach the baserunner to take an extra shuffle step when the catcher drops to his knees, which is essential to the success of the advance. The extra shuffle is possible because the catcher must recover from his kneeling down position.
5. To teach the baserunner to go if the ball kicks out or away from the catcher after taking an extra shuffle step.
6. To teach the baserunner to read the low pitch and anticipate a ball in the dirt or the catcher dropping to his knees.
7. To teach the runner that the extra shuffle step and break for the next base should be a continuous motion without hesitation.

Learn the Extra Shuffle Step

The extra shuffle step is the key to successfully advancing to the next base on balls in the dirt that are not handled cleanly by the catcher.

The extra shuffle step not only puts the runner 9 to 10 feet closer to the next base, but also puts him in motion, allowing for a fluid start. A body in motion tends to remain in motion.

The extra shuffle is made possible by the fact that the catcher has to drop to his knees and therefore is in poor throwing position.

Procedure

1. Place the catcher in full protective equipment, including protective cup, behind home plate.
2. The pitcher should be in front of the mound, 45 to 50 feet from home plate.
3. Place a protective screen in front of first base and behind second base to protect runners from errant throws.
4. Place a fielder in front of the protective screens at first and second bases to receive the catcher's throws.
5. Station baserunners at first base, three or four at a time.
6. Instruct the pitcher to throw balls in the dirt in front of the catcher.
7. The catcher attempts to block the ball and field it cleanly.
8. The baserunners take a secondary lead, then react to the ball in the dirt by taking an extra shuffle step, and if the ball "kicks out," they go hard for second base.
9. The catcher throws to the fielder in front of the protective screen at second base if the runners attempt to advance.

Setup for the Short Hop/Block and Run Drill:

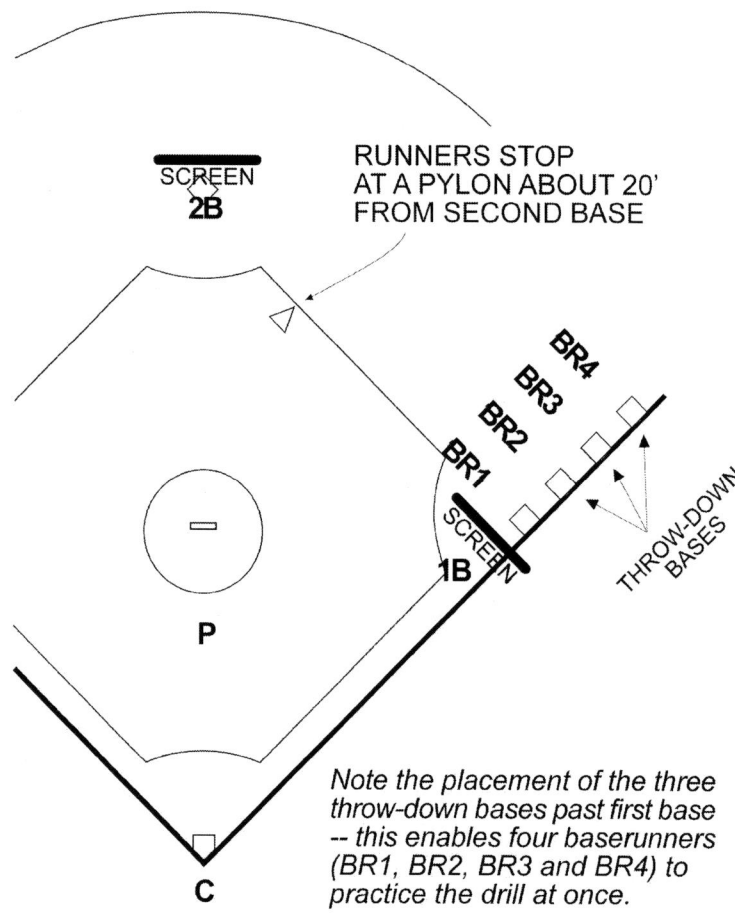

Note the placement of the three throw-down bases past first base -- this enables four baserunners (BR1, BR2, BR3 and BR4) to practice the drill at once.

The coach should evaluate whether the runners would have been safe or out, as well as the catcher's and runners' mechanics and reactions. To keep runners honest, the pitcher should occasionally throw pitches directly to the catcher, who then throws to the fielder in front of the protective screen at first base. This keeps baserunners from taking sloppy secondary leads or breaking early to second base.

Variation #1 – Runners on first and second bases:

1. Execute and set up the same as the previous drill.
2. Place baserunners at both first and second bases.
3. The runner at first base advances only if the runner at second attempts to move to third base.
4. The pitcher throws balls in the dirt in front of home plate for the catcher to block.
5. The baserunners extend their secondary leads by taking an extra shuffle step when the pitched ball is in the dirt, or the catcher drops to his knees attempting to block the ball.
6. The runner at second base learns how far the ball must "kick out" on the block attempt by the catcher to enable a safe advance to third base.
7. Again, the pitcher should occasionally throw the ball directly to the catcher, who attempts a pickoff throw to first base; this keeps the baserunners honest.
8. The baserunner at second base learns to advance to third base whenever the catcher throws behind him on a pickoff attempt at first base.

Variation #3 – Bases loaded:
1. Execute and set up the same as the previous drills.
2. Place runners at first, second, and third bases.
3. The pitcher throws balls in the dirt in front of home plate for the catcher to block.
4. The runners at first and second base advance only if the runner on third attempts to score.
5. The baserunners at first and second base extend their secondary leads by taking an extra shuffle step when the pitched ball is in the dirt, or the catcher drops to his knees to block the ball.
6. The runner at third practices the "walking lead" and learns how far the ball must kick out on the catcher's attempt to block the ball to enable him to advance and score a run.

Extra Runs Equals Extra Wins

This drill will pay dividends—it will result in countless advances and extra bases during the course of the season. Extra bases translate into extra runs, and extra runs mean extra wins.

When a runner is on first base, it usually takes two hits to score a run. But if the runner is able to advance to second base, one hit will most likely score him. This drill fosters alert and aggressive baserunning.

Good Luck!

The Bent Leg Slide

"I carry my cigars in my back pocket and was afraid I'd break them." – Philadelphia A's infielder Jimmy Dykes, on why he didn't slide on a particular play

---

The most knowledgeable and dynamic instructor I had the good fortune to meet during my minor league playing days was Bernie DeViveiros, a scout and instructor for the Detroit Tigers. Bernie was a creative and innovative thinker with a great passion and love for the game of baseball. His great teaching talent revolved around his enthusiasm for the game and a genuine desire to help players improve their talent and develop to their full capacity.

Bernie had the knack of making each player he was teaching feel *important,* which developed the player's self-confidence. "As long as you will listen and accept my instruction, I will help you," he would say. His message was simple, direct and easy to understand, and all he asked in return was an attentive ear.

Bernie helped the likes of Al Kaline, Harvey Kuenn and Maury Wills, and he was the scout who signed Mickey Lolich. Bernie continued to share his knowledge with me well after my playing days were over, and he charged me with a great deal of responsibility when he said, *"Jack, it is your responsibility to pass this knowledge on to future generations and to keep it alive."*

One of the things Bernie advocated strongly was the Bent Leg Slide, and he was instrumental in reviving its popularity. It was not uncommon to see Bernie, at age seventy-five, on the floor of a hotel lobby demonstrating how the Bent Leg Slide should be executed to a group of interested coaches.

Bernie's Notes on the Bent Leg Slide:

Here are the notes Bernie DeViveiros gave me on the mechanics of the Bent Leg Slide:

- Remove your spike shoes to prevent injury while learning and practicing. Run in stocking feet or tennis shoes.
- Use dry lawn, the shorter cut the better (and brown if possible), as a sliding pit.
- Inside, use the gym floor or any carpeted surface.
- Do not wet down the sliding area. It's a mess. Dampness makes you stick.
- Use protective pants or a pair of coveralls over a clean uniform to prevent soiling, and to prevent the annoying strawberry (a skin burn caused on the side of the rump by friction, if you are not sliding on the *calf of the bottom leg*).
- Use knee-length jockey shorts or any kind of sateen pants light in weight. Tight-fitting shorts are best—they cannot roll up and expose the skin to the slide if the player leans too far back. Throw the old-type sliding pads away.

THE BENT LEG SLIDE

- A sateen slip sewed into the uniform on the inside from the belt and hung loosely to the knee, 18 inches long and 12 inches wide. The cotton side is to the body and the sheen side rides with the pants. They never ravel up the run. Wilson and McGregor Sporting Goods Company did this for Jack Homel, the former trainer of the Detroit Tigers. You could make up a pair and tie. This will prevent any chance of burning when leaning too far back on a slide and not on *the calf of the bottom leg*.

- All slides are made in a half-sitting position. All slides are made on *the calf of the bottom leg*, which is bent under. Bend them both, if you like, in learning. All tags of the base are made with the top leg, which is held about six inches off the ground and in a relaxed position. You cannot hurt the top leg; it is the bottom leg which must be *bent under*. You just ride the calf of the bottom leg. Be relaxed in all slides. Do not fight it—a slide is a glide.

- Most important: As a rule of thumb, you have only one good side and it is *your master side*. It can be either your right or left side. Just sit down and nature will put it under for you. You can feel it—it is more comfortable. In other words, always slide on the side that is best for you and stay on that side for the rest of your life. *Most broken legs are the result of sliding on the wrong side*. Some people just cannot bend both legs under, and if the bottom leg is straight out, you are in trouble. Some people are ambidextrous and can use both sides. Be doubly sure—take no chances. A broken leg is the worst thing that can happen to you, so do it right!

- With the Bent Leg Slide, you cannot get hurt if you wanted to.

- Slide straight in and tag the bag with the top leg. That is the quickest way in, and the toughest to tag. Forget the hook slide, which has caused more broken legs than any other slide. It has caused the loss of many great stars, my reason of getting it out of baseball.

- To do a slide: First place a loose bag on the lawn. Then start at a short distance and be sure you bend the leg that is right for you. You will slide on the calf of this leg, and not on the rump. The first thing you do as you go into your slide is to throw your hands in the air, with your head slightly back. This will put you on or about a 30 degree angle and will bring your knee up, to avoid jamming it into the ground and preventing the knee burn, which will happen if you slide too much in a forward position. The knee burn is caused because you have no protection over your knee. Wear your socks high to the knee, forget the fancy role, and keep the socks high and flat to the knees. Wear a kneepad if the trouble is consistent.

- Throwing your arms up will also prevent you from jamming your hand in the ground and straining your wrist and fingers.

- Start your slide about six to eight feet from the bag. Do not slide late. It is best to have someone stand over the bag at the beginning, as it will bring you down better. *All slides are made with speed at the base of the slide; all slides are made close to the ground, to bring lightness*.

- Keep the bag loose on the ground. Do not slide uphill; a downgrade is better. *Do not hesitate in your slide; it can hurt you. When you are in doubt, always slide.* Do not let a baseman hold you up; *slide, slide, slide*.

- If you are late in your slide, just try raising your body into a pop-up slide as you hit the bag. This will take all the jar out of the slide when the base is anchored down.

- *To do a pop-up slide*, just sort of lift yourself up like taking a deep breath as you slide along, the speed will bring you up. Do not try to come up too quick—slide along and gradually come up, with the top foot on the bag, ready to run again.

- A slight push with the bottom hand will bring you up, but this is temporary. Learn to do it with your arms up. Speed is the trick—it will bring you up.

- A slide is a glide. It is not a leap or a jump. It is a glide.

- Learn to slide on both sides of the bag and tag the bag with the hands and not the foot.
- Always slide on your good side no matter which side of the bag you go to.
- Forget the headfirst slide. It can hurt you and you fool no one.
- Sliding is fun… enjoy it! You can make many slides on the grass and not feel it. Practice, practice, practice…it is simple, learn to do it good.

Signed, Bernie DeViveiros, D.S. (Doctor of Sliding).

Master Side Drill

Purpose: To have each player determine which side of his body is his "master side" (the side he will slide on) when using the Bent Leg Slide.

Procedure:
1. Have players sit on the ground assuming the Bent Leg Slide position. They will naturally choose one side over the other, which will be their master side.
2. Players assume the Bent Leg Slide position and push themselves along the ground to become familiar with their master side and how it makes contact with the ground.
3. The coach makes appropriate suggestions and corrections.

Partner Pull Drill

Purpose: To have each player learn to slide on his master side.

Procedure:
1. Divide players into groups of two.
2. One player sits on the ground in the Bent Leg Slide position. The other stands in front of him.
3. The standing player grasps the hands of his partner and pulls him along the ground so that he can feel how the slide should be executed.
4. The coach makes appropriate suggestions and corrections, then players switch positions.

Pop-up Slide Drill

Purpose: To teach players the pop-up slide.

Procedure:
1. Follow steps 1-2 of the Partner Pull Drill above.
2. The standing player grasps the hands of his partner and pulls him along the ground so that he can feel how the slide should be executed.
3. On the coach's command "Up!" the standing player pulls his partner to his feet, completing the pop-up slide. The partner on the ground (the slider) uses his momentum to help with the pop-up.
4. The coach makes appropriate suggestions and corrections, then players switch positions.

Good Luck!

The Measured Leadoff

"If you don't know where you are going, you might wind up someplace else." – Yogi Berra

---

In baseball, as in life, it is important to know where we are. Global Positioning System (GPS) devices have been developed to help us know our location; however, when taking a *primary lead* away from first base, most baserunners have no idea where they are.

Their primary lead varies and is rarely the same distance from the base, regardless of who the pitcher is. Because no GPS device is available to tell the baserunner where he is when leading off first base, the "measured lead" becomes the baserunner's GPS.

The measured lead is a method of determining distance from a base by taking a prescribed number of steps away from that base—in this case, first base.

The measured lead method of leading off base was first introduced to me by Tom Trebelhorn, a former high school student and player of mine. Tom is a very bright and intelligent individual, and following his graduation from Portland State University he entered professional baseball. Tom managed both the Milwaukee Brewers and Chicago Cubs, and has also been the bench coach for the Baltimore Orioles.

Advantages of the Measured Lead

▶ The baserunner knows his exact distance from the base at all times.

▶ The baserunner takes the same lead off the base *every time*… and then can adjust.

▶ It eliminates haphazard leads off base.

▶ The baserunner does not have to look back toward the base to see where he is—looking back makes him vulnerable to the pickoff.

▶ It standardizes the primary lead regardless of playing field conditions (a skinned infield vs. grass).

How to Take a Measured Lead

When leading off first base, the baserunner takes a prescribed number of steps off the base to establish his primary lead, as follows:

STEP….CROSSOVER….ADJUST

STEP: With the *left foot* in contact with first base and the body square to and facing the infield, the baserunner takes a *sideways, lateral step* with his right foot directly toward second base.

CROSSOVER: After the right foot hits the ground, a quick *crossover step* directly toward second base with the left foot follows. It is absolutely essential that the baserunner's body remains facing the infield and does not turn toward second base while making the crossover step. (Turning the body toward second base during the crossover step would result in a loss of lateral movement and make the baserunner vulnerable to being picked off first base.) The crossover step is done very quickly and alertly. If done correctly, a pickoff is highly unlikely.

ADJUST: The *adjustment step* completes the initial sequence. After the crossover step is completed, the baserunner brings his left foot to his right foot in a closing action. The left foot replaces the right foot and the baserunner steps out with his right foot toward second base and into an athletic stance.

Once the baserunner completes the measured leadoff sequence, his left foot will be approximately 9 to 10 feet from first base. From this distance, a return to first base can be made standing up.

Extending the Primary Lead

To extend the primary lead, the baserunner moves his right foot toward second base and then closes with his left foot, using a quick half-step. The half-step enables the baserunner to maintain body control and quick lateral movement.

The extended lead will place the baserunner's left foot approximately 12 to 15 feet from first base. The limit of an individual baserunner's leadoff will depend upon his ability and quickness and the pitcher's pickoff move to first base. Trebelhorn stated, "When the baserunner passes the nine-foot mark, his legs must be ready to respond to an attempted pickoff throw from the pitcher."

The baserunner must have his left foot on first base until he is *certain* the pitcher has the baseball, or he sees that the pitcher steps on the pitching rubber. (If the pitcher steps on the rubber without the baseball, it is a balk.)

The baserunner takes his measured lead when the pitcher steps on the pitching rubber and is getting his sign from the catcher. The primary lead is taken early, before the pitcher goes into his stretch. This safeguards against the pitcher making a quick pickoff move while taking his stretch and catching the baserunner off balance.

Returning to First Base

The crossover step is the quickest and most powerful way to return to first base. The return to first base begins with a left-foot pivot and a strong right-leg crossover step.

Returning from a nine-foot lead: From this distance, a return to first can be made standing up. A left-foot pivot and a right-leg crossover step followed by a step with the left foot to the back half of the base enables the baserunner to return to first base standing up.

Returning from an extended lead of 12 to 15 feet: Once the baserunner extends his primary lead past nine feet, he must dive back to first base. The dive back to first base is a pivot on the left foot, followed by a strong right-leg crossover step and a dive to the right field side of first base. The base is touched with the outstretched right hand. The left hand should be outstretched to prevent finger injuries that could result if the left hand is under the body.

Methods of Leading off First Base

The baserunner takes his lead when the pitcher steps on the rubber and is getting his sign from the catcher. There are three slightly different "lines" he can take when leading off the base, and they each come with their own pros and cons:

▶ **Leading off the front edge of first base:** The baserunner takes his primary lead off first base with his toes on a line that runs from the inside of first base to the inside of second base. The advantage of this method is that it creates an optical illusion—the runner appears to be closer to the base than he actually is. Since the primary lead appears shorter, there are fewer pickoff attempts by the pitcher. The disadvantage of this method is that the baserunner is closer to the first baseman's tag, and reaching for the base is more difficult as the first baseman may block off the baserunner's access to the base.

▶ **Leading off the back edge of the base:** The baserunner takes his primary lead off first base on a line that runs from the outside edge of first base to the outside edge of second base. The advantage of this method is that the baserunner is not obstructed by the first baseman and is farther from his tag when returning to first base on a pitcher's pickoff attempt. The disadvantage is that the baserunner appears to have a longer lead off the base and will likely draw more pickoff throws.

▶ **Leading off even with the base:** Joe Morgan made this statement, *"Be sure in leading off that you stay in a line even with the base, or a little bit forward of it. If you lead off behind the imaginary line between first and second it not only costs you extra steps, but to the pitcher, it makes it seem as if there is a wider distance between you and the bag than there actually is. As a result, he's more likely to throw over."* Leading off even with the base and in a direct line toward second base is probably the most satisfactory method for the majority of baserunners. It is a compromise between the other two extremes. Returning from this position to the back of the base is no problem and the leadoff does not provoke an inordinate number of pickoff attempts.

Learn the Measured Lead

The measured lead enables the baserunner to develop a uniform and consistent lead off first base. It also enables the baserunner to adjust his primary lead according to his individual quickness and daring.

Good Luck!

Stealing Second Base Using a Moving Lead

"A good base stealer should make the whole infield jumpy. Whether you steal or not, you're changing the rhythm of the game. If the pitcher is concerned about you, he isn't concentrating enough on the batter." – Joe Morgan

---

A highly effective way to *steal second base against a right-handed pitcher* involves using a short lead off first base in combination with a *moving lead*. Its advantages:

*1) The **short lead off** does not look like one from which the baserunner will attempt a steal.*

*2) The **moving lead** gives the baserunner the extra jump necessary to steal the base.*

By adjusting his leadoff at first base from a long to a short lead, the smart baserunner can often dupe and then exploit the pitcher, enabling him to steal second base with relative ease. If the pitcher is a "rhythm pitcher," the baserunner has an additional advantage that can also be exploited.

The adjusted lead will enable a runner with average speed or below-average speed to become a good base stealer. The baserunner does not appear to the defense to be a base-stealing threat, and the defense often becomes complacent. Once the runner takes a short lead off first base, this complacency is reinforced.

Setting Up the Pitcher Using the Long One-Way Lead

The measured lead off first base is *step, crossover, and adjust* (see the previous chapter). This maneuver will place the runner approximately 9 to 10 feet from first base. The baserunner takes his measured lead off first base and then adds an additional shuffle step. This will result in the runner having a slightly longer-than-usual lead off the base.

The runner's lead off first base is "one way"—that is, he is physically and mentally prepared to dive back into first base. He is anticipating a pickoff throw by the pitcher. The runner's lead away from first base should be long enough to entice the pitcher to throw over to first base, but short enough to allow the runner to dive back to the base safely.

When utilizing the one-way lead, the baserunner must interpret any movement by the pitcher as a pickoff attempt and return to first base quickly.

Cashing In With the Short Leadoff

After the pitcher makes a pickoff attempt or two at first base, the runner should adjust his lead off the base from *long to short*. Using the measured lead, the baserunner's leadoff at first base is **step…crossover…with no adjustment step.** This will appreciably shorten his primary lead.

This short lead off should lull the pitcher into a sense of complacency. Feeling that his pickoff attempts have intimidated the runner, resulting in the runner shortening his leadoff, the pitcher is now vulnerable for exploitation by the alert baserunner.

The short leadoff is a good decoy because it does not look like one from which the baserunner will attempt to steal. It should be noted that the majority of pitchers will throw to first base a maximum of two times when attempting a pickoff. Rarely, if ever, will a pitcher make three attempts. Consequently, many coaches instruct their runners to steal second base on the *pitcher's first movement* after two pickoff attempts have been made.

Rhythm Pitchers

Many pitchers develop a rhythm: *one, two, three, and throw*. The alert runner can exploit this.

The baserunner should count "1001, 1002." It may be necessary to add a count or two ("1003, 1004") or subtract a count to get the correct timing. If the pitcher throws on 1003, take a short controlled shuffle step, bringing the left leg under after counting "1001, 1002." If the timing is correct, step out with the right foot and break hard for second base.

If the timing is wrong…hold up! Don't go! The shuffle step will put the runner back to his normal primary lead. If the pitcher throws to first base, push off the right foot and dive back into the bag.

Study and time the pitcher so that you can out-guess him. This will enable the average runner to become a base-stealing threat, often stealing second base standing up.

A Great Combination

The *short lead off first base* combined with the *moving lead* against the right-handed rhythm pitcher will enable the baserunner to get an extra-good jump. When timed correctly, a stolen base is almost guaranteed.

Good Luck!

Offensive Strategy

Hitting Strategies

"I have observed that baseball is not unlike a war, and when you come right down to it, we batters are the heavy artillery." – Tyrus Raymond Cobb

Taking the Pitch

To *take* simply means to not swing at a pitch. When taking a pitch, the batter should always stride through with the pitch. This makes the pitch appear higher than if the batter simply stands there, and increases the batter's chances of the pitch being called a ball.

When is it a good idea to *take*?

- A 3-0 count is an automatic take.
- Take a strike when the pitcher is wild. Do not help him by swinging at bad pitches.
- Take if your team is behind late in the game.
- Take if the first batter in the inning makes an out on the first pitch—we do not want two outs on two pitches. Make the pitcher work.
- Take if the pitcher walks the hitter ahead of you on four pitches.
- Take the first pitch if the pitcher has walked two batters in a row. If the pitch is a ball, take a strike.
- If it is important enough to take with the count 2-0, then you should also take on 3-1.

> **COACHING KEY:**
> *Be sure your players know what it means to **"take a strike."***
>
> *Simply put, it means the hitter doesn't have the option to swing until there is one strike in the count. If the count is 0-0, 1-0, 2-0 or 3-0, the hitter is taking the pitch.*

Leadoff Man Philosophy

In baseball, the term *leadoff man* has dual meaning. Yes, it refers to the hitter in the number-one slot in the lineup. But how many innings during a game does this player actually lead off? One, maybe two? Three innings at the most?

The term *leadoff man* also refers to the first player batting in any inning. If the cleanup hitter starts the second inning, he is said to be *leading off* the inning. Other than the first inning, *any* player in the lineup can be your leadoff man. And when I speak of "Leadoff Man Philosophy," I'm speaking of a philosophy for the first hitter of an inning, not just the hitter in the number-one slot in the lineup.

Many coaches often overlook this valuable offensive strategy. When leading off an inning, players should remember:

- The primary concern is to get the first man in each inning on base.

- The leadoff man in each inning takes a pitch if the count is either 2-0 or 3-1. (Of course, a 3-0 count is an automatic take.)
- Using Leadoff Man Philosophy increases the pitcher's pitch count, which may tire him in later innings.
- The Leadoff Man Philosophy in many instances forces the pitcher to throw three consecutive strikes, which creates pressure for the pitcher. (The odds of the batter walking are usually greater than his batting average.)
- You may not want to use the Leadoff Man Philosophy late in the game with a powerful hitter at bat and the game tied, or when the pitch count is less important.

Catch-up Strategy

When a team is trailing in the late innings (the final three scheduled innings of the game), it can adopt a "Catch-up Strategy." Communication with players is simplified once players understand the concept. When the coach says, "We're in catch-up," the players immediately know what the coach's strategy is, thus avoiding detailed instruction.

- In Catch-Up Strategy, the hitter may swing at the first pitch if it is to his liking (a good strike).
- If the first pitch is a ball, take a strike.
- The hitter must take when the count is 2-0 or 3-1. (*Possible exception:* There are runners in scoring position and you need the runs.)

Against the Curve

Make the pitcher prove to you that he has control of his curveball. Take the curveball on the first pitch and look for a fastball. Too many hitters swing at curveballs out of the strike zone on the first pitch and are then behind in the count. Now they are vulnerable for more curveballs.

If the first pitch is a curveball for a ball, lay for the fastball on the next pitch—99% of catchers and/or coaches will call for the fastball to even the count.

And take notice—does the pitcher give any visual checks or tip off the fact that he is throwing a curveball? Does he change his arm angle, adjust the grip in his glove, or have any abnormal twisting or curling of his wrist? Do not guess curveball unless you are absolutely 100% sure!

> ### *In Wake of the Fake Take, the Hitter Can Rake*
>
> The hitter should look for the take sign on 2-0 and 3-1 counts. The third base coach may be able to get the hitter a good pitch to hit by *faking* the take sign—making the opponent think the take sign is on! The pitcher may then throw the ball down the middle of the plate. A little good acting by both the coach and the hitter is helpful.

Fake the Suicide Squeeze

The purpose of a *fake suicide squeeze* is to force the pitcher to throw a ball when he thinks the suicide squeeze play is on. The best time to use this play is when the count is either 2-0 or 3-1 and there is a runner on third base. It's a great play to use with the bases loaded. Another result of the fake suicide squeeze is that it will enable you to squeeze when necessary by making the pitcher think you are faking.

There are two ways a fake suicide squeeze can be handled:

1) As the pitcher's arm drops down and starts forward, the hitter should turn as though bunting and take the pitch. The runner at third base must make a legitimate fake toward home plate to give the play realism. On the other hand, he should avoid being picked off base by the catcher—to do this, he should start his fake break with a shorter lead than normal to avoid being too far down the baseline.

2) The purpose of this play is to avoid the double play with runners on first and third bases with one out and a slow runner at bat. Fake the suicide squeeze and steal the runner from first base. The defense will direct its attention to the runner at third base and will concede the steal of second base as it attempts to defend the squeeze play. With runners now on second and third bases, the slow runner at bat is no longer a double play concern.

For more details on faking the suicide squeeze, see page 241.

A Few Specific Times to Be Aggressive

▶ **With two outs and a runner at second:** With two outs and a runner at second base, if the hitter drives a base hit into the outfield, have the batter continue on to second base as the outfielder throws the ball to home plate. If the infielder cuts the throw to play on the batter/runner, you have a run. And if the throw goes to home plate and the runner from second base is safe, you have scored a run and have a runner in scoring position at second base. *If there is no legitimate play at home plate, the batter/runner should not run into a sure out at second base.*

If the throw to home plate is cut off and a play is made on the batter/runner, the batter/runner should get into a rundown until the runner from second base has crossed home plate. *Do not get tagged out before the run scores.* This play forces the cutoff man to make a decision on a close play at home plate.

▶ **Also with two outs and a runner at second:** When there is a runner on second base with two outs and a single is hit to the outfield, send the runner home *if his chances of scoring are greater than the next hitter's batting average.* You must always think ahead!

This gamble has its disadvantages: you lose a possible first-and-third offensive situation, and you may start the next inning with a weak hitter at bat, if the runner is thrown out. The advantage is that you force the defense to "play the game at home plate" where they cannot make *any* mistakes.

▶ **On a two-out single to the outfield:** It is a good gamble for the batter/runner to try for two bases, if he is fast and if the defensive team has an outfielder who is slow and/or lazy in getting to the ball. The pressure is on the outfielder to make a perfect throw to second base.

Players: Do Not Do Your Own Umpiring

Tell your players: Do not leave a base until they know for sure that they are out. If they guess wrong, they may be called out. If there is any doubt whether they are safe or out, or they did not see the umpire's call, they should ask the umpire to be sure of their status before leaving the base. If they are unsure whether a ball is fair or foul, play the ball as if it is fair—the umpire only verbalizes on foul balls, and the worst thing that can happen is the hitter will have to come back.

If you're guessing and you guess wrong, you may cost your team a hit, an out, a run or the game.

Good Luck!

Baserunning Strategies

"Baserunning can win and lose games. It's something that's very simple that at times gets overlooked." – Chase Utley

---

At Portland State University, our offensive philosophy was predicated upon getting runners to third base with fewer than two outs. Here is why this is important:

- Runs can be scored without base hits!
- A run can be scored on a fair fly ball.
- A run can be scored on a foul fly ball.
- A run can be scored on a ground ball.
- A run can be scored on a suicide squeeze.
- A run can be scored on a safety squeeze.
- A run can be scored on a wild pitch.
- A run can be scored on a passed ball.
- A run can be scored on an error, either fielding or throwing.
- A run can be scored on a balk by the pitcher.
- A run can be scored by stealing home.
- A run can sometimes be scored on a dropped third strike by the catcher while he is throwing to first base.

Also, the defensive team must decide whether to play the infield in or back. Playing the infield back concedes a run on most ground balls to the infield. Playing the infield in doubles the batter's chances of getting a hit.

Going from First to Third

Advancing to third base from first base on a base hit to the outfield is the most common way for a runner to reach third. Therefore, the runner on first base must thoroughly understand the conditions necessary to justify an attempt to advance to third base.

The runner on first base should consider the following:

▶ **The number of outs:** With no outs or two outs, take no chances. If you cannot make third base standing up with no outs or two outs, don't go! If you are thrown out at third base with no outs, you destroy the possibility of a big inning. And do not make the third out at third base, because you are already in scoring position at second. On the other hand, gamble with one out! If you have a 50/50 chance of being safe and the score is close or your team is ahead, *go for it!*

▶ **The outfield:** How deep are they playing? How well does the outfielder who is fielding the ball throw? *Know in advance where the outfielders are playing!*

▶ **Other things to consider:** How hard is the ball hit? What is the condition of the playing field? (A wet baseball is difficult to throw accurately.) What is the score of the game? How important is your run? (If way behind in the score, *play it safe!* Don't take your team out of the inning.)

▶ **Advance to third base on a hit to the outfield if:**

- The angle the outfielder must go to field the ball is extreme.
- The angle of the outfielder is away from third base and to his glove side.
- The outfielder has not fielded the ball as the runner approaches second base and his momentum is away from third base.
- The outfielder has a very weak throwing arm.
- The ball is hit moderately deep and to the center fielder's left.
- The catcher fails to cover third base when the third baseman charges to field a sacrifice bunt.

▶ **Do not advance to third base on a hit to the outfield if:**

- There are no outs or two outs and you cannot make it standing up.
- The ball is hit sharply right at the outfielder.
- The outfielder is fielding the ball as you approach second base.
- Your team is way behind in the score, and if there is any doubt whether you will be safe, regardless of the number of outs.

On a long fly ball to the outfield that you are uncertain will drop in safely, advance as far toward second base as you know you can get back safely, so that you can score or at least make third base safely if the ball is not caught. If you have passed second base and the ball is caught, you must retouch second base on your return to first.

On singles to the right field side of the diamond, you should pick up the third base coach when you are about 30 feet from second base (or 20 feet in youth league), or look back over your shoulder to find the ball before you approach second base without slowing down.

Going from Second to Third

▶ **Advance from second to third base if:**

- A ground ball passes the pitcher and takes the shortstop to his left.
- The ball is a slow roller that brings the shortstop or third baseman in on the grass.
- The third baseman is playing very deep and the ball takes him into the hole.
- The shortstop goes deep into the hole—advance on his throw to first base. "Read white"—that is, see the ball leave the shortstop's hand before advancing.

▶ **Do not advance from second to third if:**

- The ball is hit directly back to the pitcher.
- The ball is hit directly to the shortstop.
- The ball is hit directly to the third baseman.

With no outs, tag up on fly balls to the outfield so that you may advance to third base after the catch and be there with one out. On short fly balls, go part way (as far as you know you can get back safely)—if you're tagging up on a short fly ball, you can't advance after the catch, but you may be able to advance if the ball drops safely.

With one out, go part way on any fly ball that you are uncertain will be caught—if the ball drops in you will have a chance to score. On fly balls to the outfield with one out, when it becomes apparent the ball will be caught, tag up and advance after the catch.

Apply the Pressure

Being able to advance to third base consistently is true "pressure baseball." It is the manifestation of intelligent, aggressive, and controlled baserunning. It also reflects how well-coached a team is, and the players' understanding of the game.

We have only scratched the surface of the baserunning game. The sole purpose was to touch upon the importance of being on third base with fewer than two outs, and how runs can be scored without base hits.

Good Luck!

"Think and Grow Rich"

"Just hold them for a few innings, fellas. I'll think of something." – Charlie Dressen

---

Napoleon Hill was a famous philosopher of personal achievement. One of the books he authored was titled *Think and Grow Rich,* based on the Andrew Carnegie formula for making money.

In a baseball context, "Think and Grow Rich" means scoring more runs, which in turn should equate to more wins. Successful coaching demands that the coach recognize and then take advantage of as many situations as possible during the course of a game and season.

Do you recognize a situation and then take advantage of it? Or do you allow it to slip by? By Thinking, the coach and team Grow Rich in terms of runs and wins.

In this chapter, we'll elaborate on two more situations on which you can capitalize.

Two by Two

Let's say, with *two outs* and a runner on second base (or runners on second and third bases), a base hit to the outfield results in an outfielder making a throw to the plate in an attempt to get the runner from second. *In this spot, the hitter should continue on to second base.*

This action will force the cutoff man to make a decision to either cut the ball off and play on the batter/runner advancing toward second, or allow the throw to go through to home plate.

If the cutoff man chooses to cut the ball off, a *run will score.*

If the cutoff man allows the throw to go through to the plate and the runner attempting to score from second is thrown out, the batter/runner advancing toward second base is of no consequence. However, if the runner attempting to score from second is safe at home plate, the offensive team will have a runner in scoring position, where he will likely score on a base hit to the outfield.

Failure to advance in this situation and remaining at first base would normally require two base hits to score a run, which has a low probability of occurring.

▶ **The coach's responsibilities:** The coach must have a prearranged sign to remind the hitter that he is to advance. And this situation must be practiced during "Situation Hitting Drills" so that the hitter understands his responsibilities.

▶ **The hitter's responsibilities:** The hitter must *read the ball* to be sure that a play or throw will be made to home plate. If there is no play on the runner scoring from second base, stay at first base. He must *go hard* to prevent an easy putout. He must *go looking* to see the cut-off man's decision. And he must *get hung up* if necessary—if the defense cuts off the throw from the outfield and the batter/runner is obviously going to be out at second base, he must stay in the rundown long enough to allow the runner to score before the third out is made. This is absolutely critical—do not make the third out before the runner crosses home plate.

▶ **The runner's responsibilities:** It's simple—the runner from second runs hard and attempts to score.

Exploit This Similar Situation

Let's say, with runners at first and third, a routine fly ball is hit to left field, deep enough that the runner at third will tag up and attempt to score, but shallow enough that the outfielder will have a legitimate chance to throw the runner out at home plate.

When the runner at first base realizes that the outfielder will likely attempt to throw to the plate, *he should tag up at first base and break hard for second.* The runner at first must "read white" before breaking toward second base—that is, he must see the ball leave the outfielder's hand before advancing. This will protect him against a fake throw or a change of mind by the outfielder and a subsequent throw to second base.

As in the situation we previously discussed, this play forces the cutoff man to make a decision. If he cuts the ball off to play on the runner advancing toward second base, a run will score. If he allows the ball to go through to home plate, the runner at first will advance to second (unless, of course, the runner from third is thrown out for the final out of the inning).

Again, by advancing the runner to second base in this spot, the offensive team will likely score a run on a hit to the outfield. Remaining at first base would require two hits to score a run, a low probability for success.

> **COACHING KEY:**
> When a runner is **tagging up**, it must be noted that once the outfielder touches the ball, the runner is free to leave the base and attempt an advance to the next base.
>
> If the outfielder juggles the ball, the baserunner may advance the moment initial contact with the ball is made. The outfielder does not have to catch the ball cleanly or have complete control of the ball before the runner may advance. Otherwise, the fielder could juggle the ball all the way into the infield, thus freezing the runner.

The runner from first must *go hard* to prevent an easy out. He must *go looking* to see the cutoff man's decision. And he must *get hung up* if necessary—if the defense cuts off the throw from the outfield and the runner from first is obviously going to be out at second base, he must stay in the rundown long enough to allow the runner to score before the third out is made. Again, do not make the third out before the runner crosses home plate.

If the fly ball is too shallow, neither baserunner should attempt to advance—this play does not exist. Instead, the baserunner at first base must go as far as he can get back safely.

▶ **The coach's responsibilities:** The coach must have his team practice this situation during "Situation Hitting Drills" so that runners understand their responsibilities. And he must have a prearranged verbal sign to remind the baserunner at first base that he must tag-up and advance on a *routine fly ball*.

▶ **Responsibilities of the runner at third base:** Tag up on all fly balls to the outfield, either fair or foul; attempt to score if instructed by the third base coach; and *go hard*.

▶ **Responsibilities of the runner at first base:** Tag-up at first base on routine fly balls to the outfield, either fair or foul; "read white" before advancing to second base; and *go hard, go looking, and if necessary, get hung up.*

A Good Trade

Give these situations serious thought. They will pay real dividends during the course of the season. When the runner at second base represents an important run, trading a run for an out is a fair exchange. The pressure is on the defense to make the right decision.

Good Luck!

The Hit-and-Run

"Man may penetrate the outer reaches of the universe, he may solve the very secret of eternity itself, but for me, the ultimate human experience is to witness the flawless execution of the hit-and-run."
– Branch Rickey

The hit-and-run was originally designed by John McGraw to decrease the possibility of the double play. With a slow runner at bat, the runner at first base attempts to steal second base, and the hitter protects the runner by swinging at the pitch regardless of its location. If the ball is hit on the ground, there will be no play at second base even though the ball is fielded cleanly by an infielder. The offensive team has thus avoided the double play and has advanced the baserunner into scoring position. If the hitter is successful and drives the ball through the infield for a hit, the runner from first base most likely will advance to third base, or score if the hit goes for extra bases.

The hit-and-run is a do-or-die play and should not be used indiscriminately. Paul Richards, the onetime Baltimore Orioles manager who was considered an excellent strategist, made the following comments relative to the hit-and-run play as an offensive tactic:

"Keep a record as to how many times the play worked, as against how many times it failed for any of the following reasons."

- The batter swings at a bad ball at the wrong time (with a count of 3-1, 3-2, 2-0).
- There is a line drive at an infielder, resulting in a double play.
- The defensive team calls a pitch-out.
- Either the runner or the hitter misses the sign.
- An infielder moving to cover second base fields a ball that would have been a hit.

Richards' conclusion: "The hit-and-run probably takes you out of more innings than it creates."

Don't Use the Hit-and-Run with:
- A high-average line drive hitter.
- A power hitter.
- Two outs (you want the extra-base hit in this situation).
- A slow runner on first (if the hitter swings and misses the slow runner will be thrown out).
- A fast runner at bat (the chances are the fast runner will not hit into a double play).

The hit-and-run play places the burden on the hitter and many players do not like to have to hit a particular pitch.

On the other hand, Earnshaw Cook in his book *Percentage Baseball* states, "The only defense against the hit-and-run is the pitch-out, eschewed by most managers and pitchers with the count against them. The play assuredly deserves more serious and frequent attention than it normally receives."

Advantages of the Hit-and-Run:

- It avoids the double play if the ball is hit on the ground.
- It allows the runner on first base to advance a minimum of two bases if the hitter hits safely to the outfield.
- With runners on first and second bases and a base hit to the outfield, the runner on second base will score and the runner on first base will most likely advance to third base. This is a total of four bases advanced!
- If a team has a non-aggressive hitter who won't swing the bat, this forces him to pull the trigger.
- A weak hitter advances the runner into scoring position simply by hitting a ground ball.
- The hit-and-run play opens holes in the infield as infielders move to cover their bases. With runners on first and second bases, two positions are opened. With a runner on first base, either the second base or shortstop position is opened.
- If successful, the hit-and-run play has a very positive emotional impact upon the offensive team and is a real "bummer" for the defense.

Mechanics of the Hit-and-Run:

Responsibilities of the runner on first base:
1. The runner at first breaks for second base on the pitcher's first move to home plate as in a normal steal attempt.
2. On approximately the third or fourth step toward second base, the runner "looks in." That is, he takes a quick glance toward the hitter as the ball enters the impact zone. This glance is chin to left shoulder as the ball enters the impact zone, and is a very quick look. No staring allowed—this would jeopardize his chances of stealing second base in the event the hitter swings and misses.
3. *Read the ball off the bat as it enters the impact zone.*
4. The runner reacts to the pitch as follows:
   – On a *swing and miss:* attempt to steal second base.
   – On a *line drive to the infield:* keep going—you're doubled up anyway if the ball is caught.
   – On a *ground ball:* go hard!
   – On a *fly ball:* go as far as you can and still get back safely if it looks like it will be caught.
5. Don't be duped by an alert infielder who fakes a ground ball when the ball is actually hit in the air. (This results when the runner fails to look in on the pitch and has no idea where the ball is.)
6. Theoretically, the right-handed hitter should hit the ball to the second base position, and the left-handed hitter to the shortstop position, because these positions will be opened as the infielder evacuates his position to cover second base.

Responsibilities of the hitter:
1. The hitter must protect the runner by swinging at the pitch regardless of its location…there is *no taking!* (Exception: If the pitch is thrown at the hitter, duck!)
2. Hit the ball where it's pitched. It is difficult enough for most young players to make contact, let alone place the ball to a specific area of the field.
3. Hit the ball on the ground if possible. "Tomahawk" the high pitches—that is, bring the head of the bat over the top. This will increase the hitter's chances of hitting a line drive or ground ball.

Look-In Drill

Purpose: To teach baserunners to "look in."

Procedure:
1. The coach should be in the right-handed batter's box. Station a pitcher on the mound, a catcher behind home plate and runners at first base.
2. To facilitate the drill have two or three runners go at a time.
3. The pitcher throws out of the stretch and the runners break for second as they would if stealing.
4. "Look in"—after 3 or 4 steps, the runners should take a quick glance in toward home plate, looking at the coach who is standing in the right-handed batters box.
5. The coach points either up or down. Players must verbalize "up!" or "down!" to designate whether the fictitious batter hit the ball in the air or on the ground.
6. The coach makes necessary suggestions to runners, such as "Don't go looking" or "Quick glances only!"
7. Runners should remember: You have to steal second base if the hitter swings and misses!

Hit-and-Run Drill

Purpose: To teach hitters that they must swing at the pitch to protect the runner, and to teach runners to look in, read the ball off the bat and react accordingly.

Procedure:
1. Station a pitcher on the mound to throw batting practice. Divide the squad into 3 groups: Group 1 bats; Group 2 runs at first base; Group 3 is in the field shagging. Rotate groups after a prescribed number of times at bat.
2. *The hitter gets one pitch and one pitch only!* If he takes, he loses that time at bat.
3. The runners at first break for second base, look-in and react to the hit—read the ball off the bat!

Other Considerations

▶ **A natural hit-and-run spot:** A natural hit-and-run occurs with a runner on first base or runners on first and second bases, one out and 3-2 count on the batter—when the runners on first and second attempt to steal, two infield positions are opened. This is made more effective if the hitter is a pull hitter. The exception to the natural hit-and-run in this spot would be if the lead runner is very slow or the hitter is an easy strikeout.

▶ **Maximize your chance to score—consider not sending the runner from first base:** With runners on first and third bases, no outs, a 3-2 count and you have an important run at third base, don't send the runner from first base! Why? You must maximize your chances of scoring the runner from third. A line drive doubles up the runner and a strike-out-and-throw-out is a double play. In both cases, you have lost one opportunity to drive in the run. Instead of three chances to score, you will only have two. If the infield is back and turns the double play on a ground ball, the run scores from third base anyway. *Think about it!*

▶ **Watch the middle infielders:** If you play against a team whose middle infielders both evacuate their positions in a first-and-third steal situation, the hit-and-run is an excellent play (with one out) because both infield positions will be open, greatly increasing the hitter's chances of getting a hit on a ground ball. Well-coached and sophisticated middle infielders may flip/flop their coverage—that is, the shortstop covers second base with a right-handed hitter at bat, and the second baseman covers second base with a left-handed hitter at bat. This sometimes happens when the hit-and-run is employed too often.

▶ Well-coached middle infielders do not evacuate their positions prematurely. Consequently, it is more difficult to hit a ball through their position.

▶ The hit-and-run is a valuable offensive weapon if used intelligently and not indiscriminately!

A Dash of Logic and a Pinch of Hunch

Earnshaw Cook in *Percentage Baseball* stated that "Modern baseball strategy is nothing more than tribalistic ritual passed on from generation to generation and cannot be held up to scrutiny by the laws of probability." Coaches must realize no offensive or defensive decision will be correct one hundred percent of the time. If strategy decisions are based on logical thinking and percentages, they will be correct a greater percentage of the time than if they are made on a hunch. Yet, don't overlook your "gut feelings" upon occasion. When the pressure is on and the score is tied or you are one or two runs behind, it takes courage to make a move.

Good Luck!

First-and-Third Double Steals

"I don't set trends. I just find out what they are and exploit them." – Dick Clark

A team's personality manifests itself through its baserunning. It is on the basepaths where a player's and team's aggressiveness, alertness, and enthusiasm for the game can be seen. It is also a reflection of their understanding of offensive game strategy.

When there are baserunners on first and third bases, an exciting aspect of daring and aggressive baserunning presents itself. This situation offers an excellent opportunity for the offensive team to score a run without a base hit, and to create some real problems for a defensive team that is not prepared to deal with this situation.

There is a wide variety of tactics that may be employed in the first-and-third double steal situation. The runner at first base initiates these variations, and what he does determines the particular type of double steal play that the offensive team will be running.

The effectiveness of any double steal will vary depending upon the sophistication and maturity of the defensive team. If they are alert, well-coached, and physically capable of executing the defense correctly, the offensive team can be made to look foolish at times.

The offensive team coach must keep in mind that first-and-third double steals are "gamble plays," even though they are very difficult to defend. However, the double steal adds spice and excitement to the game, usually forcing the defense to play the game at home plate, where no mistakes can be made, or forcing the defensive team to concede a run for an out.

> **COACHING KEY:**
> When a first-and-third situation presents itself, the coach must "read the defense"—that is, he must observe the actions and responses of the defensive team, especially the middle infielders and catcher, after the pitch has passed through the impact zone. The coach can then determine which double steal has the greatest chance of scoring a run.
>
> The coach can also learn a great deal by watching pregame infield practice: teams may reveal their double steal defensive alignment.
>
> Things that can often be seen include how they will cover the base; if they throw directly to one of the middle infielders in position; or if they will send one of the middle infielders to the halfway position between the mound and second base.
>
> **Delayed steals can be run at any time, but are usually two-out plays. Remember, the object is to score a run, not to steal a base.**

Intelligent, aggressive and controlled baserunning is a great offensive weapon and will put psychological pressure on the defense. "What are they going to do next?" becomes a matter of concern for the defensive team. With two outs, the first-and-third double steal presents a better chance of scoring a run than allowing the batter to hit away, provided the defense opts to play the situation and not concede second base. If second base is conceded, the hitter now has an opportunity to drive in two runs.

Types of Double Steals

When and how the runner at first base breaks for second identifies the particular type of double steal being employed. The following are examples of first-and-third double steals that have proved to be effective offensive weapons.

▶ **The Straight Steal:** The runner on first base attempts to steal second base by breaking on the pitcher's first move toward home plate. This is a normal steal attempt, and it is done without hesitation.

▶ **The Delayed Steal:** So named because the runner on first base delays his break for second until the pitcher has released the ball to home plate, or until the catcher begins to throw the ball back to the pitcher. Delayed steals are designed to exploit the middle infielder who fails to cover second base after the ball has passed through the impact zone, or the lazy catcher who fails to shift into throwing position, lobs the ball back to the pitcher, or throws from his knees.

▶ **The Forced Balk (a.k.a. the "Kansas City Steal"):** The runner on first base breaks for second base as the pitcher goes into his set position. The intent is to startle the pitcher into committing a balk.

▶ **Intentional Pickoff/Long Lead:** The runner at first base takes a normal lead, then increases it to invite a pickoff attempt. When the pitcher throws to first base, the runner breaks hard for second. This forces the first baseman to make a decision—a throw to second base allows the runner on third base to score, but holding the ball moves another runner into scoring position.

▶ **Automatic Steal (Option 1):** This is primarily a one-out play with runners on first and third bases. The runner on first tags up on pop flies hit behind first base, third base, or home plate. These pop flies are usually foul balls, but may be fair. The runner on first base breaks hard for second after the catch and is prepared to be caught in a rundown. The runner on third base tags up and scores if the throw is made to second base.

▶ **Automatic Steal (Option 2):** With a runner on second base, the batter walks or strikes out, and in either case, the pitch is a passed ball or wild pitch, taking the catcher to the backstop far enough away that the pitcher must cover home plate. The batter/runner sprints to first base, touches the base, and runs full speed toward second. If the catcher throws to second and there is no cutoff man, the runner on third base will score easily.

Absolutes for the Runner at First Base

The success of all double steals is predicated upon the following "absolutes" that the runner at first base must strictly adhere to. Adherence to these absolutes will maximize the chances of scoring a run and will give uniformity and consistency in the execution of the play.

▶ **GO HARD!** "To Throw Or Not To Throw: That Is The Question." Running full speed forces the defensive player to make an immediate decision—that is, whether to play on the runner advancing to second base by making a throw there, or to concede the base by holding the ball. Throwing to second base enhances the offensive team's chances of scoring a run; holding the ball moves another runner into scoring position.

▶ **GO LOOKING!** The runner at first should be aware not to run into the tag before the runner on third base scores. This is extremely important because most first-and-third double steal attempts are made with two outs. The baserunner should steal second base while *watching* the play develop—this allows the runner to stop, reverse direction and not run into the tag. He can anticipate the play, stop in time, and prolong the rundown.

▶ **GET HUNG UP!** The runner at first base should "stay alive" as long as possible, stopping before reaching second base, and getting in a rundown. With two outs, the runner should stay in the rundown as long as possible, giving the runner on third an opportunity to score before the final out of the inning can be made.

▶ **TAKE THE BASE!** This is a corollary to the "absolutes." If the defense concedes second base, take it without hesitation. Taking the base eliminates the force play at second base, puts another runner in scoring position and prevents the defense from getting into a short rundown situation, which is fatal with two outs.

Why it is Important to "Go Hard" for Second Base

Running hard to second prevents the second baseman from "sealing off" the runner. That is, it prevents the second baseman from positioning himself in the baseline between the runner and second base and trapping the runner by creating a shorter rundown distance between first and second bases.

When the rundown is conducted in a smaller area, less time is needed to tag the runner out. And the closer the infielder is to first base, the shorter the throwing distance to home plate will be should a throw be made there.

The second baseman's ability to seal off the runner is a direct result of the runner not going full speed, which gives the second baseman enough time to get to the seal position.

Ideally, if there is a rundown, it should begin as far from first base and as close to second as possible—in other words, it should utilize as much of the 90-foot distance between first and second bases as it can. (With two outs, a smart first baseman will trail the baserunner and the rundown will take place in a shorter area. This puts the success of the play in jeopardy, as the third out can often be made before the runner can score from third base.) The farther the rundown distance is from first base, the more time it will take the defense to tag out the runner, and the longer and more awkward the throw home will be. Both of these factors increase the offense's chances of scoring a run.

SPECIFIC INSTRUCTIONS FOR THE RUNNER AT FIRST BASE

We just learned the "absolutes" for the runner at first base in a first-and-third double steal situation. Now, what about the specific actions of the runner at first, depending upon the play? Here they are:

On Straight Steals

▶ **Straight steal with no outs or one out:** In this spot, the runner's job is simply to steal the base; it is the only exception to the "Go hard, go looking, get hung up" rule. This is a no-out or one-out play—if the middle infielder attempts to tag the stealing runner out, the runner from third base will be able to score, and an out is exchanged for a run.

Remember, though, with a good hitter at the plate and no one out, a straight steal would be foolish. The offense wants to maximize its opportunities for a big inning, to score the runner on third base and keep the inning alive. And with a weak hitter at bat and runners on first and third bases with none out or one out, a safety squeeze bunt might be a better choice of strategy to score the runner from third base and advance the runner on first base into scoring position.

The straight steal is justified if the infield is playing in to cut the run off at home plate and no one can cover second base, or if the defense is incapable of defending the double steal (as is often the case with Little League or other youth teams).

▶ **Straight steal with two outs:** With two outs on a straight steal, the runner on first base breaks for second as on a straight steal, but instead he "Goes hard, goes looking and gets hung up!" If a rundown occurs, the baserunner must stay alive as long as possible to allow the runner from third base to score before the final out of the inning is made. Yet, the runner at first should not hesitate to "take the base" if the defensive team makes no play and concedes it to him.

On Delayed Steals

The success of any delayed steal is dependent on the middle infielders or catcher "falling asleep." If the catcher doesn't shift into throwing position, throws from his knees, lobs the ball back to the pitcher or is slovenly in general, he is a potential victim. Even if the catcher is alert, one of the middle infielders must cover second base after the pitch has passed the impact zone. If the middle infielder fails to cover the base (instead looking down at the ground or kicking the dirt after the pitch), or is late in covering, the delayed steal will work like a charm.

▶ **Little League Steal:** This play draws its name not because its use is limited to Little League, but because the runner at first base mimics a Little League baserunner, who isn't allowed to steal until the ball crosses the plate. In this play, the runner on first base takes a normal primary and secondary lead as the pitcher delivers the pitch. The runner delays his break for second until the ball crosses the front edge of home plate. At this point, the runner should *Go hard, go looking and get hung up.*

▶ **Scooter Play:** The runner on first base takes a normal secondary lead as the pitcher delivers the pitch; however, the secondary lead is "continued" by a series of sideways shuffle steps until the runner has reached his "release point," which is approximately thirty feet from first base. The runner then breaks for second, remembering the absolute of *Go hard, go looking and get hung up.* It is critical to the success of this steal that the runner stays low and keeps his body square to home plate before reaching the release point. If the runner stands up or releases too soon, it will immediately alert the middle infielders and the play will fail.

Each runner must know the number of "scoots" it will take him to reach the release point—this will vary depending upon the physical size and agility of the runner. The number of scoots to the release point should be determined during practice sessions. Most coaches say "take three scoots," but this is not nearly as effective as using the release point as a reference. "Three scoots" causes many runners to release too soon, destroying the play's chances for success. The middle infielders are alerted too soon and have enough time to get to second base and receive the catcher's throw. (The Scooter Play can also be run effectively as a straight steal with no runner on third base, particularly with a left-handed hitter at bat.)

The Advantages of a Left-Handed Hitter

All delayed steals are more effective with a left-handed batter up. The catcher's view is obscured by the hitter, and the runner's intentions are hidden for a longer period of time.

Also, many shortstops play too far from second base with a left-handed batter at the plate, meaning they are late covering the base, making a return throw to the plate very difficult. Read where the shortstop is playing with a left-handed batter up and a runner on first base—to be forewarned is to be forearmed.

▶ **Delay on Catcher's Throw to Pitcher:** The runner on first takes a normal secondary lead with no false starts to alert the defense. He does not return to first base after the catcher receives the pitch, but may take a short scoot back toward first (this action may fake out the catcher and middle infielders and avoid alerting them to the impending steal attempt). As the catcher starts his arm forward to throw the ball to the pitcher, the runner on first breaks hard for second. *Go hard, go looking and get hung up!*

▶ **Walking Lead:** The runner takes a normal primary lead off first. As the pitcher releases the ball, instead of taking a normal secondary lead, the runner takes three walking steps toward second base. After completing the third step, he breaks hard for second. *Go hard, go looking and get hung up.* The Walking Lead delayed steal may catch the defense unaware if they are keyed in on the Scooter Play and Little League Steal. The disadvantage of this play is that the baserunner doesn't cover enough distance before breaking for second, which gives the middle infielder a chance to recover and get to the base in time. To compensate, the runner should continue walking until he reaches his release point, as detailed above in the Scooter Play.

On Other Plays

▶ **The Forced Balk:** This is an attempt to startle the pitcher into committing a balk, and it is especially effective against a nervous or inexperienced pitcher, or against a careless pitcher who does not watch the runner at first base when going into his stretch. On this play, the runner at first base breaks hard for second when the pitcher starts his hands up. (Key on the pitcher's hands because pitchers use different styles to get into their set positions.) The runner must go hard, go looking and get hung up. This is a good tactic *with the bases loaded, two outs and two strikes on a weak hitter*—it creates a rundown situation that probably will have a greater chance of scoring a run than having the weak hitter swing away, and it may force the pitcher to balk.

▶ **Intentional Pickoff/Long Lead:** In this play, the runner at first takes a normal lead off the bag and increases it as the pitcher is coming into his set position. This can be done by slowly taking an additional adjustment step. The runner should place all of his weight on his right leg (a one-way lead). Be subtle and "set a trap," particularly if the pitcher is left-handed. Invite a pickoff attempt. When the pitcher throws to first base, break hard for second. *Go hard, go looking and get hung up.* If the pitcher steps off the rubber, return to first base. And remember, the lead should not be so obvious that the second baseman moves into the "seal position" and ruins the play.

Another variation of this play occurs when there is a left-handed pitcher. The runner should take his lead off first base as described above and attempt to lure the pitcher into a pickoff attempt. The runner should key on the pitcher's front foot, then break hard for second *as soon as the pitcher lifts the foot.* Again, *Go hard, go looking and get hung up.*

▶ **Automatic Steal (Option 1):** This play can be used with no outs or one out. When a pop fly is hit behind first base, home plate or third base (these are usually foul balls), the runner at first base tags up and breaks for second base after the catch. *Go hard, go looking and get hung up.*

The following problems are created for the defense when this play is used:

> *On a pop fly to the catcher:* If the catcher must leave home plate to catch the ball, the pitcher will cover home plate. If the catcher opts to play on the runner advancing to second base by throwing there, the runner on third base will score easily if the defense fails to have a cutoff man in position between the catcher and second base.

> *On a pop fly to the first baseman:* If the first baseman, after making the catch, opts to play on the runner advancing to second base by throwing there, the runner on third base will score easily if the defense fails to have a cutoff man in position between the first baseman and second base. This ball is usually foul and often between home plate and first base, but may be anywhere in the general area as long as the catch is not made too close to second base.

> *On a pop fly hit into short right field (fair or foul):* With runners on first and third bases and less than two outs, a pop fly hit into short right field behind first base (fair or foul) that forces both the first baseman and second baseman to pursue the ball presents an extremely difficult play to defend. It offers an excellent opportunity for the offense to score a run or advance another runner into scoring position. If the defensive player making the catch throws to second base, the runner on third base will surely score. If he holds the ball or throws to home plate, the runner on first base advances to second base.

▶ **Automatic Steal (Option 2):** Although this play occurs with a runner at second base instead of runners on first and third, it is listed in this chapter because it becomes a first-and-third situation as the play develops. This play happens when 1) there is a runner on second base; 2) there is a passed ball or wild pitch on strike three or ball four; and 3) as a result of the wild pitch or passed ball, the runner at second goes to third base and the batter/runner goes to first.

This play can be run regardless of the number of outs. The batter/runner must hustle to first base to beat the throw and/or prevent the defense from adjusting into the "seal position." After arriving at

228 FROM THE THIRD BASE COACH'S BOX

first base safely, the batter/runner breaks hard for second, remembering to *Go hard, go looking and get hung up.*

The players must be taught to recognize this situation. They must realize that once the runner on second advances to third and the batter reaches first safely, the first-and-third double steal is in order. The coach must have a verbal signal to communicate his desire to run the "automatic double steal."

Automatic Steal (Option 1):

This diagram happens to show a popup behind home plate near the backstop, although a similar opportunity for the offense exists on popups down the lines past first and past third.

On the play depicted here, if the defensive team does NOT station a cutoff man between the catcher and second base (somewhere near the "X"), they will be forced to concede second base to the runner breaking from first, or by throwing through to second, they will allow the runner on third to score.

This play can be run with none out or one out.

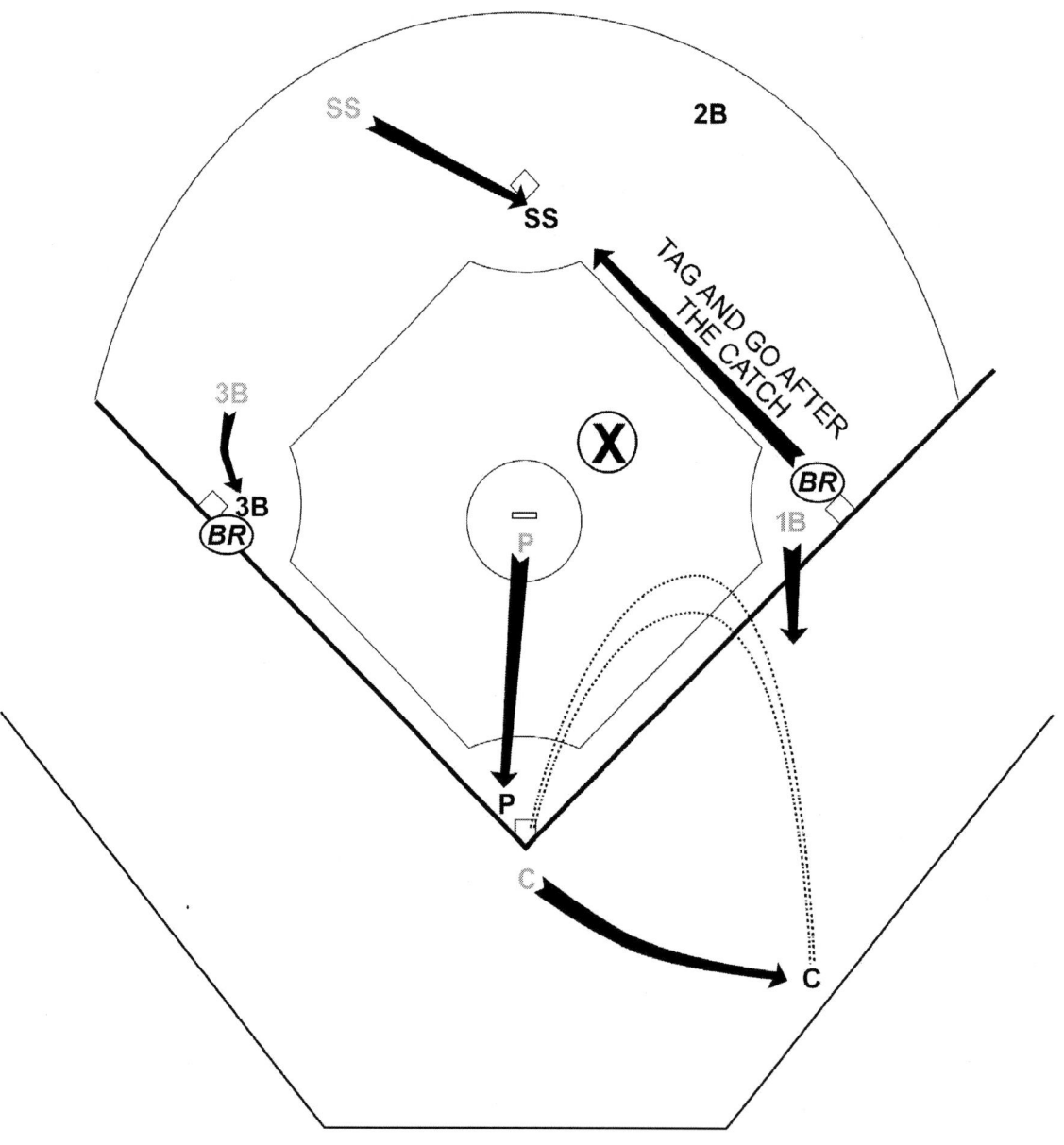

Automatic Steal (Option 2):

This play occurs with a runner at second on a wild pitch or passed ball that is ALSO either ball four or strike three. The hitter runs hard around first and breaks for second. Similar to Automatic Steal Option 1, if the defensive team does NOT station a cutoff man between the catcher and second base (somewhere near the "X"), they will be forced to concede second base, or by throwing through to second, they will allow the runner rounding third to score.

This play can be run regardless of the number of outs.

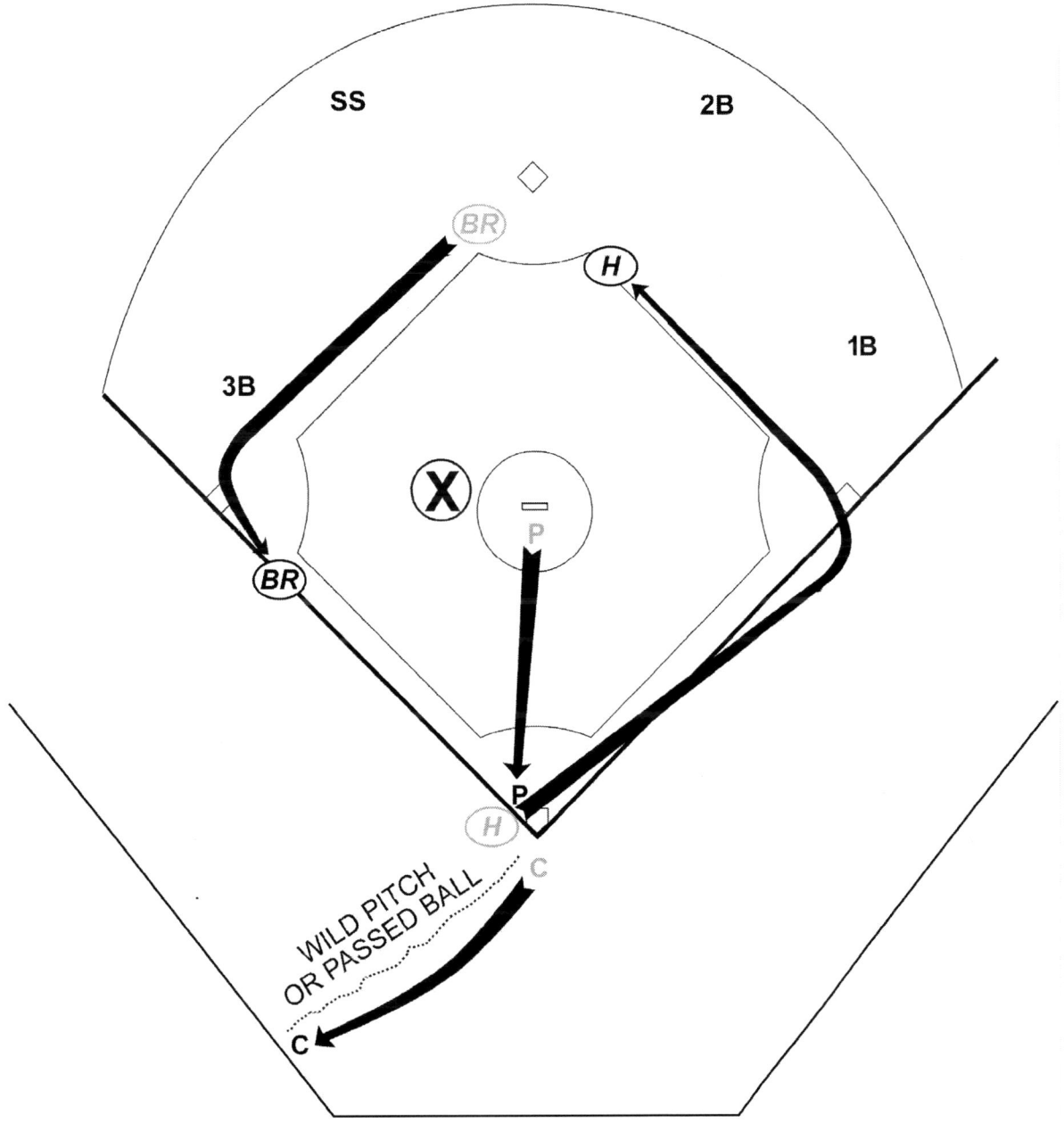

SPECIFIC INSTRUCTIONS FOR THE RUNNER AT THIRD BASE

In many instances, the runner at third has not been given proper instruction, and is instead left mostly to his own devices. This results in a high percentage of runners being picked off third or being thrown out at the plate.

Keys to Scoring a Run

The runner at third must be aware of several keys to maximize his chances of scoring a run:

1. He must read the catcher. If the catcher looks at the runner at third, he will probably throw through to second base. If he *doesn't* look at the runner at third, it could mean: he's going to execute a full-arm fake; throw it directly to the pitcher, who will cut it off; throw it directly to third (the "Third Base Right Now" play); throw directly to the shortstop or second baseman; or it could simply mean he's a dumb catcher.

2. He must "read white"—that is, he must see the ball actually leave the catcher's hand before advancing. He must be sure the ball is thrown before breaking for home plate, or he is liable to be picked off after a full-arm fake. "Read white" is an excellent word picture to communicate, reinforce and remind the runner to see the ball leave the defensive player's hand before committing to home plate.

3. If the catcher throws down to second base, the runner at third must be certain the ball clears the pitcher's head (key on the button of the pitcher's cap—if the ball passes this point, it won't be cut off by the pitcher). The runner can get an early jump by reading the trajectory of the catcher's throw—if the catcher has a weak arm, it may be apparent early that the throw will clear the pitcher's head. Watch the catcher throw during pregame infield practice.

4. *Finally, he must make a full commitment to score.* He must make the defense throw him out at home plate. *No rundowns! No hesitations from third base!* The defense either makes the play or doesn't. The odds of getting out of a rundown are very slim, so force the defense to make an accurate, pressure throw to home plate.

On the Straight Steal and Delayed Steal

▶ **Breaking for home:** The primary lead for the runner at third can be the same distance as the third baseman plays from the base. The runner should take a walking lead in foul territory as the pitcher delivers the ball to home plate, then take as long a secondary lead as possible without being picked off. Then, after the ball has passed through the impact zone, the runner should move into the baseline—this will block the catcher's view of third base, making it difficult for him to judge the length of the runner's lead. (If the batter has been given the take sign, the baserunner should take his lead on the base line. His feet should be on the foul line with his body facing the infield when the catcher receives the ball, blocking the catcher's view of third base.)

The runner should take a rocker step back toward third base with a slight inward turn of the shoulder as the catcher looks at him. This may be helpful to generate momentum and make the catcher think the runner is returning to third. Catchers are taught to "read the runner" at third base—that is, they're taught that an open chest (facing the catcher) means the runner is coming, and that a closed chest (facing the infield) means the runner is not coming.

▶ **On a rundown between first and second:** If the runner at third does not get a jump on the catcher's throw to second base and was not able to break for home, he may do either of the following:

1. Wait until the middle infielder starts the rundown, then take three scoots toward home plate, stay low and square to the baseline, then release and make an all-out break for home plate.

2. Wait until the middle infielders are in poor throwing position or just as the ball is being released (such as the first baseman tossing to the second baseman, or vice versa). Break hard for home plate at this moment. *This is an all-out commitment to score*—you are either safe or out at home plate. Make the defense "play the game at home plate," particularly with two outs.

On the Forced Balk

On this play, the runner at third takes as long a primary lead as possible because he will not be able to take a secondary lead. If the pitcher steps off the rubber and looks at him after the runner at first base makes his break, *freeze*. At this point, four options are available:

1. The moment the pitcher throws the ball to second base, break for home plate. *Read white!* Don't get caught by a full-arm fake by the pitcher. See the ball leave the pitcher's hand.

2. Take three scoots or shuffle steps if the pitcher throws to first base—don't chicken out. Break for home if the first baseman throws to second base or throws to third base. Return to third base immediately if the first baseman fakes a throw to either second or third base, or if the first baseman runs at you. Again, read white—don't get caught by a full-arm fake by the first baseman.

3. Break for home as the runner on first base breaks for second base. Key on the runner at first. This option is effective against a righthander who steps off and turns his back to third base, runs at the baserunner and/or makes a full-arm fake, and also against a lefthander who doesn't check third base before he throws to first. The runner will beat the first baseman's throw home, or will score if the first baseman throws to second base.

4. If you do not get a jump on the pitcher's throw to second base, wait until the middle infielder starts the rundown—take three scoots and then break full-speed for home plate. Stay low and square while scooting. Wait until the middle infielders are in poor throwing position or just as the ball is being released (such as when the first baseman tosses to the second baseman or vice-versa). Break hard for home plate at this moment. *This is an all-out commitment to score.*

On the Automatic Steals

▶ **On Automatic Steal Option 1:** On this play, with no outs or one out, a pop fly is hit behind first base, third base, or home plate (these are usually foul balls). The runner should tag up and begin walking off third base after the catch. The length of the lead depends on where the catch is made—a catch made behind home plate or first base will permit a bigger lead than a catch made down the third base line. Take a 25-30 foot lead off third base if the catch is made behind home plate or in the first base area—*invite a throw!* Then, break for home if a throw is made to second base and there is no cutoff man, or the first baseman or catcher throws to third base. The runner can score before a throw can be made to third base and then back to home plate. Return to third base if either the catcher, first baseman or third baseman runs at you after making the catch or makes a full-arm fake.

▶ **On Automatic Steal Option 2:** On a passed ball/wild pitch on ball four or strike three with a runner on second base (regardless of the number of outs), the runner on second advances to third when the ball gets past the catcher. The pitcher will cover home plate. The runner rounds third base and takes as long a lead as possible, usually 25 to 30 feet. Break for home on the catcher's throw to second base (if there is no cutoff man). Break for home on the catcher's throw to third base, if the throw comes from the first base side of the diamond or the deep backstop area. Return to third base if the catcher runs at you, or full-arm fakes a throw.

> ### Make It Automatic
>
> Automatic Steals offer an opportunity to score a run on what normally would be considered a routine out for the defense. How often can a team score a run on a pop fly to the catcher or first baseman? It can in the first-and-third situation if the offense recognizes its opportunity and the defense doesn't.
>
> **Opportunity meets preparation—be prepared! You should have the automatic series in your repertoire.**

On the Intentional Pickoff/Long Lead

▶ **Against a left-handed pitcher:** With a left-handed pitcher on the mound, the runner at third takes a primary lead as far as the third baseman is from the base. When the pitcher checks him, he should "look dumb"… pose no threat… stand still. Allow the pitcher to focus all his attention on the runner at first base. As the pitcher goes into his stretch, the runner at third should begin a cautious walk toward home plate. The pitcher's attention should be directed toward the runner at first base, if the runner at third seems to be of no concern. Here the play differs depending upon the number of outs in the inning:

1. With *two outs*, the runner at third should break for home plate *as soon as the pitcher has committed to throw a pickoff to first base.* Key on the pitcher's front (stride) foot. The runner should be able to beat the return throw from the first baseman to the plate.

2. With *one out* and a left-handed pitcher on the mound, the runner at third should break hard for home plate *on the pitcher's first move* (as the runner on first simultaneously breaks for second). Key on the pitcher's front, or stride foot—as he lifts his stride foot to throw, go all out for home plate! If the pitcher's throw is to first base, the runner should be able to beat the first baseman's return throw to the plate and score a run. If the pitcher's throw is to home plate, it is an

automatic squeeze situation. (The squeeze bunt sign should be given in conjunction with the long lead sign and *acknowledged* by the hitter.)

▶ **With two outs and a right-handed pitcher on the mound:** In this spot, the runner at third should take a primary lead as described above. If the pitcher attempts a pickoff at first base, take three scoots/shuffle steps toward home plate and hold. Break for home if the first baseman throws to second base or throws to third base. Return to third base immediately if the first baseman executes a full-arm fake to either second or third base, or runs toward you.

A FINAL POINT

Remember, these are high-risk plays. But if the double steal presents a better chance of scoring a run than the hitter's batting average, particularly with two outs, *GO FOR IT!*

Good Luck!

Spin 'Em and Keep the Infield Honest

"For every punch that you or your opponent throws there's always a counter shot or two which you have to be ready to fire or defend." – Boxing great Alexis Arguello

One area of defensive baseball that is often misplayed is the sacrifice bunt defense. Players often become careless in their fielding responsibilities, and some coaches fail to insist upon perfection of their team's defensive execution when the sacrifice bunt is in order. Whatever the cause, the end result is a defense that is vulnerable to exploitation by the alert coach.

An offensive weapon that can be used to exploit these mistakes is the Spin 'Em offense, more commonly known as the slash, slug bunt or slap bunt. We relabeled it "Spin 'Em" in order to paint a clear picture in the minds of our players—the hitters are told to spin the over-charging infielders around.

For the Spin 'Em offense to be effective, it should not be used indiscriminately. It should be predicated upon a well-thought-out philosophy, which dictates when its use is appropriate and justifiable.

Reasons to Use the Spin 'Em Offense

– To be able to sacrifice bunt when necessary.
– To exploit over-charging infielders who are too close too soon and lose their lateral movement.
– To exploit infielders who evacuate their positions early, leaving those positions wide-open.

It is the coach's responsibility to be alert and *read* the opponent's defensive alignment, then exploit it if the opportunity presents itself.

Mechanics of the Spin 'Em Offense

If the players understand the philosophy of the Spin 'Em offense, it will make mastery of the mechanics much easier. In teaching the mechanics of the Spin 'Em offense, the following points are emphasized:

1. Stand forward in the batter's box—the back foot should be at the break in home plate.
2. *Turn early* and be in a bunting stance as the pitcher stretches. The defense won't be able to determine if you are going to bunt or slap bunt.
3. Make a legitimate bunt fake.
4. Feet should be in an open stance at 45 degrees (toes pointing toward the mound).

5. Key on the pitcher's front foot—as he lifts it to deliver the pitch, turn from bunting position into the "slap bunt" stance. This will give the hitter the right amount of time to get into hitting position. Do not move the feet from the original bunting stance—just rotate the body at the waist while staying low and compact.
6. Bat control is a must! Change from a bunt grip to a slap bunt (Spin 'Em) grip by sliding the top hand down to the bottom hand. The bottom hand is placed one hand-width up the bat from the knob and does not move, and the top hand slides down the bat handle when making the transition from bunt to hit. Spacing the hands one or two inches apart greatly increases bat control.
7. *Hit down on the ball* with a hard three-quarters swing. *Do not break your wrists.* Drive the ball into the ground toward the shortstop or second baseman's position. A fly ball is the only way you can be hurt offensively—fly balls result from assuming the Spin 'Em position too late, standing up and not staying compact, taking a full swing or trying to hit the ball too hard.
8. Rotate your back heel up and out—this allows your hips to rotate for maximum power. Failure to rotate the heel is a common mistake—watch this closely.
9. Hit only strikes unless the hit-and-run is on.

Making contact with the ball is of paramount importance in the execution of the Spin 'Em offense. The hitter must be able to hit the ball into the ground—if the defense fields the ball, it is almost impossible for them to turn a double play, because they are out of position and probably surprised and confused on the play. But even if the defense is successful in forcing the runner at second base or turning the double play, they will be doubly apprehensive about charging the hitter the next time the bunt is in order. The slap bunt has then served its purpose by keeping the infield honest—by keeping them back.

Effective coaching of a particular skill involves three factors: philosophy, mechanics, and drills to implement the mechanics. Following are some of the drills we have found to be effective to implement the Spin 'Em mechanics.

Dry Hitting Spin 'Em Drill

The players are grouped in as many lines as necessary. Each player has a bat and uses his glove as home plate. For safety purposes, the players should be at least six to eight feet apart, with the lines ten to twelve feet apart.

Players face the coach, assume the Spin 'Em stance, and then go through each of the mechanics step-by-step. Once the players understand the mechanics, a pitcher (without a ball) is placed in front of the group. He is in the set position and the players key on his delivery and dry-run the execution.

The coaches should circulate among the players to make certain each player thoroughly understands all aspects of the mechanics and executes them in the prescribed manner. It is also advisable to reiterate the philosophy for the use of the slap bunt so that there is no misunderstanding as to its purpose.

Spin 'Em Toss Drill

There are two phases to this drill: the *knee phase* and the *standing phase*, and in both cases the procedure is essentially the same. Players are paired off, rotating from hitter to tosser after a prescribed number of swings. The hitter is about five feet from a screen. The thrower is in front of him at approximately a 45-degree angle, down on one knee, and tosses the ball to the hitter. It is important that the ball be tossed out in front of the hitter so that it is hit correctly.

The tosser's responsibilities:

1. Present the ball with an extended arm.
2. Drop the arm and the ball.
3. Have a slight delay.
4. Toss the ball.

(See page 154 for basics on the execution of the Toss Drill, particularly the responsibilities of the tosser.)

The hitter's responsibilities: The hitter keys on the tosser. When the tosser presents the ball to the hitter with his arm extended, the hitter assumes the bunt stance. When the tosser drops his arm and the ball, the hitter rotates his body into the Spin 'Em stance and brings his bat back into the hitting position. Allowing for a short delay, the tosser then flips the ball to the hitter, who drives it into the screen.

The Knee Phase: In the knee phase of the drill, the procedure is the same as described above, except that the hitter is down on his back knee with his front foot at a 45-degree angle. The purpose of this phase is to teach weight retention—many hitters are unable to slap bunt effectively because they have a tendency to lunge. This drill helps them learn to wait for the ball.

The Standing Phase: Once the player becomes proficient with the knee drill, the standing phase should be implemented. The hitter and tosser execute this drill exactly as they did the knee drill, except that the hitter is standing. He should not be allowed to move his feet. He must hit virtually flat-footed; at most, he should just pick his front foot up and set it down in order to generate rhythm. (But be sure to rotate the back heel up and out.)

Live Hitting Drill

Once you are satisfied that your players are fundamentally sound in their execution, have them slap bunt using live pitching. Set pylons halfway between the mound and the third base line and halfway between the mound and the first base line—these pylons serve as reference points for the hitters.

Also important during this live hitting is weight retention and keying on the pitcher's front foot. Many hitters are late in assuming the slap bunt stance and this results in failure to make contact or popping the ball up. Keying on the pitcher's front foot assures the hitter of being in his hitting stance in time.

Spin 'Em to Set Up the Sacrifice

The Spin 'Em offense is particularly effective with runners on first and second bases, no outs and the bunt in order. The hitter turns early to bunt and keys on the shortstop—if the shortstop evacuates to cover third base (the "wheel play"), the slap bunt is automatic. The wheel play is particularly vulnerable to the Spin 'Em offense.

Use this attack as a key tool in putting opponents on the defensive. Take advantage of even the slightest defensive miscues, and increase run-production by exploiting the lack of perfection in the opponent's bunt defense. The Spin 'Em offense adds a great deal of versatility against bunt defenses because it keeps the opponent guessing all the time.

And most importantly, Spin 'Em will allow you to sacrifice bunt effectively when you need to—once opponents learn you have the slap bunt in your arsenal, they can't take liberties when you actually do lay down a bunt.

Good Luck!

The Suicide Squeeze

"If you don't risk anything, you risk even more." – Novelist Erica Jong

---

There is a saying in coaching circles that states, "Real coaching class is when they're running you out of town on a rail, and you make it look like you're leading a parade." Put the suicide squeeze play on late in the game and have it fail, and you may have an opportunity to test this thesis firsthand.

The suicide squeeze is exciting. A momentum-changer. When executed correctly, it gives the offensive team a real boost, and it's a real bummer for the defense.

When it fails, the defense gains momentum, and it's disaster for the offense.

Signaling for the suicide squeeze is a gutsy call by the manager or coach.

Disadvantages of the Suicide Squeeze

1. The suicide squeeze play is often employed with a weak hitter at bat. An inability to make contact with the ball characterizes the weak hitter, and having to make contact in a pressure situation regardless of the pitch's location compounds the batter's woes and increases the chance of failure.

2. Like the hit-and-run, the suicide squeeze forces the batter to offer at the pitch regardless of its location, in or out of the strike zone.

3. If it's not handled correctly, the runner at third base may not know the play is on, and may fail to break for home plate. Or, he may break for the plate too soon, tipping off the play—the pitcher then throws inside to the right-handed batter (a knockdown pitch) or throws a pitch-out to the left-handed batter. The play is thwarted and the runner is tagged out.

4. The batter may not know the play is on and takes the pitch, leaving the runner stranded. Or, the batter turns too early, tipping off the play—the pitcher throws inside to a right-handed batter or throws a pitch-out to the left-handed batter and the runner is tagged out.

Advantages of the Suicide Squeeze

1. When executed correctly, the play is indefensible.

2. When executed correctly, the play is a momentum-changer.

3. It adds excitement and daring to the offense.

Execution and Responsibilities

Aptly named, the suicide squeeze play is an all-out, all-or-nothing play designed to score the runner from third base with a bunt. The success of the suicide squeeze is dependent upon the coach, the batter and the runner at third base executing their responsibilities flawlessly.

Responsibilities of the coach:
The coach must develop a communication system in the form of both physical and verbal signs to let the runner at third base and the batter know that the suicide squeeze play is on.

A verbal sign is used to get the attention of the runner and batter—such as "You're the doctor" or "Drive one out of the park!" A physical sign usually follows the verbal sign, but can be given simultaneously. A simple sign such as covering the letter on the cap or covering the belt buckle will suffice.

Once both the verbal and physical signs have been given by the coach, the runner at third base and the batter *must acknowledge* that they have the sign.

> **COACHING KEY:**
> If the batter fails to acknowledge the suicide squeeze sign, the play is **off** and the runner at third base does not go.
>
> **Remember: No acknowledgment = no play!**

Because the runner at third base is close to the third base coach, the acknowledgment could be as simple as a wink of the eye to the coach or a brush down the pants to the batter. The batter might acknowledge receiving the signal by running his top hand up the bat (this should be done slowly and deliberately) or digging his rear cleats into the dirt (an exaggerated movement that should be done slowly and deliberately). Other examples of acknowledgments include touching the button on the cap, clenching the fist, tugging on the ear, touching the nose, etc.

Responsibilities of the runner on third base:
1. The runner at third must acknowledge the sign with the coach and the batter.
2. The runner on third base must not tip the play off by breaking too early. He should key on the pitcher's front foot, breaking hard for the plate as the pitcher's front foot hits the ground—at this point, the pitcher cannot change the direction of his pitch.
3. If the pitcher uses a full wind-up, the runner at third base should walk quickly toward home plate and break full-speed when the pitcher's front foot hits the ground.
4. If the pitcher throws from the stretch position, the runner at third base must be more conservative, similar to the lead used when leading off first base. The runner should lead off third as far as the third baseman plays from the base. If the third baseman plays *on* third base, use a measured lead of *step, crossover and adjust* (see page 201 for an explanation).
5. Be aware of a pickoff attempt by the pitcher. If the pitcher swings his free foot past the back edge of the pitcher's rubber, it is a balk if he attempts a pickoff at third base.

Responsibilities of the batter:
1. The batter must acknowledge the sign with the coach and runner at third base (see examples of acknowledgments above).

2. Subtly move forward in the batter's box (toward the pitcher) to the break in the plate—this increases the chances of bunting a fair ball.
3. Like the runner at third, the batter *keys on the pitcher's front foot.* The batter must not turn too early, which would tip off the play. The batter turns to bunt as the pitcher's front foot hits the ground. At this point, the pitcher cannot change the direction of his pitch.
4. *The hitter must bunt the ball regardless of its location.*
5. Bunt the ball into fair territory—do not attempt to place the ball into a particular area. "Catch the ball on the bat"—don't just jab at it.

When to Use It

The suicide squeeze play is often used late in the game, when the runner on third base represents the tying or winning run. It is best used with one out and when the batter is ahead in the count or when the pitcher must throw a strike. Those with courage may call for the play on the first pitch.

The most common Suicide Squeeze play is that mentioned above. However, there are several variations that can be employed by the gutsy coach.

Double Suicide Squeeze Play

With runners on second and third bases, if the coach feels the suicide squeeze is an appropriate play, an attempt to score both runners (if there is one out) *isn't that big a gamble.*

If the batter pops the ball up in his attempt to bunt, the runner breaking from third base will be doubled up, and the runner advancing from second base will be of no consequence, because the inning will be over. (This is presupposing the play is run with *one out.* If the play is run as a *no-out* play, the offensive team is in danger of bunting into a triple play.) If the batter fails to bunt the ball, the runner breaking from third base will most likely be out at home plate—the offense will now have a runner on third base with two outs and an opportunity to score one run.

The responsibilities of the coach, the batter and the runner at third are all the same as detailed above in the regular suicide squeeze play.

The runner on second base breaks for third as if attempting to steal the base. He rounds the base, and if the ball is bunted into fair territory, continues on to home plate as the fielder makes his throw to first base.

The play works best if the ball is bunted to the third baseman. The runner from second base rounds third base and comes down the line (while staying behind), almost as far as the third baseman must go to field the ball, and then attempts to score on the third baseman's throw to first. The third base coach must be aware that an alert shortstop will cover third base, making the runner vulnerable if the third baseman bluffs a throw to first.

Like the other players involved in the play, the runner at second must acknowledge that he has the sign by giving a reply, such as brushing down the pants, tugging on the ear or nose, touching the bill of the cap, etc.

The timing of the break for the runner at second is important. There are two methods of execution: the runner can break for third as the pitcher starts his move to home plate; or, he can take a series of rapid sideways shuffle steps as the pitcher starts his move to the plate, then break full-speed when the pitcher's striding foot hits the ground. The early break may tip off the defense and result in a pitch-out, although if the infield is playing in, the chances of this are less likely.

Even though a ball bunted to third base is ideal, the batter's first priority is to bunt the ball into fair territory. A bunt to third base is a bonus.

With one out, the Double Suicide Squeeze is no more risky than the Single Suicide Squeeze. In either case, a pop fly results in a double play, and the runner on second base is of no consequence. But remember, if it's run with no outs, a pop fly would result in a triple play.

Advantages of Faking the Suicide Squeeze

Faking the suicide squeeze can be used to gain two advantages: to draw a walk or get ahead in the count; and to protect the offensive team against a double play.

▶ **To draw a walk or get ahead in the count:** This play is designed to force the pitcher into throwing a ball. It is used when the count is 2-0 or 3-1.

When the coach gives the sign for the Fake Suicide, the runner on third acknowledges the sign with a reply. He takes a short lead off the base—one step (three feet) maximum. He then breaks hard toward home plate, using a specific, controlled break as detailed below, when the pitcher's knee reaches the top of his balance position. (Faking a break when the pitcher is at the top of his balance point allows the pitcher time to adjust his throw to the batter.)

The controlled break is three full steps and one half step: left, right, left, and then one half-step right. Taking a half step enables an easy change of direction back to third base to avoid being picked off. The runner must be alert to score if the pitcher throws a wild pitch in his haste to defend what he thinks is a suicide squeeze attempt.

The batter, meanwhile, acknowledges the sign with a reply, then turns and assumes a bunting stance when the pitcher's knee reaches the top of the balance position. He fakes the bunt and takes the pitch.

Fake the fake suicide?

As opponents become aware that you have the Fake Suicide Squeeze in your repertoire, they will inform their pitchers not to take the bait when the batter turns early, and to throw the ball over the plate.

This means that turning early when the suicide squeeze play is actually being run could result in the batter getting a good ball to bunt, rather than a knockdown pitch.

However, when the suicide squeeze play is actually being employed, the runner at third base must not break early and must time his break to the pitcher's stride foot.

If run correctly, the pitcher can be duped into thinking the suicide squeeze play is being executed. Pitchers will disregard the count on the batter and throw an unhittable ball, walking the batter or creating a 3-0 count.

▶ **To protect the offensive team against the double play:** With runners on first and third bases, one out and a double play man (a slow runner) at bat, the offensive team may choose to run the Fake Suicide Squeeze. The objective is to have the runner on first base steal second base while the runner at third base and the batter fake the suicide squeeze. If the defense is concerned with the squeeze play, the runner stealing second base will be disregarded. If successful, there are runners on second and third base and the double play is no longer in order unless the defense chooses to walk the next hitter.

Once the coach gives the sign for the Fake Suicide Squeeze with runners at first and third, the responsibilities of the runner at third are the same as in the example above (he takes a short lead and breaks when the pitcher's knee is at the top of his balance position, taking a three-and-a-half step fake). The batter turns to fake a bunt when the pitcher's knee is at the top of his balance position. To add realism, the batter can "bunt through" the pitch—intentionally missing the ball to lock the defense into the play.

The runner on first base acknowledges the steal sign, steals second base, and "looks in" to be able to see the play develop.

If all goes well, the double play will no longer exist and the defense will have to decide whether to play the infield in (increasing the hitter's chance for success), play back and concede a run, or intentionally walk the next batter.

Other Options with Runners on First and Third

When there are runners on first and third bases, other interesting suicide squeeze options are available to the offensive team. The alert coach must recognize these opportunities when they present themselves and be prepared to capitalize on them when appropriate.

▶ **Run-and-Bunt Suicide Squeeze Play:** This play incorporates the suicide squeeze (for the runner at third) and the Run-and-Bunt Play (for the runner at first). It is usually attempted with one out. The objective is to score the runner from third base and advance the other runner into scoring position.

The runner on third base executes the suicide squeeze while the runner on first base simultaneously attempts to steal second base. This play is no more risky than a single suicide squeeze play—if the batter pops the ball up and it is caught by one of the defensive players, a double play will result. The runner at first base attempting to steal second will be of no consequence, because the inning will be over.

The responsibilities of the coach, batter and runner on third are the same as in the Single Suicide Squeeze and the Double Suicide Squeeze.

The runner on first, meanwhile, acknowledges that he has the sign by giving a reply—brushing down his pants, tugging on his ear or nose, touching the bill of his cap, etc. He steals on the pitch, and on the third or fourth step, he "looks in" to see if the ball has been bunted and to determine if an advance to third base is feasible. *But remember, if the runner is thrown out at first base, there will be two outs, and two-out strategy kicks in—take no chances, and don't make the third out at third base!*

The runner on first attempts an advance to third base if one of the following occurs: if the third baseman fields the bunt and is one-third of the way (30 feet or more) from third base toward home plate; if the third baseman fields the bunt and the catcher fails to cover third base; or if the first baseman has a weak arm or isn't alert.

The runner on first does not advance to third (that is, he stays at second base) if the batter fails to bunt the ball, if the ball is bunted hard to a fielder other than the third baseman, or if the third baseman covers the base.

▶ **Long Lead / Intentional Pickoff and Suicide Squeeze Play (against a left-handed pitcher):** This is a one-out play! It will be run either as a first-and-third double steal play or as a suicide squeeze, depending upon the pitcher's reaction to the situation. If the left-handed pitcher chooses to pick the runner off first base, the play becomes a double steal for the offense. If the pitcher chooses to ignore the runner at first base and instead delivers the ball to home plate, the play becomes a suicide squeeze for the runner at third base and the batter—and a run-and-bunt play for the runner at first.

The runner at first base acknowledges the coach's sign by giving a reply, then takes a normal lead off first and increases it as the pitcher is coming into his set position. As in the regular Long Lead / Intentional Pickoff Play (see page 227), he invites a pickoff attempt! This can be done by slowly taking an additional adjustment step toward second base as the pitcher is coming set. The runner should place all his weight on his right leg. Be subtle and *set a trap.* Lure the pitcher into a pickoff attempt. The lead should not be so obvious that the second baseman goes into the "seal position" and ruins the play.

The runner on first keys on the pitcher's front foot, and breaks hard for second as the pitcher lifts it. (If the pitcher steps off the rubber, return to first base.) If the pitcher attempts a pickoff play at first base, the situation becomes a double steal play and the rules for the double steal prevail—Go Hard! Go Looking! Get Hung Up! If the pitcher ignores the runner at first base and delivers the ball to home plate, the situation becomes a run-and-bunt play and the run-and-bunt rules prevail.

The runner at third base acknowledges the sign, and takes a primary lead off third as far as the third baseman plays from the base, or uses a measured leadoff of step, crossover and adjust (see page 201). When the pitcher checks the runner at third, he "looks dumb" and poses no threat! He stands still and allows the pitcher to focus all of his attention toward the runner at first base.

Remember, a left-handed pitcher will have his back to the runner at third base. As the pitcher goes into his stretch, the runner at third begins a cautious walk toward home plate. Key on the pitcher's front (stride) foot, and break hard for home plate when he lifts it! Go all-out for the plate—if the pitcher's throw is to first base, the runner at third should be able to beat the first baseman's throw to home plate and score a run. If the pitcher delivers the ball to home plate, the squeeze play is on! (The suicide squeeze bunt sign should be given in conjunction with the Long Lead Steal sign and acknowledged by the batter.)

The batter's responsibilities are the same as in the regular squeeze play: he keys on the pitcher's front foot and avoids turning too early and "tipping off" the play; he turns to bunt as the pitcher's front foot hits the ground; he must bunt the ball regardless of its location; and he bunts the ball into fair territory, avoiding an attempt to place the ball into a particular area. Remember: *catch the ball on the bat*—don't jab at it.

This play is an all-out gamble. It is designed to exploit the fact that the left-handed pitcher has his back to the runner at third base and a desire to pick runners off first base. Because of these two facts, the runner on third base breaks for home plate earlier than he would on a normal suicide squeeze play.

Use them Wisely

Suicide squeeze plays are risky at best, and it takes courage by the coach to put the play on. To increase the chances for success, the suicide squeeze must be practiced regularly, and all players must thoroughly understand the keys and fundamentals of proper execution.

Good Luck!

The Safety Squeeze

"I think there's a difference between a gamble and a calculated risk." – Edmund H. North, screenwriter for the movie Patton

---

The "safety squeeze" has been given little attention in most coaching manuals. What instruction exists usually says, *"The runner at third base decides if the bunt is well-placed, and if it is he attempts to score."*

With this limited instruction, the runner at the third base has no guidelines to decide when an attempt to score is justified. Consequently, a great deal of indecision results, rendering the safety squeeze virtually ineffective. It's no wonder most coaches don't have it in their offensive schemes.

Instead, most teams opt for the highly risky suicide squeeze, which puts pressure on both the hitter and the baserunner. If either the hitter or runner tips off the play, it will fail; however, if run correctly it is indefensible.

The much-neglected safety squeeze offers many advantages and is worthy of consideration. If run correctly and if the runner at third base is given clear guidelines about when an attempt to score is justified, this little-used weapon becomes a highly efficient method of scoring runs.

Advantages of the Safety Squeeze

Here are some reasons to consider making the safety squeeze a part of your offensive game:

1. It isn't as risky as the suicide squeeze, yet can produce runs.
2. It enables weak hitters to drive in runs when the situation presents itself.
3. It is not a disaster if the hitter takes the pitch—it allows the hitter to pick his own pitch to bunt. Neither the hitter nor the runner are committed to a specific pitch.
4. It can be used early in the game.
5. It is a tough play to defend with runners on first and third bases, even if the ball is bunted poorly.
6. It is very forgiving—a poor bunt with runners on first and third advances the runner on first base into scoring position. The defense concedes second base to the runner because of its concern that the runner on third base might score.
7. It is an easy way to score a run with a weak hitter when the infield is playing back.
8. It can be used again on the next pitch even if tipped off on the previous pitch—particularly with runners at first and third, because the first baseman must hold the runner on first base.
9. When used with runners at first and third and the middle infield in double-play depth, it makes it possible to score the runner from third base and advance the runner on first base to second base. The hitter may be safe at first because the second baseman (playing in double play depth) may not be able to cover first base in time. And, the runner on first may be able to go to third if the third baseman charges the bunt and the shortstop fails to cover third—the catcher is locked into home plate for a possible play there.

The Key to Success

The runner at third base is the key to the success of the safety squeeze, and the key to *his* success is removing indecision from his mind about when an attempt to score is and is not justified.

The runner at third base attempts to score on any bunted ball *except* one that is bunted hard back to the box, or a ball that the catcher can step out in front of the plate and field easily.

With a proper lead off third base and a fairly well-placed bunt, with runners on first and third bases the run will score a very high percentage of the time (about 90%). There will be times when someone makes a super defensive play and the runner is thrown out at home plate or the runner from third base makes a mistake in judgment and attempts to score when he shouldn't. Don't let this deter you, as the percentages are overwhelmingly in your favor that you will score a run.

Mechanics of the Safety Squeeze

The runner at third base: Once the runner thoroughly understands his reads and knows when to attempt to score, it is imperative that proper baserunning fundamentals be executed for the play to be consistently successful.

"Down in Foul, Back in Fair."

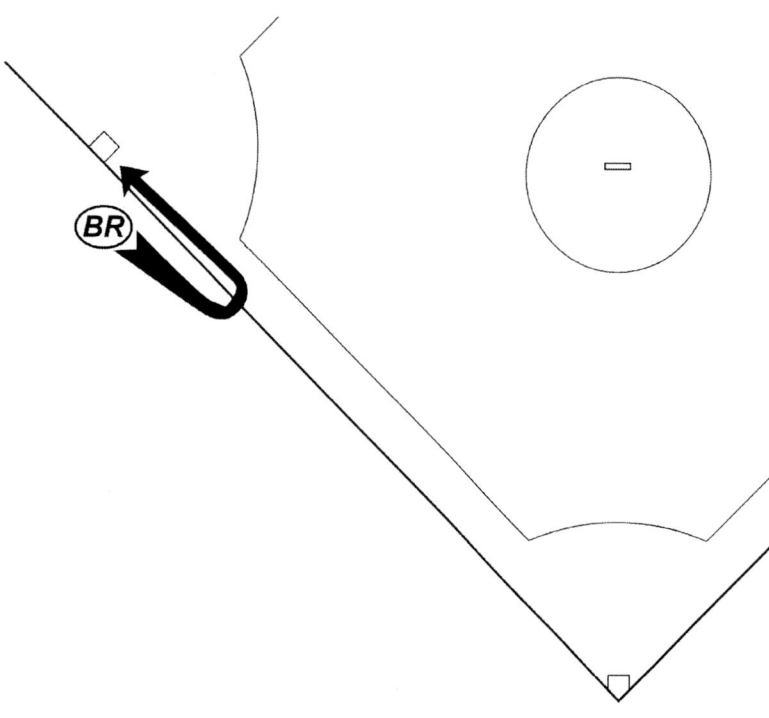

Leading off the bag: The runner's lead off of third base is critical to the success of the play. His primary lead should be in foul territory about one foot off the line (if the runner is hit with a batted ball while in foul territory, he is not out). Remember, the leadoff from third is "down in foul, back in fair territory" to block the catcher's view of third base. The length of the leadoff is determined by how far the third baseman plays from the base—the runner can be the same distance from the base as the third baseman. If the third baseman stands on the base, the runner should lead off as though leading off first base.

The secondary lead is a walking lead, and its mastery is imperative. The runner should follow this four-step sequence: crossover with the left leg, then a step with the right leg followed by left and right steps. Steps one and two are momentum steps, while steps three and four are timing steps. The runner is walking directly toward the hitter in foul territory during this sequence. If done correctly, the weight will land on the right foot as the ball enters the impact zone. The right foot then becomes the "accelerator or brake." The walking secondary lead and subsequent break to home plate should be a continuous fluid movement with no hesitation as the ball is bunted. This fluid motion maximizes the runner's chances of scoring and makes him extremely difficult to throw out. A body in motion tends to remain in motion!

With the pitcher from the windup: If the pitcher throws out of the windup, the secondary lead is a four-step sequence. The runner must not start the secondary lead too soon, but should allow the pitcher some "swing time." Begin walking as the pitcher's pivot foot steps in front of the rubber. Walking too soon will result in the runner being too far down the line too soon. The runner then must stop, lose momentum and destroy the play.

With the pitcher from the stretch: This will probably result in a two-step secondary lead, eliminating the momentum steps. The runner should be sure the pitcher throws to home plate and doesn't have a pickoff move to third base before taking the secondary lead. Begin the lead when the pitcher's throwing arm is even with his body, a split-second before his stride foot hits the ground. This will eliminate the pickoff possibility. The secondary lead will have to be done quickly to insure proper timing and a large-enough lead.

On a hard bunt to third base: When the ball is bunted *extra hard* toward third base and the third baseman is playing in, the baserunner may have difficulty scoring. In this situation, the runner may be better off waiting until the third baseman makes his throw to first base before attempting to score. If the runner chooses this option, he should follow the third baseman up the baseline, remaining a few feet behind him, and attempt to score when the throw is made to first base. Beware, though, of a full-arm fake by the third baseman and the shortstop sneaking behind to cover third base and receive the third baseman's throw. Remember to "read white"—that is, see the ball out of the third baseman's hand before attempting to score.

Remember: The runner goes on any bunted ball other than one bunted hard back to the box or one that the catcher can field easily.

Responsibilities of the bunter: The hitter executes a normal sacrifice bunt, but *must not turn too early*, lest he will tip off the play. The hitter should turn to bunt when the *pitcher's stride foot hits the ground.* No sooner.

The hitter should bunt only strikes, and should give himself up—at no time should he attempt to make a base hit out of the bunt. *Don't bunt in motion! Bunt the ball first, and then run! See the ball down!*

The hitter should bunt the ball toward first base with runners on first and third bases—the first baseman, who has been holding the runner, will be deeper and slightly slower to the ball.

Clap Drill

Purpose: To learn the walking lead at third base by clapping hands as ball enters the "impact zone."

Procedure:
1. Station a pitcher on the mound and a catcher behind home plate.
2. Three players assume their primary lead at third base.
3. The pitcher delivers the ball to the catcher.
4. During the wind-up, the runners practice the four-step walking lead.
5. Players clap their hands as their right foot (on its fourth step) hits the ground and the ball enters the impact zone.

Variation: The pitcher throws from the stretch position. Players execute the two-step lead and clap their hands together as their right foot hits the ground and the ball enters the impact zone.

Bunting Drill

Purpose: To teach the hitter to turn at the correct time and bunt into the proper areas of the field.

Procedure:
1. Station a pitcher on the mound and a catcher behind home plate in full gear.
2. Place pylons halfway between the foul lines and the pitcher's mound, approximately thirty feet from home plate—one on each side of the field.
3. The hitter bunts the ball between the pylon and the foul line.

Safety Squeeze Drill

Purpose: To learn to execute the safety squeeze correctly.

Procedure:
1. Station a pitcher on the mound and a catcher behind home plate in full gear.
2. Place pylons halfway between the foul lines and the pitcher's mound, approximately thirty feet from home plate—one on each side of the field.
3. Divide the squad into two groups—runners and bunters. Rotate groups periodically.
4. Use three runners at a time at third base to maximize running opportunities.
5. The runners at third base practice the correct walking lead and running keys.
6. The hitter turns at the correct time and bunts the ball between the pylon and the foul line.

A Great Option

Remember, the runner at third must master the walking lead, then break for the plate on any ball other than one bunted hard back to the box or one the catcher can field easily. The bunter must turn when the pitcher's stride foot hits the ground. When run correctly, the safety squeeze can be a real asset to any team's offensive game.

Good Luck!

Part Three:

ORGANIZATION AND OTHER THOUGHTS

Practice Organization

"In a balanced organization, working toward a common objective, there is success."
– British historian Arthur Helps

To have a baseball program where each player and each team develops to its maximum ability is a fundamentally sound coaching objective. If these goals are attained, every player and every team can be considered successful regardless of what their individual statistics or team standing might be.

Optimizing the player's and team's abilities can most easily be achieved through well-organized practice sessions and hard work.

Disorganized practice limits learning! But the well-designed practice schedule will yield many benefits:

- It makes maximum use of limited practice time.
- It creates a better teaching and learning environment.
- It enables practice to progress more smoothly and in a logical manner.
- It enables more instruction to take place, keeping players busy at all times.
- It stresses that a successful season is contingent upon hard work.
- It helps players think, act, and feel more confident in their ability.
- It aids players in becoming more receptive to learning and to assimilate more information.
- It forces players to approach practice in a more businesslike manner.
- It enables critical areas of play to be taught more thoroughly and in a logical sequence.
- It allows players to have a feeling of growth and accomplishment.
- It allows players to have more fun.
- It improves knowledge and understanding of the game.
- It hones skills and teaches better responses to game situations.

Practice Organization Guidelines

▶ Use multiple drills wherever possible. This allows several things to be accomplished simultaneously.

▶ Practice the skills and situations that occur most often and allot time in proportion to their relative importance. Avoid spending too much time on situations that rarely occur in the course of a game.

▶ Repeat basic drills at regular intervals. More learning will take place if key fundamental situations are practiced

> **COACHING KEY:**
> At the beginning of practice, have your team arrive on the field as a group, instead of straggling in one-by-one. This promotes good team discipline.

at regular intervals for short periods instead of longer sessions that occur less often. As players become familiar with drills, less time is wasted implementing them. Drills then become highly efficient.

▶ Take the time to build the foundation—it will pay dividends. Establishing a basic format for practice will enable the players to become familiar with a routine, which will result in very productive, efficient practices. The weather may modify practice from time to time and force improvisation by the coach.

▶ A good rule of thumb is to limit practice sessions to two and a half hours. As the players tire mentally and physically, their ability to absorb knowledge declines rapidly.

▶ **Practices can include the following segments:**

1. **Warm-up period:** To increase body temperature, blood flow, flexibility, and prepare the body for practice.
2. **Throwing period:** To warm up the throwing arm and to improve individual and team throwing skills.
3. **Fundamentals session:** To teach various aspects of team defense and offense that occur during the course of a game.
4. **Bunting session:** To teach the mechanics of the sacrifice bunt, safety and suicide squeeze plays, and the correct baserunning techniques for each.
5. **Batting practice session:** To teach the fundamentals of hitting, to provide opportunities to practice hitting skills, and to gain confidence.
6. **Infield practice:** To practice fielding and throwing and to conclude practice on a snappy upbeat note that builds confidence.
7. **Baserunning practice:** To teach various baserunning skills and situations, and to act as a conditioning drill.

A Sample Practice

Within each segment of this sample practice schedule, there is an example of a multiple drill or drills. Each drill is designed to practice several fundamentals at one time.

This is a highly efficient method of teaching and coaching. Use your imagination and devise drills that meet your needs and the needs of your players.

Remember, what follows is just a *sample practice.* You will bring many other specific elements into practice besides the things that are listed here. For example, in the "Fundamentals session," instead of Double Steal Defense and Situational Hitting, on any given day you might have Bunt Defense, Pop Fly Priorities, Rundown Drills, or any other drills you like.

Create and practice those situations you feel are important.

1. **Warm-up period**
   - Two laps around the field
   - Calisthenics
   - Stretching
   - Box Baserunning Drill
2. **Throwing period**
   - Warm-up arm by playing catch; observe "Rules for Playing Catch" on page 18.
   - Knee Drill
   - Rapid Fire Drill
   - Tandem Relay Drill
3. **Fundamentals session**
   - Double Steal Defense
   - Situational Hitting
4. **Bunting session**
   - Sacrifice bunt/Safety squeeze
   - Suicide squeeze/Double suicide squeeze
5. **Batting practice session**
   - Toss Drill runs concurrently with batting practice
   - Two rounds of hitting per group
   - Additional baserunning practice occurs during batting practice
6. **Infield practice**
   - Outfield phase
   - Infield phase
7. **Baserunning practice**
   - Arkansas Quick Drill

Running a Productive Batting Practice Session

What follows, again, is *just one example* of how a productive batting practice portion of your practice might be run. There are many options you can work in.

Purpose: To teach the fundamentals of hitting, to provide opportunities to practice hitting skills, and to gain confidence.

Procedure:
1. Divide hitters into groups of four or five players—this number will vary depending upon how many hitting warm-up stations you have available. Post the hitting order to expedite practice.
2. Each hitter should be given a prescribed number of swings. While waiting for his turn in the cage, a hitter should take warm-up swings by hitting off a batting tee or by executing a variation of the Toss Drill (see chapter on "The Toss Drill" for details).
3. Then, in the on-field batting cage, each player will have two rounds of hitting.
   - The first round consists of two bunts, two slap bunts, one hit-and-run and eight swings.
   - The second round consists of eight swings.
4. After a player's first round, he jumps into the baserunning phase of the batting practice. After the last swing, the hitter should run the ball out. Once at first base, he reacts to all balls hit by the next

batter, advancing or tagging up as the situation dictates. After two starts at each base, the player returns for a second round of hitting.
5. After a player's second round of hitting, he returns to his position.
6. When not hitting, each player should be in his fielding position and should play each pitch as he would in a game—by doing so, he can work on getting a jump on the ball. This element of surprise is lacking when fielding fungoed balls.

Running a Productive Bunting Session

Again, this is just a sample of a productive bunting practice. Once the skills are learned, bunting can be incorporated into the batting practice section. This will facilitate practice time.

Purpose: To teach the mechanics of the sacrifice bunt, safety and suicide squeeze plays, and the correct baserunning techniques for each.

Procedure:
1. Divide the squad into three groups.
2. Practice mechanics of the Sacrifice Bunt and Safety Squeeze
    – Group 1 – Bunters – Work on the correct mechanics of sacrifice bunting.
    – Group 2 – Runners at first base – practice basic running techniques for the sacrifice bunt.
    – Group 3 – Runners at third base – practice "Safety Squeeze" baserunning techniques.
3. Rotate groups so that all players practice at all stations.
4. Practice mechanics of the Suicide Squeeze and Double Suicide Squeeze.
    – Group 1 – Bunters – Work on correct mechanics of the Suicide Squeeze.
    – Group 2 – Runners at third base – practice basic running techniques for the Suicide Squeeze.
    – Group 3 – Runners at third base – practice "Double Suicide Squeeze" running techniques.
5. Rotate groups so that all players practice at all stations.

Running a Productive Infield Practice

Purpose: To practice fielding and throwing, and to wind down practice on a snappy, upbeat note that builds confidence.

Procedures:
1. Place players in their positions. Catchers should be in full gear.
2. The "outfield phase" should precede the "infield phase." The coach hits fungoes to the outfielders from the area around the pitcher's mound. Outfielders should not throw from too deep a distance.
3. Each outfielder throws twice to one of the bases and twice to home plate. The left fielder throws twice to second base and twice to home plate. The center fielder throws twice to third base and twice to home plate. And the right fielder throws twice to third base and twice to home plate.
4. An assistant coach hits fly balls to outfielders during the infield phase of practice.
5. Next, the infield phase begins. The coach fungoes ground balls from home plate.
    – The first three rounds are designed to execute a putout at first base.
    – The second three rounds are for execution of the double play.
    – The remaining two rounds are designed to give infielders practice fielding the slow roller and throwing to first base, and fielding and throwing to home plate.

6. Hit the ball directly at the infielder on the first round, to his right on the second round, and to his left on the third round. This gives the player a chance to practice moves in all directions. *Hitting the ball too hard during infield practice is a major fault to be avoided*—infield practice is a warm-up period designed to instill confidence in the players.
7. Catchers should return the throw to the player who fielded the ground ball. (The coach should decide on the exact throwing routine to be used during infield practice.)

A Great Baserunning Drill to Wrap Up Practice

This is the "Arkansas Quick Drill," and it's an outstanding way to end a great practice session. There are numerous drills that can be used during this time—this is just one example of a multiple drill that teaches baserunning techniques and acts as a conditioning drill. (I learned this drill from the *College Baseball Coaches Quarterly Digest*, July 1979.)

Purpose: To teach various baserunning skills and situations, and to act as a conditioning drill.

Procedure:
1. Station a pitcher at the mound, a catcher behind home plate and one infielder near one of the bases. (The infielder should be out of the direct line of the base so that runners will not be hit with the throw.) The coach serves as the "batter."
2. Divide the rest of the squad into four groups, and put one group at each base, including home plate.
3. The pitcher throws out of the stretch position, and one runner from each group will lead off a base—one runner at first, one at second and one at third. The runners take their primary leads from each base as normal. One runner from the group at home plate runs from a point near the home plate area as if breaking from the batter's box.
4. The pitcher throws to the plate, and the runners take their secondary leads from each base, as they would during a game.
5. When the pitch crosses home plate, the coach may do one of two things: take a full swing (do *not* hit the ball) or take a check-swing.
6. If the coach takes a check-swing, the catcher will fire a "pickoff throw" to the infielder stationed somewhere on the infield (but not at one of the bases). The runners have to get back to their bases *before the infielder catches the ball!* If a runner gets back to his base *after* the infielder catches the ball, that runner must take one lap around the field. (If the coach takes a check-swing, the runner near home plate does nothing.)
7. If the coach takes a full swing (again, don't hit the ball), the runners release from their secondary lead and run hard—the runner at first goes two bases (to third), the runner at second goes two bases (to home) and the runner at third tags and goes home. The runner starting at home plate goes two bases (to second).
8. If the runner from second base gets to home plate before the runner tagging from third base gets there, the runner from third base takes a lap.
9. After the "play," the runner who started at first base returns to second base, the runner who started at second base returns to third base, the runner who started at third base stays at home, and the runner who started at home returns to first base.

Setting Up for the "Arkansas Quick Drill":

The team is divided into four groups (A,B,C and D below), and each group starts at a base. Note that group A starts from a point up the first base line away from home plate.

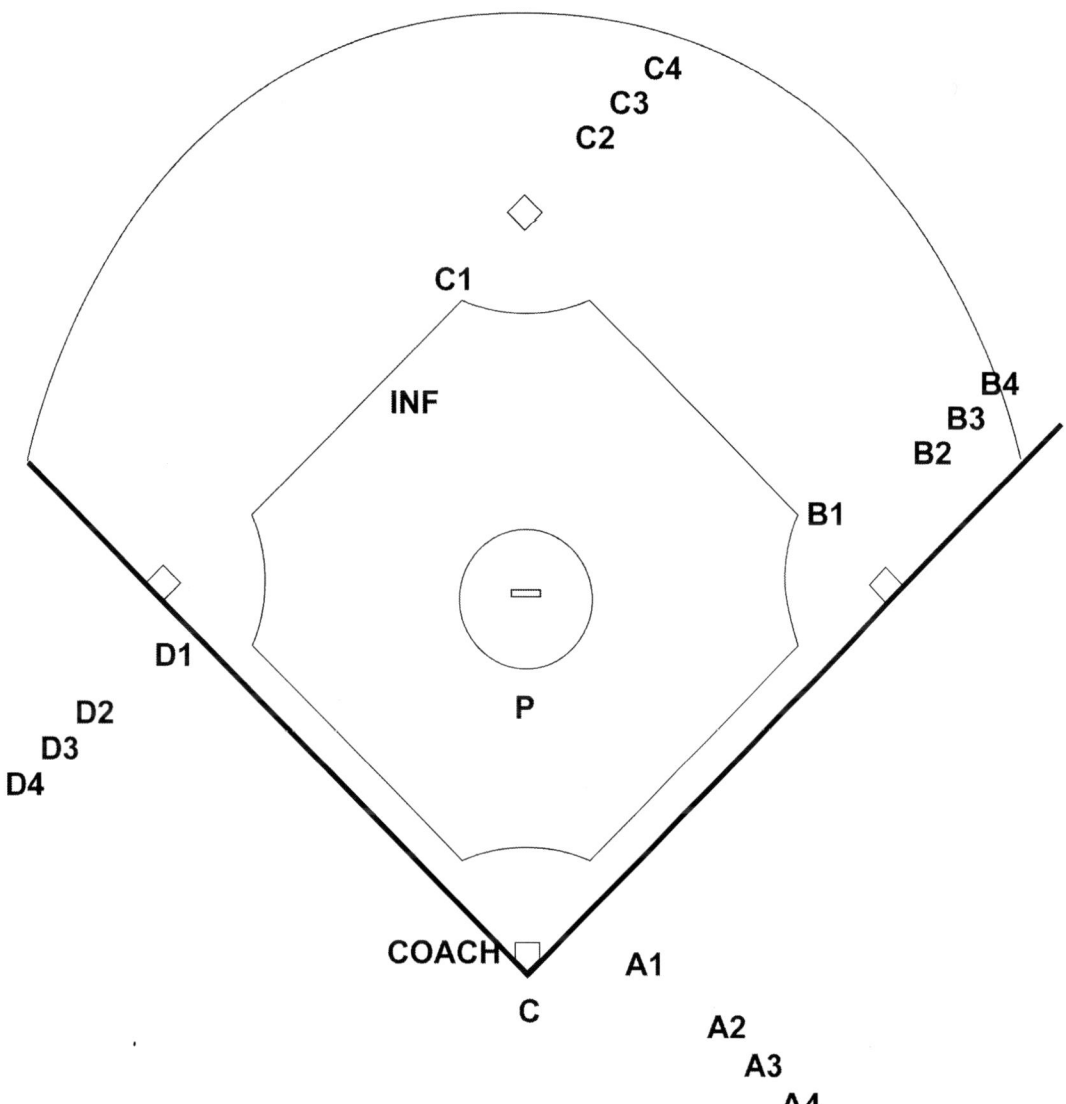

Pick, Choose and Combine

Pick and choose your drills—this will give practice sessions variety. Don't attempt to do every drill in this book in every practice session. There just isn't enough time.

Many aspects of the practice schedule can be incorporated into one segment of the practice—this will facilitate the learning process. Multiple drills should be used whenever possible for better time utilization. For example: Situation Hitting Drills (see page 160) will enable the team to take batting practice, play defense and react to baserunning situations *all* under game-like conditions. This drill could take the place of batting practice, infield practice and baserunning drills.

Good Luck!

The Timed Pitching Scrimmage

"An absolutely new idea is one of the rarest things known to man." – Thomas More

---

A genuine challenge for the well-organized coach is how to control the intrasquad scrimmage so that it fits neatly into the practice schedule.

Intrasquad scrimmages are essential during the preseason to get the team "playing ready," to allow the pitchers to throw to hitters under game conditions, and to enable the hitters to hone their timing by hitting off live pitching.

Using a scrimmage format where each pitcher throws a prescribed number of innings creates an uncontrollable time monster. The length of time to complete an inning will vary greatly from pitcher to pitcher. The amount of time needed to complete the scrimmage is unknown and many pitchers scheduled to throw may not get an opportunity to pitch if the scrimmage drags on too long.

This is an inefficient method of developing a pitching staff. And the unpredictability and uncertainty of its length results in a somewhat disorganized practice session.

The Solution

So, what should you do? Rob Nelson, my former pitching coach at Portland State University, came up with the answer: use an intrasquad scrimmage format where each pitcher throws for *a predetermined amount of time,* rather than a number of innings.

This way, you'll be in complete control of the scrimmage, blending it naturally into the total practice schedule.

The advantages of the timed pitching scrimmage are many:

– Pitchers know the exact starting time they will begin pitching, and for how long.
– Pitchers know they will not miss their assignment.
– The length of the scrimmage can be predetermined.
– The scrimmage does not preclude other phases of the practice schedule.
– A master pitching plan can be developed.

How to Run the Timed Pitching Scrimmage

▶ Assign each pitcher a specific starting time and a specific number of timed pitching segments. Each pitching segment is six minutes in length—this corresponds roughly to one-half inning and limits the total number of pitches per inning to a reasonable amount.

▶ The coach should designate one individual to act as the "timer." The timer monitors the six-minute pitching segments and announces pitching changes. He also alerts the pitcher on the sidelines one minute before he will enter the scrimmage.

▶ The coach should post pitching times in advance to facilitate the scrimmage. (See the section below detailing the Master Pitching Chart.)

▶ Each pitcher should warm up in the bullpen and be ready to pitch at his assigned pitching time.

▶ Pitchers work in pairs until their assigned pitching segments are completed. *One pitches while the other rests.* Each pitcher should begin throwing on the sideline one minute before replacing his pitching partner, or *longer if necessary.* This brief period corresponds to his between-inning warm-up pitches.

▶ Upon entering (or re-entering) the scrimmage, the new pitcher will be allowed two warm-up pitches from the game mound. The new pitcher then will pick up the count on the batter and game situation as it exists when he entered the scrimmage.

▶ *Stay on schedule.* All pitching segments must be carefully timed and strictly adhered to for maximum time-control to be realized.

The Master Pitching Chart

Develop and post a Master Pitching Chart for the timed pitching scrimmage—this will allow pitchers to know when they will be pitching and how many segments they will pitch. This advance notice will give them time to warm-up properly in the bullpen.

Increase the number of pitching segments for each pitcher as the preseason progresses and the pitchers' conditioning improves. And develop relief pitchers by having them throw one or two segments on consecutive days, or every other day.

As individual pitching segments increase, the number of pitchers who will throw during that day's scrimmage will decrease. Because the time needed for the scrimmage can be predetermined and controlled, the scrimmage will consume only a portion of the practice schedule.

On the next page is a sample chart. Write in the day of the week and the date on the line at the top of the chart, and the names of the pitchers in the left-hand column. The numbers in the boxes indicate the number of six-minute segments a pitcher will throw on that day.

The chart can be posted on the bulletin board in advance of practice, or copies may be passed out to individual pitchers.

	Mon 3/5	*Tue* 3/6	*Wed* 3/7	*Thu* 3/8	*Fri* 3/9	*Sat* 3/10	*Sun* 3/11	*Mon* 3/12	*Tue* 3/13	*Wed* 3/14	*Thu* 3/15
Adams	2	X	2	X	2	X	X	4	X	X	X
Baltus	X	2	X	2	X	2	X	X	X	4	X
Baumer	2	X	2	X	2	X	X	X	4	X	X
Baysinger	X	2	X	2	X	2	X	X	X	4	X
Brown	X	2	X	2	X	2	X	X	X	4	X
Daniell	X	2	X	2	X	2	X	X	X	4	X
Ginsberg	X	2	X	2	X	2	X	X	X	X	4
Inman	X	2	X	2	X	2	X	X	X	X	4
Johansen	X	2	X	2	X	2	X	X	2	X	2
Minder	2	X	2	X	2	X	X	4	X	X	X
Nelson	X	2	X	2	X	2	X	X	4	X	2
Nichols	2	X	2	X	2	X	X	X	4	X	X
Peterson	2	X	2	X	2	X	X	4	X	X	X
Prentice	2	X	2	X	2	X	X	1	1	X	1
Williams	2	X	2	X	2	X	X	1	1	X	1
Wittcke	2	X	2	X	2	X	X	2	X	X	2
START TIME	2:45	2:45	2:45	2:45	2:45	9:30	---	2:45	2:45	2:45	2:45

Daily Pitching Chart

Then, each day, post a more detailed chart, similar to the one below, outlining that day's pitching duties. The first two columns show the exact times pitchers will throw *that day*. The next two columns indicate the total minutes pitchers will throw the next day (exact times posted the next day):

Mon 3/5		Tue 3/6	
PITCHER	**TIME**	**PITCHER**	**TOTAL TIME**
Baumer	2:45-2:51 / 2:57-3:03	**Brown**	12 minutes
Nichols	2:51-2:57 / 3:03-3:09	**Daniell**	12 minutes
Minder	3:09-3:15 / 3:21-3:27	**Baysinger**	12 minutes
Wittcke	3:15-3:21 / 3:27-3:33	**Inman**	12 minutes
Peterson	3:33-3:39 / 3:45-3:51	**Baltus**	12 minutes
Williams	3:39-3:45 / 3:51-3:57	**Johansen**	12 minutes
Adams	3:57-4:03 / 4:09-4:15	**Ginsberg**	12 minutes
Prentice	4:03-4:09 / 4:15-4:21	**Nelson**	12 minutes

You can also post the following instructions at the bottom of the Daily Pitching Chart:

PITCHERS:
1. Be warmed-up and ready to pitch at your assigned time.
2. Begin throwing on the sidelines one (1) minute before replacing your pitching partner… *longer if necessary.*
3. You will be allowed two (2) warm-up pitches when you enter the game.
4. You will pick up the count and situation as it exists when you enter the game.

Other notes

The above scrimmage schedule consumes 96 minutes. Allowing time to get organized, more than an hour of practice time in a two-and-a-half hour practice session should be available to work on other aspects of the game.

Note that it is not necessary to have two complete teams to scrimmage effectively. In fact, the timed pitching scrimmage runs more effectively if you *don't* have two complete teams. Place a defensive team in the field which remains there during the entire scrimmage—this saves the time it takes to change from defense to offense. Rotate players between defense and offense so that all players get an opportunity to do both. Change catchers every four pitching segments (24 minutes). When the catching change is made, the new catcher should be in full catching gear, warmed up and ready to step in with no delay.

For variety, and to help the pitchers develop their change-ups, have pitchers throw only fastballs and change-ups during a given day—no breaking balls. This will force pitchers to use the change-up under game conditions, helping them gain confidence in it.

Make it Part of Your Routine

The timed pitching scrimmage is a highly efficient and effective way to scrimmage. Pitchers and hitters both perform under game conditions and the scrimmage does not lag, because pitchers are not required to get a certain number of outs.

The timed pitching scrimmage can be any length of time the coach desires, depending upon the number of pitchers who need work.

This format can also be used with two full teams in a more conventional game-like situation, but will require more time because of the time consumed changing from offense to defense.

Good Luck!

Occupational Hazards

"Too bad all the people who know how to run this country are busy running taxicabs or cutting hair." – George Burns

---

So, you're the coach…

Reflecting back upon 19 years of coaching high school baseball, 18 years of coaching American Legion baseball, and 20 years of Division I college baseball, it is apparent to me that two major problems are common to all of us coaching baseball and softball at all age levels. If we agree with the thesis that "misery loves company" (that is, having companionship while experiencing discomfort serves to make that discomfort lighter) it should be reassuring to recognize these two major problems:

> **1. Everyone's an authority.**
> **2. Parental interference.**

Beginning coaches may feel their problems are unique. With experience, however, it will become apparent that these problems are common to most coaching situations. It is hoped that experienced coaches will gain some solace as they recognize and identify with the problems presented here.

Everyone's An Authority

Baseball is peculiar in that it is a relatively easy game to understand. There are no complicated offenses or defenses as exist in other sports—the action is slower and easier to follow. Furthermore, most people have played some form of baseball or softball during their life, or are engaged in coaching some youth teams. These circumstances cause many fans to believe they are qualified to make judgments concerning the conduct of the game.

Consequently, one of the occupational hazards of being a baseball or softball coach is that you will be second-guessed. (Remember: you have one guess… everyone else has two!)

From a more positive standpoint, the appeal of baseball or softball can very well be attributed to the fact that fans do feel they understand the game, even if not to the degree they may presume. Realistically, they do not have the knowledge, the ability to implement that knowledge, or the organizational talent necessary to field a team that will play to its capacity.

We should be concerned only with those individuals who overstep the bounds of propriety and openly challenge our judgment or authority. These people, thank goodness, are in the minority, but they tend to destroy team morale. Most of them know everything about baseball and coaching, except how little they know. They must be confronted, won over if possible, and if not, at least silenced.

Parental Interference

This problem exists at all levels of play, but to varying degrees. The lower the organizational or age level, the more problems you will have. There are more problems with parental interference at the Little League level than at the high school level, and high school has many more problems of this type than the college level of play.

Players are an extension of their parents' ego, and many parents are vicariously playing the games or reliving their lives through their children. This is fine, but a problem results when a parent gets overly involved emotionally and creates a negative situation out of what otherwise would be a positive experience for their child.

This usually occurs when their child is not playing regularly, and rather than admit that he or she may not have sufficient ability, or may not be physically mature enough to merit more playing time, the parent projects the blame upon the coach, and the coach becomes the scapegoat for the athlete's inability to measure up to the hopes and aspirations of the parent. If the player is led to believe that he or she should be playing more or starting, the player will feel cheated, become bitter and may harbor resentment toward the coach. This is grossly unfair to both the athlete *and* the coach. In reality, the animosity toward the coach is a manifestation of the parent's own frustrations.

Ideally, parents must be objective in terms of the athlete's abilities. The sole criterion for success should be, "Does the athlete play to his or her capabilities?" and not the parent's ego. It may take more effort for one player to "make the end of the bench" than it does for another to play regularly or star. Therefore, the benchwarmer is as successful as the star when *effort* is the yardstick.

So relax! Give yourself credit for the knowledge you possess. You're a professional in your field. You're the one willing to put your time in and you're the one making it possible for the kids to have a team, a league, and a place to play.

Nice going! We need more people like you!

Good Luck!

Play Smart: Know the Rules

"You have to learn the rules of the game. And then you have to play better than anyone else."
– Albert Einstein

Would you like to coach a smarter, more alert, more efficient ballclub? Sure you would! Then take the time to teach your players the basic rules of the game. This is an area of play often missing from many lesson plans.

By having a basic understanding of the rules, baseball becomes more fun to play. It helps alleviate frustration and hostility toward the umpire, cuts down on griping, and generally leads to a more positive approach to the game. With a bit of luck, *a more relaxed, happier player results.*

When players are well-versed in the rules of play, fewer costly mental mistakes occur. They understand, for example, the infield fly rule, what to do if two runners are on the same base, and what it means if the umpire makes no call on a play at any base.

When players have been taught the basic rules of the game, they are less likely to feel cheated when the umpire makes a decision involving them that is based on rule interpretation. Furthermore, teaching the rules to your team is an excellent rainy day activity and should be included in your practice schedule sometime during the preseason.

Judgment calls—such as balls, strikes, safe, or out—are part of the game and subject to human interpretation and possible error. Each player and coach must learn to live with and adjust to this fact. *Umpire calls tend to balance out over the course of the season, so relax!*

Invite your Umpires Association to discuss the rules with your team. They will jump at the chance. The better informed the coaches and the players are, the less hassle the umpires will experience during the season and the better prepared your team will be.

Remember: Each organization has its own variation of the rules, and you should be familiar with those that are unique to your organization and age group.

The following are a few of the rules we taught and discussed at the beginning of each season, and reinforced from time to time during the course of the season. Compile your own list of rules by choosing those that you feel are appropriate for your level of play and age group. Then, *teach them thoroughly.*

Do Not Do Your Own Umpiring

One over-riding principle that each player must understand is "Don't do your own umpiring!" This simply means *do not* leave the base or stop running until you are certain of what the umpire's call was. If uncertain as to your status after sliding into a base, stay on the base and ask the umpire "Am I safe or out?"

If you hit a ball and are uncertain as to whether it is fair or foul, run the ball out! Whether you are on offense or defense, if you are uncertain if a ball is fair or foul, *play it as if it is fair!*

Fair or Foul?

Some things to know about fair and foul balls:

- A fair ball is a legally batted ball that settles on or over fair territory.

- A fair fly is judged according to the position of the ball and the foul line and not with respect to the fielder at the time of contact.

- The foul lines are in fair territory, as is home plate.

- *The umpire will verbalize only on a foul ball and will remain mute on a fair hit.*

- A ball that hits or bounces over first or third base in fair territory is a fair ball even if it moves into foul territory beyond the base.

Infield Fly Rule

The Infield Fly Rule becomes possible *when there are fewer than two outs and either the bases are loaded or there are runners on first and second.* In this situation, when the batter hits a fair popup (*not* including a line drive or attempted bunt) which can be caught by an infielder with ordinary effort, *the batter is declared automatically out* by the umpire, regardless of whether or not the ball is caught. (The umpire will yell something like, "Infield fly, batter's out," or, if the ball is along the foul line, "Infield fly, if it's fair.")

This rule is designed to protect the offensive team. Declaring the batter automatically out means that if the ball is dropped, the runners *do not* have to run. If there were no Infield Fly Rule, the defensive team could let the ball drop, and then easily get force-outs on at least two runners.

With the Infield Fly Rule, the runners don't have to advance to the next base if the ball is dropped, but they are allowed to advance if they so choose—and they do so at their own risk.

Note that the Infield Fly Rule can include very shallow fly balls to the outfield, as long as an infielder can catch the ball with normal effort. Note also that the Infield Fly Rule does not preclude an outfielder from being allowed to attempt to make the catch—the rule will still be in effect (or should be, if the umpire calls it correctly) if an infielder could have made the catch with normal effort.

Make sure your team fully understands the intent and function of this rule, as well as the following:

– If runners attempt to advance, whether the ball is caught or dropped, they must be *tagged out* because the force-out no longer exists.

– Teach the players the offensive and defensive implications of the Infield Fly Rule. Knowing this rule will prevent your baserunners from running into a trap if the opposition intentionally or inadvertently drops the popup.

– Conversely, your defense may be able to set a trap for the offense by intentionally dropping the popup when the Infield Fly Rule is in effect. *Remember, the force-out no longer exists and any advancing baserunner must be tagged out.*

The Running Lane

This situation usually occurs on bunted or topped balls fielded in front of home plate.

Let's say, in running the last half of the distance from home plate to first base while the ball is being thrown to first, the batter/runner runs outside the three-foot restraining line, or inside the foul line, and in so doing interferes with the ball or the fielder taking the throw at first base. In this case, the batter/runner is out. (See page 189 for a diagram of the running lane.)

There is one problem with this rule, however: *first base is in fair territory.* At some point, the runner will *have* to cross the foul line to touch the base.

So, the question to ask the Umpires Association in your area is this: "At what point does the runner have the right to leave the running lane and cross the first base foul line so that he can step on first base and not be in jeopardy of being called out for interference?"

At one time, American League umpires agreed that once the batter/runner reached the "dirt area" in front of first base (usually 13 feet in front of the bag), he could leave the running lane and cross the foul line to step on first base risk-free. This seems logical.

Baseball rules are often vague or totally remiss in addressing this aspect of the "running lane rule." *Be sure you know how your Umpires Association will interpret this rule!*

When your team is on offense, be sure your players run inside the three-foot running lane. And when they're on defense, be sure your pitchers, catchers, and infielders alert the umpire when the batter/runner is outside the three-foot running lane when making a play to first base.

Foul Tip

A batted ball that travels directly from the bat to the catcher's hands and is caught legally *is a strike and the ball is in play.* If a runner is stealing a base, the play continues as if the batter had swung and missed the pitch. If the situation presents itself, have your infielders tell the runner, "foul ball!" If he doesn't know the rule or doesn't "look in" when stealing, he may leave the base. If so, *tag him out.*

Conversely, remind your players that if they're the baserunner, "Don't do your own umpiring!"

Return to First Base

First base is, of course, the only base a runner may over-run—that is, he can run past first base without fear of being tagged out, provided he does not show intent to advance to the next base.

Once he crosses first and the play is over, the runner may turn either left or right to return to first base. To avoid confusion, especially with younger players, they should be taught to turn to their right after crossing first to play it safe.

If the runner makes an obvious move to advance, he can be tagged out. Tell your infielders to tag the baserunner if there is any doubt about an attempted advance, then ask the umpire for a call.

Dropped Third Strike with a Runner on First

The batter is out when a third strike is not caught by the catcher, provided a runner occupies first base and there are fewer than two outs. *No throw by the catcher to first base is necessary.*

Two Runners on the Same Base

When two runners occupy the same base, the runner closer to home plate is entitled to the base. The back runner is out if touched with the ball.

This presents a golden opportunity for an alert defensive player to dupe the other team. Tell your infielders to tag both runners (the back runner is then out), then tell the front runner "You are out!" When the front runner (who is actually safe) steps off the base, the infielder should tag him again. Double play!

And again, remind your players: if you're the baserunner in this spot, *"Don't do your own umpiring!"*

Retouching the Bases

The runner must, of course, touch each base in legal order (first, second, third, home plate). And when obliged to return while the ball is in play, he must retouch the base or bases in reverse order.

For example, if a runner at first base advances beyond second base on a deep fly ball to the outfield and the outfielder makes the catch, the runner must *retouch* second base on his attempt to return to first base.

Avoiding a Tag

A baserunner is out if, while trying to avoid being tagged out, he runs more than three feet left or right from a direct line between the base and the location of the runner at the time the play is being made on him.

The rule of thumb to determine if a baserunner is out of the baseline: The reference point for the defensive player is the *center of his body to the tip of his outstretched arm* on either side of his body. If the baserunner is beyond these parameters, he is out of the baseline. Call this to the umpire's attention! Yet, don't do your own umpiring—*make the play*.

Tagging Up on a Fly Ball

The baserunner, while touching his base, may advance on the first touching of the ball by the fielder. *First contact!* Otherwise, the fielder could juggle the ball all the way into the infield and freeze the runner.

Catcher's Interference

If a play follows catcher's interference, the offensive team may elect to ignore the interference and accept the play. However, if the batter reaches first base and all other runners advance at least one base, the interference is ignored

Offensively, it's a free play. Defensively, *play the ball as if no interference had occurred!*

Balk Followed by a Pitch**

If a balk is immediately followed by a pitch that permits the batter and each baserunner to advance a minimum of one base, the balk is ignored and the ball remains alive. *The offensive team has a "free swing.* Defensively, play the ball as if no balk had occurred.

** In high school rules, the ball is dead immediately when a balk occurs.

Interference

Interference is the act of an offensive player, umpire, or nongame person hindering or confusing any fielder attempting to make a play. Check your rule book for penalties.

Obstruction

Obstruction is the act of a fielder, while not in possession of the ball and not in the act of fielding the ball, impeding the progress of any runner. Obstruction may be called on a defensive player who blocks off a base, baseline, or home plate from a baserunner while not in possession of the ball or in the immediate act of catching the ball.

Some "cute" infielders (when not involved in the play) like to stand close to their base in an attempt to make the baserunner miss the base or make an extraordinarily wide turn. This is obstruction and should be called to the umpire's attention. Check your rule book for penalties.

Passing a Runner

The runner is out when he passes an unobstructed preceding runner before such runner is out.

Runner Hit by Batted Ball

If a runner is hit in fair territory by a batted fair ball before it has passed all infielders other than the pitcher, the runner is out, the ball is dead, and the batter is credited with a base hit. On the other hand, if the ball hits the runner after passing the infielder (going through his legs) the ball is alive and runners may advance.

Umpire Makes No Call

If a close play occurs on the bases and the umpire makes no signal, it means that the runner has not touched the base, nor has he been tagged or forced out by the defense. Defensively, when the umpire makes no call at home plate and the runner has missed the plate, *tag him out.* It will save a run. Reading the umpire can work to your advantage.

Ground Rules

Be sure the players know the ground rules of their home park!

Use the Rule Book to Your Advantage

Baseball rules vary from organization to organization. Check your league's rules. Discuss those rules that will enhance your team's play. The rules I have cited were taken primarily from the *N.C.A.A. Baseball Rule Book.* So, *check your league rules* to find out if there are any discrepancies with what has been written here.

And remember: you can drive a car without knowing the rules, just like you can play baseball without knowing the rules. But to be safe and smart you had better know both!

Good Luck!

Nervousness: Make it Work *for* You

"Nervousness is good. I tell the team that. You want to be nervous; you want to be a little tight. It gets your senses better. You get more focused, more zeroed in on what you have to do. If you go in and act like this is no big deal, you're going to lose." – Basketball coach John Calipari

It is our job, as coaches, to teach the fundamentals of play, as well as a myriad of offensive and defensive situations that will occur during a game and season. However, one aspect of play that confronts our athletes every time they are called upon to perform, we fail to deal with or discuss. That one aspect is *nervousness*. Call it fear, anxiety, or butterflies… but nervousness will manifest itself in tense muscles, sweaty palms, and a dry mouth—all of which adversely affect performance.

What is Nervousness?

It behooves us to teach our players to recognize nervousness for what it is. Nervousness is simply a *desire to do well*.

Many athletes do not understand this concept and believe that because they are nervous or have butterflies that they are somehow "choking." As a consequence of this negative thinking, they become tense and their performance suffers.

Dale Murphy, the former Atlanta Braves outfielder and a two-time National League Most Valuable Player, was a player of mine during his high school years. Dale said, *"Coach, I have butterflies my first time at bat in every game."* Surely, athletes of the caliber of Dale Murphy do not "choke!" They have learned to make their butterflies work for them.

Recognizing that nervousness is simply a "desire to do well," Dale changed his perception of it, and was then able to utilize the extra adrenaline that his nervousness made available to him in a positive rather than negative manner. The sting of a negative response was gone and his nervousness became an asset rather than a liability.

Our athletes must understand that everyone who puts their talents on display and holds them up for public scrutiny experiences nervousness. Success or failure is determined by how they deal with their nervousness—in a positive or negative manner.

Psychology tells us that the arousal of emotion depends upon the situation's having significance to the individual.

How Can the Athlete Deal with Nervousness?

Coping with nervousness effectively can be accomplished by using both a mental and physical approach. The mental approach utilizes *mental imagery* (preprogramming) and *positive self-talk*.

The physical approach is a more immediate tension reliever and involves correct *breathing, swinging the bat while on deck,* and *progressive relaxation.*

Mental Approach

▶ **Mental Imagery:** An excellent way to lessen nervousness, anxiety, or tension is through the use of mental pictures. This is commonly called *mental imagery.*

The athlete should develop a clear mental picture or visualization of himself/herself performing at his/her very best, free from nervousness, anxiety, or tension. This can be done during periods of relaxation or in bed prior to falling asleep.

Rick Wolff in his book *The Psychology of Winning Baseball* states: "Imaging is the practice of visualizing in your mind precisely what you expect to do on the field. Imaging allows the athlete to practice certain positive thoughts in his/her mind just as they practice their swing or pitching form on the field!"

Wolff goes on to say, "During this period of imaging, the athlete must view the game's events in a positive frame of mind! He must not visualize any nervousness, anxiety, or tension of any kind."

Astronauts, great stage performers, skilled surgeons, and championship athletes practice flawless techniques in their minds over and over; again and again, they discipline their thoughts to create the habit of superb performance. Thus, preprogramming or the ability to practice within makes performing the task easier.

▶ **Positive Self-Talk:** To enhance performance, concentrate only on those internal comments that are positive. Eliminate all negative comments and thoughts by treating yourself as you would a doubles partner in tennis. Winning self-talk should go something like this: *Of course I can do it! I've practiced it mentally a thousand times.*

Physical Approach

The late Charley Lau was considered baseball's premier hitting instructor. Lau, who authored *The Art of Hitting .300* and *The Winning Hitter* wrote, "If you are tense mentally, you will be tense physically. Your muscles tighten and you begin to grip the bat so hard your knuckles turn white."

Harvey Dorfman, author of *The Mental Game of Baseball,* stated, "The monster, fear, breaks down our confidence, brainwashes us, makes us play a losing game!"

Here are a few simple but effective techniques that can be used by players to combat their nervousness during competition.

▶ **Breathing Exercise:** It sounds simple, and it is: breathing can alleviate tension. That is, a specific breathing technique can be utilized to alleviate tension. This technique is as follows:

1. Take several full and complete breaths. Inflate the chest and abdomen.
2. Inhale and exhale through the nose. Exhaling through the nose allows for a slower release of air, which maximizes physiological benefits.
3. Several complete breaths tend to relax the body by making a greater amount of oxygen available.
   – *Inhale* = Relaxation.
   – *Exhale* = Elimination of stress.

Use this technique while on deck waiting to bat; while batting (step out of the batter's box, turn your back to home plate, and take a few complete breaths); while pitching (step off the rubber, turn your back to the hitter, and take several complete breaths.); or while in the field (do breathing exercises between pitches).

▶ **On-Deck Swings:** While on deck, prior to stepping into the batter's box, take several practice swings. These swings will relieve tension and prepare the body for actual hitting.

▶ **Squeeze and Release:** Grip the bat and squeeze it tightly for a few seconds, then release your grip. Do this several times. *Squeeze and release* is part of what is known as progressive body relaxation, where relaxation is achieved by tensing and then releasing the muscles in various parts of the body in a progressive manner, e.g.: feet, calves, thighs, buttocks, back, etc.

"I Gotta Goals": Real Tension Builders

Harvey Dorfman states: "Goal setting makes the player's purpose clear and gives direction. The successful player sets goals in order to stimulate himself to act in a way to achieve his objectives. Game-day athletic goals can cause tension if their emphasis is placed incorrectly upon the *result* rather than the function or action."

"I Gotta Goals" build tension: I gotta get a hit… I gotta throw a strike… *I gotta… I gotta*. The emphasis here is placed upon a result over which the athlete has no control.

A pitcher may throw a perfect strike on the knees outside and the batter hits the ball out of the park. A batter may hit a bullet line drive right at a defensive player. These examples show that the athlete cannot control the result of what may occur. Nervousness and tension are the only things "I Gotta Goals" accomplish.

Dorfman makes the point that to lessen tension, "the emphasis or focus should be on the function or immediate action." *Hit the ball up the middle… keep your head down… see the ball… nice low fast ball… good balance point.*

By focusing on the action, rather than the result, tensions are eased.

What You *Think* is Important

What you are *thinking* manifests itself in a *physical equivalency*. So, if you think you are "choking," muscle tensions build and performance suffers. So remember:

- Nervousness is common to all performers.
- You're not "choking" because you are nervous or have butterflies.
- Nervousness is a desire to do well.
- Practice mental imagery and positive self-talk.
- To alleviate tension, take full and complete breaths, take practice swings while in the on-deck circle, and practice "squeeze and release" techniques.

If an athlete never gets nervous, never has butterflies or is "too cool"... he either isn't smart enough to realize what kind of a *jam* he's in or doesn't give a *damn*.

For a more complete discussion of how to deal with attitudes, emotions, tension, etc. see the following:

1. Dorfman, H.A. *The Mental ABC's of Pitching*. Diamond Communications Inc., South Bend, Indiana, 2000

2. Dorfman, H.A. and Kuehl, Karl. *The Mental Game of Baseball*. New York: Rowman and Littlefield Publishing Group, 2002

3. Wolff, Rick. *The Psychology of Winning Baseball*. Parker Publishing Company, Inc. West Nyack, New York, 1986

Good Luck!

The Game Ball Sponsor Program

"You gotta have two things to win. You gotta have brains and you gotta have balls. – Paul Newman as Eddie Felson in The Color of Money

---

An excellent and easy way to raise funds for your team is through the *Game Ball Sponsor Program*.

Compile a list of businesses, parents and individuals who are interested in supporting your baseball program. Mail them a "Dear Neighbor" letter (another idea of my former pitching coach, Rob Nelson), along with the details of how the Game Ball Sponsor Program works.

When compiling your list of supporters, you may want to ask each team member to submit the names of 5 or 10 potential Game Ball Sponsors: parents, grandparents, aunts and uncles are normally very generous. They will respond to help their child and your program.

A Sample Letter

Here is an example of the "Dear Neighbor" letter. Of course, use appropriate letterhead.

Dear Neighbor:

Portland State's baseball season is just around the corner. This year the Vikings will be competing for the tenth year in the prestigious "PAC-10" Northern Division. Once again, Coach Dunn's Viks will play more games (60) on fewer dollars than any other Division I University in the Northwest.

As you know, people like you have helped the battle of the "budget crunch" in recent years. I would like to ask you to consider helping out Portland State Baseball again this year. Now more than ever you can make a difference by becoming a *"Game Ball Sponsor."*

The details of how the *Game Ball Sponsor Program* works are described on the enclosed sheet. I have also enclosed a self-addressed envelope for you to use should you decide to help Viking Baseball again this year.

Your *tax-deductible contribution* will help a winning team keep on winning... And, forty hungry ballplayers will really appreciate your support.

Sincerely,
Steve Candello
Assistant Head Baseball Coach*

P.S. Just a reminder, we certainly will not reject anyone's request to sponsor more than one home game!

* By having the "Dear Neighbor" letter signed by your assistant coach, it will be possible to say things about the program that might be awkward to say otherwise.

Substitute your school or team name and field name where appropriate. Include your team's schedule along with the following page that gives the detailed explanation of "How the Game Ball Sponsor Program Works."

Sample Information Sheet

How the program works:

1. The concept of the *"Game Ball Sponsor"* is simple. An individual or business can volunteer to pay for the baseballs used in one or more of the P.S.U. Home Games at Civic Stadium.

2. The cost of the baseballs for one game is $50.

The benefits to you – the "Game Ball Sponsor"

1. The name of each game's sponsor will be announced several times during the game at Civic Stadium. For example, Butch Paulson of JKP Sports in Tualatin, Oregon has chosen to sponsor game #3 against Pacific University on March 1.

2. Three times during that game it will be announced, "Butch Paulson has kindly provided the baseballs for today's game. Thanks for your help, Butch. The Vikings would not be able to play today without your valuable assistance."

3. The sponsor will receive a *"Family Season Pass,"* which is good for all P.S.U. Home baseball games. The sponsor can choose his game's *"Designated Bat Person"* who will sit in the dugout and assume the duties of the official bat person for the game.

How you can become a "Game Ball Sponsor."

1. Check off the home game(s) listed that you wish to sponsor.

2. Make check payable to *P.S.U. Baseball* for the amount of $50.00 if you are sponsoring one game, $100.00 for two games, etc...

3. Using the enclosed stamped envelope, mail the bottom part of this sheet and your check to Coach Dunn. Your *"Family Season Pass"* will be sent to you upon Coach Dunn receiving your contribution. Thanks for helping Viking Baseball stay on top!

**Portland State University
Home Baseball Schedule**

I would like to be the "Game Ball Sponsor" for the following PSU Home Game(s):

_____	W.O.S.C. – February 28	_____	Oregon State – April 7
_____	W.O.S.C. – February 28	_____	Lewis & Clark – April 15
_____	Pacific – March 1	_____	Eastern Washington – April 18
_____	George Fox – March 3	_____	Eastern Washington – April 18
_____	Washington – March 4	_____	Washington State – April 19
_____	Concordia – March 10	_____	Washington State – April 19
_____	Willamette – March 11	_____	Linfield – April 21
_____	Lewis & Clark – March 12	_____	Pacific Lutheran – May 5
_____	Portland – March 15	_____	Washington – May 8
_____	Oregon State – March 31	_____	Washington – May 8
_____	Gonzaga – April 5	_____	Portland – May 9
_____	Gonzaga – April 5	_____	Portland – May 9
_____	Hawaii-Hilo – May 11		

*NAME:*_____
*STREET:*_____
*CITY:*_____
*STATE:*_____
*ZIP:*_____
*PHONE:*_____

Mail the "Dear Neighbor" letter and "How the Game Ball Sponsor Program Works" to the list of supporters you have compiled. Enclose a stamped return envelope to increase your chances of success by making it easier for your supporters to respond.

The psychology of this program is very good, as the "Game Ball Sponsors" receive public recognition for their generosity by having their name announced several times during the game.

If you do not have a public address system at your field, you can recognize your "Game Ball Sponsors" by some other means. For example, publish their names on your schedule, noting the game or games they sponsored. Also, make signs and post them around the grandstand area to recognize these donors.

It is possible to have more than one "Game Ball Sponsor" per game, just be certain that each sponsor is recognized properly.

This program really works!

Good Luck!

About the Author

Jack Dunn, a 39-year veteran of the coaching ranks, is a sports legend in Oregon. He retired in 1994 after 20 straight winning seasons at Portland State University. His two high school programs, Cleveland and Wilson, were the class of the Portland City League for 19 years, and his American Legion summer teams dominated Oregon for two decades. He was selected State of Oregon Coach of the Year in 1973 after his team placed third in the American Legion World Series. At one stretch, Dunn's Legion team went four and a half years without losing a game in league play.

He has been inducted into the State of Oregon Hall of Fame, the Oregon High School Coaches' Hall of Fame, the Portland Interscholastic League Hall of Fame, Cleveland High School Hall of Fame, and the Portland State University Hall of Fame.

At Portland State, Jack compiled a record of 630 wins against 439 losses, winning conference championships in the NCAA Division I North Pacific League and PAC-10 Northern Division. The Vikings won the 1984 PAC-10 North title and placed in the upper division eight times in 11 years while competing against better-funded programs Oregon State, Washington, Washington State, University of Portland, and Gonzaga. His 1977 club advanced to the NCAA Regional at Arizona State. Nonleague opponents included Michigan, Fordham, Wichita State, Hawaii, Yale, Central Florida, Eastern Kentucky, Bradley, and Tulane, just to name a few. In both 1984 and 1986, Portland State teams won 39 games, at the time the state's collegiate record.

Thirty-five of Dunn's players signed professional baseball contracts, including major league pitchers Steve Olin, Jeff Lahti, Joel Kramer, and Eric Gunderson. Two-time National League Most Valuable Player and seven-time all-star Dale Murphy and major league manager Tom Trebelhorn were mentored by Jack in high school.

Nationally, Jack Dunn was a member of the American Baseball Coaches Association's Coaching and Teaching Aids Committee for 10 years and was also NCAA District 7 Representative. For 20 years, he ran the Portland State University Coaches Clinic, the major clinic in the state of Oregon and Southwest Washington—the clinic's philosophy was "Teachers Teaching Teachers."

He chaired the committee that organized the Oregon State High School Baseball Coaches Association, served as its President, and directed numerous baseball clinics for its membership.

In 1985, Dunn was honored by the American Red Cross with the Presidential Citation for Life-saving after administering CPR to a heart-attack victim during a flight to Honolulu. He received the Distinguished Career Award from The Oregonian, Portland's major newspaper. Dunn writes regularly for Collegiate Baseball, sharing his seven decades of knowledge with younger coaches. He has authored several instructional manuals for the Jugs Pitching Machine Company, and written 90 instructional articles for Jugs' monthly internet publication, available to the general public. He also continues to conduct a Little League summer baseball camp, as he has for 40 years.

One of Oregon's leading baseball ambassadors, he is in demand as a speaker at tournaments, banquets and clinics. He was primary clinician in the Little League International Baseball Congress meeting held in Portland, Oregon in 1972, was featured speaker and clinician at the Best in the West Clinic in Seattle, and spoke at the American Legion Baseball World Series banquet in 1992. He is also active in the Oregon Old-Timers Baseball Association and the Heart Association of Oregon.

Coach Dunn offers a bit of friendly advice

Dunn graduated with honors from the University of Oregon in 1955 with a Bachelor's Degree in history and a Master's Degree in Secondary Education. He also attended Portland State University and Oregon State. Before dedicating his life to teaching and coaching, he played 10 years of professional baseball, four in the Brooklyn Dodgers organization, and six with the Salem Senators of the Northwest League.

Jack Dunn's 39-year coaching career included:
– ABCA Baseball Coaches Association Committee on Coaching and Teaching Techniques
– NCAA District 7 At-Large Selection Committee
– Oregon Clinic Chairman at the NCAA National Convention
– Chairman of the founding committee of the Oregon High School Coaches Association
– President of the Oregon High School Baseball Coaches Association
– Conducted the Portland State University Coaches Clinic for high school coaches for 20 years
– Member of the Executive Board of the Oregon Active and Old Timers Baseball Association
– Coach of PAC-10 North All-Star team to The Netherlands, 1984 and 1990
– Literary contributor to the Athletic Journal, Collegiate Baseball, and Coaches Quarterly
– Currently writing a series of articles on coaching techniques for Collegiate Baseball

– Guest speaker at the 1993 American Legion World Series banquet
– Co-Director of Little League Summer Baseball Camp for 35 years
– Conducted clinic for International Little League Congress in 1971
– Sponsored and hosted USA All-Stars versus Japanese, Portland, Oregon, 1989

Honors won by Jack Dunn:
– State of Oregon Coach of the Year, 1973
– State of Oregon Sports Hall of Fame
– Portland State University Hall of Fame
– Oregon High School Baseball Coaches Hall of Fame
– Oregonian's Distinguished Career Award
– Won the Rollie Truitt Award for contribution to baseball in Oregon in 1972
– American Red Cross Presidential Citation for Life-Saving
– Cleveland High School Hall of Fame
– Portland Interscholastic Hall of Fame
– 2009 inductee into the American Baseball Coaches Association Hall of Fame

Jack Dunn with the 1956 Salem Senators